The
Pergamon
Dictionary of
Perfect Spelling

CHRISTINE MAXWELL

WHEAT☢N

A DIVISION OF PERGAMON PRESS

A. Wheaton & Company Limited
A Division of Pergamon Press
Hennock Road, Exeter EX2 8RP

Pergamon Press Ltd,
Headington Hill Hall, Oxford OX3 0BW, England

Pergamon Press, Inc.,
Maxwell House, Fairview Park, Elmsford, New York 10523, U.S.A.

Pergamon of Canada Ltd,
75 The East Mall, Toronto, Ontario M8Z 2L9, Canada

Pergamon Press (Australia) Pty Ltd,
19a Boundary Street, Rushcutters Bay, N.S.W. 2011, Australia

Pergamon Press GmbH,
6242 Kronberg/Taunus, Pferdstrasse 1, Federal Republic
of Germany

First edition 1977

Library of Congress Cataloging in Publication Data

Maxwell, Christine.
The Pergamon dictionary of perfect spelling.

1. Spellers. I. Title.
PE1146.M345   1977   428'.1   77-23541
ISBN 0-08-021425-8
ISBN 0-08-021902-0 pbk.
ISBN 0-08-021426-6 non net
ISBN 0-08-021427-4 pbk. non net

Printed in Great Britain by A. Wheaton & Co. Ltd, Exeter

Contents

Preface

This dictionary, the first of its kind in Great Britain (as far as the compiler knows), and its accompanying booklet, *Practise Your Spelling*, aim at being of service to children and adults of all ages who are weak at spelling and who therefore fail to locate quickly and easily the words they seek in standard dictionaries.

Compilers and publishers of English-language dictionaries overseas have long recognised this problem, and have successfully provided phonetically-arranged dictionaries to help pupils overcome these serious difficulties which so impede their progress.

Recent experience gained as a teacher in an Oxford middle school (age-group 9–13) and with students learning English as a foreign language has brought the compiler face to face with the problem. This has made her aware of the inordinate amount of time that has to be spent by teachers helping students with spelling difficulties which they could so easily have overcome for themselves had they had access to a phonetically-arranged dictionary.

The compiler gratefully acknowledges the co-operation of teachers and students in Oxfordshire schools for their help in testing the dictionary and its accompanying booklet, *Practise Your Spelling*, in a classroom environment. These successful tests, which were also carried out in several establishments that teach English as a foreign language, have revealed the following:

I. Students who assisted with the tests quickly understood that words printed in RED were incorrectly spelt and that only words printed in BLACK were correctly spelt. In tests which involved several hundred students, not one copied down incorrect spellings. Some teachers' initial concern over the possible negative effect of showing students incorrect spellings has proved unfounded.

II. Teachers (besides saving themselves time) found that regular use of the dictionary and the exercise booklet improved their pupils' ability to locate words easily and quickly and spell them correctly.

The mis-spellings (mainly phonetic) are printed in RED (RED is wrong), with the correct spellings given alongside in BLACK (BLACK is right). Even when users are unsure of the first two letters in a word, they may still find its correct spelling with the help of this dictionary. For instance, the word 'pheasant' will be found under the phonetic groups <u>fes</u> and <u>fez</u> as well as in its correct alphabetical place under <u>phe</u>:

fesant	pheasant
fezant	pheasant

pheasant

Some of the commonest spelling errors are made in adding suffixes and in forming derivatives from root words which in themselves may be quite easy to spell. In a conventional dictionary a student may be able to find the spellings of infinitives like 'picnic', 'abandon' and 'span', but may encounter difficulties spelling their present and past participles. How is one to know that the words 'spanning' and 'spanned' are not spelt 'spaning' and 'spaned'? There may be no indication that one must insert 'k' after 'picnic' in order to spell 'picnicking' and 'picnicked' correctly. This dictionary leaves no room for error in this respect, as difficult and irregular word derivatives are included. \

It is hoped that this dictionary (and its accompanying booklet) will prove to be of practical, daily help, solving spelling problems and helping to increase the spelling skills of both children and adults—in the classroom, at home and at work.

Oxford, July 1977   CHRISTINE MAXWELL

On Choice of Words, Spelling and Arrangement of Entries

The words in this dictionary have been chosen because they are difficult to spell. Accordingly, many common words are omitted. Obsolete and highly technical words have also been left out, though special attention has been given to the selection of scientific and technical words. Very few proper names are given and foreign words are included only if they have passed into common use.

Where alternative spellings exist these have mostly been omitted. In the case of words ending in -ise, -isation, the -ize and -ization versions have not been given (nor have they been given as mis-spelt versions since they cannot be counted as such). In a very few instances two spellings have been given; where only one spelling is given the reader can assume that it is widely accepted as being correct. To help the user decide upon the correct spelling, brief word definitions are given in the case of words that are (1) pronounced alike but differ in meaning and spelling, (2) often mispronounced to give the same or almost the same sound but are entirely different in meaning and spelling, e.g.:

(1) sail (of boat)   (2) poplar (tree)
    sale (of goods)   popular (well known)

The spellings and mis-spellings in the dictionary are arranged in alphabetical order.

Endings of words: It has not been possible to put in every derivation and many comparative endings have been excluded. In many cases there has been insufficient space for all the derivatives to be placed in one entry. They have therefore been split up in what the author considers to be the most obvious and practical way, e.g.:

abnormal /ly
abnormalit*y* /ies

Abbreviations Used in the Dictionary

adj(s).   adjective(s)
fem.   feminine
n.   noun
pl(s).   plural(s)
v.   verb

How to Use the Dictionary

1. Think hard about the word you wish to spell and try to decide with which two letters it starts.

2. Find the two letters in the dictionary and look down the <u>left-hand column</u> under these two letters until you find the word you want. If you find the word printed in BLACK, then you have found the correct spelling. However, if the word is printed in RED, then you are not spelling the word correctly, but if you look across the same line you will find the correct spelling printed in BLACK, e.g.:

palis   palace

3. (a) It may be necessary to add the word endings which are individually separated by oblique strokes (/) in order to build up the complete word you want. In the example below you can see how this works:

neat /er/est/ly/ness

    By adding <u>er</u> to <u>neat</u> you spell <u>neater</u>.
    By adding <u>est</u> to <u>neat</u> you spell <u>neatest</u>.
    By adding <u>ly</u> to <u>neat</u> you spell <u>neatly</u>.
    By adding <u>ness</u> to <u>neat</u> you spell <u>neatness</u>.

(b) Where the last letter or letters of a word are in *italics* these <u>must</u> be left off before adding the endings, e.g.:

nast*y* /ier/iest/ily/iness

Here, the *y* must be left off before making:

nastier, nastiest, nastily, nastiness

(c) The plurals of most nouns may be formed by simply adding the letter **s**. Only where this does not apply, or where the spelling of a plural often gives trouble, is the plural spelling noted, e.g.:

dais*y* /ies	(daisies)		cello /s	(cellos)
cargo /es	(cargoes)		minutia /e	(minutiae)
circus /es	(circuses)			

4. NOTE

If the correct spelling given alongside a mis-spelling has a ⁺ sign after it, then this means that all other given derivations of the word may only be found by looking up the correct spelling again, but in its PROPER ALPHABETICAL PLACE, e.g.:

hapen   happen[1]
hapier   happier[+]
hapless
happen[1]
happi*er* /est/ly/ness

Where the word <u>happier</u> occurs in its correct alphabetical place other forms of the word are given:

happiest, happily, happiness

If you thought that the word <u>elastic</u> began with an **i** you would find that you are spelling the word wrongly and, as the following example shows, the correct spelling of <u>elastic</u> has a ⁺ sign after it:

ilastic   elastic[+]

Now if you look up elastic under **e** instead of **i** you will find that other forms of the word are given:

elastic /ally/ity

5. All the words with the number ¹ or ² or ³ or ⁴ after them are verbs (doing words) or may be used as verbs. If you require the word to end in either <u>ed</u> or <u>ing</u>, then you must remember the following:

(a) If you see ¹ after a word you may add <u>ed</u> or <u>ing</u> to the word without changing it, thus:

add¹   add <u>ed</u>   add <u>ing</u>

(b) If you see ² after a word ending in **e**, the **e** must be dropped before adding <u>ed</u> or <u>ing</u>, thus:

name²   nam <u>ed</u>   nam <u>ing</u>

(c) If you see ³ after a word you must double the final consonant (the last letter) before adding <u>ed</u> or <u>ing</u>, thus:

pat³   patt <u>ed</u>   patt <u>ing</u>

(d) If you see ⁴ after a word (all words with a ⁴ after them end in **y**) you MUST change the **y** to an **i** before adding <u>ed</u>, but you may add <u>ing</u> to the word without changing it, thus:

carry⁴   carri <u>ed</u>   carry <u>ing</u>
cry⁴   cri <u>ed</u>   cry <u>ing</u>

BEWARE

A word having an asterisk (*) after it has the same sound, or almost the same sound, as another word, but it has a different meaning and spelling.

Explanations in brackets (not exact definitions) are only included where the words occur in their correct alphabetical place in the book, e.g.:

berr*y* * (fruit) /ies
berry   bury⁴*
bury⁴* (cover)

If you want to check the meaning of the word <u>bury⁴*</u>, you must look it up in its correct alphabetical place under <u>bu</u> and not under <u>be</u>.

NOTES. (1) Where a dagger (†) appears after the *, the word definition is given on the next line, e.g.:

farth *er* *† /est
†(distant)

(2) The **hyphen** (-) is a sign used to join words and must not be left out, e.g.:

far /-fetched/-flung (far-fetched, far-flung)
fire-engine

KEY TO DICTIONARY SYMBOLS

A list of meanings of the various symbols used appears on the inside back cover of the dictionary.

Dictionary Exercises

Although the instructions on the use of the dictionary are set out clearly enough for a pupil to follow and understand, it would be helpful for the teacher to read through the rules with the pupils and make them do the exercises set out below. There is an exercise to help reinforce each rule, and the final exercise (V) gives the pupil practice in the use of all the rules.

Most pupils will quickly learn how to use the dictionary and the teacher can check whether they are using it accurately simply by giving a verbal test requiring written answers. For those who may need further practice, the teacher may use the exercises set out in *Practise Your Spelling* (O. B. Gregory/C. Maxwell, Wheaton, 1977), which exploit further the special features of the dictionary—and are designed to aid spelling, word study and development of vocabulary.

EXERCISE I

Look up the following words and write out in full all the other words that you can make up from the information you find. (The first question has been done for you.)

1. bite *(biting, bitten)*
2. abundant
3. bleak
4. bush
5. door
6. feeble
7. wealth
8. luck
9. sharp
10. tooth

EXERCISE II

Remember: When the last letter or letters of a word are in *italics*, these must be LEFT OFF before adding the other endings, e.g.:

nast*y* /ier/iest/ily/iness

The *y* in <u>nasty</u> must be left off before making the words

nastier, nastiest, nastily, nastiness

Look up the following words and write out in full all the other words that you can make up from the information you find. (The first question has been done for you.)

1. difficulty *(difficulties)*
2. rowdy
3. geography
4. giddy
5. mightier
6. lady
7. someone
8. greedier
9. busier
10. army

EXERCISE III **Using the numbers 1, 2, 3, and 4**

Use the following example as a guide,

Verb	Past participle	Present participle
peck	pecked	pecking

and write out the corresponding parts of the verbs listed in the following sections A–D. (The first items of sections A–D, respectively, have been done for you.)

A. Using the number 1
1. tick *(ticked, ticking)*
2. bang
3. dismay
4. help
5. thump
6. link
7. lisp
8. hurl
9. shatter
10. drill

10

B. Using the number **2**
1. cripple *(crippled, crippling)*

2. mime	5. slope	8. fuse
3. rinse	6. tremble	9. chuckle
4. blaze	7. wrestle	10. ache

C. Using the number **3**
1. dab *(dabbed, dabbing)*

2. skid	5. jar	8. zigzag
3. beg	6. chip	9. prod
4. whiz	7. hum	10. expel

D. Using the number **4**
1. dignify *(dignified, dignifying)*

2. satisfy	5. busy	8. try
3. disqualify	6. marry	9. fry
4. pity	7. terrify	10. crucify

EXERCISE IV
Combination of numbers and other word endings: e.g. dance ² /r
In the above entry the ² tells us that we can write <u>dancing</u> and <u>danced</u>.
If we add the **r** to the main word <u>dance</u>, we get <u>dancer</u>.
 See if you can do this exercise. Write out in full as many forms of the words
as you can from the information given. (The first question has been done for you.)

1. attract *(attracting, attracted, attraction)*

2. coach	5. guide	8. thin
3. narrow	6. hedge	9. mouth
4. dissatisfy	7. learn	10. travel

EXERCISE V
You are now ready to tackle an exercise containing a mixture of all the rules.
 Look up the following words and write out as many words as you can from the
information given. (The first question has been done for you.)

1. close *(closed, closing, closure)*

2. further	5. young	8. wide
3. playful	6. clever	9. knife
4. run	7. police	10. water

 Your teacher will now ask you to spell a number of words, and if you use the
dictionary correctly, you will get every word right.
 You may also work with another member of your group or class, taking turns to
ask each other how to spell words that you are presently using, until you are quite
confident that you can use the dictionary successfully.

 Remember, on the inside back cover there is a key to the symbols used in this
dictionary.

A

à la carte
aback
abac *us* /i (pl.)
abait   abate[2+]
abanden   abandon[1+]
abandon[1] /ment
abash /ed
abate[2] /ment
abawd   aboard
abawshun   abortion[+]
abawt   abort[1+]
abawtion   abortion[+]
abayans   abeyance[+]
abbey /s
abb *ot* /ess (fem.)
abbreviat *e*[2] /ion
abdicat *e*[2] /ion
abdomen
abdomin *al* /ally/ous
abduct[1] /ion/or
abet[3] /tor
abetor   abettor
abeyan *ce* /t
abeyans   abeyance[+]
abhaw   abhor[3+]
abhor[3] /rence
abhorence   abhorrence
abhorens   abhorrence
abhorent   abhorrent[+]
abhorrent /ly
abidans   abidance
abid *e*[2] /ance
abilit *y* /ies
abismal   abysmal[+]
abiss   abyss
abject /ion/ly/ness
ablative
ablbodid   able-bodied

able /-bodied/r/st
ablie   ably
ably
abnawmal   abnormal[+]
abnawmalitey   abnormality[+]
abnormal /ly
abnormalit *y* /ies
aboard
abode
aboli *sh*[1] /tion
abolishun   abolition
A-bomb
abominabl *e* /y
abominabul   abominable[+]
abominashun   abomination
abominat *e*[2] /ion
abord   aboard
aborigin *al* /es
aborshun   abortion[+]
abort[1] /ive
abortion /ist
abound[1]
about
above /-board
abownd   abound[1]
abowt   about
abracadabra
abrashun   abrasion[+]
abras *ion* /ive
abrawd   abroad
abreast
abrecadabra   abracadabra
abrest   abreast
abreviashun   abbreviation
abreviate   abbreviate[2+]
abreviation   abbreviation
abridge[2] /ment
abrige   abridge[2+]

abroad		abyewse	abuse [2+]
abrord	abroad	abysmal /ly	
abrupt /ly/ness		abyss	
absaloot	absolute [+]	abyusiv	abusive
absawb	absorb [1+]	abzawb	absorb [1+]
absawbency	absorbency [+]	abzawbent	absorbent
absawbensey	absorbency [+]	abzolv	absolve [2+]
absawbent	absorbent	acacia	
absawpshun	absorption [+]	academic /al/ally	
abscess /es		academician	
abscond [1] /er		academishun	academician
absent /ee/eeism		academ*y* /ies	
abserd	absurd [+]	acapuncture	acupuncture
abserditey	absurdity	accede [2] /nce	
absess	abscess [+]	accelerat*e* [2] /ion/or	
absolushun	absolution	accent [1] /ual	
absolut*e* /ely/ism		accentuat*e* [2] /ion	
absolution		accept [1] /ability	
absolv*e* [2] /able		acceptabl*e* /y	
absorb [1] /able		acceptabul	acceptable [+]
absorben*cy* /t		acceshun	accession [+]
absorbensey	absorbency [+]	access /ibility/ible	
absorpshun	absorption [+]	accessar*y* ★ (legal) /ies	
absorpt*ion* /ive		accession /al	
abstain [1] /er		accessor*y* ★† /ies	
abstayn	abstain [1+]	†(accompaniment)	
abstemious /ness		accident /al/ally	
abstemius	abstemious [+]	acclaim [1] /er	
abstenshun	abstention	acclamashun	acclamation [+]
abstention		acclamat*ion* /ory	
abstinen*ce* /t		acclaym	acclaim [1+]
abstinens	abstinence [+]	acclimatis*e* [2] /ation	
abstract [1] /ion/or		accolade	
abstroos	abstruse [+]	accommodat*e* [2] /ion	
abstruse /ness		accompani*st* /ment	
absurd /ity/ities		accompany [4]	
abul	able [+]	accomplice	
abundanc*e* /y		accomplish [1] /ment	
abundans	abundance [+]	accompliss	accomplice
abundant /ly		accord [1] /ance/ingly	
abundent	abundant [+]	accordion /ist	
abunduns	abundance [+]	accordyun	accordion [+]
abus*e* [2] /ive/iveness		accost [1]	
abut [3] /ment		account [1] /ancy/ant	
abuv	above [+]	accountab*le* /ility	

14

accountabul	accountable +
accoutrements	
accredit[1] /ation	
accru *e*[2] /al	
accumpany	accompany[4]
accumulat *e*[2] /ion/or	
accumulative	
accuracy	
accurasey	accuracy
accurate /ly/ness	
accursed /ly/ness	
accusative	
accus *e*[2] /ation/er	
accustom[1]	
ace	
acer	acre +
acerige	acreage
acetate	
acetic	
acetone	
acetylen *e* /ic	
ache[2]	
achevabul	achievable
acheve	achieve[2]+
achievable	
achieve[2] /ment/r	
achromatic	
acid /ic/ity	
acidul *ate*[2] /ous	
acknoledge	acknowledge[2]+
acknolidge	acknowledge[2]+
acknowledge[2] /ment	
aclaim	acclaim[1]+
aclamashun	acclamation +
aclamation	acclamation +
aclaym	acclaim[1]+
acme	
acne	
acolight	acolyte
acolyte	
acommodate	accommodate[2]+
acomodate	accommodate[2]+
acompaniment	accompaniment
acompany	accompany[4]
acompliss	accomplice

acootrements	accoutrements
acord	accord[1]+
acorn	
acost	accost[1]
acount	account[1]+
acoustic /s	
acownt	account[1]+
acquaint[1] /ance	
acquiesce[2] /nce/nt	
acquire[2] /ment	
acquisit *ion* /ive	
acquit[3] /tal	
acre /age	
acrid /ity/ness	
acrimonious /ly	
acrimonius	acrimonious +
acrimony	
acrobat /ic/ically	
acromatic	achromatic
acronim	acronym
acronym	
acropolis	
across	
acseed	accede[2]+
acselerate	accelerate[2]+
acselerater	accelerator
acsent	accent[1]+
acsentuate	accentuate[2]+
acsept	accept[1]+
acseptable	acceptable +
acsesary	accessary *+
acsesary	accessory *+
acseshun	accession +
acsess	access +
acsessorey	accessory *+
acshun	action +
acsident	accident +
act[1] /able	
actini *c* /um	
action /able	
activat *e*[2] /ion/or	
active /ly/ness	
activis *m* /t	
activit *y* /ies	
act *or* /ress (fem.)	

actual /ly		adhearence	adherence
actualit*y* /ies		adhere² /nce/nt	
actuar*y* /ies		adheshun	adhesion⁺
actuat*e*² /ion/or		adhes*ion* /ive	
acumen		adicshun	addiction
acumpany	accompany⁴	adiction	addiction
acumpliss	accomplice	adidge	adage
acumulate	accumulate²⁺	adieu	
acupuncture		adige	adage
acupunkcher	acupuncture	adikwacy	adequacy
acuracy	accuracy	adikwat	adequate⁺
acustic	acoustic⁺	adiquacy	adequacy
acurate	accurate⁺	adiquate	adequate⁺
acustum	accustom¹	adishun	addition⁺
acute /ly/ness		adition	addition⁺
ad	add¹	adjacent /ly	
ad hoc		adjectiv*e* /al	
ad infinitum		adjoin¹	
ad lib.³		adjourn¹ /ment	
adage		adjudge²	
adagio /s		adjudicat*e*² /ion/or	
adamant /ine		adjunct /ion/ive	
adament	adamant⁺	adjust¹ /able/ment	
adapt¹ /ation/ive		adjutan*cy* /t	
adaptab*le* /ility		adle	addle²
adaptabul	adaptable⁺	administ*er*¹ /rable	
adapter ⋆ (person)		administrat*e*² /ion/or	
adaptor ⋆ (electric)		administrater	administrator
add¹		administrative	
addend*um* /a (pl.)		admirabl*e* /y	
addenoids	adenoids	admirabul	admirable⁺
adder		admiral /ty	
addict¹ /ion/ive		admirashun	admiration
addition /al/ally		admir*e*² /ation/er	
addle²		admirul	admiral⁺
address¹ /ee/er		admishun	admission⁺
ade	aid¹⁺	admisibul	admissible⁺
adement	adamant⁺	admissib*le* /ility	
adendum	addendum⁺	admiss*ion* /ive	
adenoids		admit³ /tedly	
adept /ly/ness		admitance	admittance
adequacy		admitans	admittance
adequasey	adequacy	admittance	
adequate /ly/ness		admonish¹ /er/ment	
adhear	adhere²⁺	ado	

16

adobe	
adobi	adobe
adolescen *ce* /t	
adolesence	adolescence +
adolesens	adolescence +
adolesent	adolescent
adoor	adore ²+
adopshun	adoption
adopt ¹ /er/ion/ive	
adorabl *e* /y	
adorabul	adorable +
ador *e* ² /ation	
adorn ¹ /ment	
adrenal /in	
adrift	
adroit /ly/ness	
adsorpshun	adsorption +
adsorpt *ion* /ive	
adue	adieu
adul	addle ²
adulashun	adulation
adulat *e* ² /ion/or	
adult /hood	
adulterat *e* ² /ion/or	
adulterus	adulterous
adulter *y* /er/ous	
advance ² /ment	
advans	advance ²+
advencher	adventure ²+
advencherous	adventurous +
advencherus	adventurous +
advent	
adventishus	adventitious +
adventitious /ly/ness	
adventure ² /some	
adventurous /ly/ness	
adverb /ial	
adversar *y* /ies	
adverse /ly/ness	
adversit *y* /ies	
advertise ² /ment	
advice ★ (a suggestion)	
advisabl *e* /y	
advisabul	advisable +
advise ² ★ (suggest)	

advis *edly* /er/ory	
advocacy	
advocasey	advocacy
advocat *e* ² /or	
advurse	adverse +
advurtisment	advertisement
aegis	
aerat *e* ² /ion/or	
aerial /ly	
aerobatics	
aerodrome	
aerodynamics	
aerofoil	
aeronaut /ical/ics	
aeroplane	
aerosol	
aesthet *e* /ic/icism	
afable	affable +
afabul	affable +
afair	affair
afare	affair
afecshun	affection
afecshunate	affectionate +
afect	affect ¹+
afectation	affectation
afection	affection
afectionate	affectionate +
afective	affective
afeild	afield
afeld	afield
aferm	affirm ¹+
afermativ	affirmative +
affab *le* /ility/ly	
affair	
affect ¹ /ion/ive	
affectation	
affectionate /ly/ness	
affidavit	
affiks	affix ¹+
affiliat *e* ² /ion	
affinit *y* /ies	
affirm ¹ /ation	
affirmative /ly	
affix ¹ /er	
afflict ¹ /ion	

affluen *ce* /t		after	
affluens	affluence [+]	afterbirth	
afford [1] /able		afterburth	afterbirth
afforest [1] /ation		aftermath	
affray /s		afternoon	
affront [1]		afterthort	afterthought
afid	aphid [+]	afterthought	
afidavit	affidavit	afterwards	
afield		afterwerds	afterwards
afiks	affix [1+]	afurm	affirm [1+]
afiliashun	affiliation	afurmashun	affirmation
afiliate	affiliate [2+]	afurmation	affirmation
afiliation	affiliation	afurmativ	affirmative [+]
afinitey	affinity [+]	again	
afire		against	
afirm	affirm [1+]	agast	aghast
afirmativ	affirmative [+]	agate	
afix	affix [1+]	agayn	again
aflaim	aflame	age [2] /less	
aflame		agen	again
aflicshun	affliction	agenc *y* /ies	
aflict	afflict [1+]	agenda	
afliction	affliction	agensey	agency [+]
afloat		agenst	against
aflote	afloat	agent /ial	
afluence	affluence [+]	agglomerat *e* [2] /ion	
afluens	affluence [+]	aggrandise [2] /ment	
afluent	affluent	aggravat *e* [2] /ion	
aford	afford [1+]	aggregat *e* [2] /ely/ion	
aforesaid		aggreshun	aggression [+]
aforest	afforest [1+]	aggress *ion* /or	
aforestashun	afforestation	aggressive /ly/ness	
aforestation	afforestation	aggrieved	
aforism	aphorism [+]	aghast	
aforistic	aphoristic	agil *e* /ity	
aforsed	aforesaid	agitat *e* [2] /ion/or	
afrade	afraid	aglomerashun	agglomeration
afraid		aglomerate	agglomerate [2+]
afray	affray [+]	aglomeration	agglomeration
afrayd	afraid	aglow	
African		agnostic /ism	
Afrikaans		agonie	agony [+]
Afrikans	Afrikaans	agonis *e* [2] /ingly	
afrodisiac	aphrodisiac	agon *y* /ies	
afront	affront [1]	agorafobia	agoraphobia

agoraphobia		air hostess /es	
agrafobia	agoraphobia	airial	aerial +
agrandise	aggrandise ²⁺	airily	
agrarian		airline /r	
agravate	aggravate ²⁺	air-lock	
agree /d/ing/ment		airmail ¹	
agreeabl e /y		airmale	airmail ¹
agregate	aggregate ²⁺	airobatics	aerobatics
agrement	agreement	airodinamics	aerodynamics
agreshun	aggression +	airodrome	aerodrome
agresion	aggression +	airofoil	aerofoil
agresiv	aggressive +	airofoyl	aerofoil
agression	aggression +	aironort	aeronaut +
agreved	aggrieved	aironortics	aeronautics
agriculcher	agriculture +	airoplane	aeroplane
agricultur e /al/ally		airosol	aerosol
agrieved	aggrieved	air-pocket	
aground		airport	
agrownd	aground	air raid	
agu e /ish		airworth y /iness	
ahead		airy /-fairy	
ahed	ahead	aisle ★ (passage)	
ahoi	ahoy	aisle	isle ★
ahoy		ajar	
aid ¹ /er		ajasent	adjacent +
ail ¹★ (trouble)		ajectiv	adjective +
ail	ale ★	ajency	agency +
ailment		ajenda	agenda
aim ¹ /less/lessly		ajensey	agency +
air ¹★ (gases)		ajent	agent +
air	ere ★	ajile	agile +
air	heir ★	ajilitey	agility
airate	aerate ²⁺	ajitashun	agitation
airborne		ajitate	agitate ²⁺
air-brake		ajoyn	adjoin ¹
aircondishner	air-conditioner	ajudicate	adjudicate ²⁺
air-conditioner		ajunct	adjunct +
air-cooled		ajurn	adjourn ¹⁺
aircraft		ajusment	adjustment
aires	Aries	ajust	adjust ¹⁺
airey	airy +	ajustable	adjustable
airfeild	airfield	ajutancy	adjutancy +
airfield		akimbo	
air force		akin	
air-gun		aksiomatic	axiomatic +

19

aksis	axis +	alegation	allegation
aksium	axiom	alege	allege 2+
akwaintance	acquaintance	alegiance	allegiance
akwalung	aqualung	alegians	allegiance
akwamarine	aquamarine	alegorey	allegory +
akwaplane	aquaplane	alegorical	allegorical +
akwarium	aquarium +	alelooya	alleluia
akwarius	Aquarius	aleluia	alleluia
akwatic	aquatic	alergey	allergy +
akwatint	aquatint	alergic	allergic
akwiduct	aqueduct	alert 1 /ly/ness	
akwiesence	acquiescence	aleviate	alleviate 2+
akwiesent	acquiescent	alfa	alpha
akwiline	aquiline	alfabet	alphabet +
akwire	acquire 2+	alfabetical	alphabetical
akwisition	acquisition +	alfresco	
akwisitiv	acquisitive	alga /e (pl.)	
akwit	acquit 3+	algebra	
akwital	acquittal	algibra	algebra
alabaster		ali	ally 4+
alack		aliance	alliance
alacrit y /ous		alians	alliance
alagro	allegro	alias /es	
alah	Allah	alibi /s	
alarm 1 /ist		aliby	alibi +
alas		alien /able	
alay	allay 1+	alienat e 2 /ion/or	
albatross		aligater	alligator
albeit		alight 1	
albeno	albino +	align 1 /ment	
albino /s		alike /ness	
album		alimenta ry /tion	
albumen *†		alimentrey	alimentary +
†(white of egg)		alimony	
albumin *†		aline	align 1+
†(soluble protein)		alite	alight 1
alchem y /ist		aliterashun	alliteration
alcohol /ic/ism		aliterate	alliterate 2+
alcove		aliteration	alliteration
alder		alive	
alderman /cy		alkali /s	
ale * (drink)		alkalin e /ity	
ale	ail 1*	alkemey	alchemy +
alegashun	allegation	alkemist	alchemist
alegater	alligator	all * (everyone)	

20

all	awl ★	almon *er* /ry	
Allah		almost	
allay¹ /er		alms ★ (charity)	
allegashun	allegation	alms	arms ★
allegation		alms-house	
allege² /dly		alocate	allocate²⁺
allegiance		alocation	allocation
allegorical /ly		aloft	
allegor*y* /ies		aloi	alloy¹
allegro		alone	
alleluia		along /side	
allergic		alood	allude²★
allerg*y* /ies		aloof /ness	
alleviat*e*² /ion		alot	allot³⁺
alley /s/way		alotment	allotment
alli	ally⁴	aloud	
alliance		alow	allow¹⁺
allians	alliance	alowable	allowable
alligator		alowabul	allowable
alliterat*e*² /ion/ive		alowance	allowance
allmost	almost	alowans	allowance
allocat*e*² /ion		alowd	aloud
allot³ /ment		aloy	alloy¹
allotropes		alp /ine	
allow¹ /able/ance		alpaca	
alloy¹		alpaka	alpaca
all right		alpha	
allrite	all right	alphabet /ical/ically	
allso	also	alpine	
allude²★ (refer to)		already	
allude	elude²★	alredy	already
allure² /ment		alright	all right
allushun	allusion ★	alrite	all right
allusion★ (reference to)		alsashun	Alsatian
allusion	illusion ★	Alsatian	
allusive ★† /ly/ness		also	
† (suggestive)		altar ★ (church)	
allusive	elusive ★⁺	altarpiece	
allusive	illusive ★	alter¹★ (change)	
alluvi *al* /um		altera *ble* /tion	
all*y*⁴ /ies		alterabul	alterable⁺
ally	alley ⁺	alterashun	alteration
almanac		altercat*e*² /ion	
almighty		alternashun	alternation
almond		alternat*e*² /ion/or	

21

alternative /ly	
alterpeace	altarpiece
alterpiece	altarpiece
altho	although
although	
altimeter	
altitude	
alto /s	
altogether	
altrooism	altruism
altrooist	altruist [+]
altrooistic	altruistic
altruism	
altruist /ic/ically	
alude	allude [2]★
alum	
aluminium	
aluminum	aluminium
alure	allure [2+]
alurt	alert [1+]
alushun	allusion ★
alusion	allusion ★
alusiv	allusive ★+
always	
amaise	amaze [2+]
amalgam	
amalgamashun	amalgamation
amalgamat *e* [2] /ion	
amass [1] /able/ment	
amater	amateur [+]
amateur /ish/ism	
amaze [2] /ment	
Amazon /ian	
ambasader	ambassador [+]
ambassador /ial	
amber	
ambiant	ambient
ambidekstrus	ambidextrous
ambidextrous	
ambidextrus	ambidextrous
ambien *ce* /t	
ambiens	ambience [+]
ambiguit *y* /ies	
ambiguous /ly/ness	
ambiguus	ambiguous [+]

ambishun	ambition
ambishus	ambitious [+]
ambit	
ambition	
ambitious /ly/ness	
ambivalen *ce* /t	
amble [2] /r	
amboosh	ambush [1+]
ambrosia /l	
ambul	amble [2+]
ambulance	
ambulans	ambulance
ambulat *e* [2] /ory	
ambush [1] /er	
ame	aim [1+]
ameba	amoeba
amelierashun	amelioration
amelierate	ameliorate [2+]
ameliorat *e* [2] /ion	
amen	
amenabl *e* /y	
amenabul	amenable [+]
amend [1] /ment	
amenit *y* /ies	
American	
ameter	ammeter
amethyst /ine	
amfibian	amphibian
amfibious	amphibious [+]
amfibius	amphibious [+]
amfitheater	amphitheatre
amiab *le* /ility/ly	
amiabul	amiable [+]
amicab *le* /ility/ly	
amicabul	amicable [+]
amid /st	
amiss	
amiter	ammeter
amitey	amity
amithist	amethyst [+]
amity	
ammeter	
ammonia /c/cal	
ammonya	ammonia [+]
ammunishun	ammunition

ammunition	
amnest *y* /ies	
amoeba	
amoner	almoner +
among /st	
amonia	ammonia +
amonya	ammonia +
amoral /ity/ly	
amorfus	amorphous +
amorous /ly	
amorphous /ly/ness	
amortise 2	
amorus	amorous +
amount 1	
amownt	amount 1
ampar	ampere +
amper *e* /age	
amperige	amperage
amphibian	
amphibious /ly/ness	
amphitheatre	
ampl *e* /y	
amplie	amply
amplifi	amplify 4+
amplif *y* 4 /ier	
amplitude	
ampool	ampoule
ampoule	
ampul	ample +
amputashun	amputation
amputat *e* 2 /ion	
amulet	
amung	among +
amunishun	ammunition
amunition	ammunition
amuse 2 /ment/r	
anachronism	
anachronistic /ally	
anaconda	
anacronism	anachronism
anacronistic	anachronistic +
anaemi *a* /c	
anaesthe *sia* /tic/tist	
anaesthetis *e* 2 /ation	
anagram /matic	

anakey	
anakronism	
anal	
analgesi *a* /c	
analise	analyse 2+
analisis	analysis +
analist	analyst
analitic	analytic +
analog	analogue
analogey	analogy +
analogous /ly	
analogue	
analogus	analogous +
analog *y* /ies	
anals	annals
analyse 2 /r	
analys *is* /es (pl.)	
analyst	
analytic /al/ally	
anarchi *c* /sm/st	
anarch *y* /ical	
anarkey	anarchy +
anarkick	anarchic +
anarkism	anarchism
anarkist	anarchist
anathema	
anatomic *al* /ally	
anatomise 2	
anatom *y* /ist	
ancest *or* /ress (fem.)	
ancestr *y* /al	
anchor 1 /age	
anchov *y* /ies	
ancient /ly/ness	
ancillar *y* /ies	
andante	
androginus	androgynous +
androgyn *ous* /y	
anecdot *e* /al/ic	
aneks	annex 1★
aneks	annexe ★
aneksashun	annexation
aneksation	annexation
anemia	anaemia +
anemic	anaemic

anarchy +
anachronism

anemomet *er* /ry	
anemone	
anemya	anaemia [+]
aneroid	
anesthesia	anaesthesia [+]
anesthetic	anaesthetic
anesthetise	anaesthetise [2+]
anesthetist	anaesthetist
anew	
angel ★ (heavenly)	
angel	angle [2]★
angelic /al/ally	
angena	angina
anger	
angina	
angle [2]★ (geometry)	
angler	
Anglican /ism	
anglicise [2]	
anglisise	anglicise [2]
anglosaksen	Anglo-Saxon
Anglo-Saxon	
angora	
angrie	angry [+]
angr *y* /ier/iest/ily	
angsietey	anxiety [+]
anguish [1]	
angular /ity	
anguler	angular [+]
angwish	anguish [1]
anhidrus	anhydrous
anhydrous	
anihilate	annihilate [2+]
aniilate	annihilate [2+]
anilen	aniline
aniline	
animal /ism/istic	
animashun	animation
animat *e* [2] /ion	
animatedly	
animosit *y* /ies	
animul	animal [+]
aniseed	
aniversarey	anniversary [+]
anjelic	angelic [+]

anjelical	angelical
anker	anchor [1+]
ankerage	anchorage
ankerige	anchorage
ankle /bone/t	
ankshous	anxious [+]
ankshus	anxious [+]
ankul	ankle [+]
annals	
anneal [1]	
annex [1]★† /ation	
† (take possession of)	
annexe ★ (of house)	
annihilat *e* [2] /ion	
anniversar *y* /ies	
Anno Domini	
annon	anon
annotat *e* [2] /ion/or	
announce [2] /ment/r	
announs	announce [2+]
annoy [1] /ance/ingly	
annoyans	annoyance
annual /ly	
annuit *y* /ies	
annul [3] /ment	
annular /ity	
annunciat *e* [2] /ion	
Ano domini	Anno Domini
anod *e* /al	
anodine	anodyne
anodyne	
anoi	annoy [1+]
anoiance	annoyance
anoians	annoyance
anoint [1] /er/ment	
anomaley	anomaly [+]
anomalous /ly	
anomalus	anomalous [+]
anomal *y* /ies	
anon	
anonimitey	anonymity
anonimous	anonymous [+]
anonimus	anonymous [+]
anonymity	
anonymous /ly/ness	

24

anorak	
anotashun	annotation
anotate	annotate [2+]
anotation	annotation
another	
anounce	announce [2+]
anouns	announce [2+]
anounser	announcer
anownce	announce [2+]
anowns	announce [2+]
anoy	annoy [1+]
anoyance	annoyance
anoyans	annoyance
anoynt	anoint [1+]
anser	answer [1+]
anserable	answerable
anserabul	answerable
ansester	ancestor [+]
ansestrul	ancestral
ansestry	ancestry [+]
anshent	ancient [+]
ansilarey	ancillary [+]
answer [1] /able/er	
ant /-eater/-hill	
ant	aunt [+]
antacid	
antagonis e [2] /m	
antagonist /ic/ically	
Antarctic	
antasid	antacid
anteceden ce /t	
antecedens	antecedence [+]
antechamber	
antedate [2]	
antediluvian	
anteek	antique [+]
antelope	
antena	antenna [+]
antenatal	
antenna /e (pl.)	
anterier	anterior
anterior	
anteroom	
anthem	
anther	

antholog y /ies/ist	
anthracit e /ic	
anthraks	anthrax
anthrasite	anthracite [+]
anthrax	
anthropoid /al	
anthropologey	anthropology [+]
anthropologist	
anthropolog y /ical	
anthropoyd	anthropoid [+]
anti-aircraft	
antibiotic	
antibod y /ies	
antic	
antichamber	antechamber
antichrist	
anticiclone	anticyclone [+]
anticipat e [2] /ion/ory	
anticlimaks	anticlimax [+]
anticlima x /ctic	
anticyclon e /ic	
antidate	antedate [2]
antidiloovian	antediluvian
antidot e /al/ally	
anti-freeze	
antihistamine	
antikwarian	antiquarian
antikwate	antiquate [2]
antikwerey	antiquary [+]
antikwitey	antiquity [+]
antilope	antelope
antimon y /ial	
antinatul	antenatal
antipathey	antipathy [+]
antipath y /etic	
antipodes	
antiquar y /ies/ian	
antiquate [2]	
antique /ness	
antiquit y /ies	
antiroom	anteroom
antisedens	antecedence [+]
anti-semiti c /sm	
antiseptic /ally	
antisiclone	anticyclone [+]

antisipashun	anticipation	aparishun	apparition
antisipate	anticipate [2+]	aparition	apparition
antisipation	anticipation	apart	
antisocial /ly		apartat	apartheid
antisoshal	antisocial [+]	apartheid	
antithes *is* /es (pl.)		apartied	apartheid
antithisis	antithesis [+]	apartment	
antitoksic	antitoxic [+]	apase	apace
antitoksin	antitoxin	apathetic /al/ally	
antitoxi *c* /n		apathy	
antler /ed		ape [2]	
anu	anew	apeace	apiece
anual	annual [+]	apeal	appeal [1+]
anuitey	annuity [+]	apear	appear [1+]
anul	anal	apearance	appearance
anul	annul [3+]	apearans	appearance
anular	annular [+]	apease	apiece
anulment	annulment	apeel	appeal [1+]
anunciashun	annunciation	apeer	appear [1+]
anunciate	annunciate [2+]	apeice	apiece
anunciation	annunciation	apeks	apex [+]
anunsiashun	annunciation	apellant	appellant [+]
anunsiate	annunciate [2+]	apellashun	appellation
anunsiation	annunciation	apellation	appellation
anus		apend	append [1+]
anuther	another	apendage	appendage
anvil		apendicitis	appendicitis
anxiet *y* /ies		apendige	appendage
anxious /ly/ness		apendiks	appendix [+]
any		apendisitis	appendicitis
anybody		apendix	appendix [+]
anyhow		aperance	appearance
anyone		aperans	appearance
anything		apercher	aperture
anyual	annual [+]	apergey	apogee [+]
anyway		aperitif	
anywere	anywhere	apertain	appertain [1]
anywhere		aperture	
aorta		apetiser	appetiser
apace		apetising	appetising [+]
Apache		apetite	appetite
apal	appal [3+]	ap *ex* /exes/ices (pls.)	
aparatus	apparatus [+]	aphid /ian	
aparel	apparel [+]	aphoris *m* /tic	
aparent	apparent [+]	aphrodisiac	

apiar *y* /ies	
apiece	
apissul	epistle +
apitite	appetite
aplaud	applaud [1]
aplause	applause
aplawd	applaud [1]
aplawse	applause
aple	apple +
apli	apply [4]
apliance	appliance
aplians	appliance
aplicable	applicable +
aplicabul	applicable +
aplicant	applicant
aplicashun	application
aplication	application
aplom	aplomb
aplomb	
apocalips	apocalypse +
apocalyp *se* /tic	
apocrifal	apocryphal
apocryphal	
apoge *e* /an	
apoint	appoint [1+]
apologetic /ally	
apologey	apology +
apologise [2]	
apolog *y* /ies/ist	
apoplectic /ally	
apopleksey	apoplexy
apoplexy	
aporshun	apportion [1+]
aportion	apportion [1+]
aposishun	apposition
aposit	apposite
aposition	apposition
aposle	apostle +
apost *le* /olate/olic	
apostrofey	apostrophe
apostrophe	
aposul	apostle +
apothecar *y* /ies	
apoynt	appoint [1+]
appal [3] /ingly	

apparatus /es	
apparel /led	
apparent /ly	
apparishun	apparition
apparition	
appeal [1] /ingly	
appear [1] /ance	
appease [2] /ment/r	
appella *nt* /tion	
append [1] /age	
appendices (pl.)	
appendicitis	
appendiks	appendix +
appendix /es (pl.)	
appertain [1]	
apperture	aperture
appetiser	
appetising /ly	
appetite	
applaud [1]	
applause	
applawd	applaud [1]
applaws	applause
apple /-cart/-pie	
appli	apply [4]
appliance	
applians	appliance
applicab *le* /ility	
applicant	
applicashun	application
application	
apply [4]	
appoint [1] /ment	
apporshun	apportion [1+]
apportion [1] /ment	
apposishun	apposition
apposite	
apposition	
appreciabl *e* /y	
appreciabul	appreciable +
appreciat *e* [2] /ion/ive	
apprehend [1]	
apprehenshun	apprehension
apprehension	
apprehensive /ly/ness	

apprentice ² /ship	
apprentis	apprentice ²⁺
apprise ²	
approach ¹ /able	
approbation	
approch	approach ¹⁺
appropriate ² /ly/ness	
appropriat*ion* /or	
approval	
approve ²	
approximashun	approximation
approximate ² /ly	
approximation	
aprehend	apprehend ¹
aprehenshun	apprehension
aprehensiv	apprehensive ⁺
apren	apron ¹
aprentis	apprentice ²⁺
apreshabul	appreciable ⁺
apreshiable	appreciable ⁺
apreshiativ	appreciative
apresiashun	appreciation
apricot	
April	
aprise	apprise ²
aprize	apprise ²
aproach	approach ¹⁺
aprobashun	approbation
aprobation	approbation
aproch	approach ¹⁺
aprochabul	approachable
aproksimashun	approximation
aproksimat	approximate ²⁺
aproksimation	approximation
apron ¹	
aproov	approve ²
aprooval	approval
apropo	apropos
apropos	
apropriashun	appropriation ⁺
apropriate	appropriate ²⁺
apropriation	appropriation ⁺
aproval	approval
aprove	approve ²
aproximate	approximate ²⁺

aproximation	approximation
apt /ly/ness	
aptitude	
aptley	aptly
apul	apple ⁺
aqualung	
aquamarine	
aquaplane	
aquarelle	
aquari*um* /a/ums (pls.)	
Aquarius	
aquatic	
aquatint	
aqueduct	
aqueous	
aquiline	
aquius	aqueous
ar	are ⁺
arabel	arable
arabesk	arabesque
arabesque	
Arabi*an* /c	
arable	
arabul	arable
araign	arraign ¹⁺
arain	arraign ¹⁺
Aramaic	
arange	arrange ²⁺
arant	arrant ⁺
aray	array ¹⁺
arayn	arraign ¹⁺
arber	arbour
arbiter	
arbitrar*y* /ily/iness	
arbitrashun	arbitration
arbitrat*e* ² /ion/or	
arbour	
arc ★ (curved line)	
arc	ark ★
arcade	
arch /es/ly/ness	
archaeolog*y* /ical/ist	
archai*c* /sm	
archangel	
archaologey	archaeology ⁺

archbishop
archdeacon
archduke
archeologey   archaeology +
archer /y
archetype
archfeind   archfiend
archfiend
archipelago /s
architect /ure
architectural /ly
archiv es /ist
archley   archly
archway
arcipeligo   archipelago +
arcitect   architect +
arcitectural   architectural +
arcives   archives +
arc -lamp /-light
Arctic
ardent /ly
arder   ardour
ardewus   arduous +
ardour
arduous /ly/ness
arduus   arduous +
are /n't
area * (surface)
area   aria *
arears   arrears
arees   Aries
arena
arent   aren't
arest   arrest [1]+
argew   argue [2]+
argu   argue [2]+
arguabul   arguable
argu e [2] /able/ably
argument /ative
ari   awry
aria * (song)
aria   area *
arial   aerial +
arid /ity
Aries

aright
ariley   airily
arina   arena
arise /n
aristocracy
aristocrasey   aristocracy
aristocrat /ic
arite   aright
arithmetic /ian
arithmetical /ly
arival   arrival
arive   arrive [2]+
arizen   arisen
ark * (floating vessel)
ark   arc *
arkade   arcade
arkaic   archaic +
arkangel   archangel
arkiologey   archaeology +
arkiologist   archaeologist
arkipeligo   archipelago +
arkitect   architect +
arkitectural   architectural +
arkives   archives +
arktic   Arctic
arktipe   archetype
arm [1] /ful/let
armada
armadillo /es
armament
armchair
armer   armour +
armey   army +
armistice
armistis   armistice
armoner   almoner +
armour /ed
arms * (limbs)
arms   alms *
arm y /ies
arnt   aren't
arogance   arrogance +
arogans   arrogance +
arogant   arrogant
arogate   arrogate [2]+

aroma /s/tic	
arora	aurora
aroroot	arrowroot
arose	
around	
arouse [2]	
arow	arrow [+]
arownd	around
arowroot	arrowroot
arowse	arouse [2]
arpeggio /s	
arpejo	arpeggio [+]
arraign [1] /ment	
arrange [2] /ment	
arrant /ly	
array [1] /s	
arrears	
arrest [1] /er	
arrival	
arrive [2] /r	
arrogan ce /t/tly	
arrogans	arrogance [+]
arrogat e [2] /ion	
arrow /-head	
arrowroot	
arsenal	
arsenic /al	
arsnic	arsenic [+]
arson /ist	
artefact	
arter y /ies	
arteshun	artesian
artesian	
artful /ly/ness	
arthriti c /s	
arthropod	
artichoke	
article [2]	
articul	article [2]
articular	
articulat e [2] /ion	
artifice /r	
artificial /ity/ly	
artifis	artifice [+]
artifishal	artificial [+]

artiller y /ies	
artisan	
artist * (painter)	
artiste * (performer)	
artistic /ally	
artistry	
artizan	artisan
artless /ly/ness	
asail	assail [1+]
asailant	assailant
asalant	assailant
asale	assail [1+]
asalt	assault [1+]
asassin	assassin
asassinashun	assassination
asassinate	assassinate [2+]
asassination	assassination
asault	assault [1+]
asay	assay [1+]
asayl	assail [1+]
asbestos /is	
ascend [1] /ancy/ant	
ascenshun	ascension
ascension	
ascent * (rise)	
ascent	assent [1*]
ascertain [1] /able	
ascetic /ally/ism	
ascrib e [2] /able	
ase	ace
asemblage	assemblage
asemble	assemble [2+]
asembley	assembly [+]
asemblige	assemblage
asembul	assemble [2+]
asend	ascend [1+]
asendancy	ascendancy
asendansey	ascendancy
asendant	ascendant
asenshun	ascension
asension	ascension
asent	ascent *
asent	assent [1*]
asep sis /tic	
asershun	assertion

asert	assert [1+]	asistance	assistance
asertain	ascertain [1+]	asistans	assistance
asertane	ascertain [1+]	asistant	assistant
asertayn	ascertain [1+]	asitic	acetic
asertion	assertion	ask [1]	
asertive	assertive	askance	
asess	assess [1+]	askans	askance
asesser	assessor	askew	
asessment	assessment	asku	askew
aset	asset	asleep	
asetic	ascetic [+]	asma	asthma [+]
aseticism	asceticism	asmatic	asthmatic
asfalt	asphalt	asociate	associate [2+]
asfixia	asphyxia	asociation	association
asfixiate	asphyxiate [2+]	asonance	assonance [+]
ash /es/en/-tray/y		asonans	assonance [+]
ashamed		asonant	assonant
ashfalt	asphalt	asort	assort [1+]
ashor	assure [2*]	asoshiashun	association
ashorance	assurance	asoshiate	associate [2+]
ashorans	assurance	aspadistra	aspidistra
ashore * (on beach)		asparagus	
ashore	assure [2*]	aspect	
aside		aspen	
asiditey	acidity	asperit y /ies	
asidulate	acidulate [2+]	aspershun	aspersion
asiduous	assiduous [+]	aspersion	
asiduus	assiduous [+]	asphalt	
asign	assign [1+]	asphyxia	
asignashun	assignation	asphyxiat e [2] /ion	
asignation	assignation	aspic	
asignment	assignment	aspidistra	
asilum	asylum	aspirashun	aspiration
asimetrical	asymmetrical	aspir e [2] /ation	
asimilashun	assimilation	aspirin	
asimilate	assimilate [2+]	asprin	aspirin
asimilater	assimilator	ass /es	
asimilation	assimilation	assail [1] /able/ant	
asimitrey	asymmetry [+]	assassin	
asinable	assignable	assassinat e [2] /ion	
asinabul	assignable	assault [1] /er	
asine	assign [1+]	assay [1] /er	
asinement	assignment	assembl e [2] /age	
asinin e /ity		assembl y /ies	
asist	assist [1+]	assembul	assemble [2+]

assend	ascend [1+]	astronaut /ic/ical	
assendancy	ascendancy	astronomy	
assendant	ascendant	astronort	astronaut [+]
assenshun	ascension	astronortic	astronautic
assension	ascension	astrul	astral [+]
assent [1*] (agree)		astur	astir [*]
assent	ascent [*]	asturn	astern
assert [1] /ion/ive		astute /ly/ness	
assess [1] /ment/or		asume	assume [2+]
asset		asumpshun	assumption
assiduous /ly		asumption	assumption
assign [1] /able/ation/ment		asunder	
assignee		aswage	assuage [2+]
assimilat *e* [2] /ion/or		asylum	
assine	assign [1+]	asymetrey	asymmetry [+]
assist [1] /ance/ant		asymmetr *y* /ical	
associat *e* [2] /ion		atach	attach [1+]
assonan *ce* /t		atachable	attachable
assonans	assonance [+]	atachabul	attachable
assort [1] /ment		atachay case	attaché case
assoshiate	associate [2+]	atack	attack [1+]
assuage [2] /ment		atain	attain [1+]
assum *e* [2] /able/ably		atane	attain [1+]
assumption		ate [*] (did eat)	
assumshun	assumption	ate	eight [*]
assurance		ateen	eighteen [+]
assurans	assurance	atempt	attempt [1+]
assure [2*] (make certain)		atend	attend [1+]
aster [*] (flower)		atendance	attendance
aster	astir [*]	atendans	attendance
asterisk		atendant	attendant
astern		atenshun	attention [+]
asteroid		atention	attention [+]
asthma /tic		atentiv	attentive
astigmati *c* /sm		atenuashun	attenuation
astir [*] (motion)		atenuate	attenuate [2+]
astonish [1] /ment		atenuation	attenuation
astound [1] /ingly		aterney	attorney [+]
astownd	astound [1+]	atest	attest [1+]
astral /ly		atestashun	attestation
astray		atestation	attestation
astrel	astral [+]	atey	eighty [+]
astride		atheis *m* /t/tic	
astringen *cy* /t		athiism	atheism [+]
astrolog *y* /er/ical		athiist	atheist

32

athleet	athlete	attest¹ /ation	
athlete		attic	
athletic /ism/s		attire²	
atic	attic	attitude	
atipical	atypical⁺	attorney /s	
atire	attire²	attract¹ /ion	
atitude	attitude	attractive /ly/ness	
Atlantic		attributable	
atlas /es		attribut e² /ion/ive	
atmosfere	atmosphere⁺	attrishun	attrition
atmosferic	atmospheric	attrition	
atmospher e /ic		attune²	
atom /ic/ically		atune	attune²
atomise² /r		aturney	attorney⁺
atone² /ment		atypical /ly	
atract	attract¹⁺	au pair	
atraction	attraction	aubergine	
atractiv	attractive⁺	auburn	
atribushun	attribution	aucshun	auction¹⁺
atributable	attributable	auction¹ /eer	
atributabul	attributable	audacious /ly	
atribute	attribute²⁺	audacity	
atribution	attribution	audashus	audacious⁺
atrishun	attrition	audasitey	audacity
atrition	attrition	audib le /ility/ly	
atrium		audibul	audible⁺
atrocious /ly/ness		audience	
atrocit y /ies		audiens	audience
atrofey	atrophy⁴⁺	audiomet er /ric/ry	
atroph y⁴ /ic		audio-typist	
atroshus	atrocious⁺	audio-visual	
atrositey	atrocity⁺	audishun	audition¹
attach¹ /able		audit¹	
attachabul	attachable	audition¹	
attaché case		auditor	
attachment		auditorium	
attack¹ /er		auditory	
attain¹ /able/ment		auditrey	auditory
attempt¹ /able		auger ★ (tool)	
attend¹ /ance		aught ★ (anything)	
attendant		aught	ought ★
attenshun	attention⁺	augment¹ /ation	
attent ion /ive		augur¹★ (predict)	
attenuat e² /ion		augur y /ies	
atterney	attorney⁺	August	

aunt /ie/y		availab *le* /ility	
aura		avalable	available +
aural *(of the ear) /ly		avalabul	available +
auric *le* /ular		avalanche	
aurora		avale	avail [1]
auspic *es* /ious		avarey	aviary +
auspishus	auspicious	avaric *e* /ious	
austere /ly/ness		avenew	avenue
austerit *y* /ies		avenge [2] /r	
Australian		avenue	
authentic /ally/ity		aver [3] /ment	
authenticat *e* [2] /ion		average [2] /ly	
author /ess (fem.)		averige	average [2]+
authoris *e* [2] /ation		averishus	avaricious
authoritarian /ism		averiss	avarice +
authoritative /ly		averse /ly/ness	
authorit *y* /ies		avershun	aversion
autis *m* /tic		aversion	
autobiografey	autobiography +	avert [1] /edly	
autobiografical	autobiographi-cal +	aviar *y* /ies	
autobiographical /ly		aviashun	aviation +
autobiograph *y* /ies		aviater	aviator
autocrac *y* /ies		aviat *ion* /or	
autocrasey	autocracy +	avid /ity/ly	
autocrat		avlanch	avalanche
autocratic /ally		avocado	
autograf	autograph [1]+	avocashun	avocation
autograph [1] /ic		avocation	
automat *e* [2] /ion		avoid [1] /able/ably	
automatic /ally		avow [1] /al/edly	
automatism		avoyd	avoid [1]+
automaton		avoydable	avoidable
automobile		avoydabul	avoidable
autonomous /ly		avrige	average [2]+
autonomus	autonomous +	avur	aver [3]+
autonomy		avurs	averse +
autopilot		avurshun	aversion
autops *y* /ies		avursion	aversion
autum	autumn +	avurt	avert [1]+
autumn /al		await [1]	
auxiliar *y* /ies		awake [2]	
avaidable	available +	awaken [1]	
avaide	evade [2]+	award [1] /able/er	
avail [1]		aware /ness	
		awate	await [1]

away	
awb	orb [1]
awe [2]★(fear)/some/struck	
awear	aware [+]
awful /ly/ness	
awgsiliarey	auxiliary [+]
Awgust	August
awgy	orgy [+]
awhile	
awile	awhile
awiyul	awhile
awkward /ly/ness	
awl ★ (tool)	
awning	
awoard	award [1+]
awoke	
awry	
axe [2]	
axial	
axident	accident [+]
axiom	
axiomatic /ally	
ax is /es (pl.)	
axle	
axseed	accede [2+]
axsel	axle
axselerate	accelerate [2+]
axsent	accent [1+]
axsentuate	accentuate [2+]
axsept	accept [1+]
axseptable	acceptable [+]
axseptabul	acceptable [+]
axsesorey	accessory [+]
axsess	access [+]
axsessible	accessible
axsessibul	accessible
ay ★ (yes) /es ★	
ay	eye [2★+]
ay	I ★+
aya	ayah
ayah	
aye ★ (always)	
azalea	
azalia	azalea
azure	

B

babble [2]	
babie	baby [+]
babmingten	badminton
babminten	badminton
baboon	
babul	babble [2]
bab y /ies	
baby-sitter	
baccarat	
bach	batch
bacheler	bachelor [+]
bachelor /hood	
bacill us /i (pl.)	
back [1] /ache/bone/er	
backara	baccarat
backbencher	
backbit e /er/ing	
backbone	
backcloth	
backfire [2]	
backgammon	
background	
backgrownd	background
backhand /ed/er	
backlash	
backlog	
backslid e /er/ing	
backspace [2]	
backstage	
backstitch [1]	
backstroke	
backward /ness/s	
backwater	
bacon	
bacteriological /ly	
bacteriolog y /ist	
bacteri um /a (pl.)	
bad ★ (no good) /ly	
bade ★ (asked)	
badge	
badger [1]	
badley	badly

badminton	
baffle² /r	
baful	baffle² +
bag³ /gy/gier/giest	
bagatelle	
baggage	
baggidge	baggage
baggi *ly* /ness	
bagier	baggier
bagiley	baggily +
bagpipe /r	
baige	beige
bail ★ (security, sport)	
bail	bale²★
bailee ★ (person)	
bailey ★ (castle wall)	
bailful	baleful +
bailiff	
bain	bane +
bainful	baneful
bairn	
baist	baste²
bait¹★ (fishing)	
bait	bate²★
baize	
baje	beige
Balaclava	
balad	ballad +
balalaika	
balalika	balalaika
balance² /r	
balans	balance²+
balast	ballast
balay	ballet
balcon *y* /ies	
bald ★ (no hair)	
bald	bawled ★
balderdash	
bald-headed	
bald *ing* /ness	
bale²★ (bundle)	
bale	bail ★
baleful /ly	
balerina	ballerina
balihoo	ballyhoo

balistic	ballistic +
balk¹	
balkoney	balcony +
ball ★ (dance) /room	
ball	bawl★
ballad /ry	
ballast	
ball-bearing	
ballerina	
ballet	
ballistic /s	
balloon¹ /er/ist	
ballot¹	
ball-point	
ballyhoo	
balm /y ★ (mild)	
balmoral	
baloney	
baloon	balloon¹+
balot	ballot¹
balsa	
balsam	
baluster	
balustrade	
bamboo	
bamboozle² /r	
bamboozul	bamboozle²+
ban³	
banal /ity/ities	
banalitey	banality
banana	
band ★(stripe, group)/s★	
band	banned ★
bandage²	
bandanna	
bandey	bandy +
bandie	bandy +
bandige	bandage²
bandit /ry	
bands	banns ★
bandstand	
bandwagon	
bandy /-legged	
bane /ful/fully	
baner	banner

bang [1]	
bangle	
bangul	bangle
banish [1] /ment	
banister	
banjo /s	
bank [1] /er/note	
bankrupt [1] /cy	
bankwet	banquet [1]
banned * (barred)	
banner	
banns * (marriage)	
banquet [1]	
bans	banns *
bantam /-weight	
banter [1] /ingly	
Bantu	
baonet	bayonet [3]
baptis e [2] /m	
bar /red * (stop) /ring *	
barack	barrack [1]
barb	
barbarian	
barbar ic /ism/ous	
barbarit y /ies	
barbarus	barbarous
barbecue	
barbed wire	
barber	
barbican	
barbique	barbecue
barbiturate	
bard * (poet)	
bard	barred *
bare [2]* (naked) /foot	
bare	bear *
bareback	
barefaced	
bareheaded	
barel	barrel [3]+
barelegged	
baren	baron *+
baren	barren *+
bareskin	bearskin
bargain [1] /er	

barge [2] /-pole	
bargen	bargain [1]+
baricade	barricade [2]
barier	barrier
barige	barrage
baring * (exposing)	
baring	barring *
baring	bearing *
barister	barrister
baritone	
barium	
bark [1] /er	
barley /-sugar	
barly	barley +
barm	balm +
barmade	barmaid
barmaid	
barmy * (crazy)	
barmy	balmy *
barn /yard	
barn	bairn
barnacle /d	
barnicul	barnacle +
barograf	barograph
barograph	
barok	baroque
baromet er /ric	
baron * (noble) /et/y	
baroness (fem.)	
baroque	
barow	barrow
barrack [1]	
barrage	
barrel [3] /ful	
barren * (empty) /ness	
barricade [2]	
barrier	
barrister	
barrow	
barter [1] /er	
barul	barrel [3]+
basalt	
base * (station, foundation)	
base	bass *

baseball	
base *less* /ly/ness	
basement	
baset	basset
bashful /ly/ness	
basic /ally	
basillus	bacillus +
basin /ful	
basis * (groundwork)	
basit	basset
bask [1]	
basket /ball/ful/ry	
baskit	basket +
basoon	bassoon
bas-relief	
bass * (deep tone)	
bass clef	
bass drum	
basset	
bassoon	
bastard /ly	
bastardis *e* [2] /ation	
baste [2]	
basterd	bastard +
bastion	
bastyun	bastion
bat [3] /sman	
batalion	battalion
batalyun	battalion
batch	
bate [2]* (lessen)	
bate	bait [1]*
baten	baton *
baten	batten [1]*
bater	batter [1]
baterey	battery +
batering ram	battering-ram
bathe [2] /r	
bathroom	
batie	batty +
batik	
batle	battle [2]+
baton * (staff of office)	
battalion	
batten [1]* (wood, grow fat)	

batter [1]	
battering-ram	
batter *y* /ies	
battle [2] /dress/ship	
battle-axe	
batt *y* /ier/iest	
batul	battle [2]+
baty	batty +
bauble	
baubul	bauble
bauxite	
bawble	bauble
bawdie	bawdy
bawdi *ly* /ness	
bawd *y* /ier/iest	
bawk	balk [1]
bawksite	bauxite
bawl * (cry)/ed * /ing	
bawl	ball *
bawl-baring	ball-bearing
bawldedash	balderdash
bawldheded	bald-headed
bawldness	baldness
bawlpoint	ball-point
bawlroom	ballroom
baylif	bailiff
bayonet [3]	
bayth	bathe [2]+
bazaar	
bazar	bazaar
bazooka	
be * (is-[verb]) /ing	
be	bee *
beach [1]* (shore) /es	
beach	beech *+
beachcomber	
beachhead	
beacon	
bead /y	
beadle	
beadul	beadle
beaf	beef +
beafeter	beefeater
beafstake	beefsteak
beagl *e* /ing	

beagul	beagle +	bed ³ /ridden/rock	
beak /er		bedaub ¹	
beam ¹		bedawb	bedaub ¹
bean * (vegetable)		beday	bidet
bean	been *	bedevil ³	
beanstalk		bedlam	
bear * (carry, animal)		bedouin	
bear	bare ²*+	bedowin	bedouin
bearback	bareback	bedraggle ²	
beard¹		bedragul	bedraggle ²
bearfased	barefaced	bedriden	bedridden
bearfoot	barefoot	bedroom	
bearheded	bareheaded	bed-sitter	
bearing * (carrying)		bedspread	
bearing	baring *	bedstead	
bearleggid	barelegged	bedtime	
bearskin		bee * (insect) /hive	
beast /ly		beech * (tree) /es	
beastli er /est/ness		beech	beach ¹*+
beat * (strike) /en		beechcomer	beachcomber
beat	beet *	beechhed	beachhead
beatif y ⁴ /ic/ication		beecon	beacon
beatitude		beed	bead +
beatle	beetle	beedle	beadle
beatroot	beetroot	beef /y	
beatul	beetle	beefeater	
beau * (dandy)		beefi er /est/ly/ness	
Beaufort scale		beefsteak	
beauteous		beegle	beagle +
beautician		beek	beak +
beautie	beauty +	beekun	beacon
beautiful /ly		beeline	
beautify ⁴		Beelzebub	
beautishun	beautician	beem	beam ¹
beaut y /ies		been * (past of be)	
beaver		been	bean *
becalmed		beenstork	beanstalk
became		beer * (drink)	
becarmed	becalmed	beer	bier *
because		beerd	beard ¹
beck		beest	beast +
beckon ¹ /ingly		beestlier	beastlier +
becom e /ing		beeswaks	beeswax
becon	beacon	beeswax	
becos	because	beet * (vegetable)	

beet	beat *+	bel	bell *
beetle		bel	belle *
beetroot		belaber	belabour [1]
beetul	beetle	belabour [1]	
beever	beaver	belated /ly	
befall /en		belay [1]	
befell		belch [1]	
befier	beefier +	beleaf	belief
befit [3]		beleager	beleaguer [1]
before /hand		beleaguer [1]	
befrend	befriend [1]	beleavabul	believable +
befriend [1]		beleave	believe [2+]
befuddle [2]		belfrey	belfry +
befudul	befuddle [2]	belfr y /ies	
beg [3]		Belgian	
began		beli	belie *+
beger	beggar [1+]	belicose	bellicose +
beggar [1] /liness/ly		belie * (untruth) /d	
begile	beguile [2+]	belief	
begin /ner/ning		believabl e /y	
begone		believe [2] /r	
begot /ten		beliful	bellyful
begrudge [2]		beligerence	belligerence +
beguile [2] /ment/r		beligerency	belligerency
begun		beligerent	belligerent
behalf		beline	beeline
beharf	behalf	belittle [2] /r	
behave [2]		belittul	belittle [2+]
behavier	behaviour +	beliying	belying
behaviour /ism		bell * (rings)	
behead [1]		belle * (beauty)	
behed	behead [1]	bellicos e /ity	
beheld		belligerenc e /y	
behest		belligerent	
behind		bellow [1] /er	
behive	beehive	bellows	
behold /en/er/ing		bell y * (stomach) /ies/ied	
behove		bellyful	
beige		belong [1] /ings	
being		belose	bellows
bekoz	because	beloved	
bekweath	bequeath [1+]	below * (beneath)	
bekwest	bequest	below	billow [1*+]
bel *†		below	bellow [1+]
†(unit = 10 decibels)		belows	bellows

bely	belly*+	beril	beryl+
belying		berilium	beryllium
bemoan¹		berkelium	
bemuse²		berlap	burlap
bench /er/es		berli	burly+
bend /ing		bern	burn¹+
beneath		bernish	burnish¹+
benefaction		berr y* (fruit) /ies	
benefact or /ress (fem.)		berry	bury⁴*
beneficen ce /t		berserk	
beneficial		bersurk	berserk
beneficiar y /ies		berth¹* (moor, bunk)	
benefisens	beneficence+	berth	birth*+
benefisent	beneficent	bery	berry*+
benefisharey	beneficiary+	bery	bury⁴*
benefishul	beneficial	beryl /line	
benefit³		beryllium	
benevolen ce /t/tly		beseech¹ /er	
benevolens	benevolence+	beseige	besiege²+
benifacshun	benefaction	beset³	
benifacter	benefactor+	beside /s	
benifactress	benefactress	besiege² /ment	
benifit	benefit³	besort	besought
benign /ant/ly		besot³	
benine	benign+	besought	
bent		bespatter¹	
benum	benumb¹+	best /-seller	
benumb¹ /ment		bester	bestir³
benzene*†		bestial /ism/ly	
†(from coal-tar)		bestialit y /ies	
benzine* (from		bestir³	
mineral oils)		bestow¹ /al/er	
bequeath¹ /ment		bestrew¹ /n	
bequest		bet³	
berate²		beta particles	
beray	beret	betle	beetle
bereave² /ment		betoken¹	
bereft		betray¹ /al/er	
beret		betroth¹ /al	
bereve	bereave²+	better¹ /ment	
bergler	burglar	betul	beetle
berial	burial	between	
beriberi		betwixt	
berie	berry*+	beverage	
berie	bury⁴*	beveridge	beverage

41

beverige	beverage	bifell	befell
bevie	bevy [+]	bifocal	
bev*y* /ies		bifurcat*e*[2] /ion	
bewail[1] /er		big /ger/gest/gish	
beware		bigam*ist* /ous	
bewayl	bewail[1+]	bigamus	bigamous
bewich	bewitch[1+]	bigam*y* /ies	
bewilder[1] /ment		bigan	began
bewitch[1] /er		bighead	
beyond		bigile	beguile[2+]
bezurk	berserk	bigin	begin[+]
bi election	by-election	biginer	beginner
biannual *† /ly		bigining	beginning
† (twice a year)		bigon	begone
biannual	biennial *[+]	bigone	bygone[+]
bias[1] /es		bigot /ed/ry	
biatifi	beatify[4+]	bigrudge	begrudge[2]
biatitude	beatitude	bigun	begun
Bibl*e* /ical		biharf	behalf
bibliografey	bibliography[+]	bihave	behave[2]
bibliografic	bibliographic[+]	bihavier	behaviour[+]
bibliographic /al		bihed	behead[1]
bibliograph*y* /ies/er		bihest	behest
bibul	Bible[+]	bihove	behove
bicalmed	becalmed	bike	
bicame	became	bikweath	bequeath[1+]
bicarbonate		bikwest	bequest
bicarmed	becalmed	bil	bill[1]
bicentenar*y* /ies		bilaber	belabour[1]
bicentennial		bilated	belated[+]
bicentenyul	bicentennial	bilateral /ism/ly	
biceps		bilaw	by-law
bich	bitch[+]	bilay	belay[1]
bicicle	bicycle[2+]	bilberie	bilberry[+]
biciclist	bicyclist	bilberr*y* /ies	
bicker[1] /er		bild	build[+]
bicycl*e*[2] /ist		bilding	building
bide[2]		bile	
bidet		bileager	beleaguer[1]
bidevil	bedevil[3]	bileavable	believable[+]
biennial *† /ly		bileavabul	believable[+]
† (every two years)		bileave	believe[2+]
biennial	biannual *[+]	bileger	beleaguer[1]
bier	beer *	bileif	belief
bier	byre *	bilet	billet[1]

42

bilge		biografical	biographical +
bilief	belief	biographical /ly	
bilingual /ism/ly		biograph y /ies/er	
bilingwal	bilingual +	biokemist	biochemist +
bilious		biologey	biology +
bilittle	belittle 2+	biological /ly	
bilitul	belittle 2+	biolog y /ist	
bilius	bilious	biopsey	biopsy +
bilk 1 /er		biops y /ies	
bill 1		biparti te /san	
billabong		bipartizan	bipartisan
billet 1		bipass	by-pass 1
billiards		biped	
billion /aire		biplane	
billit	billet 1	biplay	byplay
billow 1★ (wave) /y		bipolar /ity	
bilong	belong 1+	biproduct	by-product
bilow	below ★	birate	berate 2
bilow	billow 1★+	birch /es	
biluvd	beloved	bird	
bilyards	billiards	birdie	
bilyon	billion +	bird's-eye	
bilyus	bilious	bireft	bereft
bimetalli c /sm		bireve	bereave 2+
bimoan	bemoan 1	birode	byroad
bimonthly		birth ★ (born) /day	
bimuse	bemuse 2	birth	berth 1★
bin ★ (box)		biscuit	
bin	been ★	bisecshun	bisection
binacle	binnacle	bisect 1 /ion/or	
binacul	binnacle	biseech	beseech 1+
binary		biseege	besiege 2+
bind /er/ery/ing		biseksual	bisexual +
bineath	beneath	bisentenary	bicentenary +
bineeth	beneath	bisentenial	bicentennial
binge		bisentenyal	bicentennial
bingo		biseps	biceps
binine	benign +	biset	beset 3
binnacle		bisexual /ly	
binocular /s		bishop /ric	
binomial		bisicle	bicycle 2+
binum	benumb 1+	bisiclist	bicyclist
biochemist /ry		biside	beside +
biografer	biographer	bisier	busier +
biografey	biography +	bisiley	busily

43

biskit	biscuit	blaber	blabber
bismuth		black [1] /out	
bisness	business [+]	black-beetle	
bison		blackberie	blackberry [+]
bisort	besought	blackberr *y* /ies	
bisot	besot [3]	blackbird	
bispatter	bespatter [1]	blackboard	
bistander	bystander	blacken [1]	
bistow	bestow [1+]	blackguard	
bistowal	bestowal	blackleg [3]	
bistru	bestrew [1+]	blacklist [1]	
bistur	bestir [3]	blackmail [1] /er	
bisun	bison	blacksmith	
bisy	busy [4]	bladder	
bitch /es		blade	
bit *e* /ing/ten		blader	bladder
biter	bitter [+]	blagard	blackguard
bitoken	betoken [1]	blaid	blade
bitray	betray [1+]	blaim	blame [2+]
bitrayal	betrayal	blaimless	blameless [+]
bitroth	betroth [1+]	blair	blare [2]
bitter /est/ly/ness		blaise	blaze [2]
bitum *en* /inous		blaizer	blazer
bitween	between	blam´*e* [2] /able	
bitwixt	betwixt	blameless /ly	
bivalve		blameworthy	
bivouac /ked/king		blamonge	blancmange
bivuac	bivouac [+]	blanch [1]	
biwail	bewail [1+]	blancmange	
biware	beware	bland /ly/ness	
biwayul	bewail [1+]	blank /ly	
biwear	beware	blanket [1]	
biwhich	bewitch [1+]	blare [2]	
biwich	bewitch [1+]	blarney	
biwilder	bewilder [1+]	blasfeim	blaspheme [2+]
biword	byword	blasfemey	blasphemy [+]
biyond	beyond	blasfemus	blasphemous
bizar	bizarre [+]	blasphem *e* [2] /ous	
bizarre /ly/ness		blasphem *y* /ies	
bizier	busier [+]	blast [1] /-off	
biziley	busily	blast-furnace	
bizmuth	bismuth	blatancy	
bizness	business [+]	blatansey	blatancy
bizy	busy [4]	blatant /ly	
blab [3] /ber		blaze [2]	

blazer		blo	blow +
blazon¹ /er		bloat¹ /edness	
bleach¹ /er		bloater	
blead	bleed +	blob³	
bleak /er/est/ly/ness		bloc ★ (group)	
blear¹ /y		blochie	blotchy
bleari er /est/ly		block ★† /age	
bleat¹ /er		†(solid piece, stop)	
bled		block	bloc ★
bleech	bleach ¹+	blockade² /r	
bleed /er/ing		blockhead /ed	
bleek	bleak +	blond /ish/ness	
bleer	blear ¹+	blone	blown
bleerey	bleary	blood¹ /y	
bleerier	blearier +	blood pressure	
bleet	bleat ¹+	blood vessel	
blemish¹ /er		bloodhound	
blench¹ /er		blood ied /ier/iest	
blend¹ /er		bloodi ly /ness	
bless¹		blood shed /shot	
blest		bloodthirst y /iness	
blew ★ (wind)		bloom¹ /ers	
blew	blue ★+	blossom¹ /y	
blewbell	bluebell	blosum	blossom ¹+
blewberie	blueberry +	blot³ /ter	
blewbery	blueberry +	blot	bloat ¹+
blew-chip	blue-chip	blotch¹ /y	
blewish	bluish	bloter	bloater
blewprint	blue-print	bloter	blotter
·blight¹ /er		blouse	
blind¹ /est/ly/ness		blow /er/ing/n/y	
blinder /s		blowse	blouse
blind-man's-buff		blowter	bloater
blink¹		blowze	blouse
bliss /ful/fully		blowzey	blowzy +
blister¹		blowz y /ier/iest	
blite	blight ¹+	blu	blue ★+
bliter	blighter	blubber¹ /y	
blith	blithe +	blubell	bluebell
blithe /ly/ness		bluberie	blueberry +
blithering		blubery	blueberry +
blits	blitz¹	blud	blood ¹+
blitz¹		blud presher	blood pressure
blizard	blizzard	blud vesel	blood vessel
blizzard		bludey	bloody

45

bludgen	bludgeon [1]	bob-sled	
bludgeon [1]		bob-sleigh	
bludhound	bloodhound	boby	bobby [+]
bludhownd	bloodhound	boch	botch [1+]
bludid	bloodied [+]	bode [2]	
bludie	bloody	bodice	
bludily	bloodily [+]	bodie	body [+]
bludshed	bloodshed [+]	bodi *ed* /ly	
bludshot	bloodshot	bodigard	bodyguard
bludthurstey	bloodthirsty [+]	bodiley	bodily
blue ★ (colour) /bell		bodiss	bodice
blue	blew ★	bodkin	
blueberr *y* /ies		bod *y* /ies	
bluebottle		bodyguard	
blue-chip		bogey ★ (golf)	
blue-print		bogey	bogy ★[+]
bluf	bluff [1+]	boggle [2]	
bluff [1] /er		bogul	boggle [2]
bluish		bogus	
blummers	bloomers	bog *y* ★ (devil) /ies	
blunder [1] /er		bohemian	
blunderbuss		boi	boy ★
blunt /er/est/ly/ness		boi	buoy [1★+]
blur [3] /riness/ry		boiansey	buoyancy [+]
blurb		boiant	buoyant
blurie	blurry	boicot	boycott [1+]
blurt [1]		boil [1] /er	
blush [1] /es/ingly		boisterous /ly	
bluster [1] /y		boisterus	boisterous [+]
boa-constrictor		boks	box [1+]
boar ★ (swine)		Boksing Day	Boxing Day
boar	boor ★	bolard	bollard
boar	bore [2★+]	bolaro	bolero
board [1] /er ★ (lodger)		bold	
boarding /-house/-school		bolder ★ (braver)	
boast [1] /er		bolder	boulder ★
boastful /ly/ness		bold *ly* /ness	
boat [1] /-house/-race		bole ★ (tree trunk)	
boater		bole	bowl [1★]
boatswain		bolero	
bobbin		bollard	
bobb *y* /ies		boloney	
bobie	bobby [+]	Bolshevi *k* /sm/st	
bobin	bobbin	bolster [1] /er	
bobslay	bob-sleigh	bolt [1]	

bom	bomb ¹⁺	boraks	borax
bomb ¹ /er		borasic	boracic
bombard ¹ /ment		borax	
bombardier		bord	board ¹⁺
bombast /ic/ically		border ¹* (edge) /line	
bomberdeer	bombardier	border	boarder *
bomer	bomber	bording	boarding ⁺
bona fide		bordum	boredom
bonanza		bordy	bawdy ⁺
bond ¹ /age		bore ²*† /dom	
bondige	bondage	† (drill, dull)	
bon e ² /y		bore	boar *
bonet	bonnet	bore	boor *
bonfire		born * (birth)	
bonie	bonny	borne * (carried)	
bonier	bonnier ⁺	boron	
bonit	bonnet	borough * (town)	
bonnet		borow	borrow ¹⁺
bonni er /est/ly/ness		borrow ¹ /er	
bonny		borstal	
bonus /es		bort	bought
bony	bonny	bos	boss ¹⁺
boo ¹ /er		bosie	bossy
boobie	booby ⁺	bosier	bossier ⁺
boob y /ies		bosily	bossily
boodwar	boudoir	bosn	bosun
book /able/ish/let		bosn	boatswain
bookay	bouquet	bosom	
bookie		boss ¹ /es/y	
boolvar	boulevard	bossi er /est/ly/ness	
boomerang		bost	boast ¹⁺
boor * (bad-mannered)		bostful	boastful ⁺
boor	boar *	bosun	
boorgwa	bourgeois	bosy	bossy
boost ¹ /er		bot	boat ¹⁺
boot /ee * (shoe) /less		botaney	botany ⁺
booteek	boutique	botanical /ly	
booth		botan y /ist	
bootie	booty *	botch ¹ /y	
bootik	boutique	boter	boater
bootleg ³ /ger		both	
booty * (spoils)		bother ¹ /ation/some	
booty	bootee *	botherashun	botheration
booze ² /r		bothersum	bothersome
boracic		botom	bottom ⁺

bottle[2]		boy	buoy[1]★
bottom /less/most		boyancy	buoyancy[+]
botul	bottle[2]	boyansey	buoyancy[+]
boudoir		boyant	buoyant
bough ★ (tree)		boycott[1] /er	
bough	bow[1]★	boykot	boycott[1+]
bought		boyl	boil[1+]
boukay	bouquet	boysterus	boisterous[+]
boulder ★ (big rock)		brace[2]★ (strap up)	
boulder	bolder ★	bracelet	
boulevard		bracken	
bounc e[2] /y		bracket[1]	
bound[1] /er		brackish	
boundar y /ies		brackit	bracket[1]
boundless		brade	braid[1]
bounteous		brag[3] /gart	
bountius	bounteous	braget	braggart
bount y /ies/iful		Brahm a /in	
bouquet		brai	bray[1]
bourgeois		braid[1]	
bourgwa	bourgeois	brail	Braille
bout		Braille	
bouteek	boutique	brain /wave/y	
boutique		brain-drain	
bovine		braini er /est/ly	
bow[1]★ (bend, arrow)		brainwash[1]	
bow	beau ★	braise[2]★ (cook)	
bow	bough ★	braise	braze[2]★[+]
bowel		braisen	brazen[+]
bower		brakable	breakable
bowl[1]★ (cricket, basin)		brakabul	breakable
bowl	bole ★	brake[2]★ (stop)	
bownce	bounce[2+]	brake	break ★[+]
bownd	bound[1+]	brakedown	breakdown
bowndarey	boundary[+]	braken	bracken
bowndless	boundless	brakeneck	breakneck
bowncy	bouncy	brakethrew	breakthrough
bowns	bounce[2+]	brakethrough	breakthrough
bowntey	bounty[+]	brakewater	breakwater
bowntiful	bountiful	brakige	breakage[+]
bowntius	bounteous	braking	breaking
bowt	bout	brakish	brackish
box[1] /er/es/-office		brale	Braille
Boxing Day		brama	Brahma[+]
boy ★ (lad)		brambl e /y	

brambul	bramble +	breadth	
bramin	Brahmin	break * (destroy) /able	
branch[1] /es		break	brake[2]*
brand[1] /-new		break *age* /er/ing	
brandie	brandy +	breakdown	
brandnu	brand-new	breakfast	
brandy /-snap		breakneck	
brane	brain +	breakthrew	breakthrough
branedrain	brain-drain	breakthrough	
branewash	brainwash[1]	breakwater	
branier	brainier +	bream	
bras	brass +	breast[1] /bone/plate	
brase	brace[2]*	breast stroke	
brase	braise[2]*	breath /less/lessly	
brase	braze[2]*+	breathalyse[2] /r	
brash /ly		breathe[2] /r	
brasier	brassiere *	breathtaking	
brasier	brazier *	bred * (reared)	
braslet	bracelet	bred	bread *
brass /ier/iest/ily/y		bredth	breadth
brassiere *†		breech * (part of gun)	
†(undergarment)		breech	breach[1]*
brasy	brassy	breed /er/ing	
brasyer	brazier *	breef	brief[1]+
brat		breef case	brief-case
bravado		breem	bream
brave[2] /ly/ry		breez*e*[2] /ily/iness	
bravo		breez*y* /ier/iest	
bravoora	bravura	breif	brief[1]+
bravrey	bravery	breif case	brief-case
bravura		brekfast	breakfast
brawd	broad +	Bren-gun	
brawl[1] /er		brest	breast[1]+
brawn /ier/iest/y		brestbone	breastbone
bray[1]		brestplait	breastplate
brayd	braid[1]	breststroke	breast stroke
braze[2]* (solder) /r		breth	breadth
braze	braise[2]*	breth	breath +
brazen /ly/ness		brethalise	breathalyse[2]+
brazier * (fire basket)		brethless	breathless
breach[1]*†		brethren	
† (gap, violation)		brethtaking	breathtaking
breach	breech *	brevit*y* /ies	
bread * (food)		brew[1] /er	
bread	bred *. *	brewer*y* /ies	

breze	breeze ²⁺	brisket	
brezy	breezy ⁺	brisle	bristle ²⁺
briar		bristl e ² /y	
bribabul	bribable	brisul	bristle ²⁺
brib e ² /able/er		brite	bright ⁺
briber y /ies		briten	brighten ¹
bric-à-brac		brittle /ness/r/st	
brick /bat/yard		britul	brittle ⁺
bricklay er /ing		broach ¹ *†	
bridal * (of bride)		† (tool, discuss)	
bridal	bridle ²*⁺	broach	brooch *⁺
bride /groom		broad /ly	
bridel	bridal *	broadcast	
bridel	bridle ²*⁺	broadcloth	
bridelpath	bridle-path	broaden ¹	
bridesmaid		broadside	
bridge ² /able		broad ways /wise	
bridle ² *† /-path		brocade ²	
†(for a horse)		broccoli	
bridle	bridal *	broch	broach ¹*
brief¹ /s/ly		broch	brooch *⁺
brief-case		brochure	
brigade		brock	
brigadear	brigadier	brocoli	broccoli
brigadier		brog	brogue
brigand /age		brogue	
brige	bridge ²⁺	broil¹ /er	
bright /ly/ness		broke /r	
brighten¹		broken /-hearted	
brillianc e /y		bromide	
brilliant /ly		bromine	
brilliantine		bronchial	
brilyance	brilliance ⁺	bronchitis	
brilyancy	brilliancy	bronco	
brilyans	brilliance ⁺	bronkitis	bronchitis
brilyansey	brilliancy	bronkiul	bronchial
brilyant	brilliant ⁺	bronkyul	bronchial
brilyantine	brilliantine	bronze ²	
brim ³ /ful		brooam	brougham
brimstone		brooch * (clasp) /es	
brindled		brood¹ /iness/y	
brin e /y		brook¹ /let	
bring /ing		broom /stick	
brink		broonet	brunette
brisk /ly/ness		broose	bruise ²⁺

broot	brute +	buccaneer /ing	
brootal	brutal +	buck [1]	
brootalitey	brutality +	buckaneer	buccaneer +
brorn	brawn +	bucket /ful	
brornie	brawny	buckle [2] /r	
brorny	brawny	buckshot	
brort	brought	buckskin	
brosher	brochure	buckwheat	
broth		bucolic	
brothel		Buddhis m /t	
brother /hood		budge [2]	
brother(s)-in-law		budgerigar	
brotherl y /iness		budget [1] /ary	
brougham		budgigar	budgerigar
brought		Budism	Buddhism +
brow /s ★ (eyebrows)		budist	Buddhist
browbeat /en/ing		buf	buff
brown [1] /er/est		bufalo	buffalo +
browney	brownie	bufer	buffer [1]
Brownian motion		bufet	buffet [1]
brownie		buff	
browse [2]★ (read) /r		buffalo /es	
broyl	broil [1]+	buffer [1]	
brud	brood [1]+	buffet [1]	
brudy	broody	buffoon [1]	
bruer	brewer	buffooner y /ies	
bruerey	brewery +	bufit	buffet [1]
bruise [2] /r		bufoonerey	buffoonery +
brunet	brunette	bufune	buffoon [1]
brunette		bufunerey	buffoonery +
brunt		bug [3] /bear	
bruse	bruise [2]+	bugbare	bugbear
brush [1] /wood		bugerigar	budgerigar
brusk	brusque +°	buget	budget [1]+
brusque /ly/ness		bugg y /ies	
Brussels sprouts		bugie	buggy +
brutal /ly		bugl e /er/ing	
brutalis e [2] /ation		bugul	bugle +
brutalit y /ies		bugy	buggy +
brut e /ish		build /er/ing	
bubbl e [2] /y		built	
bublie	bubbly	buksom	buxom +
bubly	bubbly	buksomness	buxomness
bubonic plague		bulb /ous	
bubul	bubble [2]+	bulbus	bulbous

buldoze	bulldoze ²⁺	bungul	bungle ²⁺
bulet	bullet ⁺	bunie	bunny ⁺
buletin	bulletin	bunion	
bulfinch	bullfinch ⁺	bunk ¹	
bulfite	bullfight	bunker ¹	
bulg e ² /y		bunkum	
bulie	bully ⁴⁺	bunn y /ies	
bulit	bullet ⁺	Bunsen burner	
bulit proof	bullet-proof	buny	bunny ⁺
bulk /ier/iest/iness/y		bunyon	bunion
bulkey	bulky	buoy ¹★ (float)	
bulkhead		buoyan cy /t	
bull /fight		buoyansey	buoyancy ⁺
bulldoze ² /r		bur	
bullet /-proof		bura	borough ★
bulletin		burble ² /r	
bullfinch /es		burbul	burble ²⁺
bullion		burch	birch ⁺
bullock		burd	bird
bullring		burden ¹ /some	
bull's-eye		burdey	birdie
bull y ⁴ /ies		burdie	birdie
bulock	bullock	burds eye	bird's-eye
bulring	bullring	bureau /x (pl.)	
bulrush		bureaucrac y /ies	
bulseye	bull's-eye	bureaucrat /ic	
bulwark		burgandey	Burgundy
buly	bully ⁴⁺	burger	burgher
bulyon	bullion	burgher	
bumbelbe	bumble-bee	burglar	
bumble-bee		burglar y /ies	
bump ¹ /er/ily/iness		burgle ²	
bumpey	bumpy ⁺	burgler	burglar
bumpkin		burgul	burgle ²
bumpshus	bumptious ⁺	Burgundy	
bumptious /ly/ness		burial	
bump y /ier/iest		burlap	
bumshus	bumptious ⁺	burlesk	burlesque ²⁺
bunch ¹ /es/y		burlesque ² /r	
bundle ²		burlie	burly ⁺
bundul	bundle ²	burl y /ier/iest/iness	
bung ¹ /-hole		burn ¹ /able/er/t	
bungalow		burnish ¹ /er	
bungkum	bunkum	buro	bureau ⁺
bungle ² /r		burocracy	bureaucracy ⁺

burocrasey	bureaucracy +	butress	buttress [1]+
burocrat	bureaucrat +	butrey	buttery +
buro	bureau +	butt [1] * (end)	
burow	burrow [1]*+	butter [1] /-fingered	
burra	borough *	buttercup	
burrow [1]* (hole, dig) /er		butterey	buttery +
burrow	borough *	butterfly	
bursar /y		buttermilk	
burser	bursar +	butterscotch	
burst /ing		butter y /ies	
burth	birth *+	buttock	
burthday	birthday	button [1] /hole	
bur y [4]* (cover)		buttress [1] /es	
bus [3] /es		buxom /ness	
busbie	busby +	buy *† /ing/er * †(purchase)	
busb y /ies		buy	by *
bush /ily/iness		buy	bye *
bushel		buzz [1] /es	
bushie	bushy +	buzzard	
bush y /ier/iest		by * (near)	
busi er /est/ly		by	buy *+
business /-like		by	bye *
bust		by-and-by	
bustle [2] /r		bycicle	bicycle [2]+
busul	bustle [2]+	byciclist	bicyclist
busy [4]		bye * (sport)	
but * (however)		by-election	
but	butt [1]*	byer	buyer
butcher [1] /y		byfocal	bifocal
buten	button [1]+	bygone /s	
buter	butter [1]+	bying	buying
buter fingerd	butter-fingered	byke	bike
butercup	buttercup	by-law	
buterfly	butterfly	byle	bile
butermilk	buttermilk	bylore	by-law
buterscotch	butterscotch	bymetalic	bimetallic +
butey	beauty +	bymonthly	bimonthly
butician	beautician	bynomial	binomial
butify	beautify [4]	byopsey	biopsy +
butique	boutique	bypartisan	bipartisan
butishun	beautician	bypartite	bipartite +
butler		by-pass [1]	
butn	button [1]+	byped	biped
butock	buttock	byplane	biplane
buton	button [1]+		

byplay	
bypolar	bipolar [+]
by-product	
byre ★ (barn)	
byroad	
byrode	byroad
bysecshun	bisection
bysect	bisect [1+]
bysection	bisection
byseksual	bisexual [+]
bysexual	bisexual [+]
bystander	
byvalv	bivalve
byword	

C

cab /man	
cabal [3]	
cabaray	cabaret
cabaret	
cabbage	
cabbidge	cabbage
cabb y /ies	
cabie	cabby [+]
cabin /-boy	
cabinet	
cable [2] /gram/way	
cabul	cable [2+]
cacao	
cach	catch [+]
cachay	cachet
cache [2]★ (hidden store)	
cache	cash [1]★
cachet	
cachou	cashew
cachwerd	catchword
cackle [2]	
cacofony	cacophony [+]
cacophon y /ous	
cact us /i (pl.)	
cacul	cackle [2]
cad /dish	
cadaver /ous	

caddey	caddie ★
caddie ★ (golf)	
caddis /-worm	
cadd y [4]★ (for tea) /ies	
cadence	
cadens	cadence
cadentsa	cadenza
cadenza	
cadet corps	
cadge [2]	
cadis	caddis [+]
cadmium	
Caesar	
Caesarean	
caesium	
café /s	
cafene	caffeine
cafeteria	
caffeine	
cafiene	caffeine
cafiteria	cafeteria
cage [2] /y	
cagi er /est/ly/ness	
cain	cane [2+]
cairn	
cairngorm	
caison	caisson
caisson	
cajole [2] /ry	
cake [2]	
calabash	
calamine	
calamit y /ies/ous	
calcareous	
calcarius	calcareous
calcif y [4] /ication	
calcin e /ation	
calcium	
calculable	
calculabul	calculable
calculashun	calculation
calculat e [2] /ion/or	
calculus	
cale	kale
Caledonian	

calendar ★ (time)	
calender ¹★ (machine)	
cal f /ves (pl.)	
caliber	calibre
calibrashun	calibration
calibrat e ² /ion/or	
calibre	
calicks	calyx
calico /es	
calif	caliph ⁺
californium	
caligrafey	calligraphy ⁺
caligraphy	calligraphy ⁺
calipers	callipers
caliph /ate	
calipso	calypso
calix	calyx ⁺
calk ¹★ (horseshoe)	
calk	caulk ¹★
call ¹★ (cry out)	
call	caul ★
calligraph y /er/ist	
callipers	
callisthenics	
callosity	
callous ★ (unfeeling)	
callous ly /ness	
callow	
callus ★ (hard skin)	
calm ¹ /ly/ness	
calomel	
calorie /s	
calorific	
calorif y ⁴ /ier	
calorimet er /ric/ry	
calory	calorie ⁺
calositey	callosity
calow	callow
calsify	calcify ⁴⁺
calsine	calcine ⁺
calsium	calcium
calumniat e ² /ion/or	
calumn y /ies/ious	
calus	callous ★
calus	callus ★

Calvary	
calve ²★ (produce a calf)	
calve	carve ²★
Calvinis m /t/tic	
calypso	
calyx /es	
cam /shaft	
camaflage	camouflage ²
camaraderie	
camber ¹	
Cambrian	
cambric	
came	
camellia	
camelya	camellia
Camembert	
cameo /s	
camera /man	
camerarderey	camaraderie
camfor	camphor ⁺
camforated	camphorated
camio	cameo ⁺
camisole	
camombare	Camembert
camomile	
camouflage ²	
camp ¹ /-follower	
campaign ¹	
campain	campaign ¹
campanile	
campanology	
camphor /ated	
campus /es	
can ³ /not/'t ★	
canabis	cannabis
Canadian	
canal	
canalis e ² /ation	
canar y /ies	
cancan	
cancel ³ /lation	
cancer /ous	
cancerus	cancerous
candela	
candelabrum	

cander	candour	cantankerous /ly/ness	
candey	candy +	cantata /s	
candid * (frank)		canteen	
candid	candied *	canter [1]	
candidac y /ies		cantilever /ed	
candidat e /ure		cantle	
candie	candy +	canton [1] /al/ment	
candied * (sugared)		cantul	cantle
candle /light/stick		canvas * (cloth) /es	
candour		canvass [1]* (solicit)	
candul	candle +	cany	canny
cand y /ies		canyon	
cane [2] /-sugar		caolin	kaolin
canery	cannery +	caos	chaos +
cangaroo	kangaroo	caotic	chaotic
canibal	cannibal +	cap [3]	
canibalise·	cannibalise [2]+	capabilit y /ies	
canie	canny	capabl e /y	
canine		capabul	capable +
canister		capacious /ly/ness	
canker [1]		capacit ance /ive/or	
cannabis		capacitans	capacitance +
canner y /ies		capacitate [2]	
cannibal /ism/istic		capacit y /ies	
cannibalis e [2] /ation		capashus	capacious
cannon [1]* (gun)		capasitey	capacity +
cannonade		capasitor	capacitor
canny		cape	
canoe [2] /s		caper [1]	
canoeist		capilarey	capillary +
canon * (law) /ical		capillar y /ies	
canon	cannon [1]*	capital /ism/ly	
canonaid	cannonade	capitalis e [2] /ation	
canonis e [2] /ation		capitalist /ic	
canonry		capitashun	capitation
canooist	canoeist	capitation	
canop y [4] /ies		capitulat e [2] /ion	
cansel	cancel [3]+	capon	
canselashun	cancellation	capric e /ious	
canselation	cancellation	Capricorn	
canser	cancer +	caprishus	capricious
canserus	cancerous	capshun	caption [1]
cant * (hypocrisy)		capshus	captious
cant	can't *	capsiz e [2] /able	
cantaloup		capstan	

capsul*e*² /ar		careful /ly	
captain¹ /cy		careless /ly/ness	
capter	captor	caress¹	
captin	captain¹⁺	caret ★ (mark)	
caption¹		caret	carat ★
captious		caretak*er* /ing	
captivashun	captivation	cargo /es	
captivat*e*² /ion		cariage	carriage⁺
captiv*e* /ity		caribou	
captor		caricacher	caricature²⁺
capture² /r		caricatur*e*² /ist	
car /park		caricter	character
caracter	character	caricteristic	characteristic⁺
caracteristic	characteristic⁺	caridge	carriage⁺
carafe		carie	carry⁴⁺
caramel		carier	carrier
carat ★ (unit of gems)		carion	carrion
carat	caret ★	carisma	charisma
carate	karate	carkey	khaki
caravan³		carki	khaki
caraway		carm	calm¹⁺
carbine		carmine	
carbohydrate		carnage	
carbolic		carnal /ity/ly	
carbon /aceous/ate		carnashun	carnation
carbon dioxide		carnation	
carbon monoxide		carngorm	cairngorm
carbonis*e*² /ation		carnidge	carnage
carbuncle		carnival	
carbuncul	carbuncle	carnivor*e* /ous	
carbureter	carburettor	carol³ /ler	
carburettor		carot	carrot⁺
carcass		carous*e*² /al	
carcino*ma* /genic		carowsal	carousal
card /board		carowse	carouse²⁺
cardiac		carp¹ /er	
cardigan		carpent*er*¹ /ry	
cardinal		carpet¹	
cardiograf	cardiograph⁺	carpus	
cardiogram		carriage /way	
cardiograph /y		carrier	
care² /worn		carrion	
careen¹		carrot /y	
career¹ /ism/ist		carr*y*⁴ /ier	
carefree		carryon	carrion

carsinoma	carcinoma [+]	casserole [2]	
cart [1] /-horse		casset	cassette
cartel		cassette	
cartilage		cassock	
cartilidge	cartilage	cast ★ (throw) /ing	
cartografer	cartographer	cast iron	
cartografey	cartography [+]	castanet	
cartograph y /er/ic		castaway	
carton		caste ★† /less	
cartoon [1] /ist		† (social class)	
cartridge		castigat e [2] /ion/or	
cartrite	cart-wright	castle [2]	
cart-wheel		cast-off	
cart-wright		castor	
carve [2]★ (cut)		castor-oil	
carve	calve [2]★	castrashun	castration
cary	carry [4+]	castrat e [2] /ion	
cascade [2]		casual /ly/ness	
cascara		casualt y /ies	
case [2]		casuist /ic/ry	
casein		cat /tish/ty/walk	
casement		catabolism	
caserole	casserole [2]	cataclysm /ic	
casette	cassette	catacomb	
cash [1]★ (money)		catacoom	catacomb
cash	cache [2]★	catalep sy /tic	
cashay	cachet	catalise	catalyse [2+]
casheer	cashier [1]	catalisis	catalysis [+]
cashew		catalist	catalyst
cashier [1]		catalitic	catalytic
cashmere		catalog	catalogue [2+]
cashoo	cashew	catalogue [2] /r	
cashual	casual [+]	catalys e [2] /ation	
cashuist	casuist [+]	cataly sis /tic	
cashultey	casualty [+]	catalyst	
casing		catamaran	
casino /s		catapiler	caterpillar
cask ★ (wine)		catapult [1]	
cask	casque ★	catar	catarrh [+]
caskaid	cascade [2]	cataract	
casket		catarrh /al	
caskit	casket	catastrofey	catastrophe
casock	cassock	catastrofic	catastrophic [+]
casque ★ (helmet)		catastrophe	
cassel	castle [2]	catastrophic /ally	

catcall [1]	
catcawl	catcall [1]
catch /ing/ment	
catchword	
catechis e [2] /m	
categoric /al/ally	
categorise [2]	
categor y /ies	
cater [1] /er	
caterpillar	
caterwaul [1]	
catgut	
cathar sis /tic	
cathedral	
Catherine-wheel	
cathod e /ic	
catholic /ism	
caticise	catechise [2+]
catigorey	category [+]
catigoric	categoric [+]
catigorise	categorise [2]
catikism	catechism
catish	cattish
catkin	
catle	cattle
catnap [3]	
cat-o'-nine-tails	
cat's-eye	
cattle	
catul	cattle
caucashun	Caucasian
Caucasian	
caucus /es	
caught ★ (did catch)	
caught	court [1]★
cauk	caulk [1]★
caul ★ (membrane)	
caul	call [1]★
cauldron	
cauliflower	
caulk [1]★ (seal)	
caulk	calk [1]★
causal	
causat ion /ive	
cause [2] /less	

causeway	
caustic /ally	
cauteris e [2] /ation	
caution [1] /ary	
cautious /ly/ness	
cavalcade	
cavalier	
cavalr y /ies	
cave [2] /man	
cavern /ous	
caveson	
caviare	
cavil [3]	
cavisun	caveson
cavit y /ies	
cavort [1]	
caw [1]★ (cry of a crow)	
caw	core ★
caw	corps ★
cawcashun	Caucasian
cawcasian	Caucasian
cayenne	
cazm	chasm
cease [2] /-fire/less	
cedar	
cede [2]★ (give up)	
cede	seed [1]★
ceder	cedar
cedilla	
ceeling	ceiling ★
ceese	cease [2+]
cefalic	cephalic [+]
ceiling ★ (top)	
ceiling	sealing ★
celandine	
celebrant	
celebrashun	celebration
celebrat e [2] /ion	
celebrit y /ies	
celerey	celery
celerity	
celery	
celestial /ly	
celiba cy /te	
celibasey	celibacy [+]

celibrant	celebrant	centileter	centilitre
celibrate	celebrate [2+]	centilitre	
cell ★ (prison, unit)		centime	
cell	sell ★+	centimeter	centimetre
cellar ★ (cave)		centimetre	
celler	seller ★	centipede	
cellist		centor	centaur
cello /s		central /ity/ly	
cellophane		centralis e [2] /ation	
cellular		centre [2] /board	
cellule		centre-forward	
celluler	cellular	centrifugal /ly	
celluloid		centrifuge	
cellulose		centripetal	
celofane	cellophane	centuple	
Celsius		centupul	centuple
Celt /ic		centurion	
cement [1] /ation		centur y /ies	
cemeter y /ies		cephali c /tis	
cemetrey	cemetery +	ceramic /s	
cemical	chemical +	circuler	circular
cemist	chemist +	cercumcise	circumcise [2+]
cemistrey	chemistry	cercumference	circumference
cenotaf	cenotaph	cercumferens	circumference
cenotaph		cercumflex	circumflex
censer ★ (for incense)		cercumnavigate	circumnavi-gate [2+]
censer	censor [1]★+		
censership	censorship	cercumscribe	circumscribe [2]
censher	censure [2+]	cercumscripshun	circumscription
censor [1]★† /ious/ship †(moral overseer)		cercumscription	circumscription
		cercumsise	circumcise [2+]
censur e [2] /able		cercumspect	circumspect +
census /es		cercumstance	circumstance
cent ★ (money)		cercumstans	circumstance
cent	scent [1]★	cercumstanshul	circumstantial +
cent	sent ★	cercumstantial	circumstantial +
centaur		cercumvent	circumvent [1+]
centeem	centime	cercus	circus +
centenarian		cereal ★ (grain)	
centenar y /ies		cereal	serial ★+
centennial /ly		cerebellum	
center	centre [2+]	cerebra l /tion	
center forwud	centre-forward	cerebrum	
centigrade		ceremonial /ly	
centigram		ceremonious /ly	

ceremonius	ceremonious +	chalenge	challenge 2+
ceremon y /ies		chalet	
cerial	cereal *	chalice	
cerial	serial *+	chalinge	challenge 2+
ceribelum	cerebellum	chalis	chalice
ceribrum	cerebrum	chalk 1 /y	
cerise		challenge 2 /r	
cerkit	circuit 1+	chamber /-music	
cert		chamberlain	
certain /ly		chamberlin	chamberlain
certaint y /ies		chambermade	chambermaid
certen	certain +	chambermaid	
certifiabl e /y		chameleon	
certifiabul	certifiable +	chamie	chamois
certificat e 2 /ion		chamois	
certif y 4 /ier		champ 1	
certinty	certainty +	champagne	
certitude		champain	champagne
cervical		champion 1 /ship	
cervicul	cervical	champyun	champion 1+
cerviks	cervix +	chamwa	chamois
cervix /es		chanc e 2 /y	
cesashun	cessation	chancel	
cesation	cessation	chanceller y /ies	
ceshun	cession *	chancellor	
ceshun	session *	chancelor	chancellor
cespit	cesspit	chancelrey	chancellery +
cespool	cesspool	chancer y /ies	
cessation		chandelier	
cession * (yielding)		chandler	
cession	session *	chane	chain 1+
cesspit		chane reacshun	chain-reaction
cesspool		chanel	channel 3
chacoal	charcoal	change 2 /able/-over	
chafe 2* (rub)		changeling	
chaff * (grain husks)		channel 3	
chaffer 1		chans	chance 2+
chaffinch /es		chansel	chancel
chagrin /ed		chanseler	chancellor
chain 1 /-gang		chanselrey	chancellery +
chain-armour		chanserey	chancery +
chain-mail		chansey	chancy
chain-reaction		chansie	chancy
chain-store		chant 1	
chair 1 /man		chao s /tic	

61

chap³		chat³ /ty	
chapel		chateau /x (pl.)	
chaperon¹ /age		chater	chatter¹+
chaplain /cy		chaterbox	chatterbox
chaplet		chattel	
chaplin	chaplain+	chatter¹ /er	
chapter /-house		chatterbox	
char³ /woman/women		chaty	chatty
character		chauffeur	
characteris e² /ation		chauvinis m /t/tic	
characteristic /ally		cheap ★ (inexpensive)	
charade		cheap	cheep¹★
charcoal		cheap ish /ly/ness	
chare,	chair¹+	chear	cheer¹+
charey	chary+	chearful	cheerful+
charge² /able		chease	cheese+
chargé-d'affaires		cheat¹ /er	
charger		check¹★ (stop) /er	
charie	chary+	check	cheque★+
chariot /eer		Check	Czech★
charisma		checkmate²	
charitabl e /y		check-up	
charitabul	charitable+	Cheddar	
charit y /ies		cheder	Cheddar
charlatan		cheef	chief+
charlot	charlotte	cheek y /ier/iest/ily/iness	
charlotte		cheep¹★ (bird sound)	
charm¹ /er		cheep	cheap★
charman	chairman	cheer¹ /less	
chart¹		cheerey	cheery+
charter¹ /er		cheerful /ly/ness	
chartis m /t		cheerie	cheery+
char y /ily/iness		cheerio	
chas ed ★ (pursued) /ing		cheer y /ier/iest/ily/iness	
chased	chaste★	chees e /y	
chasen	chasten¹	cheesecake	
chasis	chassis	cheese-cloth	
chasm		cheet	cheat¹+
chassie	chassis	cheeta	cheetah+
chassis		cheetah /s	
chaste ★ (pure)		cheeter	cheetah+
chaste	chased★	chef	
chasten¹		chef-d'oeuvre	
chastise² /ment		cheif	chief+
chastity		cheiften	chieftain+

chelist	cellist	chilli er /est/ly/ness	
chelo	cello +	chime 2	
chemical /ly		chimeric /al	
chemise		chimney /-piece	
chemist /ry		chimnie	chimney +
chemistrey	chemistry	chimpanzee	
cheque *† /-book		chin	
†(money)		china /-clay	
cherie	cherry +	Chinese	
cherio	cheerio	chink 1	
cherish 1		chintz /es	
cheroot		chip 3	
cherp	chirp 1+	chipendale	Chippendale
cherr y /ies		chipmunk	
cherub /ic		chipolata	
chery	cherry +	Chippendale	
ches	chess +·	chiropod y /ist	
chesbord	chessboard	chirp 1 /y	
chess /board		chirrup 1	
chest		chisel 3 /ler	
Chesterfield		chit /-chat	
chestnut		chivalrus	chivalrous
chevalier		chivalr y /ous	
chevron		chive	
chew 1 /ing-gum		chlorate	
chic * (stylish)		chloride	
chicanery		chlorinat e 2 /ion	
chicory		chlorine	
chick *† /weed		chlorofill	chlorophyll
†(baby bird)		chloroform 1	
chide 2		chlorophyll	
chief /s		chloroplast	
chieftain /cy		chock /-a-block	
chiffon		chock-full	
chil	chill 1+	choclut	chocolate
chilblain		chocolate	
child /ren (pl.)		choice /st	
childbaring	childbearing	choir * (singers)	
childbearing		choir	quire *
child birth /hood		chois	choice +
child ish /less/like		choke 2 /r	
chili * (food) /es		choler * (rage) /ic	
chilie	chilly *	choler	collar 1*+
chilier	chillier +	cholera	
chill 1 /y * (cold)		cholester in /ol	

choo	chew [1]+	chub /by	
choos e /ing/y		chubbi er /est/ly/ness	
chop [3] /per		chubier	chubbier +
chopp y /ier/iest		chuck [1]	
chopsooey	chop-suey	chuckle [2]	
chopstick		chucul	chuckle [2]
chop-suey		chug [3]	
chopy	choppy +	chukker	
choral ★ (singing) /ly		chum [3] /my	
chorale ★ (metric hymn)		chump	
chord ★ (music)		chunk /y	
chord	cord ★+	church /es/warden	
chore		churl /ish	
choreograph y /er		churn [1]	
chorister		churp	chirp [1]+
chork	chalk [1]+	chute ★ (drop)	
chortle [2]		chute	shoot ★+
chortul	chortle [2]	chutney	
chorus [1] /es		chyle	
chose /n		chyme	
chow		cianide	cyanide
chrisalis	chrysalis +	cibernetics	cybernetics
chrisanthemum	chrysanthemum	cicada	
Christ		cicatrice	
christen [1]		cicatricks	cicatrice
Christendom		ciclamate	cyclamate
Christian /ity		ciclamen	cyclamen
Christmas /sy		cicle	cycle [2]
chromate		ciclic	cyclic +
chromatic /ally		ciclist	cyclist +
chromatin		ciclometer	cyclometer
chromatograf	chromatograph +	ciclone	cyclone +
chromatogram		ciclops	Cyclops
chromatograph /y		ciclostile	cyclostile
chrom e /ic/ium		ciclotron	cyclotron
chromosome		cicul	cycle [2]
chronic /ally		cider	
chronicle [2] /r		cifer	cipher [1]
chronicul	chronicle [2]+	cigar /ette	
chronograph /ic		cigaret	cigarette
chronological /ly		cignet	cygnet ★
chronolog y /ies		cignet	signet ★
chronometer		cilestial	celestial +
chrysalis /es		cilinder	cylinder
chrysanthemum		cilindrical	cylindrical +

cilium		circus /es	
cimbal	cymbal ★+	cirosis	cirrhosis
cimbal	symbol ★+	cirrhosis	
ciment	cement [1]+	cirro-cumulus	
cinamon	cinnamon	cirro-stratus	
cinch /es		cist	cyst +
cinder		cistern	
Cinderella		cistitis	cystitis
cine camera		citadel	
cinema /tic		cit *e* [2]★ (quote) /ation	
cinematograph /er/y		cite	sight [1]★+
cinerama		cite	site [2]★
cinic	cynic +	citie	city +
cinical	cynical +	citizen /ship	
cinicul	cynical +	citologey	cytology
cinima	cinema +	citric acid	
cinimatograf	cinematograph +	citr *on* /ate/ic	
cinimatograph	cinematograph +	citrus	
cinnamon		cit *y* /ies	
cinosure	cynosure	civet	
cipher [1]		civic /ism/s	
cipress	cypress	civil /ian/ly	
circa		civilis *e* [2] /ation	
circit	circuit [1]+	civilit *y* /ies	
circle [2]		civit	civet
circuit [1] /ous/ry		clad /ding	
circul	circle [2]	claim [1] /able/ant	
circular		clairvoyan *ce* /t	
circularis *e* [2] /ation		clam	
circulat *e* [2] /ion		clamant	
circulator /y		clamber [1]	
circumcis *e* [2] /ion		clame	claim [1]+
circumference		clamer	clamour +
circumferens	circumference	clamerous	clamorous
circumflex		clamerus	clamorous
circumfrence	circumference	clamm *y* /ily/iness	
circumnavigat *e* [2] /or		clamo *ur* /rous	
circumscribe [2]		clamp [1]	
circumscription		clamy	clammy +
circumspect /ion		clan /nish	
circumstance		clandestine /ly	
circumstans	circumstance	clang [1] /our	
circumstanshul	circumstantial +	clank [1]	
circumstantial /ly		clansman	
circumvent [1] /ion		clap [3] /per	

claptrap		clew [1]★ (thread)	
claret		clew	clue ★+
clarify [4] /ication/ier		clichay	cliché
clarinet /tist		cliché	
clarion		click [1]	
clarity		client /ele	
clark	clerk +	cliff /s	
claryun	clarion	climactic /ally	
clash [1]		climaks	climax [1]+
clasify	classify [4]+	climat e /ology	
clasroom	classroom	climatic /ally	
class [1] /less/y		climax [1] /es	
classic /al/ally/s		climb [1]★ (go up) /er	
classicis m /t		clime ★ (climate)	
classif y [4] /ication/ier		clinch [1]	
classroom		cling /ing	
clatter [1]		clinic /al/ally	
clause		clink [1]	
claustrofobia	claustrophobia	clinker /-built	
claustrophobia		cliontell	clientele
clavichord		clip [3] /per	
clavic le /ular		cliqu e /ish/y	
clavicord	clavichord	clitoris	
clavicul	clavicle +	cloak /room	
claw [1]		clobber [1]	
clay /more		cloche	
claym	claim [1]+	clock [1] /wise/work	
clean [1] /able/liness/ly		clod /-hopper	
cleanse [2]		clog [3]	
clear [1] /ance/ly/ness		cloister [1]	
cleave [2] /age		clorate	chlorate
cleavidge	cleavage	clore	claw [1]
cleek	clique +	cloride	chloride
clef		clorinate	chlorinate [2]+
cleft		clorine	chlorine
clematis		clorofill	chlorophyll
clemen cy /t		cloroform	chloroform [1]
clemensey	clemency +	clorophil	chlorophyll
clench [1]		cloroplast	chloroplast
clenliness	cleanliness	clos e [2] /ure	
clense	cleanse [2]	closet [1]	
clergy /man		closher	closure
cleric /al/alism		clot [3]	
clerk /ship		cloth	
clever /er/est/ly		cloth e [2] /ier	

cloud [1] /ier/less/y	
clout [1]	
clove /n	
clover /-leaf	
clowd	cloud [1]+
clown [1] /ish	
club [3] /bable	
cluch	clutch [1]
cluck [1]	
clue * (guide) /less	
clue	clew [1]*
clump [1]	
clumsi *ly* /ness	
clums *y* /ier/iest	
clung	
cluster [1]	
clutch [1]	
clutter [1]	
coach [1] /ful/man	
coagulant	
coagulat *e* [2] /ion/or	
coaks	coax [1]
coal /field/mine	
coala	koala
coalesans	coalescence
coalesce [2] /nce/nt	
coalesent	coalescent
coaless	coalesce [2]+
coalishun	coalition +
coalition /ist	
coal-scuttle	
coarse * (rough) /ly/ness	
coarse	course *+
coarsen [1]	
coast [1] /al	
coast *guard* /line	
coat [1] /ee	
coax [1]	
cob	
cobalt	
cobble [2] /r	
cobra	
cobul	cobble [2]+
cobweb /bed	
coca	

cocaine	
cocane	cocaine
coccyx /es	
coch	coach [1]+
cochineal	
cock [1] /crow/erel	
cockato	cockatoo
cockatoo	
cockchafer	
cocker	
cocket	coquette +
cocketrey	coquetry
cock-eyed	
cockle	
cockney /ish/ism/s	
cockpit	
cockroach	
cockscomb	
cockshore	cocksure
cocksis	coccyx +
cocksure	
cocktail	
cockul	cockle
cock *y* /ier/iest/ily	
coco * (palm tree)	
coco	cocoa *
cocoa * (cacao powder)	
coconut	
cocoon	
cocotte	
cod [3] /ling	
codak	Kodak
coddle [2]	
code [2]	
codecks	codex +
codeine	
cod *ex* /ices (pl.)	
codger	
codicil	
codif *y* [4] /ication/ier	
codisil	codicil
codle	coddle [2]
co-educate [2]	
co-education /al	
coefficient	

coefishent	coefficient	coinidge	coinage
coegsist	coexist ¹⁺	coinside	coincide ²
coequal /ity/ly		coinsidence	coincidence ⁺
coerc e ² /ible		coinsidens	coincidence ⁺
coerc ion /ive		coinsident	coincident
coerse	coerce ²⁺	coir ⋆ (coconut fibre)	
coershun	coercion ⁺	coir	choir ⋆
coersive	coercive	coit us /ion	
coexist ¹ /ence/ent		coke ²	
cofee	coffee	coket	coquette ⁺
cofer	coffer	cokoon	cocoon
cofey	coffee	col	
coff	cough ¹⁺	cola	koala
coffee		colaborate	collaborate ²⁺
coffer		colage	collage
coffin		colander	
cog ³ /-wheel		colaps	collapse ²⁺
cogen cy /t		colate	collate ²⁺
coger	codger	cold /er/est/ly/ness	
cogitat e ² /ion		cold-blooded	
cognac		cold-shoulder ¹	
cognate		cole	coal ⁺
cognisabl e /y		colean	colleen
cognisan ce /t		colecshun	collection
cognishun	cognition ⁺	colect	collect ¹⁺
cognition /al		colectabul	collectable ⁺
cognitive		colection	collection
cognomen		colectiv	collective ⁺
cohabit ¹ /ation		coleeg	colleague
cohear	cohere ²⁺	colege	college ⁺
cohearent	coherent ⁺	colegian	collegian
cohere ² /nce		colegiate	collegiate
coherent /ly		coler	choler ⋆⁺
coheshun	cohesion ⁺	coler	collar ¹⋆⁺
cohes ion /ive		colera	cholera
cohort		coleric	choleric
coifer	coiffeur ⋆⁺	colesterin	cholesterin ⁺
coiffeu r ⋆† /se (fem.)		colesterol	cholesterol
†(hairdresser)		colic /ky	
coiffure ⋆ (hair style)		colide	collide ²
coifur	coiffure ⋆	colier	collier
coil ¹		colinder	colander
coin ¹ /age/er		colinear	collinear
coincide ²		colishun	collision
coinciden ce /t		colision	collision

colitis	
collaborat *e* ² /ion/or	
collage	
collaps *e* ² /ible	
collar ¹*† /-bone	
†(seize, neckband)	
collar	choler *+
collat *e* ² /ion/or	
collateral	
colleague	
collect ¹ /ion/or	
collect *able* /edly	
collectiv *e* /ism/ist	
colleen	
colleg *e* /ian/iate	
coller	choler *+
coller	collar ¹*+
collide ²	
collie	
collier	
collinear	
collision	
collocate ²	
colloid /al	
colloquial /ism/ly	
colloqu *y* /ies	
collude ²	
collus *ion* /ive	
colly	collie
colokwey	colloquy +
colokwial	colloquial +
colon	
colonade	colonnade
colonel * (officer)	
colonial /ism	
colonis *e* ² /ation/er	
colonnade	
colon *y* /ies/ist	
coloqual	colloquial +
coloquy	colloquy +
color	colour ¹+
coloration	
colorful	colourful +
colossal /ly	
colossus /es	

colour ¹ /less	
colourful /ly	
coloyd	colloid +
colt /ish	
colude	collude ²
colum	column +
columbine	
column /ar/ist	
colushun	collusion +
colusion	collusion +
coma * (deep sleep)	
coma	comma *
comand	command ¹+
comandment	commandment
comando	commando +
comb ¹	
combat ¹ /ant/ive	
combinashun	combination
combin *e* ² /ation	
combuschun	combustion
combustib *le* /ility	
combustibul	combustible +
combustion	
com *e* /ing	
come	comb ¹
comedi *an* /enne (fem.)	
comed *y* /ies	
comel *y* /ier/iest	
comemorashun	commemoration
comemorate	commemorate ²+
comence	commence ²+
comend	commend ¹+
comendabul	commendable +
comendashun	commendation
comendation	commendation
comens	commence ²+
comenshurate	commensurate
coment	comment ¹+
comentater	commentator
comentrey	commentary +
comerce	commerce
comercial	commercial +
comercialise	commercialise ²+
comercialism	commercialism
comerse	commerce

comershal	commercial +	commit ³ /ment/tal	
comershalise	commercialise ²+	committee * (body)	
comershalism	commercialism	commity	comity *
comestibles		commod e /ious	
comet		commodit y /ies	
comfert	comfort ¹+	commodore	
comfort ¹ /er/less		common /er/est/ly	
comfortabl e /y		Common Market	
comic /al/ally		commonplace	
comicalit y /ies		Commons	
comiserate	commiserate ²+	Commonwealth	
comiserey	commissary +	commoshun	commotion
comishun	commission ¹+	commotion	
comission	commission ¹+	communal /ly	
comit	comet	communalise ²	
comit	commit ³+	commune ²	
comital	committal	communicable	
comitey	comity *	communicat e ² /ion	
comitment	commitment	communicat ive /or	
comittal	committal	communikay	communiqué
comittey	committee *	communi on /cant	
comit y *(courtesy)		communiqué	
comma *(punctuation)		communis m /t/tic	
comma	coma *	communit y /ies	
command ¹ /ant/er		commute ² /r	
commandeer ¹		comode	commode +
commandment		comodious	commodious
commando /s		comodity	commodity +
commemorat e ² /ion		comodius	commodious
commence ² /ment		comodoor	commodore
commend ¹ /ation		comon	common +
commendabl e /y		Comon Market	Common Market
commensurate		Comonwelth	Commonwealth
comment ¹ /ator		comoshun	commotion
commentar y /ies		comotion	commotion
commentrey	commentary +	compact	
commerce		compair	compère ²*
commercial /ism/ly		companion /ship	
commercialis e ²/ation		compan y /ies	
commershal	commercial +	companyun	companion +
commershalise	commercialise ²+	comparabl e /y	
commiserat e ² /ion		comparabul	comparable +
commissar /iat		comparative /ly	
commissar y /ies		compare ²* (liken to)	
commission ¹ /aire/er		compare	compère ²*

70

comparison	
compartment	
compashonate	compassionate
compashun	compassion [+]
compass [1] /es	
compassion /ate/ately	
compatib *le* /ility	
compatibul	compatible [+]
compatriot	
compel [3]	
compendium	
compensat *e* [2] /ion	
compensator /y	
compère [2]* (presenter)	
competant	competent
compet *e* [2] /ition	
competen *ce* /t	
competit *ive* /or	
compil *e* [2] /ation	
complacenc *e* /y	
complacens	complacence [+]
complacent /ly	
complain [1] /ant/t	
complane	complain [1+]
complasense	complacence [+]
complasent	complacent [+]
complement [1]*† /ary	
† (balance)	
complete [2] /ly	
completion	
complex	
complexion /ed	
complexit *y* /ies	
complian *ce* /t	
complicat *e* [2] /ion	
complicity	
compliment [1]*† /ary	
† (praise)	
compl *y* [4] /iable	
component	
comport [1] /ment	
compose [2]	
composher	composure
composishun	composition
composite /ly	

composition	
compositor	
compost	
composure	
compot	compote
compote	
compound [1] /able	
comprehen *d* [1] /sible	
comprehens *ion* /ive	
compress [1] /ion/or	
compressib *le* /ility	
compris *e* [2] /able	
compromise [2]	
compulshun	compulsion [+]
compuls *ion* /ive	
compulsor *y* /ily	
compulsrey	compulsory [+]
compuncshun	compunction
compunction	
comput *e* [2] /ation/er	
computeris *e* [2] /ation	
comrad	comrade [+]
comrade /ly/ship	
comunal	communal [+]
comunalise	communalise [2]
comune	commune [2]
comunicable	communicable
comunicant	communicant
comunicashun	communication
comunicate	communicate [2+]
comunication	communication
comunikay	communiqué
comunion	communion[+]
comunism	communism [+]
comunist	communist
comunitey	community [+]
comunyun	communion[+]
comute	commute [2+]
con [3]	
concave	
concavit *y* /ies	
conceal [1] /ment	
concede [2]	
conceit /ed	
conceivabul	conceivable

71

conceiv *e* [2] /able/ably
concentrat *e* [2] /ion
concentric /ity
conception
concept /ual/ually
concern [1]
concert /ina
concerto /s
concession /ary
conch
concherto — concerto [+]
conciet — conceit [+]
concievabul — conceivable
concieve — conceive [2+]
conciliat *e* [2] /ion
conciliator /y
concise /ly/ness
conclave
conclude [2]
conclus *ion* /ive
concoct [1] /ion
concomitant
concord /ance/ant
concorse — concourse
concourse
concrete /ly/ness
concubine
concur [3]
concurren *ce* /t/tly
concuss [1] /ion
condemn [1] /ation
condens *e* [2] /ation/er
condescen *d* [1] /sion
condiment
condisend — condescend [1+]
condisenshun — condescension
condisension — condescension
condishun — condition [1+]
condit — conduit
condition [1] /al/ally
condole [2] /nce
condon *e* [2] /ation/er
conduc *e* [2] /ive
conduct [1] /ion
conductiv *e* /ity

conduct *or* /ress (fem.)
conduit
cone
conect — connect [1+]
conerbashun — conurbation
conerbation — conurbation
confabulat *e* [2] /ion
confection /er/ery
confederac *y* /ies
confederasey — confederacy [+]
confederat *e* [2] /ion
confer [3] /ment
conference
confeser — confessor
confess [1] /or
confession /al
confetti
confidant *† /e (fem.)
  †(trusted friend)
confide [2] /nce
confidenshal — confidential [+]
confident *† /ly
  †(self-assured)
confidential /ity/ly
configerashun — configuration
configuration
confine [2] /ment
confirm [1] /ation
confirmat *ive* /ory
confiscat *e* [2] /ion
conflagration
conflict [1]
conform [1] /able/ation
conform *ist* /ity
confound [1]
confownd — confound [1]
confurm — confirm [1+]
confus *e* [2] /ion
confut *e* [2] /ation
congeal [1]
congenial /ity/ly
congenital /ly
conger /-eel
congest [1] /ion/ive
conglomerat *e* [2] /ion

congratulat *e* [2] /ions/ory

congregat *e* [2] /ion

congregational /ist

congress /ional

conic /al/ally

conifer /ous

conjectcher   conjecture [2+]

conjectur *e* [2] /al

conjoin [1] /t

conjucive   conducive

conjugal

conjugat *e* [2] /ion

conjuice   conduce [2+]

conjuncshun   conjunction

conjunction

conjunctiv *e* /itis

conjur *e* [2] /ation/er

conker*(horse chestnut)

conker   conquer [1*+]

conkwest   conquest

connect [1] /ion/ive

conneser   connoisseur

conning-tower

conniv *e* [2] /ance/er

connoisseur

connot *e* [2] /ation

connubial /ly

conosseur   connoisseur

conote   connote [2+]

conquer [1]*(defeat) /or

conquest

consanguin *eous* /ity

conscience

conscienshus   conscientious [+]

conscientious /ly

conscious /ly/ness

conscript [1] /ion

conseal   conceal [1+]

conseat   conceit [+]

consecrat *e* [2] /ion

consecutive

consekwence   consequence [+]

consensus

consent [1]

consequen *ce* /t

consequential /ly

conservancy

conservansey   conservancy

conservashun   conservation

conservation

conservat *ive* /ism

conservatoire

conservator *y* /ies

conservatrey   conservatory [+]

conserv *e* [2]

consider [1] /able/ably

considerat *e* /ion

considrabul   considerable

consign [1] /ment

consiliate   conciliate [2+]

consine   consign [1+]

consise   concise [+]

consist [1] /ence

consistenc *y* /ies

consistensey   consistency [+]

consolabul   consolable

consolashun   consolation

consol *e* [2] /able/ation

consolidat *e* [2] /ion

consommé

consonan *ce* /t

consonans   consonance [+]

consort [1] /ium

conspicuous /ly/ness

conspirac *y* /ies

conspirasey   conspiracy [+]

conspirater   conspirator [+]

conspirator /y

conspire [2]

constable

constabul   constable

constabular *y* /ies

constan *cy* /t

constansey   constancy [+]

constelashun   constellation

constellation

consternat *e* [2] /ion

constipat *e* [2] /ion

constituenc *y* /ies

constituensey   constituency [+]

constituent
constitute [2]
constitution /al/ally
constrain [1] /t
constrict [1] /ion
construct [1] /ion
constructive /ly
constru *e* [2] /able
consul /ar/ate
consult [1] /ant
consultat *ion* /ive
consumashun   consummation
consum *e* [2] /able/er
consummate [2] /ly
consummation
consumpt *ion* /ive
consumshun   consumption [+]
consumtion   consumption [+]
contact [1] /or
contag *ion* /ious
contagus   contagious
contain [1] /er/ment
contaminat *e* [2] /ion
contemplat *e* [2] /ion
contemplative /ly
contemporaneous
contemporar *y* /ies
contempt /ible/uous
contend [1]
content [1] /ment
content *ion* /ious
contest [1] /able/ant
context
contigu *ous* /ity
continence
continens   continence
continent /al
contingenc *y* /ies
contingensey   contingency [+]
contingent
continual /ly
continua *nce* /tion
continu *e* [2] /ity
continuous /ly
contorshun   contortion [+]

contort [1]
contortion /ist
contour
contraband
contracept *ion* /ive
contract [1] /ion/or
contractual /ly
contradict [1] /ion/ory
contralto /s
contrapshun   contraption
contraption
contrar *y* /ily/iness
contrast [1]
contraven *e* [2] /er/tion
contribut *e* [2] /ion
contributor /y
contrit *e* /ion
contriv *e* [2] /ance
control [3] /lable/ler
controvershal   controversial [+]
controversial /ly
controvers *y* /ies
contus *e* [2] /ion
conurbation
convalesce [2] /nce/nt
convaless   convalesce [2+]
convalessence   convalescence
convect *ion* /ive/or
convene [2] /r
convenien *ce* /t
conveniens   convenience [+]
convenshun   convention
convenshunal   conventional [+]
convent
convention
conventional /ism/ly
converge [2] /nce/nt
conversant
conversation /al/alist
converse [2] /ly
conversion
convert [1] /er/ible
convex /ity
convey [1]
conveyanc *e* /ing

conveyor belt		coral ★ (sea life)	
convict [1] /ion		coral	choral ★+
convinc e [2] /ingly		coral	corral [3]★
conviscate	confiscate [2]+	corcus	caucus +
convivial /ity/ly		cord ★ (rope) /age	
convocashun	convocation	cord	chord ★
convocation		cordial /ity/ly	
convoke [2]		cordite	
convolut e [2] /ion		cordon [1]	
convoy [1]		cordon bleu	
convuls e [2] /ion		corduroy	
convulsive /ly		core ★ (centre)	
con y /ies		core	caw [1]★
conyac	cognac	core	corps ★
coo [1]		corecshun	correction
cooger	cougar	corect	correct [1]+
cook [1] /able		corection	correction
cooker /y		corectiv	corrective
cool [1] /ant/est/ness		corespond	correspond [1]+
coolie ★ (labourer)		corespondence	correspondence
coolly ★ (calmly)		corespondens	correspondence
coop [1]		co-respondent	
co-op		coridoor	corridor
cooper /age		coriografey	choreography +
co-operat e [2] /ion/or		corispondence	correspondence
co-operative /ly/ness		corispondens	correspondence
co-opt [1] /ion		corister	chorister
co-ordinat e [2] /ion		cork /age/screw	
co-partner /ship		corm	
cope [2]		cormorant	
copeck		corn /flour	
Copernican system		cornea /l	
co-pilot		corner [1] /-stone	
copious /ly		cornet [1]	
copiss	coppice	cornia	cornea +
copper /plate		cornice	
coppice		cornucopia	
copra		corny	
copse		coroborate	corroborate [2]+
copulat e [2] /ion		coroborativ	corroborative +
cop y [4] /ies/ier		corode	corrode [2]+
copyright		corollary	
copyrite	copyright	corona	
coquetry		coronary	
coquett e /ish		coronashun	coronation

coronation		corterise	cauterise ²⁺
coroner		cort *ex* /ices (pl.)	
coronet		cortion	caution ¹⁺
coroshun	corrosion ⁺	cortious	cautious ⁺
corosion	corrosion ⁺	cortisan	courtesan
corosiv	corrosive	cortisone	
corporal		cortship	courtship
corporat *e* /ion		cortyard	courtyard
corporeal		corugate	corrugate ²⁺
corps ★ (army)		corupt	corrupt ¹⁺
corpse ★ (body)		coruptible	corruptible ⁺
corpulen *ce* /t		coruptibul	corruptible ⁺
corpus		corus	chorus ¹⁺
corpusc *le* /ular		corvet	corvette
corpussel	corpuscle ⁺	corvette	
corral ³ ★ (animal pen)		cosecant	
corral	coral ★	coset	cosset ¹
correct ¹ /ion/ive/or		cosh ¹	
correlat *e* ² /ion		cosi *er* /est/ly/ness	
correlative /ly		co-signator *y* /ies	
correspond ¹ /ence/ent		cosine	
corridor		cosmetic /ian	
corrigend *um* /a (pl.)		cosmic /ally	
corrigible		cosmografey	cosmography ⁺
corroborat *e* ² /ion		cosmograph *y* /ic	
corroborative /ly		cosmolog *y* /ical	
corrod *e* ² /ible		cosmonaut	
corros *ion* /ive		cosmonort	cosmonaut
corrugat *e* ² /ion		cosmopolitan /ism	
corrupt ¹ /ive/ness		cosmos	
corruptib *le* /ility		cosmotron	
corsashun	causation ⁺	co-sponsor	
corsation	causation ⁺	Cossack	
corse	coarse ★⁺	cosset ¹	
corse	course ★⁺	cost ¹ /ly	
corsen	coarsen ¹	cost	coast ¹⁺
corset /ed		costgard	coastguard ⁺
corshun	caution ¹⁺	costive	
corshus	cautious ⁺	costli *er* /est/ness	
corslet		costum *e* /ier	
corstic	caustic ⁺	cosy	
cort	caught ★	cot	
cort	court ¹★	cotage	cottage ⁺
cort marshal	court-martial ³⁺	cotangent	
cortège		cote	coat ¹⁺

coterie	
cotidge	cottage [+]
coton	cotton [+]
cottage /r	
cotton /wool	
cou dayta	coup d'état
couch [1] /es	
cougar	
cough [1] /er	
could /n't	
coulomb	
council ★ (assembly)	
councillor ★ (member of assembly)	
counsel [3]★ (advice)	
counsellor ★ (adviser)	
count [1] /ess (fem.) /less	
countenance	
counter [1] /foil	
counteract [1] /ion	
counter-attack [1]	
counterbalance [2]	
counter-charge [2]	
counter-claim [1]	
counter-clockwise	
counterfeit [1] /er	
countermand [1]	
countermine [2]	
counterpane	
counterpart	
counterpoint	
counterpoise [2]	
countersign [1]	
countersine	countersign [1]
counterway	counter-weigh [1]
counter-weigh [1]	
countie	county [+]
countr y /ies	
countryside	
count y /ies	
coup d'état	
couple [2] /t	
coupon	
courage /ous/ously	
courier	

cours e ★† /ing †(conduct, passage)	
course	coarse ★[+]
coursen	coarsen [1]
court [1]★ (law)	
court	caught★
courtesan	
courtes y /ies	
courtier	
courtley	courtly [+]
courtl y /iness	
court-martial [3] /s	
courtship	
courtyard	
cousin	
covalent bond	
cove	
coven	
covenant	
Coventry	
cover [1] /age/let	
covert	
covet [1] /er/ous	
covey /s	
cow	
coward /ice	
cowardl y /iness	
cowboy	
cowch	couch [1+]
cower [1]	
cowerd	coward [+]
cowl /ing	
cownt	count [1+]
cowntenance	countenance
cowntenans	countenance
cownter	counter [1+]
cownteract	counteract [1+]
cowpox	
cowslip	
cox [1] /swain	
coxcomb	
coy /ly/ness	
coyn	coin [1+]
coyote	
crab [3] /-apple	

77

crack¹ /er		credence	
crackle²		credens	credence
cracknel		credential	
crackul	crackle²	credib le /ility/ly	
cradel	cradle²	credibul	credible +
cradle²		credit¹ /or	
cradul	cradle²	creditabl e /y	
craft /y		creditabul	creditable +
crafti er /est/ly/ness		crediter	creditor
craftsman /ship		credul ity /ous	
crag /gy		creed	
crain	crane²+	creek ★ (stream)	
cram³ /mer		creek	creak¹★+
cramp¹ /on		creem	cream¹+
cranberie	cranberry +	creep /er/ing/s/y	
cranberr y /ies		creepi er /est/ly/ness	
crane² /-fly		cremat e² /ion	
crani um /al		crematorium	
crank¹ /case/shaft/y		Cremlin	Kremlin
crann y /ies		crenellated	
crape		creole	
crash¹		crep	crêpe
crash-land¹		crêpe	
crass		crept	
crate²		crepuscular	
crater		crescendo /s	
cravat		crescent	
crave² /n		cresent	crescent
crawl¹ /er		cresh	crèche
crayfish		creshendo	crescendo +
crayon		cresit	cresset
craz e² /y		cresset	
crazi er /est/ly/ness		crest /fallen	
creacher	creature	cretin /ism/ous	
creak¹★ (noise) /y		cretonne	
creak	creek ★	creture	creature
cream¹ /y		crevasse	
creamer y /ies		crevice	
creami er /est/ness		crevis	crevice
crease²		crew¹ /s ★ (sailors)	
creat e² /ion/or		crews	cruise²★+
creativ e /ity		crewsifix	crucifix +
creature		crib³ /ber	
crèche		cribbage	
crecher	creature	cribidge	cribbage

crick [1]
cricket /er
crime
criminal /ity/ly
criminolog ist /y
crimson
crincul   crinkle [2+]
cringe [2]
crinkl e [2] /y
crinoline
cripple [2]
cript   crypt [+]
criptograf   cryptograph [+]
criptogram   cryptogram
criptograph   cryptograph [+]
cripul   cripple [2]
crisalis   chrysalis [+]
crisanthemum   chrysanthemum
crisen   christen [1+]
Crisendum   Christendom
Crishna   Krishna
cris is /es
Crismas   Christmas [+]
crisp /iness/ly/y
criss-cross [1]
Crist   Christ
cristal   crystal [+]
cristaline   crystalline
cristalise   crystallise [2+]
cristalografer   crystallographer [+]
Cristian   Christian [+]
Cristianity   Christianity
criteri on /a (pl.)
critic /al/ally
criticis e [2] /able
criticism
critisize   criticise [2+]
criy   cry [4+]
croak [1]
croch   crotch
crochet [1]
crock /ery
crocodile
crocus /es
croft /er

croissant
crokay   croquet
cromatic   chromatic [+]
cromatin   chromatin
cromatograf   chromatograph [+]
cromatogram   chromatogram
crome   chrome [+]
cromic   chromic
cromium   chromium
crone ★ (hag)
crone   krone ★[+]
cronic   chronic [+]
croniçul   chronicle [2+]
cronie   crony [+]
cronograf   chronograph [+]
cronograph   chronograph [+]
cronologey   chronology [+]
cronological   chronological [+]
cronometer   chronometer
cron y /ies
crood   crude [+]
crook
crooked /ly/ness
croon [1]
croop   croup
croopier   croupier
crop [3] /per
croquet
cross [1] /ly/ness
cross -breed /-bred
cross-country
cross-cut /ting
cross-examin e [2] /ation
cross-fertilis e [2] /ation
cross-fire
cross-legged
crosspatch
cross-purpose
cross-question [1]
cross-reference [2]
cross-road
crosswise
crossword
crotch
crotchet /y

crouch [1]
croup
croupier
crow [1]
crowbar
crowd [1]
crown [1]
crucial /ly
crucible

crucibul	crucible
crucifix /ion	
crucify [4]	
crude /ly/ness/st	
cruditey	crudity +
crudit y /ies	
cruel /ler/lest/ly	
cruelt y /ies	
cruet	
cruise [2]* (voyage) /r	
crum	crumb +
crumb /iness/y	
crumbl e [2]*(break up)/y	
crumbul	crumble [2]*+
crumpet	
crumple [2]* (crease)	
crumpul	crumple [2]*
crumy	crumby
crunch [1] /iness/y	
cruper	crupper
crupper	
crusade [2] /r	
crush [1]	
crushal	crucial +
crusible	crucible
crusibul	crucible
crust /y	
crustace a /an/ous	
crustasha	crustacea +
crutch	
crux /es	
cruze	cruise [2]*+
cr y [4] /ies/ier	
crypt /ic/ically	
cryptogram	
cryptograph /ic	

crysalis	chrysalis +
crystal /line	
crystallis e [2] /ation	
crystallograph er /y	
cub	
cubby-hole	
cub e /age	
cubical * (cube-shaped)	
cubicle * (small room)	
cubihole	cubby-hole
cubis m /t	
cuboard	cupboard
cuckold [1]	
cuckoo	
cucumber	
cuddle [2]	
cudgel [3]	
cudul	cuddle [2]
cue [2]* (billiards)	
cue	queue [2]*
cuff [1]	
cuisine	
culcher	culture [2]+
cul-de-sac	
culer	colour [1]+
culerashun	coloration
culinary	
culinder	colander
culinrey	culinary
cull [1]	
culminat e [2] /ion	
culpab le /ility	
culpabul	culpable +
culprit	
cult	
cultivat e [2] /ion/or	
cultur e [2] /al/ist	
culvert	
cumbersome /ly/ness	
cumbersum	cumbersome +
Cumbrian	
cumfert	comfort [1]+
cumpas	compass [1]+
cumulative	
cumulus	

cuneiform		cursive /ly	
cuniform	cuneiform	cursory	
cunning		curt /ly/ness	
cuntreyside	countryside	curtail¹ /ment	
cup³ /ful		curtain¹	
cupboard		curtale	curtail¹⁺
cupidity		curts y⁴ /ies	
cupola		curv e² /ature	
cupro-nickel		curvilinear	
cur /rish		cushion¹	
curab le /ility		cushon	cushion¹
curabul	curable⁺	cusp	
curac y /ies		cuss¹ /edness	
curant	currant ★	custard	
curasey	curacy⁺	custod y /ial/ian	
curate		custom /er	
curater	curator⁺	customar y /ily	
curator /ship		cut /ter/ting	
curb¹★ (chain in bit)		cute /ly/ness/r/st	
curb	kerb¹★	cuticle	
curd		cuticul	cuticle
curdle²		cutlass /es	
curdul	curdle²	cutlery	
cur e² /ative		cutlet	
curent	current ★⁺	cuttle-fish	
curfew		cuvenant	covenant
curiculum	curriculum⁺	cuver	cover¹⁺
curie		cuvet	covet¹⁺
curio /s		cuvey	covey⁺
curiosit y /ies		cyanide	
curious /ly/ness		cybernetics	
curium		cyclamate	
curius	curious⁺	cyclamen	
curl¹ /er/iness/y		cycle²	
curlew		cyclic /al/ally	
curnel	colonel ★	cycl ist /ometer	
currage	courage⁺	cyclon e /ic	
curragus	courageous	Cyclops	
currant ★ (fruit)		cyclostyle	
currenc y /ies		cyclotron	
currensey	currency⁺	cygnet ★ (swan)	
current ★ (flow) /ly		cygnet	signet ★
curricul um /a (pl.)		cyle	chyle
curry⁴ /comb		cylinder	
curse²		cylindrical /ly	

cymbal *† /ist	
†(musical instrument)	
cymbal	symbol *+
cynic /ism	
cynical /ly	
cynosure	
cypress	
cyst /itis	
cytology	
czar	tsar
Czech * (nationality)	
Czechoslovakian	

D

dab³ /ber	
dabble² /r	
dable	dabble²+
dabul	dabble²+
dabutant	débutant +
dace	
dachshund	
dactill	dactyl
dactyl	
daddy /-long-legs	
daffodil	
daft /er/est	
dagger	
dahlia	
dail	dale
dailie	daily +
dail y /ies	
daintie	dainty +
daint y /ier/iest/ily/iness	
dairie	dairy +
dairimade	dairymaid
dair y /ies	
dairymaid	
daisie	daisy +
dais y /ies	
daitee	deity +
dakshound	dachshund
dale	
dalia	dahlia

dalie	dally⁴+
dall y⁴ /ier	
dam³* (water)	
dam	damn¹*+
damage² /able	
damask	
dame	
damidge	damage²+
damn¹* (curse) /ation	
damnabl e /y	
damnabul	damnable +
damp /er/est/ness	
dampen¹	
damsel	
damson	
dance² /r	
dandelion	
dandie	dandy +
dandifi	dandify⁴
dandify⁴	
dandilion	dandelion
dandruff	
dand y /ies	
Dane * (from Denmark)	
dane	deign¹*
danger /ous/ously	
dangerus	dangerous
dangle² /r	
dangul	dangle²+
danjer	danger+
danjerus	dangerous
dank /ness	
danse	dance²+
daper	dapper +
daple	dapple²
dapper /ness	
dapple²	
dapul	dapple²
dare² /-devil	
dark /er/est/ly/ness	
darken¹	
darling	
darn¹ /er	
darnel	
dart¹	

dase	dace
dash¹ /board	
dastard /ly	
data	
dat e² /able	
dater	data
dative	
daub¹ /er/y	
daufin	dauphin
daughter /-in-law	
daunt¹ /less	
dauphin	
dauter	daughter +
davenport	
Davielamp	Davy lamp
davit	
Davy lamp	
dawb	daub¹+
dawdle² /r	
dawdul	dawdle²+
dawn¹	
dawnt	daunt¹+
dawter	daughter +
day /-break/s * (dates)	
daybu	début
day-dream /t/ing	
dayify	deify⁴+
dayism	deism +
dayist	deist
dayity	deity +
daylight	
daylite	daylight
day-nurser y /ies	
daytant	détente
daze ²* (stun)	
dazle	dazzle²+
dazul	dazzle²+
dazzl e² /er/ingly	
de luxe	
deacon /ess (fem.)	
deactivat e² /ion	
dead /-beat/-line	
deaden¹ /er	
dead-heat¹	
deadlock	

deadl y /ier/iest/iness	
dead-nettle	
deaf /-mute/ness	
deafen¹ /ingly	
deal /er/ing/t	
deam	deem¹
dean /ery	
deap	deep +
dear * (loved)	
dear	deer *
dear er /est/ly	
dearth	
death /-mask/-rate	
death ly /less/like	
death -trap /-watch	
débâcle	
debacul	débâcle
debar³ /ment	
debark¹ /ation	
debase² /ment	
debat e² /able/ably	
debauch¹ /ery	
debilitat e² /ion	
debility	
debit¹ /able	
debonair /ness	
deborch	debauch¹+
debree	debris
debrief¹	
debris	
debt /or * (owe money)	
debunk¹ /er	
début	
débutant /e (fem.)	
decade	
decaden ce /t	
decagon /al	
deca gram /litre/metre	
decamp¹ /ment	
decant¹ /er	
decapitat e² /ion	
decapod	
decarbonis e² /ation	
decathlon	
decay¹	

decease [2]
deceit /ful/fully/fulness
deceive [2] /r
decelerat *e* [2] /ion
December
decenc *y* /ies

decensey   decency [+]
decent ★ (good) /ly

decent   descent ★
decentralise [2]

decepshun   deception
deception
deceptive /ly/ness

decerus   decorous [+]
decibel
decide [2] /dly
deciduous

decifer   decipher [1+]
deci *gram* /litre/metre
decimal /ism
decimalis *e* [2] /ation
decimat *e* [2] /ion
decipher [1] /able
decision
decisive /ly/ness
deck [1] /-chair/-hand
declaim [1] /er

declamashun   declamation [+]
declamat *ion* /ory
declarat *ion* /ory
declare [2]
declassif *y* [4] /ication
declension
declin *e* [2] /able/ation
declivit *y* /ies
declutch [1]

decockshun   decoction
decoction
decode [2] /r

decoi   decoy [1]
décollet *é* /age
decompos *e* [2] /able/ition
decompress [1] /ion
decompress *ive* /or
decon   deacon [+]

decongestant
decontaminat *e* [2] /ion
decontrol [3]
décor

decorashun   decoration
decorat *e* [2] /ion/ive/or
decorous /ly/ness
decorum

decorus   decorous [+]
decoy [1]
decreas *e* [2] /ingly
decree /d/ing
decrepit /ude

decrese   decrease [2+]
decri   decry [4+]
decr *y* [4] /ier
ded   dead [+]
deden   deaden [1+]
dedheat   dead-heat [1]
dedicat *e* [2] /ion
dedlie   deadly [+]
dedlier   deadlier
dedlock   deadlock
dedly   deadly [+]
dednetle   dead-nettle
dednetul   dead-nettle
deduc *e* [2] /ible
deduct [1] /ible/ion
deed /-poll
deel   deal [+]
deem [1]
deen   dean [+]
deep /er
deepen [1]
deep-freez *e* /er/ing
deep-frozen
deep-fry [4]
deer ★ (animal)
deer   dear ★
de-escalat *e* [2] /ion
def   deaf [+]
deface [2] /ment
defamatory
defamatrey   defamatory
defam *e* [2] /ation

default¹ /er
defeat¹ /ism/ist
defecat *e*² /ion
defect¹ /ion/ive/or
defeet   defeat¹⁺
defen   deafen¹⁺
defence /less
defend¹ /able/ant
defens   defence⁺
defensib *le* /ility
defensibul   defensible⁺
defensive /ly/ness
defensless   defenceless
defer³★ (postpone)
deferen *ce* /tial
deferens   deference⁺
deferenshal   deferential
defesit   deficit
defi   defy⁴⁺
defian *ce* /t/tly
defians   defiance⁺
deficienc *y* /ies
deficient /ly
deficit
defile² /ment/r
defin *e*² /able/ition
definishun   definition
definit   definite⁺
definite /ly
definitive /ly
defishency   deficiency⁺
defishent   deficient⁺
defisit   deficit
deflashun   deflation
deflat *e*² /ion/ionary
deflecshun   deflection
deflect¹ /ion/ive/or
deflour   deflower¹
deflower¹
defmute   deaf-mute
deforest¹ /ation
deform¹ /ation
deformashun   deformation
deformit *y* /ies
defraud¹ /er

defray¹ /able/al
defreez *e* /ing
defrord   defraud¹⁺
defrost¹ /er
defrozen
deft /ly/ness
defunct /ive/ness
defy⁴
degeneracy
degenerat *e*² /ion
degrad *e*² /ation
degree
dehidrate   dehydrate²⁺
dehydrat *e*² /ion
de-ice² /r
deifi   deify⁴⁺
deif *y*⁴ /ier
deign¹★ (condescend)
de-ise   de-ice²⁺
deis *m* /t
deitee   deity⁺
deit *y* /ies
deject¹ /ion
dejeneracy   degeneracy
dejenerate   degenerate²⁺
dejeneration   degeneration
dekstrose   dextrose
dekstrus   dextrous
delay¹ /er
delectabl *e* /y
delectabul   delectable⁺
delegac *y* /ies
delegasey   delegacy⁺
delegat *e*² /ion
delet *e*² /ion
deleterious /ly
deliberat *e*² /ely/ion
delibratley   deliberately
delicac *y* /ies
delicate /ly/ness
delicatessen
delicious /ly/ness
deligacy   delegacy⁺
deligashun   delegation
deligate   delegate²⁺

delight [1] /ful/fully
delineat *e* [2] /ion
deliniashun   delineation
deliniate   delineate [2+]
delinkwasey   delinquency [+]
delinkwens   delinquence [+]
delinquen *ce* /t
delinquenc *y* /ies
delirious /ly/ness
delirium
delirius   delirious [+]
delishus   delicious [+]
delite   delight [1+]
deliteful   delightful
deliterius   deleterious [+]
deliver [1] /ance/er
deliver *y* /ies
delivrey   delivery [+]
dell
delouse [2]
delt   dealt
delta
delude [2]
deluge [2]
deluks   de luxe
delushun   delusion [+]
delusion /al
delus *ive* /ory
delve [2] /r
demagog   demagogue [+]
demagog *ue* /y
demand [1] /able/er
demarcat *e* [2] /ion
demarch   démarche
démarche
demean [1] /our
demeaner   demeanour
demented
demerara
demerit
demesne
demigod
demilitarise [2]
demis *e* [2] /able
demist [1] /er

demobilis *e* [2] /ation
democrac *y* /ies
democrasey   democracy [+]
democratic /ally
democratis *e* [2] /ation
demolish [1] /able
demolishun   demolition [+]
demolition /ist
demon /ic
demonstra *ble* /tive
demonstrashun   demonstration
demonstrat *e* [2] /ion/or
demoralise [2]
demot *e* [2] /ion
demur [3*] (object)
demure *(quiet, coy)/ly
denationalise [2]
dencher   denture
dendrology
deni   deny [4]
denial
denier
denigrat *e* [2] /ion/or
denim
denizen
denominat *e* [2] /or
denomination /al
denot *e* [2] /able/ation/ive
denounce [2] /ment
denownse   denounce [2+]
dense /ly/r
densitey   density [+]
densitie   density [+]
densit *y* /ies
dent [1]
dental
dentifrice
dentifriss   dentifrice
denti *ne* /tion
dentishun   dentition
dentist /ry
denture
denud *e* [2] /ation
denunciat *e* [2] /ion
deny [4]

deoderant	deodorant	deput e^2 /ation	
deoderise	deodorise $^2+$	deputey	deputy $^+$
deodorant		deputise ^{2}	
deodorise ^{2} /r		deput y /ies	
deparcher	departure	derail ^{1} /ment	
depart ^{1} /ure		derale	derail $^1+$
department /al/ally		derange ^{2} /ment	
departmentalise ^{2}		derelicshun	dereliction
depen	deepen ^{1}	derelict /ion	
depend ^{1} /able/ence		derick	derrick
dependant $\star$ (n.)		deride ^{2} /r	
dependenc y /ies		derishun	derision
dependensey	dependency $^+$	derision	
dependent $\star$ (adj.)		deris ive /ory	
depict ^{1} /ion		derivashun	derivation $^+$
depilat e^2 /ion/or		derivat ion /ive	
depilatory		derivativ	derivative
deplet e^2 /ion		deriv e^2 /able/er	
deploi	deploy $^1+$	dermatitis	
deplor e^2 /able/ably		dermatolog y /ist	
deploy ^{1} /ment		derogat e^2 /ive/ory	
depo	depot	derrick	
depopulat e^2 /ion		dert	dirt $^+$
deport ^{1} /ment		derth	dearth
deportashun	deportation	derty	dirty $^4+$
deportation		dervish	
depos e^2 /able		desalinat e^2 /ion	
deposishun	deposition	descant ^{1} /er	
deposit ^{1} /ion/or		descend ^{1} /er	
depositor y /ies		descendant $\star$ (n.)	
depositrey	depository $^+$	descendent $\star$ (adj.)	
depot		descent $\star$ (go down)	
deprav e^2 /ity		describ e^2 /able	
deprecat e^2 /ion/ory		descript ion /ive	
depreciat e^2 /ion		descry ^{4}	
depredat e^2 /ion		deseat	deceit $^+$
depresherise	depressurise ^{2}	deseave	deceive $^2+$
depreshurise	depressurise ^{2}	desecrat e^2 /ion	
depresiv	depressive	desegregat e^2 /ion	
depress ^{1} /ion/ive		desel	diesel
depressant		deselerashun	deceleration
depressurise ^{2}		deselerate	decelerate $^2+$
depricate	deprecate $^2+$	Desember	December
depriv e^2 /ation		desency	decency $^+$
depth		desend	descend $^1+$

desensitise[2]	
desent	decent *+
desent	descent *
desentralise	decentralise[2]
desershun	desertion
desert[1]* (abandon, dry land)	
desert	dessert *
desert er /ion	
deserve[2] /dly	
desese	disease +
desibel	decibel
desiccat e[2] /ion	
desiduous	deciduous
design[1] /er	
designat e[2] /ion/or	
desimal	decimal +
desimalise	decimalise[2]+
desimate	decimate[2]+
desimation	decimation
desine	design[1]+
desirab le /ility	
desirabul	desirable +
desir e[2] /ous	
desist[1]	
desk	
deskant	descant[1]+
desolat e[2] /ion	
despair[1]	
desperado /es	
desperashun	desperation
desperate /ly/ness	
desperation	
despicabl e /y	
despise[2] /r	
despite	
despoil[1] /ment	
despoliation	
despond[1] /ent	
despondenc e /y	
despondens	despondence +
despot /ism	
despotic /ally	
dessert * (food)	
dessert	desert[1]*

destinashun	destination
destination	
destine[2]	
destin y /ies	
destitut e /ion	
destroy[1] /er	
destructib le /ility	
destructibul	destructible +
destruct ion /ive	
desultor y /ily	
det	debt +
detach[1] /ment	
detail[1]	
detain[1] /ment	
detale	detail[1]
detane	detain[1]+
detecshun	detection
detect[1] /ion/or	
detective	
détente	
detention	
deter[3]* (hinder)	
deter	debtor *
deterent	deterrent
detergent	
deteriorat e[2] /ion	
determinant	
determinashun	determination
determination	
determin e[2] /able	
deterrent	
detest[1] /able/ation	
deth	death +
dethrone[2] /ment	
detiriarate	deteriorate[2]+
detonat e[2] /ion/or	
detoor	detour
detour	
detract[1] /ion/or	
detriment /al	
detrishun	detrition
detrition	
deuce	
deuterium	
deuteron	

devalu *e*² /ation
devastat *e*² /ion/or
develop¹ /er/ment
devian *ce* /t
deviat *e*² /ion
device ★ (scheme, means)
devil /ry
devilish /ly
devious /ly
devis *e*²★ (invent) /able
devitalis *e*² /ation
devius   devious⁺
devoid
devolushun   devolution
devolution
devolve²
devot *e*² /ee/ion
devour¹
devout /ly/ness
dew ★ (moisture)
dew   due ★⁺
dew *y* /-drop
dext *erity* /rous
dextrose
dextrus   dextrous
dhoti
dhow
diabetes
diabetic
diabolic /al/ally
diadem
diafanous   diaphanous⁺
diafanus   diaphanous⁺
diafram   diaphragm⁺
diagnose²
diagnos *is* /es (pl.)
diagnostic /ian
diagnostishun   diagnostician
diagonal /ly
diagram
diagrammatic /ally
dial³ /er
dialect /al/ally
dialectic /al/ally
dialisis   dialysis⁺

dialog   dialogue
dialogue
dialy *sis* /tic
diamet *er* /ral
diametric /al/ally
diamond
diapason
diaper
diaphanous /ly
diaphragm /atic
diarea   diarrhoea
diarey   diary⁺
diarrhoea
diar *y* /ies/ist
diatonic
diatribe

If you cannot find your word under **di** *look under* **de**

---

dibase   debase²⁺
dibate   debate²⁺
dibble² /r
dice² (pl. of die)
dichotom *y* /ies
diciple   disciple
dicipul   disciple
dicotomey   dichotomy⁺
dicotyledon
dicshun   diction
dicshunrey   dictionary⁺
dictafone   dictaphone
dictaphone
dictat *e*² /ion
dictator /ial
diction
dictionar *y* /ies
dictum
didactic /ally/ism
diddle² /r
didget   digit⁺
didgitalis   digitalis
didn't (did not)
didnt   didn't
die ★ (sing. of dice)
die ★ (death) /d

die-hard		dignity	
dieing	dyeing ★	digress [1] /ion/ive	
dieing	dying ★	dike [2]	
diernal	diurnal +	dil	dill
diesel		dilapidat e [2] /ion	
diet [1] /ary		dilatashun	dilatation
dietetic /s		dilat e [2] /ation/or/ory	
dietician		dilemma	
dietishun	dietician	diletant	dilettante +
difer	differ [1]★	dilettant e /i (pl.)	
diference	difference +	dilidalie	dilly-dally [4]
diferens	difference +	diligen ce /t	
diferenshal	differential +	diligens	diligence +
diferenshiate	differentiate [2]+	dill	
diferent	different	dilly-dally [4]	
diferential	differential +	dilut e [2] /ion/or	
diferentiate	differentiate [2]+	diluvial	
differ [1]★ (disagree)		dim [3] /ly/ness	
differ	defer [3]★	dime	
differen ce /t		dimenshun	dimension +
differential /ly		dimension /al	
differentiat e [2] /ion		dimer	dimmer +
difficult		diminish [1] /able	
difficult y /ies		diminuendo	
diffiden ce /t		diminut ive /ion	
diffract /ion		dimm er /est	
diffus e [2] /ion/ive		dimpl e [2] /y	
dificult	difficult	dimpul	dimple [2]+
dificultey	difficulty +	dinamic	dynamic +
difidence	diffidence +	dinamite	dynamite [2]
difident	diffident	dinamo	dynamo +
difract	diffract +	dinastey	dynasty +
diftheria	diphtheria	dinastic	dynastic +
difthong	diphthong	dine [2]★ (eat) /r	
difuse	diffuse [2]+	dine	dyne ★
difushun	diffusion	diner	dinner
difusion	diffusion	dingh y /ies	
dig [3] /ger		dingie	dinghy +
digest [1] /ion/ive		ding y /ily/iness	
digestib le /ility		dinner	
digit /al/ally		dinosaur	
digitalis		dinosore	dinosaur
dignify [4]		dioces e /an	
dignitar y /ies		diode	
dignitrey	dignitary +	diokside	dioxide

diosees	diocese +	disarange	disarrange 2+
dioxide		disaray	disarray
dip 3 /per		disarm 1 /ament	
diper	diaper	disarrange 2 /ment	
diphtheria		disarray	
diphthong		disasoshiate	disassociate 2+
diploma /s		disassociat e 2 /ion	
diplomac y /ies		disast er /rous/rously	
diplomasey	diplomacy +	disastrus	disastrous
diplomat /ist		disatisfi	dissatisfy 4+
diplomatic /ally		disavow 1 /al	
dipsomania /c		disband 1 /ment	
dire /ful/ly/r/st		disbar 3 /ment	
direcshun	direction	disbeleif	disbelief
direct 1 /ion/ive		disbeleive	disbelieve 2+
director /ate		disbelief	
director y /ies		disbelieve 2 /r	
directrey	directory +	disberden	disburden 1+
dirge /ful		disberse	disburse 2+
dirigib le /ility		disbileaf	disbelief
dirigibul	dirigible +	disbileve	disbelieve 2+
dirt /iness		disburden 1 /ment	
dirt y 4 /ier/iest/ily		disburse 2 /ment	
disabilit y /ies		disc /-brake/-jockey	
disable 2 /ment		discard 1	
disabul	disable 2+	discern 1 /ible/ment	
disabuse 2		discernibul	discernible
disadvantage /ous		discharge 2	
disadvantidge	disadvantage +	disciple	
disafecshun	disaffection	disciplinar y /ian	
disaffected		discipline 2	
disaffection		discipul	disciple
disagreabul	disagreeable +	disclaim 1	
disagree /d/ing/ment		disclaym	disclaim 1
disagreeabl e /y		disclos e 2 /ure	
disagrement	disagreement	discolor	discolour 1+
disallow 1		discolo ur 1 /ration	
disapear	disappear 1+	discomfert	discomfort 1
disapearance	disappearance	discomfort 1	
disapoint	disappoint 1+	discompos e 2 /ure	
disapoynt	disappoint 1+	disconcert 1	
disappear 1 /ance		disconect	disconnect 1+
disappoint 1 /ment		disconnect 1 /ion	
disapprov e 2 /al		disconsert	disconcert 1
disaproval	disapproval	disconsolate /ly	

discontent[1]	
discontinu *e*[2] /ance	
discontinu *ity* /ous	
discord /ance/ant	
discorse	discourse[2]
discotek	discotheque
discotheque	
discount[1] /able/er	
discountenance[2]	
discourage[2] /ment	
discourse[2]	
discourteous /ly/ness	
discourtes *y* /ies	
discourtius	discourteous +
discover[1] /er	
discover *y* /ies	
discownt	discount[1]+
discowntenans	discountenance[2]
discredit[1] /able	
discreet /ly/ness	
discrepanc *y* /ies	
discrepansey	discrepancy +
discrepant	
discreshun	discretion +
discretion /ary	
discribable	describable
discribe	describe[2]+
discriminat *e*[2] /ion	
discripshun	description +
discriptiv	descriptive
disculer	discolour[1]+
discuridge	discourage[2]+
discurs *ion* /ive	
discurtesey	discourtesy +
discurtius	discourteous +
discus ⋆† /es	
†(heavy disc)	
discushun	discussion
discuss[1]⋆ (debate)	
discussion	
disdain[1] /ful/fully	
dise	dice[2]
disease /d	
diseave	deceive[2]+
disecshun	dissection

disect	dissect[1]+
disembark[1] /ation	
disembarrass[1] /ment	
disemble	dissemble[2]+
disembodie	disembody[4]+
disembod *y*[4] /iment	
disembowel[3] /ment	
disembroil[1]	
disembul	dissemble[2]+
diseminashun	dissemination
diseminate	disseminate[2]+
disenchant[1] /ment	
disengage[2] /ment	
disenshent	dissentient
disenshun	dissension
disentangle[2] /ment	
disentient	dissentient
disentrey	dysentery
disern	discern[1]+
disernible	discernible
disernibul	discernible
disertashun	dissertation
disertation	dissertation
diserviss	disservice
disfaver	disfavour[1]
disfavour[1]	
disfiger	disfigure[2]+
disfigure[2] /ment	
disfranchise[2] /ment	
disgise	disguise[2]+
disgorge[2] /ment	
disgrace[2] /ful/fully	
disgruntled	
disguise[2] /r	
disgust[1]	
dish /-cloth/ful	
dishabille	
disharmoney	disharmony +
disharmon *y* /ious	
disharten	dishearten[1]
dishearten[1]	
dishevel[3]	
dishonest /ly/y	
dishonour[1] /able/ably	
dishonrabul	dishonourable

disidence	dissidence +	disobey¹	
disidens	dissidence +	disoblige²	
disident	dissident	disoloot	dissolute +
disillusion¹ /ment		disoluble	dissoluble
disilushun	disillusion¹+	disolute	dissolute +
disimilar	dissimilar +	disolution	dissolution
disimulashun	dissimulation	disolve	dissolve²+
disincentive		disonance	dissonance +
disinclinashun	disinclination	disonans	dissonance +
disinclin e² /ation		disonant	dissonant
disinfect¹ /ant/ion		disone	disown¹
disinherit¹ /ance		disoner	dishonour¹+
disinsentiv	disincentive	disonerabul	dishonourable
disintegrat e² /ion		disonest	dishonest +
disinter³ /ment		disonist	dishonest +
disinterest¹		disonrabul	dishonourable
disintigrate	disintegrate²+	disorder¹ /ly	
disipate	dissipate²+	disorganis e² /ation	
disiple	disciple	disorientate²	
disiplin	discipline²	disoshiate	dissociate²+
disiplinarey	disciplinary +	disown¹	
disipul	disciple	disparage² /ment	
disjoint¹		disparate /ly/ness	
diskwiet	disquiet¹+	disparidge	disparage²+
diskwolification	disqualification	disparige	disparage²+
diskwolify	disqualify⁴+	disparitey	disparity +
dislik e² /able		disparit y /ies	
dislocat e² /ion		dispashonate	dispassionate +
dislodge² /ment		dispassionate /ly	
disloge	dislodge²+	dispatch¹ /er	
disloial	disloyal +	dispel³ /ler	
disloialtey	disloyalty	dispensar y /ies	
disloyal /ly/ty		dispens e² /ation/er	
dismal /ly		dispepsia	dyspepsia +
dismantle²		dispeptic	dyspeptic
dismantul	dismantle²	dispers e² /al	
dismast¹		dispershun	dispersion
dismay¹		dispersion	
dismember¹ /ment		dispirit¹	
dismisal	dismissal	displace² /ment	
dismiss¹ /al		displase	displace²+
dismount¹		display¹	
dismownt	dismount¹	displeas e² /ure	
disobay	disobey¹	displese	displease²+
disobedien ce /t		displesher	displeasure

disport [1]
dispos *e* [2] /able/al
disposeshun — dispossession
disposess — dispossess [1+]
disposishun — disposition
disposition
dispossess [1] /ion
disproof
disproov — disprove [2]
disproporshun — disproportion [+]
disproportion /ate
disprosium — dysprosium
disprove [2]
dispursal — dispersal
dispurse — disperse [2+]
dispurshun — dispersion
disputashun — disputation [+]
disputat *ion* /ious
disput *e* [2] /able
disqualif *y* [4] /ication
disquiet [1] /ude
disregard [1] /ful
disrepair
disreputabl *e* /y
disrepute
disrespect /ful/fully
disrigard — disregard [1+]
disripair — disrepair
disrispect — disrespect [+]
disrobe [2] /ment
disrupt [1] /ion/ive
dissapear — disappear [1+]
dissapoint — disappoint [1+]
dissaproov — disapprove [2+]
dissatisf *y* [4] /action
dissect [1] /ion/or
dissemble [2] /r
disseminat *e* [2] /ion/or
dissension
dissent [1]* (disagreement)
dissentient
dissentious
dissertation
disservice
dissiden *ce* /t

dissidens — dissidence [+]
dissimilar /ity/ities
dissimulat *e* [2] /ion
dissipat *e* [2] /ion
dissociat *e* [2] /ion
dissoluble
dissolute /ly/ness
dissolution
dissolve [2] /nt
dissonan *ce* /t
dissuade [2]
dissuas *ion* /ive
distaff
distance
distans — distance
distant /ly
distaste /ful/fully
distemper [1]
distend [1]
distenshun — distension
distens *ible* /ion
distensibul — distensible [+]
disterb — disturb [1+]
disterbance — disturbance
distil [3] /lation/ler
distiller *y* /ies
distinct /ive/ly
distinction
distinguish [1] /able
distingwish — distinguish [1+]
distorshun — distortion
distort [1] /ion
distracshun — distraction
distract [1] /ion
distrain [1] /t
distrane — distrain [1+]
distraught
distrawt — distraught
distress [1] /ful
distribut *e* [2] /ion
distribut *ive* /or
district /nurse
distrort — distraught
distrust [1] /ful
disturb [1] /ance

disunion	
disunit *e* [2] /y	
disurn	discern [1+]
disurnible	discernible
disuse [2]	
diswade	dissuade [2]
diswashun	dissuasion [+]
diswasion	dissuasion [+]
diswasiv	dissuasive
ditch [1] /er	
dither [1] /y	
ditie	ditty [+]
dito	ditto
ditto	
ditt *y* /ies	
dity	ditty [+]
diurnal /ly	
divan	
dive [2] /r	
diverge [2] /nce/nt	
divergens	divergence
divers	diverse [+]
diverse /ly	
divershun	diversion
diversifi	diversify [4+]
diversif *y* [4] /ication	
diversion	
diversitey	diversity [+]
diversity /ies	
divert [1] /er	
divest [1]	
divide [2] /r	
dividend	
divin *e* [2] /ation/ely/er	
divinitey	divinity [+]
divinit *y* /ies	
diviser	divisor
divishun	division [+]
divis *ible* /ive/ively	
divisibul	divisible [+]
division /al	
divisiv	divisive
divisor	
divorce [2] /é/ée (fem.)	
divorse	divorce [2+]

divulge [2] /nce/r	
dizier	dizzier [+]
dizmal	dismal [+]
dizolve	dissolve [2+]
dizy	dizzy
dizzi *er* /est/ly/ness	
dizzy	
do ★ (perform) /er/ing	
do ★ (music) /s ★ (pl.)	
do	doe ★[+]
docile /ly	
docility	
dock [1] /er/yard	
docket [1]	
dockit	docket [1]
docter	doctor [1+]
doctor [1] /ate/ial	
doctrin	doctrine [+]
doctrinair	doctrinaire
doctrin *e* /aire/al	
document [1] /ation	
documentar *v* /ies	
documentrey	documentary [+]
dodder [1] /er/y	
dodecagon	
doder	dodder [1+]
dodg *e* [2] /er/y	
dodgi *er* /est/ness	
doe ★ (deer) /s ★ (pl.)	
doe	do ★[+]
doe	dough ★[+]
does ★ (do-[verb])	
doesn't (does not)	
doff [1]	
dofin	dauphin
dog [3] /fight/fish	
dog-eared	
dogeared	dog-eared
dogeral	doggerel
dogfite	dogfight
doggerel	
dogma /tic/tically	
dogmatis *e* [2] /m	
doilie	doily [+]
doil *y* /ies	

doldrum	
dole²	
doleful /ly	
doler	dollar
dolerus	dolorous⁺
dolfin	dolphin
doll¹ /y	
dollar	
doller	dollar
dollop	
dolman	
dolomite	
dolorous /ly/ness	
dolorus	dolorous⁺
dolphin	
domain	
domane	domain
dome	
Domesday Book	
domestic /ally	
domesticate²	
domesticity	
domestisitey	domesticity
domicil e /iary	
dominan ce /t	
dominans	dominance⁺
dominat e² /ion/or	
dominear	domineer¹
domineer¹	
dominion	
domino /es	
dominyon	dominion
domisile	domicile⁺
don³*† /nish	
†(put on, tutor)	
donat e² /ion/or	
done * (finished)	
doner	donor
donkey /s	
donky	donkey⁺
donor	
donut	doughnut
dooch	douche²
doodle² /r	
doodul	doodle²⁺

doom¹	
doomsday book	Domesday Book
door /step/way	
door	dour
doordle	dawdle²⁺
doormouse	dormouse
doosh	douche²
dope² /y	
dophin	dauphin
dore	door⁺
dorman cy /t	
dormansey	dormancy⁺
dormice	
dormise	dormice
dormitor y /ies	
dormitrey	dormitory⁺
dormouse	
dorn	dawn¹
dorsal /ly	
dorter	daughter⁺
dos e² /age	
dosidge	dosage
dosile	docile⁺
dositey	docility
dossier	
dot³	
dot age /ard	
dote² /r	
doti	dhoti
dotidge	dotage⁺
dotti er /est/ly/ness	
dotty	
double² /-barrelled	
double-bass	
double-cross¹	
doublet	
doubloon	
doubly	
doubt¹ /er/less	
doubtful /ly/ness	
douche²	
dough * (bread) /nut/y	
dought y /ily	
dour	
douse²* (shower) /r	

douse	dowse ²★	draftiness	draughtiness
dout	doubt ¹⁺	drafts	draughts ★
doutey	doughty ⁺	draftsman ★ (drafter	
doutful	doubtful ⁺	of documents)	
doutless	doubtless	draftsman	draughtsman ★
dove /-cot		drafty	draughty ⁺
dovetail ¹		drag ³ /ger	
dow	dhow	dragon	
dow	doe ★⁺	dragonfl y /ies	
dow	dough ★⁺	dragoon ¹	
dowager		drain ¹ /age/er	
dowdie	dowdy ⁺	drainidge	drainage
dowd y /ily/iness		drake	
dowey	doughy	dram	
down ¹ /cast/hill		drama /s/tist	
downey	downy	dramatic /ally	
downfall /en		dramatis e ² /ation	
downgrade ²		drank	
downharted	downhearted	drape ² /r	
downhearted		draper y /ies	
downie	downy	drastic /ally	
downpoor	downpour	draught ★† /s ★	
downpour		†(air current, game)	
downright		draughtiness	
downrite	downright	draughtsman ★†	
downstairs		†(drawer of plans)	
downtrodden		draught y /ier/iest	
downward		draw /ing/n	
downwerd	downward	drawback	
downy		drawbridge	
dowrie	dowry ⁺	drawer	
dowr y /ies		drawing-room	
dowse ²★ (divine with rod)		drawl ¹ /er	
dowse	douse ²★⁺	dray ★ (low cart)	
dowt	doubt ¹⁺	dray	drey ★
dowtey	doughty ⁺	dread ¹ /ful/fully	
dowtful	doubtful ⁺	dreadnort	dreadnought
doz e ²★ (sleep) /y		dreadnought	
doze	does ★	dream ¹ /ily/less/t/y	
dozen		drearey	dreary
dozi ly /ness		drearie	dreary
drab		dreari er /est/ly/ness	
draft ¹★ (bank, military)		dreary	
draft	draught ★⁺	dred	dread ¹⁺
draftey	draughty ⁺	dredful	dreadful

dredge² /r	
drednort	dreadnought
dreem	dream¹⁺
drege	dredge²⁺
dregs	
dremt	dreamt
drench¹ /er	
drerey	dreary
drerie	dreary
drerier	drearier⁺
dresage	dressage
dresie	dressy
dresmaker	dressmaker⁺
dress¹ /er/es/iness/y	
dressage	
dressmak er /ing	
dresy	dressy
drew	
Drewid	Druid
drey ★ (squirrel's nest)	
dri	dry⁴⁺
dribble² /r	
driblet	
dribul	dribble²⁺
driclean	dry-clean¹
drift¹ /er/wood	
dril	drill¹
drill¹	
drily	
drink /able/er	
drip³ /-dry	
driv e /en/er/ing	
drivel³ /ler	
drizul	drizzle²⁺
drizzl e² /y	
droll /ness	
droller y /ies	
dromedar y /ies	
drone²	
Drooid	Druid
drool¹	
droop¹ /y	
drop³ /let	
droper	dropper
drop-out	

dropper	
dropsey	dropsy⁺
dropsie	dropsy⁺
drops y /ical/ied	
dross /iness	
drought	
drout	drought
drove /r	
drown¹	
drows e² /y	
drowsey	drowsy
drowsie	drowsy
drowsi er /ly/ness	
drowt	drought
dru	drew
drub³ /ber	
drudge² /ry	
drug³	
druge	drudge²⁺
drugery	drudgery
drugget	
druggist	
Druid	
drum³ /mer/stick	
drumedarey	dromedary⁺
drum-major	
drunk /ard/en/enness	
dr y⁴ /ier/iest	
dry-clean¹	
dryer	drier
dual ★ (two) /ism/ity	
dual	duel³★
dub³	
dubbin	
dubious /ly	
dubius	dubious⁺
duble	double²⁺
dublebareld	double-barrelled
dublet	doublet
dublie	doubly
dubloon	doubloon
dubly	doubly
ducal	
ducat	
duce	deuce

duchess /es		dun ★ (colour)	
duchey	duchy +	dun	done ★
duchie	duchy +	dunce	
duch y /ies		dune	
duck [1] /ling		dung /hill	
ducket	ducat	dungaree /s	
ducktile	ductile +	dungen	dungeon
duct /ing/less		dungeon	
ductil e /ity		dunjon	dungeon
du e ★† /ly		duns	dunce
†(owing, expected)		dunse	dunce
due	dew ★	duolog	duologue
duedrop	dew-drop	duologue	
duel [3]★ (fight)		dup e [2] /able	
duel	joule ★	dupleks	duplex +
dueler	dueller +	duplex /ity	
duelist	duellist	duplicat e [2] /ion/or	
duell er /ist		duplicity	
duet /tist		duplisitey	duplicity
duey	dewy +	durab le /ility/ly	
dufel	duffel	durabul	durable +
duffel		durashun	duration
duffer		duration	
dug /-out		duress	
dul	dull +	durge	dirge +
dulcet		during	
dulcimer		durt	dirt +
duler	duller +	durtie	dirty [4]+
dulie	duly	durtier	dirtier
dull /ard/y		durty	dirty [4]+
dull er /est/ish		dusbin	dustbin +
dulset	dulcet	duse	deuce
dulsimer	dulcimer	dusk /y	
dum	dumb +	dust [1] /er/y	
dumb /ly/ness		dust bin /man/pan	
dumb-bell		dusti er /est/ness	
dumbell	dumb-bell	Dutch /man/woman	
dumbfound [1]		dutie	duty +
dumfound	dumbfound [1]	dutifree	duty-free
dumfownd	dumbfound [1]	dutiful /ly	
dumm y /ies		dut y /ies	
dumness	dumbness	duty-free	
dump [1] /er/y		duv	dove +
dumpling		duvtail	dovetail [1]
dumy	dummy +	duvtale	dovetail [1]

duz	does ★
duzn	dozen
duznt	doesn't
dwarf¹ /ish	
dwell /er/ing	
dwelt	
dwindle²	
dwindul	dwindle²
dworf	dwarf¹⁺
dye ★† /d ★† /ing ★†	
†(change colour)	
dye	die ★⁺
dyed	died ★
dyehard	die-hard
dying ★ (death)	
dying	dyeing ★
dynamic /ally	
dynamics	
dynamite²	
dynamo /s	
dynast	
dynastey	dynasty ⁺
dynastic /ally	
dynast y /ies	
dyne ★ (unit of force)	
dysentery	
dysentrey	dysentery
dyspep sia /tic	
dysprosium	

E

each	
eager /ly/ness	
eagle /-eyed/t	
eal	eel
ear /-ache/-drum	
earie	eerie ★
earie	eyrie ★
earl /dom	
earli er /est	
early /ish	
earmark¹	
earn ¹★ (gain) /ings	

earnest /ly/ness	
ear-ring	
earshot	
earth¹ /iness	
earthen /ware	
earthl y /iness	
earthquake	
earth work /worm	
earwig	
ease²	
easel	
east /erly/ward/wards	
easten	eastern ⁺
Easter	
eastern /er	
eas y /ier/ily/iness	
easy-going	
eat /able/en/er/ing	
eau-de-cologne	
eaves	
eavesdrop³ /per	
ebb¹	
ebonie	ebony ⁺
ebon y /ite	
ebulience	ebullience ⁺
ebuliens	ebullience ⁺
ebulient	ebullient
ebullien ce /t	
eccentric /ally/ity	
ecclesiastic /al/ally	
ecentric	eccentric ⁺
ech	each
echelon	
echo¹ /es	
eclair	
eclare	eclair
eclectic	
eclesiastic	ecclesiastic ⁺
eclipse²	
ecliptic	
ecolog	ecologue
ecologey	ecology ⁺
ecological /ly	
ecologue	
ecolog y /ist	

economic /al/ally/s		efemeral	ephemeral +
economise ²		efeminacy	effeminacy
economist		efeminasey	effeminacy
econom y /ies		efeminate	effeminate +
ecsema	eczema	efert	effort +
ecsentric	eccentric +	efervesence	effervescence
ecstas y /ies		efervesent	effervescent
ecstatic /ally		efervess	effervesce ²+
ectoplasm		efface ² /ment	
ecumenical		effect ¹	
eczema		effective /ly	
edd y ⁴ /ies		effectual	
edge ² /ways/wise		effeminacy	
edgey	edgy +	effeminate /ly	
edgie	edgy +	effervesce ² /nce/nt	
edg y /ily/iness		effervess	effervesce ²+
edib le /ility		effete	
edibul	edible +	efficacious /ly/ness	
edict		efficacy	
edie	eddy ⁴+	efficashus	efficacious +
edifice		efficienc y /ies	
edifiss	edifice	efficient /ly	
edif y ⁴ /ication		effigey	effigy +
edishun	edition	effig y /ies	
edit ¹ /ion		efflorescen ce /t	
editer	editor +	effluen ce /t	
editor /ial/ially		effluvium	
educab le /ility		effort /less/lessly	
educashun	education +	effronter y /ies	
educat e ² /ive/or		effulgen ce /t	
education /al/ally/ist		effulgens	effulgence +
edy	eddy ⁴+	effus e ² /ion/ive	
eeger	eager +	eficacious	efficacious +
eegle	eagle +	eficacy	efficacy
eel		eficasey	efficacy
eer	ear +	eficashus	efficacious +
eerie ★ (strange)		eficiency	efficiency +
eerie	eyrie ★	eficient	efficient +
eeri er /est/ly/ness		efigey	effigy +
eermark	earmark ¹	efishency	efficiency +
eface	efface ²+	efishensey	efficiency +
efect	effect ¹	efishent	efficient +
efectiv	effective +	efloresence	efflorescence +
efectual	effectual	efluence	effluence +
efeet	effete	efluens	effluence +

efluent	effluent
efluvium	effluvium
efort	effort +
efronterey	effrontery +
efulgence	effulgence +
efuse	effuse 2+
efusiv	effusive
eg	egg 1+
egalitarian /ism	
ege	edge 2+
egg 1 /-cup/-shell	
Egipshun	Egyptian
Egiptian	Egyptian
egis	aegis
ego /ism/tism	
egocentric /ity	
egoist /ic/ically	
egosentric	egocentric +
egotist /ical/ically	
egress 1	

> If you cannot find your word
> under **egs** look under **ex**

egsact	exact 1+
egsamine	examine 2+
egsample	example
egsaust	exhaust 1+
egsecutive	executive
egsempt	exempt 1+
egsert	exert 1+
Egyptian	
eiderdown	
Eiffel	
eight * (number)	
eighteen /th	
eighth /ly	
eight y /ies	
einsteinium	
either	
ejaculat e 2 /ion/ory	
eject 1 /ion/or	
ejis	aegis
eke 2	
eko	echo 1+

> If you cannot find your word
> under **eks** look under **ex**

ekscavate	excavate 2+
ekschange	exchange 2+
eksclaim	exclaim 1
eksite	excite 2+
ekumenical	ecumenical
ekwable	equable +
ekwabul	equable +
ekwal	equal 3+
ekwalise	equalise 2+
ekwalitey	equality +
ekwanimitey	equanimity
ekwashun	equation
ekwate	equate 2
ekwater	equator +
ekwation	equation
ekwerey	equerry +
ekwestrian	equestrian
ekwianguler	equiangular
ekwidistant	equidistant
ekwilateral	equilateral
ekwilibrium	equilibrium
ekwine	equine
ekwinox	equinox
ekwip	equip 3+
ekwitable	equitable +
ekwitabul	equitable +
ekwity	equity +
ekwivalence	equivalence +
ekwivocate	equivocate 2+
elaborat e 2 /ely/ion	
elapse 2	
elastic /ally/ity	
elat e 2 /ion	
elbow 1 /-room	
elder /ly	
elderberie	elderberry +
elderberr y /ies	
eldest	
elect 1 /ive/or/orate	
election /eering	
electoral /ly	
electric /al/ally	
electrician	

Word	Correction
electricity	
electrif *y*[4] /ication	
electrocut *e*[2] /ion	
electrode	
electrolight	electrolyte[+]
electrolite	electrolyte[+]
electrolysis	
electrolyt *e* /ic	
electromagnet /ic/ism	
electromotive	
electron /s	
electronic /ally/s	
electroplate[2]	
electroscope	
electrovalency	
elefant	elephant[+]
elegan *ce* /t	
elegans	elegance[+]
elegey	elegy[+]
eleg *y* /ies/iac	
element /al/ary	
elephant /ine	
elevat *e*[2] /ion/or	
eleven /th	
elf /in/ish	
elfs	elves
elicit[1]* (draw out)	
elicit	illicit*[+]
eli *de*[2] /sion	
elifant	elephant[+]
eligans	elegance[+]
eligant	elegant
eligib *le* /ility	
eligibul	eligible[+]
elikser	elixir
eliment	element[+]
elimental	elemental
elimentarey	elementary
elimentrey	elementary
eliminat *e*[2] /ion/or	
elips	ellipse
elipsis	ellipsis
eliptic	elliptic[+]
elishun	elision
élit *e* /ism/ist	

Word	Correction
elivashun	elevation
elivate	elevate[2+]
elivater	elevator
elivation	elevation
elixir	
Elizabethan	
elk	
ellipse	
ellipsis	
elliptic /al/ally	
elocution /ary/ist	
elokwence	eloquence[+]
elokwens	eloquence[+]
elokwent	eloquent
elongat *e*[2] /ion	
elope[2] /ment/r	
eloquen *ce* /t	
eloquens	eloquence[+]
else /where	
elswere	elsewhere
elucidat *e*[2] /ion/or	
elude[2]* (avoid)	
elude	allude[2]*
elushun	elusion*
elusidate	elucidate[2+]
elusion* (escape)	
elusive* (evasive) /ness	
elusive	illusive*
elver	
elves (pl. of elf)	
emaciat *e*[2] /ion	
emanat *e*[2] /ion/ive	
emancipat *e*[2] /ion/or	
emansipate	emancipate[2+]
emasculat *e*[2] /ion	
emasiate	emaciate[2+]
embalm[1] /er/ment	
embankment	
embarass	embarrass[1+]
embargo[1] /es	
embark[1] /ation	
embarm	embalm[1+]
embarrass[1] /ment	
embass *y* /ies	
embattle[2]	

embatul	embattle²	eminens	eminence⁺
embed³		eminent	imminent ★⁺
embellish¹ /ment		emisarey	emissary⁺
ember		emishun	emission
embezul	embezzle²⁺	emissar*y* /ies	
embezzle² /ment/r		emission	
embitter¹ /ment		emit³ /ter	
emblazon¹		emollient	
emblem		emolument	
emblematic /ally		emoshun	emotion⁺
embodie	embody⁴⁺	emotion /al/ally	
embod*y*⁴ /iment		emotive	
embolism		empanel³	
emboss¹		emperer	emperor⁺
embrace²		emp*eror* /ress (fem.)	
embrase	embrace²	emphas*is* /es (pl.)	
embrio	embryo	emphasise²	
embriologist	embryologist⁺	emphatic /ally	
embrocashun	embrocation	empire ★ (dominion)	
embrocation		empire	umpire²★
embroider¹ /y/ies		empiric /ism/ist	
embroil¹ /ment		empirical /ly	
embryo /s/nic		empirisist	empiricist
embryolog*ist* /y		emplacement	
emend	amend¹⁺	emploi	employ¹⁺
emerald		employ¹ /able/ee/er	
emerey	emery	emporium /s	
emerge² /nce/nt		empower¹	
emergenc*y* /ies		empress	impress¹⁺
emergensey	emergency⁺	emptie	empty⁴
emergent		empti*er* /est/ness	
emerie	emery	empt*y*⁴	
emershun	emersion	emulashun	emulation
emersion		emulat*e*² /ion/ive/or	
emery		emulshun	emulsion
emetic		emulsif*y*⁴ /ication	
emfasis	emphasis⁺	emulsion	
emfasise	emphasise²	en route	
emfatic	emphatic⁺	enable² /ment	
emigrant		enabul	enable²⁺
emigrat*e*² /ion		enact¹ /able/ment	
emigray	émigré⁺	enamel³ /ler	
émigré /e (fem.)		enamer	enamour¹
eminen*ce* /t ★†		enamour¹	
†(distinguished)		encamp¹ /ment	

encapsulat *e* ² /ion
encase ² /ment
encefalic   encephalic
encephalic
enchant ¹ /ment
enchant *er* /ress (fem.)
enciclical   encyclical
enciclopedia   encyclopedia ⁺
encircle ² /ment
enclave
enclos *e* ² /ure
encompass ¹
encore ²
encounter ¹
encourage ² /ment
encownter   encounter ¹
encroach ¹ /er/ment
encrust ¹
encumb *er* ¹ /rance
encuridge   encourage ²⁺
encurige   encourage ²⁺
encyclical
encyclopedi *a* /c
end ¹ /less/lessly
endanger ¹
endear ¹ /ment
endeavour ¹
endeer   endear ¹⁺
endever   endeavour ¹
endive
endocrine
endorse ² /ment/r
endow ¹ /ment
end-product
endur *e* ² /able/ance
enema /s
enem *y* /ies
energetic /ally
energey   energy ⁺
energise ² /r
energ *y* /ies
enervat *e* ² /ion
enfebul   enfeeble ²⁺
enfeeble ² /ment
enfold ¹

enforce ² /ment
enforceab *le* /ility
enfors   enforce ²⁺
enforsible   enforceable ⁺
enforsibul   enforceable ⁺
enfranchise ² /ment
engage ² /ment
engender ¹
engine /-driver
enginear   engineer ¹
engineer ¹
English /man/woman
engraft ¹ /ment
engrain ¹
engrave ² /r
engrayn   engrain ¹
engross ¹
engulf ¹
enhance ² /ment
enhans   enhance ²⁺
eni   any
enibodie   anybody
enigma /tic/tically
enihow   anyhow
enima   enema ⁺
enithing   anything
eniware   anywhere
eniway   anyway
eniwhere   anywhere
eniwun   anyone
enjender   engender ¹
enjin   engine ⁺
enjineer   engineer ¹
enjoi   enjoy ¹⁺
enjoiable   enjoyable ⁺
enjoiabul   enjoyable ⁺
enjoiment   enjoyment
enjoin ¹
enjoy ¹ /ment
enjoyabl *e* /y
enlace ²
enlarge ² /able/ment/r
enlase   enlace ²
enlighten ¹ /ment
enlist ¹

enliten	enlighten [1+]	enterpris*e* /ing	
enliven [1]		entertain [1] /er/ment	
enmit*y* /ies		entertane	entertain [1+]
ennoble [2] /ment		enthral [3] /ment	
ennui		enthrone [2] /ment	
enobul	ennoble [2+]	enthuse [2]	
enormit*y* /ies		enthusias*m* /t	
enormous /ly/ness		enthusiastic /ally	
enormus	enormous [+]	entice [2] /ment/r	
enough		entire /ly/ty	
enquire [2] /r		entise	entice [2+]
enquir*y* /ies		entitey	entity [+]
enrage [2]		entitle [2] /ment	
enrap	enwrap [3]	entitul	entitle [2+]
enrapcher	enrapture [2]	entit*y* /ies	
enrapture [2]		entomb [1] /ment	
enrich [1] /ment		entomolog*y* /ical/ist	
enrol [3] /ment		entoom	entomb [1+]
enroot	en route	entrails	
ensconce [2]		entrain [1]	
enscons	ensconce [2]	entrales	entrails
ensefalic	encephalic	entrance [2] /ment	
ensemble		entrans	entrance [2+]
ensembul	ensemble	entrant	
ensercal	encircle [2+]	entrap [3]	
enshore	ensure [2★]	entreat [1] /ingly	
enshore	insure [2★+]	entreat*y* /ies	
enshrine [2]		entrée	
enshure	ensure [2★]	entreet	entreat [1+]
ensiclical	encyclical	entrench [1] /ment	
ensiclopedia	encyclopedia [+]	entreprener	entrepreneur [+]
ensign		entrepreneur /ial	
ensine	ensign	entrey	entry [+]
enslave [2] /ment		entrust [1]	
ensnare [2]		entr*y* /ies	
ensue [2]		entwine [2]	
ensure [2★] (make certain)		enuf	enough
ensure	insure [2★+]	enumerat*e* [2] /ion/or	
entail [1]		enunciat*e* [2] /ion/or	
entale	entail [1]	enunsiate	enunciate [2+]
entangle [2] /ment		envelop [1★†] /ment	
entangul	entangle [2+]	†(to surround)	
enteprise	enterprise [+]	envelope ★ (stationery)	
enter [1]		envenom [1]	
enteritis		envie	envy [4+]

envious /ly/ness
environ [1] /s
environment /al/ally
envisage [2]
envisidge envisage [2]
envisige envisage [2]
envius envious [+]
envoi envoy
envoy
env y [4] /iable/ier
enwrap [3]
enzime enzyme
enzyme
epaulet
epawlet epaulet
ephemeral /ly
epic /ally
epicenter epicentre
epicentre
epicure /an/anism
epidemic
epiderm is /al
epidiascope
Epifaney Epiphany
epiglottis
epigraf epigraph [+]
epigram
epigrammatic /ally
epigraph /ic
epilep sy /tic
epilog epilogue
epilogue
Epiphany
episcopacy
episcopal /ian
episcopasey episcopacy
episod e /ic/ical
epist le /olary
episul epistle[+]
epitaf epitaph
epitaph
epithet
epitome
epitomise [2]
epoch /al

epok epoch [+]
eporlet epaulet
equab le /ility/ly
equal [3] /ly
equalis e [2] /ation/er
equalitey equality [+]
equalit y /ies
equanimity
equashun equation
equate [2]
equater equator [+]
equation
equator /ial
equerr y /ies
equestrian
equiangular
equidistant
equilateral
equilibrium
equine
equinoks equinox
equinox
equip [3] /ment
equitabl e /y
equitabul equitable [+]
equit y /ies
equivalen ce /t
equivalens equivalence [+]
equivocal /ly
equivocat e [2] /ion/or
equmenical ecumenical
er err [1]
era /s
eradicat e [2] /ion/or
erand errand
erant errant
eras e [2] /er/ure
erasher erasure
erata errata
eratic erratic [+]
eratum erratum [+]
erban urban
erbane urbane [+]
erbanise urbanise [2+]
erbanitey urbanity

epoch [+]
epaulet

equality [+]

equation

equator [+]

equinox

equitable [+]

equivalence [+]

ecumenical
err [1]

errand
errant

erasure
errata
erratic [+]
erratum [+]
urban
urbane [+]
urbanise [2+]
urbanity

erchin	urchin	erudit *e* /ely/ion	
ere ★ (before)		erupt¹ /ion/ive	
erecshun	erection	erwig	earwig
erect¹ /ile/or		esay	essay¹⁺
erection		escalat *e*² /ion/or	
erer	error	escallop¹	
erge	urge²⁺	escapade	
ergency	urgency	escape² /ment	
ergensey	urgency	escapis *m* /t	
ergent	urgent	escarpment	
erie	eerie ★	eschew¹	
erie	eyrie ★	eschu	eschew¹
ering	ear-ring	escort¹	
erk	irk¹⁺	esel	easel
erksome	irksome	esence	essence
erksum	irksome	esens	essence
erl	earl⁺	esenshal	essential⁺
erlier	earlier⁺	esential	essential⁺
erly	early⁺	eshelon	echelon
ermine		eshoo	eschew¹
ern	earn¹★⁺	Eskimo /s (pl.)	
ern	urn ★	eskwire	esquire
ernest	earnest⁺	esofagus	esophagus
erode²		esophagus	
eroneous	erroneous⁺	esoteric /ally/ism	
eronius	erroneous⁺	especial /ly	
eror	error	espeshal	especial⁺
eroshun	erosion	espi	espy⁴
erosion		espionage	
erotic /a/ally/ism		esplanade	
err¹		esplanaid	esplanade
errand		espous *e*² /al	
errant		espowse	espouse²⁺
erratic /ally		espresso	
errat *um* /a (pl.)		esp *y*⁴	
erroneous /ly		esquire	
erronius	erroneous⁺	essay¹ /s/ist	
error		essence	
erstwhile		essens	essence
erstwile	erstwhile	essenshal	essential⁺
erth	earth¹⁺	essential /ly	
erthen	earthen⁺	est	east⁺
erthley	earthly⁺	establish¹ /able/ment	
erthquake	earthquake	estate	
erudishun	erudition	esteam	esteem¹

esteem [1]		eunuch	
Ester	Easter	euphemism	
estern	eastern [+]	euphemistic /ally	
esthet	aesthete [+]	euphon y /ious	
esthetic	aesthetic	euphori a /c	
estimable		Eurashun	Eurasian
estimabul	estimable	Eurasian	
estimat e [2] /ion/or		eurhythmics	
estrange [2] /ment		eurithmics	eurhythmics
estuar y /ies		European	
et cetera		euthanasia	
etch [1] /er		evacuashun	evacuation
ete	eat [+]	evacuat e [2] /ion	
eternal /ly		evacuee	
eternit y /ies		evad e [2] /able	
ether /eal		evaluat e [2] /ion	
ether	either	evangelic /al/ally	
ethic /al/ally/s		evangelis e [2] /m/t	
ethnic /ally		evanjelic	evangelic [+]
ethnolog y /ical		evaperate	evaporate [2+]
etholog y /ical		evaporat e [2] /ion/or	
ethos		evaquee	evacuee
etiket	etiquette	evashun	evasion
etimology	etymology [+]	evasion	
etiquet	etiquette	evasive /ly/ness	
etiquette		eve	
etsetera	et cetera	even [1] /ly/ness	
etymolog y /ical/ist		even song /tide	
eucalyptus /es		event /ful	
Eucharist		eventual /ly	
Euclid		eventualit y /ies	
eufemism	euphemism	ever /green/lasting	
eufoney	euphony [+]	evermore	
eufonious	euphonious	every /body/day/one	
eufonius	euphonious	every thing /where	
eufony	euphony [+]	eves	eaves
euforia	euphoria [+]	evesdrop	eavesdrop [3+]
euforic	euphoric	evict [1] /ion	
eugenic /ally/s		eviden ce [2] /tial	
Eukarist	Eucharist	evidens	evidence [2+]
Euklid	Euclid	evident /ly	
eulogey	eulogy [+]	evil /ly	
eulogis e [2] /m		evince [2]	
eulogistic /ally		evins	evince [2]
eulog y /ies		evocat ion /ive	

evoke²		excoriat *e*² /ion	
evolushun	evolution⁺	excrement	
evolushunist	evolutionist	excrescence	
evolution /ary/ist		excresens	excrescence
evolve²		excreta	
evrie	every⁺	excret *e*² /ion	
evry	every⁺	excruciating /ly	
ewe ★ (sheep)		excrushiating	excruciating⁺
ewe	yew ★	excursion /ist	
ewe	you ★	excus *e*² /able/ably	
exacerbat *e*² /ion		exebition	exhibition⁺
exacrabul	execrable	execrable	
exact¹ /itude/ly/ness		execrabul	execrable
exaggerat *e*² /ion/or		execrat *e*² /ion	
exalt¹ /ation		execut *e*² /ant/or/rix (fem.)	
examination		execution /er	
examine² /r		executive	
example		exemplary	
exampul	example	exemplif *y*⁴ /ication	
exaserbate	exacerbate²⁺	exempt¹ /ion	
exasperat *e*² /ion		exentric	eccentric⁺
excavat *e*² /ion/or		exentricitey	eccentricity
exceed¹ /ingly		exercise²	
excel³		exert¹ /ion	
excellen *ce* /t		exhal *e*² /ation	
excellenc *y* /ies		exhaust¹ /ion	
excellens	excellence⁺	exhaust *ible* /ive	
excellensey	excellency⁺	exhibit¹ /or	
excepshun	exception⁺	exhibition /er	
except¹		exhibitionis *m* /t	
exception /able/al/ally		exhilara *te* /nt/tion	
excerpt¹		exhort¹ /ation	
excess /ive/ively		exhum *e*² /ation	
exchange² /able/r		exibition	exhibition⁺
exchequer		exigence	
excis *e*² /able/ion		exigenc *y* /ies	
excitab *le* /ility		exigens	exigence
excitabul	excitable⁺	exigensey	exigency⁺
excite² /dly/ment		exigu *ous* /ity	
exclaim¹		exile²	
exclamashun	exclamation⁺	exist¹ /ence/ent	
exclamat *ion* /ory		existens	existence
exclu *de*² /sion		exit¹	
exclusiv *e* /ely/ity		exkwisit	exquisite⁺
excommunicat *e*² /ion		exonerat *e*² /ion	

110

exorbitan *ce* /t	
exorcise[2] /r	
exorcis *m* /t	
exorsism	exorcism +
exorst	exhaust[1+]
exorstibul	exhaustible +
exort	exhort[1+]
exortashun	exhortation
exoteric	
exotic /ness	
expand[1]	
expans *e* /ion	
expanshun	expansion
expansive /ly/ness	
expatriat *e*[2] /ion	
expect[1] /ation	
expectanc *e* /y	
expectans	expectance +
expectant /ly	
expedien *ce* /t	
expedienc *y* /ies	
expediens	expedience +
expedishun	expedition
expedishus	expeditious +
expedite[2] /r	
expedition	
expeditious /ly/ness	
expel[3]	
expend[1] /iture	
expendab *le* /ility	
expendabul	expendable +
expendicher	expenditure
expens *e* /ive	
experience[2]	
experiens	experience[2]
experiment[1] /ation	
experimental /ly	
expert /ise/ly	
expiat *e*[2] /ion	
expir *e*[2] /ation/y	
explain[1] /able	
explanashun	explanation +
explanat *ion* /ory	
explane	explain[1+]
explanetrey	explanatory

expletive	
explicabl *e* /y	
explicabul	explicable +
explicit /ly	
explisit	explicit +
explode[2]	
exploit[1] /ation/er	
explorashun	exploration +
explorat *ion* /ory	
explore[2] /r	
exploshun	explosion +
explos *ion* /ive	
exponent	
export[1] /ation/er	
expos *e*[2] /ure	
exposher	exposure
expostulat *e*[2] /ion	
expound[1]	
expreshun	expression +
expresibul	expressible +
expresive	expressive +
express[1]	
expressibl *e* /y	
expression /less	
expressive /ly	
expresso	espresso
expropriat *e*[2] /ion/or	
expulsion	
expunge[2]	
expurgate[2]	
expurgat *ion* /ory	
expurt	expert +
exquisite /ly/ness	
exseed	exceed[1+]
exsel	excel[3]
exselence	excellence +
exselens	excellence +
ex-service	
exstravagans	extravagance +
exsurpt	excerpt[1]
extant	
extasey	ecstasy +
extatic	ecstatic +
extempor *e* /aneous	
extemporis *e*[2] /ation	

extend [1] /ible	
extenshun	extension
extension	
extensive /ly	
extent	
extenuat *e* [2] /ion	
exterier	exterior
exterior	
exterminat *e* [2] /ion/or	
external /ly	
exterpate	extirpate [2]+
extinct /ion	
extinguish [1] /er	
extingwish	extinguish [1]+
extirpat *e* [2] /ion	
extol [3]	
extorshun	extortion +
extort [1]	
extortion /ate/er/ist	
extra	
extract [1] /ible/ion/or	
extradishun	extradition
extradit *e* [2] /able/ion	
extramural	
extraneous /ly/ness	
extranius	extraneous +
extraordinar *y* /ily	
extra-sensory	
extravagan *ce* /t/tly	
extravaganza	
extrawdinrey	extraordinary +
extream	extreme +
extreme /ly	
extremist	
extremit *y* /ies	
extricable	
extricabul	extricable
extricat *e* [2] /ion	
extrordinary	extraordinary +
extrover *t* /sion	
exuberan *ce* /t	
exuberans	exuberance +
exud *e* [2] /ation	
exult [1] /ant/ation	
exume	exhume [2]+

eye [2]*† /ball/brow/s *† †(sight)	
eyeglass /es	
eyelash /es	
eyelet * (hole for lace)	
eyelet	islet *
eye *lid* /sight	
eye-opener	
eye-witness	
eyrie * (bird's nest)	
eyrie	eerie *
eze	ease [2]
ezel	easel
ezier	easier
ezy	easy +

F

fable /d	
fabric	
fabricat *e* [2] /ion/or	
fabul	fable +
fabulous /ly	
fabulus	fabulous +
façade	
face [2] /less	
faceshus	facetious +
facet /ed	
facetious /ly	
facia * (shop-front)	
facia	fascia *
facial /ly	
facile	
facilitat *e* [2] /ion	
facilit *y* /ies	
facshun	faction +
facshus	factious
facsimile /s	
fact /ual/ually	
factio *n* /us	
factishus	factitious
factitious	
factor	
factor *y* /ies	

facultative	
facult y /ies	
fad /dish/dy	
fade ²	
faec es /al	
faeton	phaeton
fag ³ /-end	
faggot /-stitch	
fagot	faggot ⁺
Fahrenheit	
fail ¹ /ure	
failier	failure
faim	fame ²
faimus	famous ⁺
fain ★ (glad)	
fain	feign ¹★
faint ¹★ (unconscious)	
faint	feint ¹★
faint-hearted	
fair ¹★ (beauty, just)	
fair	fare ²★
fair er /est/way	
fairie	fairy ⁺
fairwell	farewell
fair y /ies	
fairy land /tale	
fait	fate ²★
faitful	fateful ⁺
faith /ful/fully	
faithless /ly	
fake ² /r ★ (deceiver)	
fakir ★ (holy man)	
fal	fall ⁺
falacious	fallacious
falacy	fallacy ⁺
falanks	phalanx ⁺
falanx	phalanx ⁺
falasey	fallacy ⁺
falashus	fallacious
falcon /er/ry	
fale	fail ¹⁺
falibility	fallibility
falible	fallible ⁺
falibul	fallible ⁺
falic	phallic

fall /en/er/ing/-out	
fallacious	
fallac y /ies	
fallasey	fallacy ⁺
fallib le /ility	
fallibul	fallible ⁺
fallow ¹	
fallus	phallus ⁺
falout	fall-out
falow	fallow ¹
fals	false ⁺
false /hood/ly/r/st	
falsetto /s	
falsif y ⁴ /ication/ier	
falsit y /ies	
falt	fault ¹⁺
falter ¹	
falure	failure
falus	phallus ⁺
fam e ²	
familey	family ⁺
familiar /ity	
familiaris e ² /ation	
familiaritey	familiarity
familier	familiar ⁺
famil y /ies	
famine	
famish ¹	
famous /ly/ness	
famus	famous ⁺
fan ³ /-belt	
fanatic /al/ally/ism	
fanatisism	fanaticism
fanci er /est/ly/ness	
fanciful /ly	
fanc y ⁴ /ies	
fane	feign ¹★
fanfair	fanfare
fanfare·	
fansie	fancy ⁴⁺
fansier	fancier ⁺
fansiful	fanciful ⁺
fansy	fancy ⁴⁺
fant	faint ¹★
fantasey	fantasy ⁺

fantasia		fascia ★ (architecture)	
fantasm	phantasm	fascia	facia ★
fantasmagoria	phantasmagoria +	fascinat *e* ² /ion	
fantastic /ally		fascis *m* /t	
fantas *y* /ies		fase	face ²+
fantharted	faint-hearted	fase	phase ²
fantom	phantom	fasees	fasces
far /-fetched/-flung		fasen	fasten ¹+
farad /ay		fasener	fastener
farc *e* ² /ical/ically		faseshus	facetious +
fare ²★ (get along)		faset	facet +
fare	fair ¹★	fasetious	facetious +
Farenheight	Fahrenheit	fasha	facia ★
Farenhite	Fahrenheit	fasha	fascia ★
farer	fairer +	fashal	facial +
farewell		fashion ¹ /able/ably	
fariland	fairyland +	fashism	fascism +
faringeal	pharyngeal +	fashist	fascist
faringitis	pharyngitis	fashon	fashion ¹+
farinks	pharynx	fashonable	fashionable
farinx	pharynx	fashonabul	fashionable
farisee	Pharisee +	fasile	facile
faritale	fairy-tale	fasilitate	facilitate ²+
farm ¹ /er/house		fasilitey	facility +
farmacist	pharmacist	fasinashun	fascination
farmacologey	pharmacology +	fasinate	fascinate ²+
farmacopea	pharmacopoeia	fasination	fascination
farmacy	pharmacy +	fast ¹	
farmasey	pharmacy +	fasten ¹ /er	
farmasist	pharmacist	fastidious /ly/ness	
farmasutic	pharmaceutic +	fastidius	fastidious +
farm *stead* /yard		fat ³ /ness/ter/test/ty	
faro	Pharaoh	fatal /ism/ly	
farse	farce ²+	fatalist /ic/ically	
farshal	farcical	fatalit *y* /ies	
far-sighted		fate ²★ (destiny)	
farth *er* ★† /est		fate	fête ²★
†(distant)		fateeg	fatigue ²
farther	father ¹★	fateful /ly	
farthing /gale		faten	fatten ¹
faryngeal	pharyngeal +	fath	faith +
faryngitis	pharyngitis	father ¹★ (parent)	
farynx	pharynx	father	farther ★+
fasade	façade	father *hood* /land	
fasces		father(s)-in-law	

father *less* /ly		febus	Phoebus
fathom¹ /able		feces	faeces⁺
fatig	fatigue²	fech	fetch¹
fatigue²		feckless	
faton	phaeton	fecund /ity	
fatten¹		fed /-up	
fatuous /ly		federal /ism/ist/ly	
fatuus	fatuous⁺	federalis *e*² /ation	
faty	fatty	federat *e*² /ion	
faucet		fee	
fault¹ /ily/less/y		feeble /r/st	
faun ★ (Roman god)		feebul	feeble⁺
faun	fawn¹★	feed /back/er/ing	
fauna		feef	fief
faux pas		feel /er/ing	
faver	favour¹⁺	feeld	field¹⁺
faverable	favourable	feend	fiend⁺
faverabul	favourable	feest	feast¹
faverit	favourite⁺	feet ★ (pl. of foot)	
faveritism	favouritism	feet	feat ★
favour¹ /able/ably		feetle	foetal
favourit *e* /ism		feetus	foetus⁺
favrable	favourable	feif	fief
fawn¹★ (young deer)		feign¹★ (invent)	
fawn	faun ★	feign	fain ★
fawna	fauna	feild	field¹⁺
fay ★ (fairy)		feildmarshal	field-marshal
fay	fey ★	feind	fiend⁺
fayton	phaeton	feint¹★ (pretend)	
fea	fee	feint	faint¹★
feacher	feature²⁺	fekless	feckless
fealty		fekund	fecund⁺
fear¹ /less/some		fekunditey	fecundity
fearful /ly		fel	fell
feasable	feasible⁺	fela	fellah
feasib *le* /ility/ly		felial	filial⁺
feasibul	feasible⁺	felicitat *e*² /ion	
feast¹		felicit *y* /ous	
feat ★ (act)		feline	
feat	feet ★	felisitate	felicitate²⁺
feather¹ /weight/y		felisitey	felicity⁺
featherbed /ding		felisitus	felicitous
feature² /less		fell	
February		fellah	
Febuary	February	fellow /ship	

felon /ious	
felon y /ies	
felow	fellow +
felt	
femail	female
female	
femer	femur
feminin e /ity	
feminis m /t	
femur	
fence ² /r	
fenel	fennel
feniks	phoenix
fenix	phoenix
fennel	
fenobarbitone	phenobarbitone
fenol	phenol
fenomenon	phenomenon +
fenomina	phenomena
fenominal	phenomenal +
fense	fence ²+
fer	fir ★
fer	fur ★
feret	ferret ¹
feric	ferric +
ferie	ferry ⁴+
feris wheel	Ferris-wheel
ferite	ferrite
ferl	furl ¹
ferlong	furlong
ferment ¹ /ation	
fermium	
fern /ery	
fernis	furnace
feroci ous /ty	
feroshus	ferocious +
ferositey	ferocity
ferous	ferrous
ferret ¹	
ferr ic /ous	
Ferris-wheel	
ferrite	
ferrule	
ferry ⁴ /ies	
ferthest	furthest

fertil e /ity	
fertilis e ² /ation/er	
fertiv	furtive +
ferule	ferrule
ferus	ferrous
ferven cy /t	
ferver	fervour
fervour	
fery	ferry ⁴+
fes	fez
fesant	pheasant
fesees	faeces +
fesible	feasible+
fesibul	feasible +
fester ¹	
festiv e /al	
festivit y /ies	
festoon ¹	
fetch ¹	
fête ²★ (festival)	
fête	fate ²★
feter	fetter ¹
fether	feather ¹+
fetherbed	featherbed +
fetherwait	featherweight
fetid	
fetish /ism/ist	
fetlock	
fetter ¹	
fettle ²	
fetul	fettle ²
feud ¹	
feudal /ism	
fever /ed/ish	
few	
fewdal	feudal +
fewdalism	feudalism
fey ★ (fated to die)	
fey	fay ★
fez	
fezant	pheasant
fial	file ²★+
fial	phial ★
fiancé /e (fem.)	
fiansay	fiancé +

fiasco /s
fib³ /ber
fiber — fibre +
fibr e /ous
fibreglass
fibrus — fibrous
fibula
fickle /ness
ficshun — fiction +
fiction /al
fictishus — fictitious +
fictitious /ly/ness
ficul — fickle +
fiddl e² /er/y
fiddlesticks
fidelity
fidget¹ /iness/y
fidle — fiddle²+
fidul — fiddle²+
fie
fief
field¹ /-day/er
field-marshal
fiend /ish
fierce /ly/ness/r/st
fierey — fiery +
fierse — fierce +
fier y /ier/iest/ily
fife
fifteen /th
fiftey — fifty +
fifth
fift y /ies/ieth
figer — figure²+
figerativ — figurative +
figerhead — figurehead
figerhed — figurehead
figet — fidget¹+
fight /er/ing
figment
figurative /ly
figure² /head
fiks — fix¹+
fiksashun — fixation +
fiksation — fixation +

fiksativ — fixative
fikscher — fixture
filament
filander — philander¹+
filanthropey — philanthropy +
filanthropic — philanthropic
filanthropist — philanthropist
filantropy — philanthropy +
filarmonic — philharmonic
filateley — philately +
filatelist — philatelist
filch¹
file²★ (tool, folder) /r
file — phial ★
filet — fillet¹
filharmonic — philharmonic
filial /ly
filibuster¹
filie — filly +
filigree
filip — fillip
filistine — Philistine
fill¹ /er
fillet¹
fillip
fill y /ies
film¹ /y
film-star
film-strip
filologey — philology +
filosofer — philosopher +
filosofey — philosophy
filosofical — philosophical +
filosofise — philosophise²
filosopher — philosopher +
filosophical — philosophical +
filosophise — philosophise²
filosophy — philosophy
filter¹★ (pass, strainer)
filter — philtre ★
filth /ier/iest/ily/iness/y
filtrat e² /ion
filum — phylum
fily — filly +
fin /ned/ny

final ★ (at last)		fisic	physic ★
finale ★ (the end)		fisic	physique ★
finalis *e*² /t		fisical	physical +
finalit *y* /ies		fisician	physician
finally		fisicist	physicist
financ *e*² /ier		fisics	physics
financial /ly		fisile	fissile
finans	finance ²+	fisiologey	physiology +
finanshul	financial +	fision	fission +
finansier	financier	fisionomey	physiognomy
finch /es		fisiotherapey	physiotherapy
find /er/ing		fisiotherapist	physiotherapist
fine ² /r/ry/st		fisique	physique ★
finerey	finery	fisishun	physician
finess	finesse	fisisist	physicist
finesse		fissile	
finger ¹ /print/tips		fission /able	
finicky		fissure	
finikey	finicky	fit ³/ment/ness/ter/test	
finish ¹ /er		fite	fight +
finite		fitful /ly	
fiord		five /pence/r	
fir ★ (tree)		fix ¹ /edly	
fir	fur ★	fixat *ion* /ive	
fire ² /arm/place/work		fixcher	fixture
fire-brigade		fixture	
fire-engine		fiy	fie
fire-escape		fizle	fizzle ²
fire-extinguisher		fizul	fizzle ²
firefl *y* /ies		fizz ¹ /y	
firm ¹ /er/est/ness		fizzle ²	
firmament		fjord	
first /-aid/-class/-rate		flabbergast ¹	
firth		flabb *y* /ier/iest/iness	
firy	fiery +	flabergast	flabbergast ¹
fiscal /ism/ly		flabie	flabby +
fiscul	fiscal +	flaby	flabby+
fiseek	physique ★	flaccid /ity/ness	
fish ¹ /ier/iest/iness/y		flag ³ /ship/staff	
fisher	fissure	flagellate ²	
fisherm *an* /en (pl.)		flagon	
fisher *y* /ies		flagrancy	
fish- *hook* /monger		flagransey	flagrancy
fishmunger	fishmonger	flagrant /ly	
fishun	fission +	flail ¹	

flair ★ (instinct)		fleat	fleet +
flair	flare ²★	flebitis	phlebitis
flak e ² /iness/y		fled	
flaks	flax +	fledgling	
flaksen	flaxen	flee ★ (run) /ing	
flaksid	flaccid +	flee	flea ★
flamable	flammable	fleec e ² /y	
flamabul	flammable	flees	fleece ²+
flamboiant	flamboyant	fleet /ing	
flamboyan ce /cy/t		flegling	fledgling
flamboyans	flamboyance +	flegm	phlegm+
flame ²		flegmatic	phlegmatic
flamingo /es		fleks	flex ¹
flammable		fleksible	flexible +
flammabul	flammable	fleksibul	flexible +
flanel	flannel ³+	flem	phlegm +
flange ²		Flemish	
flank ¹		fler de lis	fleur-de-lis
flanle	flannel ³+	flert	flirt ¹+
flannel ³ /ette/graph		flesh /iness/y	
flanul	flannel ³+	fleur-de-lis	
flap ³ /per		flew ★ (flight)	
flare ²★ (light)		flew	flu ★
flare	flair ★	flew	flue ★
flash ¹ /ier/iest/ily/y		flex ¹	
flash back /light		flexib le /ility/ly	
flask		flexibul	flexible +
flat /let/ly/test		fli	fly +
flaten	flatten ¹	flick ¹	
flater	flatter ¹+	flicker ¹	
flatten ¹		flier	flyer
flatter ¹ /er		flight /iness/y	
flatulen ce /t		flimsie	flimsy +
flatulens	flatulence +	flims y /ier/iest/ily/iness	
flaunt ¹		flinch ¹	
flautist		fling	
flaver	flavour ¹	flint /y	
flavour ¹		flipancy	flippancy +
flaw ¹★ (blemish) /less		flipansey	flippancy +
flaw	floor ¹★	flipant	flippant
flax /en		fliper	flipper
flay ¹		flippan cy /t	
flea ★ (insect)		flipper	
flea	flee ★	flirt ¹ /ation/atious	
flea-bite		flit ³	

flite	flight +	flower ¹★ (plant) /y	
flo	floe ★	flower	flour ¹★
flo	flow ¹★+	flownder	flounder ¹
float ¹		flownse	flounce ²
flock ¹ /s ★ (groups)		flowt	flout ¹
flocks	phlox ★	flox	phlox ★
floe ★ (ice)		flu ★ (cold)	
floem	phloem	flu	flew ★
flog ³		flu	flue ★
flood ¹ /-gate/lit		fluctuashun	fluctuation
floodlight /ing		fluctuat *e* ² /ion	
flooid	fluid +	flud	flood ¹+
floor ¹★ (in room)		fludlight	floodlight +
floor	flaw ¹★+	fludlite	floodlight +
flooride	fluoride	flue ★ (pipe)	
floorine	fluorine +	flue	flew ★
floot	flute	flue	flu ★
flop ³ /pily/py		fluen *cy* /t	
flora /l/lly		fluff /iness/y	
Florentine		fluid /ity	
florescen *ce* /t		fluke ²	
floresens	florescence +	fluks	flux
floresent	florescent	flummox ¹	
florid		flumuks	flummox ¹
floridate	fluoridate ²+	flumux	flummox ¹
florin		flung	
florist		fluorescen *ce* /t	
floss /y		fluoridat *e* ² /ion	
flotashun	flotation	fluori *ne* /de	
flotation		flurie	flurry ⁴+
flote	float ¹	flurish	flourish ¹
flotila	flotilla	flurr *y* ⁴ /ies	
flotilla		flurt	flirt ¹+
flotsam		flurtashun	flirtation
flotsum	flotsam	flurtation	flirtation
flounce ²		flury	flurry ⁴+
flounder ¹		flush ¹	
flouns	flounce ²	fluster ¹	
flour ¹★ (powder)		flute	
flour	flower ¹★+	flutter ¹	
flourey	flowery	fluvial	
flourish ¹		flux	
flout ¹		fl *y* /ies/yer/ying	
flow ¹★ (to move) /n		flycatcher	
flow	floe ★	flylea *f* /ves (pl.)	

fly *weight* /wheel
fo   foe +
foal ¹
foam ¹
fob ³
fobia   phobia
focal
focus ¹ /er
fodder ¹
foder   fodder ¹
foe /s
foet *us* /al
fog ³ /horn
fogg *y* /ier/iest/ily/iness
foible
foibul   foible
foier   foyer
foil ¹
foist ¹
foks   fox +
fold ¹ /er
fole   foal ¹
foliage
foliat *e* ² /ion
folie   folly +
foliidge   foliage
folio ¹ /s
folk /-dance/-song
folklor *e* /ist
follow ¹ /er
foll *y* /ies
folow   follow ¹+
foly   folly +
fome   foam ¹
foment ¹ /ation/er
fon   phon *
fond /er/est/ly/ness
fondant
fondle ²
fondul   fondle ²
fone   phone ²*
fonetic   phonetic +
fonie   phony
fonograf   phonograph +
fonografic   phonographic

fonograph   phonograph +
fonographic   phonographic
fonologey   phonology +
font
fony   phony
food /s
fool ¹ /proof
foolhard *y* /iness
foolscap
foot ¹ /fall/hold/note
football /er
foot *path* /print
foot *sore* /step/stool
fop /pish
for * (on behalf of)
for   fore *
for   four *+
for ever
forage ² /r
foram *en* /ina (pl.)
forarm   forearm ¹
forbade
forbarance   forbearance
forbare   forbear +
forbear /ance/ing
forbid /den/ding
forbode   forebode ²+
forbore
forcasel   forecastle
forcast   forecast ¹+
forcastle   forecastle
forc *e* ² /ible/ibly
forceful /ly/ness
forceps
forclose   foreclose ²+
ford ¹ /able
fore * (golf)
fore   four *+
forearm ¹
forebode ² /r
forecast ¹ /er
forecastle
foreclos *e* ² /ure
fored   forehead
forefathers

forefinger		forfront	forefront
forefoot		forfrunt	forefront
forefront		forgather [1]	
forego *(preceed)/ing*/ne*		forgave	
forego	forgo *+	forge [2] /r	
foreground		forger y /ies	
forehand		forget /table/ting	
forehead		forgetful /ness	
foreign /er/ness		forget-me-not	
foreknowledge		forgiv e /able/eness/ing	
foreland		forgo *(waive)/ing*/ne*	
foreleg		forgo	forego *+
forelock		forgot /ten	
forem an /en (pl.)		forground	foreground
foremast		forhand	forehand
foremost		forhead	forehead
foren	foreign +	forhed	forehead
forener	foreigner	forige	forage [2]+
forenoledge	foreknowledge	forin	foreign +
forensic		fork [1]	
forerunner		forland	foreland
foresail		forleg	foreleg
foresaw		forlock	forelock
foresee /able/ing/n		forlorn	
foreshadow [1]		form [1] /al/ation	
foreshorten [1]		formalis e [2] /ation	
foresight		formalit y /ies	
foresite	foresight	formally *†	
foreskin		†(conventionally)	
forest [1] /ation/er/ry		formally	formerly *
forestall [1]		forman	foreman +
foretaste [2]		format	
foretell		formative	
forethought		former /ly *†	
foretold		†(before now)	
forewarn [1]		formerly	formally *
foreword * (preface)		formic	
foreword	forward [1]*	formidabl e /y	
forfathers	forefathers	formidabul	formidable +
forfeit [1] /ure		formost	foremost
forficher	forfeiture	formula /e/s (pls.)	
forfinger	forefinger	formulat e [2] /ion	
forfit	forfeit [1]+	forn	faun *
forfiture	forfeiture	forn	fawn [1]*
forfoot	forefoot	fornicat e [2] /ion	

fornolidge	foreknowledge	forward	foreword ★
forruner	forerunner	forwarn	forewarn [1]
forsable	forcible	forwent	
forsail	foresail	forword	foreword ★
forsak e /en/ing		fosfate	phosphate
forsaw	foresaw	fosforesce	phosphoresce [2+]
forse	force [2+]	fosforescent	phosphorescent
forsee	foresee [+]	fosforess	phosphoresce [2+]
forseps	forceps	fosforus	phosphorous ★[+]
forsful	forceful [+]	fosforus	phosphorus ★
forshadow	foreshadow [1]	fosil	fossil
forshorten	foreshorten [1]	fosilise	fossilise [2+]
forsible	forcible	fosphate	phosphate
forsite	foresight	fossil	
forsithia	forsythia	fossilis e [2] /ation	
forskin	foreskin	foster [1] /-father/-mother	
forsook		foto	photo [+]
forstall	forestall [1]	fotocopy	photocopy [+]
forsythia		fotoelectric	photo-electric
fort ★ (military)		fotofinish	photo-finish
fort	fought ★	fotogenic	photogenic
fortaste	foretaste [2]	fotograf	photograph [1+]
forte ★ (strong point)		fotgrafey	photography
forteen	fourteen [+]	fotograph	photograph [1+]
fortel	foretell	fotometer	photometer [+]
forth ★ (forward)		fotometrey	photometry
forth	fourth ★	foton	photon
forthcoming		fotosinthesis	photosynthesis
forthort	forethought	fotostat	photostat
forth right /with		fototropism	phototropism
fortie	forty [+]	fought ★ (did fight)	
fortif y [4] /ication/ier		foul [1★] (dirty) /ly/ness	
Fortin barometer		foul	fowl [1★+]
fortissimo		found [1] /ation/er/ling	
fortitude		foundr y /ies	
fortnight /ly		fount	
fortnite	fortnight [+]	fountain	
fortold	foretold	four ★ (number) /th ★	
fortress		four fold /some	
fortuitous /ly		fourt	fort ★
fortuitus	fortuitous [+]	fourt	fought ★
fortun e [2] /ate/ately		fourteen /th	
fort y /ies/ieth		fourth	forth ★
forum		fourty	forty [+]
forward [1★] (advance)		fow	foe [+]

fowl [1]★ (bird) /er		frawd	fraud
fowl	foul [1]★+	frawdulence	fraudulence +
fownd	found [1]+	frawdulens	fraudulence +
fowndashun	foundation	frawdulent	fraudulent
fowndation	foundation	frawt	fraught
fowndrey	foundry +	fray [1] /s ★ (fights)	
fownt	fount	frayl	frail +
fowntain	fountain	frays	phrase [2]★+
fox-hunt /ing		freak [1] /ish	
fox-terrier		freckle [2]	
foyble	foible	frecul	freckle [2]
foyer		free /d/ing/ly/r/st	
fracshun	fraction +	freedom	
fracshus	fractious	free-hand	
fraction /al/ally		freehold /er	
fractious		freek	freak [1]+
fracture [2]		freelance [2]	
fraeltey	frailty	freelans	freelance [2]
fragile /ly		freemason /ry	
fragility		free-wheel [1]	
fragment [1] /ary/ation		freez e ★ (cold) /er/ing	
fragran ce /t		freeze	frieze ★
fragrans	fragrance +	freight /age/er	
frail /ty/ties		freind	friend +
frait	freight +	frekwency	frequency +
frame [2] /work		frekwensey	frequency +
franc ★ (money)		frekwent	frequent [1]+
franchise [2]		French /man/woman	
francium		frend	friend +
frank [1]★ (blunt) /ly/ness		frendly	friendly +
frankfurter		frendship	friendship
frankincense		frenetic	phrenetic
frankium	francium	frenologey	phrenology +
frantic /ally		frenologist	phrenologist
frase	phrase [2]★+	frenzie	frenzy +
frasologey	phraseology	frenz y /ies/ied	
frate	freight +	frequenc y /ies	
fraternal /ly		frequensey	frequency +
fraternis e [2] /ation		frequent [1] /er/ly	
fraternit y /ies		fresco /es	
fraud		fresh /er/ly/ness	
fraudulen ce /t		freshen [1]	
fraudulens	fraudulence +	fresko	fresco +
fraught		fret [3] /ful/fully	
fraut	fraught	fret -saw /work	

124

Freudian
fri | fry [4]
friable
friabul | friable
friar
fricshun | friction [+]
friction /al
friend /ship
friendl y /ier/iest/iness
frier | friar
frieze * (ornament)
frigate
fright
frighten [1]
frightful /ly/ness
frigid /ity
frill [1]
fringe [2]
fripper y /ies
frisk [1] /ily/iness/y
frite | fright
friteful | frightful [+]
friten | frighten [1]
friter | fritter [1+]
fritter [1] /er
frivol [3] /ous
frivolit y /ies
frivolus | frivolous
frizul | frizzle [2+]
frizz /y
frizzl e [2] /y
frock [1]
frog /man/men (pl.)
froidian | Freudian
frolic /some
frolick ed /ing
front [1] /age/al/ally
frontier
frontispiece
froogal | frugal [+]
frooishun | fruition
frooition | fruition
froot | fruit [1+]
frootful | fruitful [+]
frost [1] /ily/y

frostbit e /ten
froth [1] /iness/y
frown [1]
frowzie | frowzy [+]
frowz y /ier/iest
froze /n
frugal /ity/ly
fruishun | fruition
fruit [1] /ion
fruiterer
fruitful /ly/ness
fruitless /ly/ness
fruit y /ier/iest/iness
frump /ish
frunt | front [1+]
fruntal | frontal
fruntier | frontier
fruntispiece | frontispiece
frustrat e [2] /ion
frut | fruit [1+]
fruterer | fruiterer
frutful | fruitful [+]
frutie | fruity [+]
frutier | fruiterer
fry [4]
fu | few
fucher | future [+]
fucherist | futurist [+]
fucheristic | futuristic
fuchsia
fudal | feudal [+]
fudalism | feudalism
fuddle [2]
fude | feud [1]
fudge [2]
fudul | fuddle [2]
fuel [3]
fug /gy
fugitive
ful | full [+]
fulblooded | full-blooded
fulbluded | full-blooded
fulcrum
fulfil [3] /ment
full /-blooded/er/-time

125

fulscap	foolscap	furst	first [+]
fulsome /ly/ness		furstaid	first-aid
fulsum	fulsome [+]	furstrate	first-rate
fumble [2] /r		furth	firth
fumbul	fumble [2+]	further [1] /more/most	
fume [2]		furtherance	
fumigat e [2] /ion/or		furtherans	furtherance
fun /nily/ny		furtive /ly	
funcshun	function [1+]	fur y /ies/ious	
funcshunrey	functionary	furze	
function [1] /ary		fus	fuss [1+]
functional /ly		fus e [2] /ion	
fund [1]		fuselage	
fundamental /ly		fusha	fuchsia
funel	funnel [3]	fusib le /ility	
funer al /eal		fusibul	fusible [+]
fung us /i (pl.)		fusie	fussy
funicular		fusier	fussier [+]
funiculer	funicular	fusilade	fusillade
funily	funnily	fusilage	fuselage
funk [1]		fusilier	
funnel [3]		fusilige	fuselage
funn y /ier/iest/ily		fusillade	
fur ★ (coat)		fuss [1] /y	
fur	fir ★	fussie	fussy
furie	furry [+]	fussi er /est/ly/ness	
furie	fury [+]	fustie	fusty [+]
furier	furrier	fust y /ier/iest/ily/iness	
furious /ly		fusy	fussy
furius	furious [+]	futil e /ity	
furl [1]		futur e /ism/ity	
furlong		futurist /ic	
furm	firm [1+]	fuzz /ily/iness	
furmament	firmament	fwayay	foyer
furment	ferment [1+]	fyord	fiord
furmentashun	fermentation	fyord	fjord
furmentation	fermentation	fysical	physical [+]
furn	fern [+]	fysically	physically
furnace		fysician	physician
furnicher	furniture	fysicist	physicist
furnis	furnace	fysick	physic ★
furnish [1] /er		fysick	physique ★
furniture		fysicks	physics
furrow [1]		fysicley	physically
furr y /ier/iest/iness		fysiologey	physiology [+]

126

fysionomey	physiognomy	galery	gallery +
fysiotherapey	physiotherapy	Galic	Gaelic ★
fysiotherapist	physiotherapist +	Galic	Gallic ★
fysique	physique ★	galie	galley
fysishun	physician	galium	gallium
fysisist	physicist	galivant	gallivant 1
		gall 1	
		gallant /ry	
G		galler y /ies	
		galley	
gabardine		Gallic ★†	
gabble 2★ (talk) /r		†(of Gaul, French)	
gable 2★ (on roof)		gallic	Gaelic ★
gabul	gabble 2★+	gallium	
gabul	gable 2★	gallivant 1	
gad 3 /about		gallon	
gadget /ry		gallop 1 /er	
gadolinium		gallows	
gael	gale	galon	gallon
Gaelic ★ (language)		galop	gallop 1+
gaf	gaffe	galore	
gaffe		galoshes	
gag 3		galows	gallows
gaga		galvanic	
gage	gauge 2+	galvanis e 2 /ation/m	
gagercounter	Geiger counter	galvanometer	
gaget	gadget +	galy	galley
gaggle 2		gambit	
gagit	gadget +	gamble 2★ (games) /r	
gagul	gaggle 2	gambol 3★ (frolic)	
gai ety /ly		game /-bird/-cock	
gain 1 /er/ful/fully		gamekeeper	
gait ★ (walk)		gamesmanship	
gait	gate 2★+	gamie	game +
gaiter /ed		gaming	
gaitey	gaiety +	gammon	
gal	gall 1	gamon	gammon
gala		gamut	
galactic		gamy	game +
galaksey	galaxy +	gander 1	
galant	gallant +	ganet	gannet
galantrey	gallantry	gang 1 /er	
galaw	galore	gangling	
galax y /ies		gang-plank	
gale		gangreen	gangrene +

gangren *e* /ous		gash [1]	
gangrenus	gangrenous	gasha	geisha
gangster /ism		gasket	
gangway		gaslight	
gannet		gaslite	gaslight
gaol [1]★ (prison) /bird/er		gasoline	
gape [2]		gasometer	
garage [2]		gasp [1]	
garantee	guarantee ★[+]	gastley	ghastly [+]
garantor	guarantor [+]	gastri *c* /tis	
garb [1]		gastronom *y* /ic/ical	
garbage		gate [2]★ (entrance) /way	
garbige	garbage	gate	gait ★
garble [2]		gate-crash [1]	
garbul	garble [2]	gater	gaiter [+]
gard	guard [1+]	gather [1] /er	
garden [1] /er		gauche	
gardenia		gaudie	gaudy [+]
gardian	guardian [+]	gaud *y* /ily/iness	
gardroom	guard-room	gauge [2] /r	
gardsman	guardsman	gaunt /let	
garet	garret	gauze	
gargantuan		gave	
gargle [2]		gawdie	gaudy [+]
gargoil	gargoyle	gawk [1] /iness	
gargoyle		gawl	gall [1]
gargul	gargle [2]	gawnt	gaunt [+]
garish		gawntlet	gauntlet
garison	garrison [1]	gawse	gorse
garland [1]		gay /er/est	
garlic /ky		gayety	gaiety [+]
garment [1]		Gaylic	Gaelic ★
garner [1]		gayn	gain [1+]
garnet		gaysha	geisha
garnish [1]		gaze [2] /r	
garnit	garnet	gazel	gazelle
garot	garrotte [2]	gazelle	
garret		gazer	geyser
garrison [1]		gazet	gazette [2]
garrot	garrotte [2]	gazette [2]	
garrotte [2]		ge gaw	gew-gaw
garrulous /ly		gear [1] /box	
garter /ed		gees	geese
garulus	garrulous [+]	geese (pl. of goose)	
gas [3] /eous/es/-mask		Geiger counter	

geisha
gel³
gelatin — gelatine⁺
gelatin *e* /ous
gelatinus — gelatinous
geld¹
gelignite
gem³ /my
Gemini
gendarme
gender¹
gene
genealog *y* /ist
genee — genie
general /ly
generalis *e*² /ation
generalit *y* /ies
generat *e*² /ion/or
generative
generic /ally
generosity
generous /ly/ness
generus — generous⁺
genetic /ally/s
geney — genie
genial /ity/ly
genie
geniologey — genealogy⁺
genital /s
genitive
geni *us* /i/uses (pls.)
genocide
genoside — genocide
genre
genteel /ism/ly
gentile
gentility
gentle² /ness/r/st
gentlem *an* /en (pl.)
gentrey — gentry
gentry
gentul — gentle²⁺
gentulman — gentleman⁺
genuin — genuine⁺
genuine /ly/ness

genus
geny — genie
geocentric
geofisical — geophysical
geofisics — geophysics⁺
geofysical — geophysical
geofysics — geophysics⁺
geografey — geography⁺
geografic — geographic
geografical — geographical⁺
geographical /ly
geograph *y* /er/ic
geological /ly
geolog *y* /ist
geometrey — geometry
geometric /al/ally
geometry
geophysic *s* /al/ist
geosentric — geocentric
geranium /s
gerd — gird¹⁺
gerder — girder
gerdle — girdle²
gerdul — girdle²
geriatric /ian/s
gerilla — gorilla ★
gerilla — guerrilla ★
gerkin — gherkin
gerl — girl⁺
gerlish — girlish
germ
German
germane
Germanic
germanium
germicid *e* /al
germinat *e*² /ion
germiside — germicide⁺
gerontology
gerth — girth
gerund /ive
gescher — gesture²
gess — guess⁺
gesswerk — guesswork
gesswork — guesswork

gest	guest ★
gesticulat *e*² /ion	
gesture²	
get /ting	
getto	ghetto +
gew-gaw	
geyser	
ghastl *y* /ier/iest/iness	
gherkin	
ghetto /s	
ghost¹ /ly	
ghoul /ish	
giant /ess (fem.)	
gibber¹ /ish	
gibbet¹	
gibbon	
gibe²★ (taunt)	
gibe	gybe²★
giber	gibber¹+
giberish	gibberish
gibet	gibbet¹
giblets	
gibon	gibbon
gidance	guidance
gidans	guidance
gidd*y*/ier/iest/ily/iness	
gide	guide²+
gidie	giddy+
gidily	giddily
gidy	giddy+
gift /ed	
gig	
gigantic /ally	
giggle² /r	
gigolo	
gigul	giggle²+
gil	gill¹
gild¹★ (gold cover)	
gild	guild ★
gilder	guilder
Gildhall	Guildhall
gile	guile+
gileless	guileless
gill¹	
giloteen	guillotine²

gilotine	guillotine²
gilt ★ (gold leaf)	
gilt	guilt ★
gilt-edged	
giltey	guilty+
gilty	guilty+
gim	gym+
gimick	gimmick+
gimkana	gymkhana
gimlet	
gimmick /ry/y	
gimnasium	gymnasium+
gimnastics	gymnastics
gin³	
ginecologey	gynaecology+
ginecologist	gynaecologist
gingam	gingham
ginger¹ /bread/ly	
gingham	
ginie	guinea+
ginifowl	guinea-fowl
ginipig	guinea-pig
ginjer	ginger¹+
ginjerbred	gingerbread
gipsey	gipsy+
gipsie	gipsy+
gipsum	gypsum
gips *y* /ies	
giraf	giraffe
giraffe	
girashun	gyration
girate	gyrate²+
giration	gyration
gird¹ /er	
girdle²	
girdul	girdle²
girl /hood/ish	
giro ★ (banking)	
giro	gyro ★+
girth	
gise	guise
gist	
gitar	guitar+
gitarist	guitarist
give /n/r	

giving		gliserin	glycerine
Giy Forks	Guy Fawkes	glisten [1]	
gizerd	gizzard	glitter [1]	
gizzard		glo	glow [1]
glacia *l* /tion		gloaming	
glacier		gloat [1]	
glad /der/dest/ly		glob *e* /al/ally	
gladden [1]		globe-trott *er* /ing	
glade		globul *e* /ar	
gladen	gladden [1]	globuler	globular
gladiater	gladiator	gloming	gloaming
gladiator		gloo	glue [2+]
gladiol *us* /i (pl.)		gloocose	glucose
glamer	glamour	glooie	gluey
glamerus	glamorous [+]	gloom /y	
glamoris *e* [2] /ation		gloomi *er* /est/ly/ness	
glamorous /ly/ness		glooten	gluten [★+]
glamour		glorie	glory [4+]
glance [2]		glorif *y* [4] /ication	
gland /ular		glorius	glorious
glanduler	glandular	glor *y* [4] /ies/ious	
glans	glance [2]	glos	gloss [1+]
glare [2]		glosarey	glossary [+]
glas	glass [+]	gloss [1] /ier/iest/iness/y	
glashal	glacial [+]	glossar *y* /ies	
glasiashun	glaciation	glote	gloat [1]
glasiation	glaciation	glotis	glottis [+]
glasier	glacier	glott *is* /al	
glass /es/ily		glove [2] /r	
glassware		glow [1]	
glaswear	glassware	glower [1]	
glaz *e* [2] /ier		glucose	
glea	glee [+]	glue [2] /y	
gleam [1]		glum /ly/mer/mest	
glean [1] /er		glut [3]	
glee /ful/fully		glut *en* [★†] /inous	
gleem	gleam [1]	†(sticky substance)	
gleen	glean [1+]	gluten	glutton [★+]
glib /ber/best/ly		glutinus	glutinous
glicerine	glycerine	gluton	glutton [★+]
glide [2] /r		glutonus	gluttonous
glimmer [1]		glutony	gluttony
glimpse [2]		glutton [★†] /ous/y	
glint [1]		†(greedy)	
glisen	glisten [1]	glutton	gluten [★+]

gluv	glove ²⁺
glycerine	
gnarl ¹	
gnash ¹	
gnat	
gnaw ¹	
gnom *e* /ish	
gnu ★ (animal)	
go /er/es/ing	
goad ¹	
go -*ahead* /-kart	
goal ★† /ie/keeper/less	
†(an aim, sport)	
goal	gaol ¹★⁺
goat /ee	
goatherd	
gobble ² /r	
go-between	
goblet	
goblin	
gobul	gobble ²⁺
gocart	go-kart
god /child/like	
god -*daughter* /son	
goddess (fem.)	
gode	goad ¹
god*father* /mother	
god*forsaken* /head	
goggle ²	
gogul	goggle ²
goiter	goitre
goitre	
gold /en/finch/fish	
goldsmith	
gole	goal ★⁺
golf ¹ /er	
golie	goalie
golliwog	
gon	gone ⁺
gondol *a* /ier	
gone /r	
gong ¹	
gonoria	gonorrhoea
gonorrhoea	
good /ly/ness/will	

good-bye	
good-humered	good-humoured
good-humoured	
goodie	goody ⁺
good-looking	
good *y* /ies	
gool	ghoul ⁺
goolash	goulash
goolish	ghoulish
goord	gourd
goormand	gourmand ⁺
goormay	gourmet
goose /flesh	
gooseberie	gooseberry ⁺
gooseberr *y* /ies	
Gordian	
Gordyan	Gordian
gor *e* ² /y	
gorge ² /r	
gorgeous /ly/ness	
Gorgonzola	
gorgus	gorgeous
gorilla ★ (ape)	
gorilla	guerrilla ★
gorse	
gosamer	gossamer
gosip	gossip ¹⁺
gosling	
gospel /ler	
gossamer	
gossip ¹ /er/y	
gost	ghost ¹⁺
gostly	ghostly
got /ten	
gote	goat ⁺
goteherd	goatherd
Gothic	
gouge ² /r	
goulash	
gourd	
gourmand /ism	
gourmet	
gout /y	
govern ¹ /able/ance	
governer	governor ⁺

132

government /al		granite	
govern *or* /ess (fem.)		grann *y* /ies	
govner	governor +	grant [1]	
gowge	gouge [2]+	granulat *e* [2] /ion	
gown		granul *e* /ar/arity	
gowt	gout +	grany	granny +
grab [3] /ber		grape /fruit/-shot	
grace [2] /less		graph [1]	
graceful /ly		graphic /al/ally	
gracious /ly/ness		graphite	
gradashun	gradation	grapholog *y* /ist	
grad *e* [2] /ation/er		graple	grapple [2]
gradient		grapnel	
gradual /ly		grapple [2]	
graduat *e* [2] /ion/or		grapul	grapple [2]
graf	graph [1]	gras	grass [1]+
graffiti		grase	grace [2]+
grafic	graphic +	grashus	gracious +
graficley	graphically	grasp [1]	
grafite	graphite	grass [1] /es/hopper	
grafiti	graffiti	grasshoper	grasshopper
grafologey	graphology +	grate [2]★ (fire) /r	
grafologist	graphologist	grate	great ★+
graft [1] /er		grateful /ly/ness	
grail		gratif *y* [4] /ication	
grain [1]		gratis	
graling	grayling	gratitude	
gramar	grammar +	gratuitey	gratuity +
gramatical	grammatical +	gratuitous /ly/ness	
gramefone	gramophone	gratuitus	gratuitous +
gramer	grammar +	gratuit *y* /ies	
grammar /ian		grave /ly/yard	
grammatical /ly		gravel [3] /ly	
gramophone		gravie	gravy
granar *y* /ies		gravitashun	gravitation +
grand /ee/eur/stand		gravitate [2]	
grandchild /ren (pl.)		gravitation /al	
grand- *daughter* /-son		gravity	
grand- *father* /-mother		gravy	
grandiloquen *ce* /t		gray	grey +
grandios *e* /ity		grayhound	greyhound
grane	grain [1]	grayhownd	greyhound
grange		grayl	grail
granie	granny +	grayling	
granit	granite	grayn	grain [1]

graz *e* ² /ier		griffin	
greas *e* ² /y		gril	grill ¹⁺
greasie	greasy	grill ¹ /-room	
greasi *er* /est/ly/ness		grim /ly/mer/mest/ness	
great ★ (big) /er/est		grimace ²	
great	grate ²★⁺	grimas	grimace ²
greatful	grateful ⁺	grim *e* ² /ier/iest/iness/y	
grede	greed ⁺	grin ³	
greed /y		grind ¹ /er	
greedi *er* /est/ly/ness		grip ³★ (hold)	
green /er/ery/ness		grip	gripe ²★
green *gage* /grocer		gripe ²★ (colic pain)	
green *horn* /house		grisel	gristle
Greenwich mean time		grisly ★ (ghastly)	
greese	grease ²⁺	grisly	gristly ★
greesie	greasy	grist	
greet ¹		gristle	
gref	grief	gristly ★ (full of gristle)	
gregarious /ly/ness		grisul	gristle
gregarius	gregarious ⁺	grit ³ /tily/ty	
greif	grief	grizul	grizzle ²
greive	grieve ²⁺	grizzle ²	
greivus	grievous	gro	grow ⁺
gremlin		groan ¹★ (moan)	
grenad *e* /ier		groan	grown ★⁺
grene	green ⁺	grocer ★ (shop) /y/ies	
grenegage	greengage ⁺	grocer	grosser ★
grengroser	greengrocer	grogg *ily* /iness/y	
grenich	Greenwich ⁺	groin	
gresier	greasier ⁺	grone	groan ¹★
grete	greet ¹	grone	grown ★⁺
grevance	grievance	groo	grew
grevans	grievance	grooel	gruel ³
greve	grieve ²⁺	groom ¹	
grevus	grievous	groop	group ¹
grew		groosum	gruesome ⁺
grey /er/est/hound		groov *e* ² /y	
grid		grope ²	
griddle ²		gros	gross ¹⁺
gridiron		groser	grocer ★⁺
gridul	griddle ²	groser	grosser ★
grief		groserey	grocery
grievance		gross ¹ /er ★ (fatter) /ly	
grievans	grievance	grotesk	grotesque ⁺
griev *e* ² /ous/ously		grotesque /ly	

groto	grotto +	gufaw	guffaw [1]
grotto /es		guffaw [1]	
ground [1] /less		guid e [2] /ance	
ground -*swell* /work		guild ★ (association)	
group [1]		guild	gild [1]★
grouse [2] /r		guilder	
grove		Guildhall	
grovel [3] /ler		guile /ful/less	
grow /er/ing		guillotine [2]	
growl [1] /er		guilt ★ (law-breaking)	
grown ★† /-up		guilt y /ier/iest/ily	
†(matured)		guinea /-fowl/-pig	
grownd	ground [1]+	guise	
growndswell	ground-swell +	guitar /ist	
growse	grouse [2]+	gul	gull [1]
growth		gulash	goulash
grub [3] /by		gulet	gullet
grubbi er /est/ly/ness		gulf [1]	
grudge [2]		Gulf-stream	
gruel [3]		gulible	gullible +
gruesome /ly/ness		gulibul	gullible +
gruf	gruff +	gulie	gully [4]+
gruff /er/est		gull [1]	
gruge	grudge [2]	gullet	
grumble [2] /r		gullib le /ility	
grumbul	grumble [2]+	gull y [4] /ies	
grumpie	grumpy +	gulp [1]	
grump y /ily/iness		guly	gully [4]+
grunt [1] /er		gum [3] /boil/my/-tree	
grusome	gruesome +	gumption	
grusum	gruesome +	gumshun	gumption
gruyare	gruyère	gun [3] /powder	
gruyère		gunl	gunwale
guano		gunner /y	
guarantee ★ (pledge) /d/ing		gunwale	
guarant or /y ★ (undertaking)		gurgle [2]	
guard [1] /sman		gurgul	gurgle [2]
guardian /ship		gush [1]	
guard-room		gust [1]	
guava		gusto	
guerrilla ★ (war)		gut [3]	
guerrilla	gorilla ★	guter	gutter +
guess /ing/work		guteral	guttural +
guessed ★ (estimated)		gutersnipe	guttersnipe
guest ★ (visitor)		gutter /snipe	

guttural /ly	
guvern	govern [1+]
guvernable	governable
guvernabul	governable
guvernance	governance
guvernans	governance
guverner	governor [+]
guverness	governess
guvernment	government [+]
guvnable	governable
guy [1] /s	
Guy Fawkes	
guzul	guzzle [2+]
guzzle [2] /r	
gwano	guano
gwave	guava
gybe [2]★ (sailing)	
gybe	gibe [2]★
gym /nast/nastics	
gymkana	gymkhana
gymkhana	
gymnasium /s	
gynaecolog y /ist	
gypsum	
gyrat e [2] /ion/ory	
gyro ★ /compass	
gyro	giro ★
gyroscop e /ic	

H

habeas corpus	
haberdasher /y	
habias corpus	habeas corpus
habichual	habitual [+]
habichuate	habituate [2+]
habitab le /ility	
habitabul	habitable [+]
habitashun	habitation
habitat	
habitation	
habitual /ly	
habituat e [2] /ion	
hach	hatch [1+]

hacherey	hatchery [+]
hachet	hatchet
hack [1] /-saw	
hackle [2]	
hackney [1]	
hackul	hackle [2]
had /n't	
haddock	
Hades	
hadock	haddock
haemofilia	haemophilia [+]
haemoglobin	
haemophilia /c	
haemoroids	haemorrhoids
haemorrhage	
haemorrhoids	
haf	half [+]
hafnium	
hafpenie	halfpenny [+]
hafpeny	halfpenny [+]
hafway	half-way
hagerd	haggard
haggard	
haggis	
haggle [2] /r	
hagis	haggis
hagul	haggle [2+]
hai	hay ★[+]
haifever	hay fever
hail [1]★ (salute, icy rain)	
hail	hale ★
hailo	halo ★[+]
hailstone	
hair ★ (on head) /line/y	
hair	hare ★[+]
hair	heir ★
hairbreadth	
hairi er /est/ness	
hair-raising	
hake	
halcion	halcyon
halcyon	
hale ★ (hearty)	
hale	hail [1]★
haleluya	hallelujah

halestone	hailstone	handkerchief /s	
hal f /ves (pl.)		handle ² /bar/r	
half -cast /-hearted		hand-made	
halfpenn y /ies		handriten	handwritten
half-wit /ted		handriting	handwriting +
halibut		handshake	
halilooya	hallelujah	handsome * (looks) /ly	
hall * (room)		handul	handle ²+
hall	haul ¹*+	handwrit ing /ten	
hallelujah		hand y /ier/iest/ily	
hall-mark ¹		hang ¹ /over	
hallo * (cry)		hangar * (shelter)	
hallow ¹* (make holy)		hanger * (for clothes)	
Hallowe'en		hangkerchif	handkerchief +
hallucinat e ² /ion/ory		hangman	
hallucinogen		hank	
halmark	hall-mark ¹	hanker ¹	
halo *(disc of light) /es		hankerchief	handkerchief +
halo	hallow ¹*	hankuf	handcuff ¹
halogens		hansom * (cab)	
halow	hallow ¹*	hansom	handsome *+
Haloween	Hallowe'en	hansum	handsome *+
halsiun	halcyon	hapen	happen ¹
halt ¹ /er/ingly		haphazard /ly/ness	
halusinate	hallucinate ²+	hapie	happy +
halusinogen	hallucinogen	hapier	happier +
halve ²		hapless	
halyard		happen ¹	
halyerd	halyard	happi er /est/ly/ness	
ham /burger		happy /-go-lucky	
hamer	hammer ¹+	hapy	happy +
ham-fisted		hara-kiri	
hamlet		harang	harangue ²
hammer ¹ /er		harangue ²	
hammock		haras	harass ¹+
hamper ¹		harass ¹ /ment	
hamster		harber	harbour ¹+
hamstring ¹		harbour ¹ /age	
hand ¹ /ful/fuls		hard /er/est/ly/ship	
handbag		harden ¹	
handcuff ¹		hard-hearted	
handicap ³		hardie	hardy +
handicraft		hardware	
handie	handy +	hardwear	hardware
handiwork		hard y /ier/iest/ily	

hare ★ (animal) /bell		hash [1]	
hare	hair ★+	hashish	
hare-brained		hasock	hassock
harem		hassock	
harico	haricot	hast e /ily/iness/y	
haricot		hasten [1]	
harier	hairier +	hat [3] /ter	
hark [1]		hatch [1] /es/way	
harlekwin	harlequin +	hatcherey	hatchery +
harlequin /ade		hatcher y /ies	
harlot /ry		hatchet	
harm [1] /ful/fully		hate [2] /ful/r	
harmless /ness		hatred	
harmonic /a/ally		hatrid	hatred
harmonious /ly/ness		haught y /ier/iest/ily	
harmonis e [2] /ation		haul [1]★ (pull in) /age	
harmonium		haul	hall ★
harmonius	harmonious +	haulm	
harmon y /ies		haunch /es	
harness [1] /er		haunt [1]	
harow	harrow [1]	hav	have +
harp [1] /ist		Havana	
harpoon [1] /er		have /n't	
harpsichord		haven	
harpsicord	harpsichord	havent	haven't
harrier		haversack	
harrow [1]		having	
harsh /ly/ness		havoc	
hart ★ (deer)		hawk [1] /er/ish	
hart	heart ★+	hawl	haul [1]★+
hartbrake	heartbreak +	hawlidge	haulage
hartbroken	heartbroken	hawlige	haulage
hartburn	heartburn +	hawm	haulm
harten	hearten [1]	hawnch	haunch +
harth	hearth	hawnet	hornet
hartie	hearty +	hawnpipe	hornpipe
hartless	heartless +	hawnt	haunt [1]
harty	hearty +	hawser	
harum-scarum		hawthorn	
harve	halve [2]	hawticulcher	horticulture +
harvest [1] /er		hawticulture	horticulture +
harvist	harvest [1]+	hawtie	haughty +
hary	hairy	hawtier	haughtier
has /-been/n't		hawty	haughty +
hasen	hasten [1]	hay ★ (grass) /cock	

hay	hey ★	heavyweight	
hay fever		Hebrew	
hayday	heyday	hebroo	Hebrew
hazard¹ /ous		heckle² /r	
haz e /ier/iest/y		heckul	heckle²⁺
hazel		hectic /ally	
hazerd	hazard¹⁺	hecto gram /litre/metre	
hazerdus	hazardous	hed	head¹⁺
hazi ly /ness		hedake	headache
he /'ll ★ (he will)		heddress	head-dress⁺
head¹ /ache/board		heder	header⁺
head -dress /way		hedge² /hog/row	
head er /less/line/y		hedland	headland⁺
head land /long/strong		hedmaster	headmaster⁺
head master /mistress		hedmistriss	headmistress
headquarters		hedonis m /t	
heal ¹★ (to cure) /er		hedquarters	headquarters
heal	heel¹★	heed¹ /ful/less	
health /y		heel¹★ (of foot)	
healthi er /est/ly/ness		heel	heal¹★⁺
heap¹		heep	heap¹
hear ★ (sound) /er/ing		heet	heat¹⁺
hear	here ★	heeth	heath
hearabouts	hereabouts	hefer	heifer
hearafter	hereafter	heftie	hefty⁺
heard ★ (sound)		heft y /ier/iest/ily/iness	
heard	herd¹★⁺	hege	hedge²⁺
hearken¹		heifer	
hearsay		height	
hearse		heighten¹	
heart ★ (body) /broken		heinous /ly/ness	
heartbreak /ing		heinus	heinous⁺
heartburn /ing		heir ★ (inheritance)	
hearten¹		heir ess /loom	
hearth		hel	hell⁺
heartless /ly/ness		held	
heart y /ier/iest/ily		helicks	helix⁺
heat¹ /edly/er/-wave		helicopter	
heath		heliocentric	
heathen /ish		heliograf	heliograph
heather		heliograph	
heave²		heliotrope	
heaven /ly		heliport	
heaviwait	heavyweight	helium	
heav y /ier/iest/ily		heli x /ces (pl.)	

hell /ish		herbivor *e* /ous	
hello /s		herbivorus	herbivorous
helm /sman		herd[1]★ (animals) /sman	
helmet		herd	heard ★
helo	hello[+]	here ★ (this place)	
help[1] /er		here	hear ★[+]
helpful /ly/ness		hereabouts	
helpless /ness		hereafter	
helpmate		here *by* /in/of	
helter-skelter		heredit *ary* /y	
helth	health[+]	hereditey	heredity
helthier	healthier[+]	hereditrey	hereditary[+]
hem[3] /stitch		heresay	hearsay
hemerige	haemorrhage	heresie	heresy[+]
hemeroids	haemorrhoids	heres *y* /ies	
hemisfere	hemisphere[+]	heretic /al	
hemispher *e* /ical		here *to* /upon/with	
hemlock		hering	herring
hemofilia	haemophilia[+]	heritage	
hemoglobin	haemoglobin	herita *nce* /ble	
hemorige	haemorrhage	heritans	heritance[+]
hemp /en		heritige	heritage
hen /pecked		herl	hurl[1]
hena	henna	hermafrodite	hermaphrodite
hence /forth		hermaphrodite	
henceforward		hermetic /ally	
hench *man* /men (pl.)		hermit /age	
henna		hernia	
henrey	henry[+]	hero /es/ic/ically/ism	
henry /s		heroin ★ (drug)	
hens	hence[+]	heroine ★ (fem. hero)	
hensforth	henceforth	heron /ry	
hensforwerd	henceforward	herring	
henus	heinous[+]	herse	hearse
hepatitis		hert	hurt[+]
heptagon /al		hertle	hurtle[2]
her /s/self		hertul	hurtle[2]
herald[1] /ic/ry		hertz	
heraldrey	heraldry	hesian	hessian
herb /age		hesitan *cy* /t	
herbaceous		hesitansey	hesitancy[+]
herbal /ist		hesitat *e*[2] /ion	
herbashus	herbaceous	hessian	
herbicide		heterodoks	heterodox[+]
herbiside	herbicide	hetero *dox* /sexual	

heterogeneous	
heterogenus	heterogeneous
heteroseksual	heterosexual
hethen	heathen +
hether	heather
heve	heave ²
heven	heaven +
hevenly	heavenly
hevie	heavy +
heviwait	heavyweight
heviweight	heavyweight
hevy	heavy +
hew ¹★ (cut) /er/n	
hew	hue ★
hexagon /al	
hexahedr on /al	
hey ★ (call out)	
hey	hay ★+
heyday	

> *If you cannot find your word*
> *under* **hi** *look under* **hy**

hi ★ (call attention)	
hi	high ★+
hiasinth	hyacinth
hiatus /es	
hibernat e ² /ion/or	
hibrid	hybrid
hiccup ¹	
hich	hitch ¹+
hichhike	hitch-hike ²+
hicup	hiccup ¹
hid /den/ing	
hide /bound/-out	
hideous /ly/ness	
hidius	hideous +
hier	higher ★
hier	hire ²★+
hierarch /ical	
hierarch y /ies	
hierark	hierarch +
hierarkey	hierarchy +
hieroglif	hieroglyph +
hieroglyph /ic	
hi-fi	

higgledy-piggledy	
high ★ (tall) /est/ly	
higher ★ (taller)	
higher	hire ²★+
highfaluting	
highland	
highlight ¹	
highness	
highway /man/men (pl.)	
hijack ¹ /er	
hike ² /r	
hil	hill +
hiland	highland
hilari ous /ty	
hilaritey	hilarity
hilarius	hilarious +
hilight	highlight ¹
hilite	highlight ¹
hill /ock	
hill y /ier/iest/iness	
him ★ (he) /self	
him	hymn ★+
hind /sight	
hinder ¹	
hindoo	Hindu +
hindrance	
hindrans	hindrance
hindsite	hindsight
Hindu /ism	
hiness	highness
hinge ²	
hint ¹	
hinterland	
hipie	hippy +
hipodrome	hippodrome
hipopotamus	hippopotamus
hippodrome	
hippopotamus	
hipp y /ies	
hipy	hippy +
hire ²★ (employ) /ling	
hire	higher ★
hiroglif	hieroglyph +
hiss ¹	
histerey	history +

141

histeria	hysteria +	holie	holly *+
histerical	hysterical +	holie	holy *
historian		holi *er* /est/ness	
historic /al/ally		holihock	hollyhock
histor *y* /ies		hollow [1]	
histrey	history +	holly * (tree) /hock	
histrionic /s		holly	holy *
hit /ter/ting		holly	wholly *
hitch [1] /es		holm * (river islet)	
hitch-hike [2] /r		holmium	
hite	height	holocaust	
hither /to		holocorst	holocaust
hive [2]		holow	hollow [1]
hiway	highway +	holster [1]	
ho * (surprise)		holy * (sacred)	
ho	hoe [2]*+	holy	holey *
hoaks	hoax [1]+	holy	holly *+
hoard [1] * (collect) /er		holy	wholly *
hoard	horde [2]*	homage	
hoarse * (voice)		home [2] * /ward/work	
hoarse	horse [2]*	home	holm *
hoarse *ly* /ness/st		home *ly* /less	
hoax [1] /es/er		homesick /ness	
hobble [2]		homicid *e* /al	
hobb *y* /ies		homige	homage
hobie	hobby +	homiley	homily
hobnob [3]		homily	
hobul	hobble [2]	homiopath	homoeopath +
hoby	hobby +	homisidal	homicidal
hochpoch	hotchpotch	homiside	homicide +
hock		homoeopath /ic	
hockey		homogene *ity* /ous	
hockie	hockey	homogenius	homogeneous
hocus-pocus		homonim	homonym +
hoe [2]* (dig) /s *		homonym /ic	
hoes	hose [2]*	homoseksual	homosexual +
hog [3] /gish		homosexual /ity	
hogshead		hone [2]	
hogshed	hogshead	honest /ly/y	
hoist [1]		honey /dew	
hold /-all/er/ing		honeycomb [1]	
hole [2]* (cavity) /y *		honeymoon [1] /er	
hole	whole *	honeysuckle	
holey	wholly *	honie	honey +
holiday /er/ing		honorari *um* /a/ums (pls.)	

honorary
honorific
honour [1] /able/ably
hony   honey +
hood [1]
hoodwink [1]
hoo *f* [1] /fs/ves (pls.)
hook [1] /-up
hooligan /ism
hoop [1]★ (circle)
hoop   whoop [1]★
hooping coff   whooping cough
hoot [1] /er
hoover [1]
hop [3] /per/scotch
hope [2] /ful/fully
hopeless /ness
horde [2]★ (swarm)
horde   hoard [1]★+
hore   whore [2]+
horer   horror
horible   horrible +
horibul   horrible +
horid   horrid +
horific   horrific +
horify   horrify [4]
horizon
horizontal /ly
hormone
horn [1] /beam/y
hornet
hornpipe
horology
horor   horror
horoscope
horribl *e* /y
horribul   horrible +
horrid /ness
horrific /ally
horrify [4]
horror
hors-d'oeuvre
horse [2]★ (animal)
horse   hoarse ★
horse *back* /-chestnut

horsely   hoarsely +
horse *power* /radish
horseshoe /s
horsewhip [3]
horswip   horsewhip [3]
horthorn   hawthorn
horticulcher   horticulture +
horticultur *e* /al/ist
hortie   haughty +
horty   haughty +
hose [2]★ (stockings, water
  down)
hose   hoes ★
hosier /y
hospitabl *e* /y
hospitabul   hospitable +
hospital
hospitalis *e* [2] /ation
hospitality
host [1] /ess (fem.)
hostage
hostel
hostelr *y* /ies
hostige   hostage
hostile /ly
hostilit *y* /ies
hot /ly/-plate/ter/test
hotchpotch
hotel /ier
hoter   hotter
hotest   hottest
hotheaded
hotheded   hotheaded
hound [1]
hour ★ (time) /ly
hour   our ★
house [2] /boat/ful
household /er
house *keeper* /master
housewi *fe* /ves (pl.)
hovel
hover [1] /craft
how /ever
howl [1] /er
hownd   hound [1]

howse	house ²⁺	humock	hummock
howsekeeper	housekeeper ⁺	humorist /ic	
howsewife	housewife ⁺	humorous * (funny)	
howshold	household ⁺	humorous	humerus *
hu	hew ¹*⁺	humour ¹	
hu	hue *	hump ¹ /back	
hubbub		humus	
huch	hutch ⁺	hunch ¹ /back/es	
huddle ²		hundred /fold/th	
hudul	huddle ²	hundredwait	hundredweight
hudwink	hoodwink ¹	hundredweight	
hue * (tint, pursuit)		huney	honey ⁺
hue	hew ¹*⁺	hung	
huf	huff ¹⁺	hunger ¹	
huff ¹ /ily/iness/y		hungrie	hungry
hug ³		hungri er /est/ly/ness	
huge /ly/r/st		hungry	
Hugeno	Huguenot	huni	honey ⁺
Huguenot		hunk	
hul	hull	hunt ¹ /er/ress (fem.)	
hulabaloo	hullabaloo	huntsman	
hulk /ing		hura	hurrah
hull		huray	hurray
hullabaloo		hurd	heard *
hum ³		hurd	herd ¹*⁺
human * (person) /ly		hurdigurdie	hurdy-gurdy
humane * (kindly) /ly		hurdle ²	
humanis e ² /ation		hurdul	hurdle ²
humanis m /t/tic		hurdy-gurdy	
humanitarian /ism		huricane	hurricane
humanit y /ies		hurie	hurry ⁴
humble ² /ness		hurl ¹	
humbly		hurmit	hermit ⁺
humbug ³		hurnia	hernia
humbul	humble ²⁺	hurrah	
humdrum		hurray	
humer	humour ¹	hurricane	
humerist	humorist ⁺	hurry ⁴	
humerus * (bone)		hurse	hearse
humerus	humorous *	hurt /ful/ing	
humid /ity		hurtle ²	
humidif y ⁴ /ier		hurtul	hurtle ²
humiliat e ² /ion		hurtz	hertz
humility		hury	hurry ⁴
hummock		husband ¹ /ry	

husel   hustle ²⁺

hush ¹ /-hush

husie

husk ¹ /ily/iness

huskie

husk y /ies

huss y /ies

hustle ² /r

husul   hustle ²⁺

husy   hussy ⁺

hutch /es

hyacinth

hybrid

hydra

hydrangea

hydranja   hydrangea

hydrant

hydraulic /ally/s

hydrocarbon

hydrochloric

hydro-electric

hydrofobia   hydrophobia

hydrofoil

hydrogen

hydrografey   hydrography

hydrography

hydrokside   hydroxide

hydrolysis

hydromet er /ry

hydropath /ic/y

hydrophobia

hydroplane

hydrostat /ic

hydrotherapy

hydrous

hydroxide

hydrus   hydrous

hyena

hygene   hygiene ⁺

hygien e /ic/ically

hygromet er /ric

hygroscopic

hym   hymn ★⁺

hymen

hymn ★ (song) /al

---

hustle ²⁺

hussy ⁺

husky ⁺

---

hyperbola ★ (curve)

hyperbole ★ (exaggerate)

hyperbolical /ly

hypermarket

hyphenate ²

hypnosis

hypnoti c /sm/st

hypnotise ²

hypochondria /c

hypocris y /ies

hypocrit e /ical

hypodermic

hypotenuse

hypothermia

hypothes is /es (pl.)

hypothetical

hysteri a /cs

hysterical /ly

I

I /'ll ★ (I will)

I   eye ²★⁺

iambic

ice ² /-apron/berg

ice -bucket /-rink

ich   itch ¹⁺

icicle

iclesiastic   ecclesiastic ⁺

iclips   eclipse ²

icliptic   ecliptic

icon

iconomey   economy ⁺

iconomist   economist

icy

idea /s

ideal /ism

idealise ²

identical

identif y ⁴ /ication

identit y /ies

ideological /ly

ideolog y /ies

iderdown   eiderdown

P.O.D.P.S.— K

idilic	idyllic	igwana	iguana
idill	idyll +	ijaculashun	ejaculation
idioc y /ies		ijaculate	ejaculate 2+
idiologey	ideology +	ijaculation	ejaculation
idiological	ideological +	ijecshun	ejection
idiom /atic		iject	eject 1+
idiosincrasy	idiosyncrasy +	ijection	ejection
idiosincratic	idiosyncratic	ikon	icon
idiosyncra sy /tic		ikwip	equip 3+
idiot /ic		ikwivocal	equivocal +
idium	idiom +	ikwivocate	equivocate 2+
idle 2★ (lazy) /ness/r		il	I'll ★
idol ★ (worship)		ilaberate	elaborate 2+
idol	idle 2★+	ilaborashun	elaboration
idolatr y /ous		ilaborate	elaborate 2+
idolise 2		iland	island +
idyl	idyll +	ilapse	elapse 2
idyll /ic		ilash	eyelash +
iface	efface 2+	ilashun	elation
ifect	effect 1	ilastic	elastic +
ifectiv	effective +	ilasticity	elasticity
ifectual	effectual	ilastisitey	elasticity
Ifel	Eiffel	ilate	elate 2+
ifeminate	effeminate +	ilation	elation
ificiency	efficiency +	ile	aisle ★
ificient	efficient +	Ile	I'll ★
ifishensey	efficiency +	ile	isle ★
ifishent	efficient +	ilect	elect 1+
ifrunterey	effrontery +	ilection	election +
igalitarian	egalitarian +	ilectoral	electoral +
igloo		ilectorate	electorate
igneous		ilectrocute	electrocute 2+
ignishun	ignition	ilectron	electron
ignit e 2 /ion		ilectronic	electronic +
ignius	igneous	ilectroplate	electroplate 2
ignoble		ilegal	illegal +
ignominious /ly		ilegalitey	illegality
ignominius	ignominious +	ilegible	illegible +
ignominy		ilegibul	illegible +
ignor	ignore 2	ilegitimacy	illegitimacy +
ignoramus		ilegitimasey	illegitimacy +
ignoran ce /t		ilegitimate	illegitimate
ignorans	ignorance +	ilet	islet ★
ignore 2		ileven	eleven +
iguana		ilicit	elicit 1★

ilikser	elixir	imaciate	emaciate [2+]
iliminashun	elimination	imaculate	immaculate
iliminate	eliminate [2+]	image [2]	
ilimination	elimination	imagin	imagine [2+]
ilips	ellipse	imaginashun	imagination
iliptic	elliptic [+]	imagin e [2] /ation	
iliptical	elliptical	imancipate	emancipate [2+]
ilisit	elicit [1]★	imansipashun	emancipation
iliteracy	illiteracy [+]	imansipate	emancipate [2+]
iliterasey	illiteracy [+]	imansipation	emancipation
iliterat	illiterate	imasculate	emasculate [2+]
ilixir	elixir	imashiate	emaciate [2+]
ill		imaterial	immaterial
illegal /ity		imature	immature [+]
illegib le /ility		imaturitey	immaturity
illegibul	illegible [+]	imbalance	
illegitima cy /te		imbalans	imbalance
illicit ★ (illegal) /ly		imbecil e /ity	
illicit	elicit [1]★	imbesile	imbecile [+]
illitera cy /te		imbibe [2]	
illogical /ity		imbue [2]	
illuminat e [2] /ion		imediacy	immediacy
illusion ★ (false idea)		imediasey	immediacy
illusion	allusion ★	imediate	immediate [+]
illusion	elusion ★	imense	immense [+]
illusive ★ (deceptive)		imensitey	immensity
illusive	allusive ★[+]	imerge	emerge [2+]
illusive	elusive ★[+]	imergence	emergence
illustrat e [2] /ion		imergency	emergency [+]
illustrious		imergens	emergence
ilogical	illogical [+]	imergent	emergent
ilope	elope [2+]	imerse	immerse [2+]
ilucidate	elucidate [2+]	imershun	immersion
ilude	elude [2]★	imersion	immersion
iluminashun	illumination	imesurable	immeasurable [+]
iluminate	illuminate [2+]	imesurabul	immeasurable [+]
ilumination	illumination	imetic	emetic
ilusidate	elucidate [2+]	imige	image [2]
ilusion	illusion ★	imigrant	immigrant
ilusive	elusive ★[+]	imigrashun	immigration
ilusive	illusive ★	imigrate	immigrate [2+]
ilustrate	illustrate [2+]	imigration	immigration
ilustration	illustration	iminent	imminent ★[+]
ilustrius	illustrious	imishun	emission
I'm (I am)		imission	emission

imit — emit [3+]
imitat *e* [2] /ion
immaculate
immaterial
immatur *e* /ity
immeasurabl *e* /y
immediacy
immediasey — immediacy
immediate /ly
immens *e* /ely/ity
immers *e* [2] /ion
immigrant
immigrat *e* [2] /ion
imminent *† /ly
  †(about to happen)
imminent — eminent *
immobil *e* /ity
immobilis *e* [2] /ation
immoderate /ly
immodest /ly/y
immoral /ity/ly
immortal /ity/ly
immortalis *e* [2] /ation
immovabl *e* /y
immun *e* /ity
immunis *e* [2] /ation
immunology
imobile — immobile +
imoderate — immoderate +
imodest — immodest +
imodestey — immodesty
imolient — emollient
imolument — emolument
imoral — immoral +
imoralitey — immorality
imortal — immortal +
imortalise — immortalise [2+]
imortalitey — immortality
imoshun — emotion +
imoshunal — emotional
imotion — emotion +
imotional — emotional
imotiv — emotive
imovable — immovable +
imovabul — immovable +

imp /ish/ishness
impact [1] /ion
impair [1] /ment
impalpabl *e* /y
imparshal — impartial +
imparshialitey — impartiality
impart [1]
impartial /ity/ly
impas — impasse
impasabul — impassable
impashence — impatience
impashens — impatience
impashent — impatient +
impashund — impassioned
impasioned — impassioned
impasiv — impassive +
impassable
impasse
impassioned
impassive /ness
impassivity
impatience
impatient /ly
impeach [1] /able/ment
impecabul — impeccable +
impeccabl *e* /y
impecunio *us* /sity
impecunius — impecunious +
impede [2]
impediment /a
impeech — impeach [1+]
impel [3] /ler
impend [1]
impenetrab *le* /ility
impeniten *ce* /t
impenitens — impenitence +
imperative /ly/ness
imperceptibl *e* /y
imperfect /ion
imperial /ism/ly
imperialist /ic
imperil [3] /ment
imperious /ly/ness
imperishable
imperius — imperious +

impermeable		imposter	impostor
impermiabul	impermeable	impostor	
imperseptible	imperceptible +	imposture	
imperseptibul	imperceptible +	impoten *ce* /t	
impersonal /ly		impotens	impotence +
impersonat *e* ² /ion/or		impound ¹	
imperterbable	imperturbable	impoverish ¹ /ment	
impertinen *ce* /t		impownd	impound ¹
impertinens	impertinence +	impracticab *le* /ility	
imperturbab *le* /ility		impracticabul	impracticable +
impervious /ly/ness		imprecat *e* ² /ion	
impervius	impervious +	imprecise /ly	
impetuosity		impregnab *le* /ility	
impetuous /ly/ness		impregnat *e* ² /ion	
impetus /es		impres	impress ¹+
impetuus	impetuous +	impresario /s	
impiety		impreshun	impression +
impinge ² /ment		impreshunism	impressionism +
impious /ly		impresible	impressible
impius	impious +	impresibul	impressible
implacabl *e* /y		impresionism	impressionism +
implacabul	implacable +	impresionist	impressionist
implant ¹ /ation		impresise	imprecise +
implement ¹ /ation		impresiv	impressive +
impli	imply ⁴+	impress ¹ /ible	
implicat *e* ² /ion		impression /able	
implicit /ly/ness		impressionis *m* /t/tic	
implisit	implicit +	impressive /ly/ness	
implore ²		imprint ¹	
impl *y* ⁴ /ication		imprison ¹ /ment	
impolite /ly/ness		improbab *le* /ility/ly	
impolitic		improbabul	improbable +
imponderable /s		impromptu	
impondrabul	imponderable +	impromtoo	impromptu
import ¹ /able/ation		improper /ly	
importan *ce* /t/tly		impropriet *y* /ies	
importans	importance +	improve ² /ment	
importunate /ly		improviden *ce* /t/tly	
importun *e* ² /ity		improvidens	improvidence +
imposcher	imposture	improvis *e* ² /ation	
impos *e* ² /able/ition		impruden *ce* /t/tly	
imposible	impossible +	imprudens	imprudence +
imposibul	impossible +	impruve	improve ²+
imposishun	imposition	impuden *ce* /t/tly	
impossib *le* /ility/ly		impudens	impudence +

impugn [1]		inapplicabul	inapplicable +
impuls e /ion/ive/ively		inappropriate /ly	
impune	impugn [1]	inapropriat	inappropriate +
impunity		inaptitude	
impure /ly		inarticulate /ly	
impurit y /ies		inasmuch	
imput e [2] /able/ation		inate	innate +
imulshun	emulsion	inatenshun	inattention +
imulsion	emulsion	inatention	inattention +
imune	immune +	inatentiv	inattentive
imunise	immunise [2]+	inattent ion /ive	
imunitey	immunity	inaudib le /ility	
imunologey	immunology	inaugural	
imurge	emerge [2]+	inaugurat e [2] /ion/ive	
in * (on inside)		inauspicious /ly	
in	inn *+	inawmus	enormous +
inability		inawspicious	inauspicious +
inaccessib le /ility		inawspishus	inauspicious +
inaccurac y /ies		inborn	
inaccurate /ly		inbred	
inacsesible	inaccessible +	inbreeding	
inacsesibul	inaccessible +	incalculab le /ility	
inacshun	inaction	incandescen ce /t	
inaction		incandesence	incandescence +
inactive /ly		incant [1] /ation	
inactivit y /ies		incapab le /ility/ly	
inacuracy	inaccuracy +	incapabul	incapable +
inacurasey	inaccuracy +	incapacitat e [2] /ion	
inacurate	inaccurate +	incapacity	
inadekwacy	inadequacy +	incapasitate	incapacitate [2]+
inadekwasey	inadequacy +	incapasitey	incapacity
inadekwat	inadequate +	incarcerat e [2] /ion	
inadequac y /ies		incarnat e [2] /ion	
inadequate /ly		incarserate	incarcerate [2]+
inadmisibul	inadmissible +	incendiar y /ies	
inadmissib le /ility		incense [2]	
inadverten ce /t		incentive	
inadvertens	inadvertence +	incept ion /ive	
inalienab le /ility		incertitude	
inalienabul	inalienable +	incessant /ly	
inane /ly		incest /uous	
inanimate		inch [1] /es	
inanit y /ies		incidence * (bearing)	
inaplicable	inapplicable +	incident /al/ally	
inapplicabl e /y		incidents * (events)	

incinerat *e* ² /ion/or
incipient
incis *e* ² /ion
incisive /ly/ness
incisor
incite ²★ (stir up)
incite   insight ★
incivilit *y* /ies
inclemen *cy* /t
inclemensey   inclemency ⁺
inclin *e* ² /ation
inclose   enclose ²⁺
inclu *de* ² /sion
inclusive /ly
incognito
incoheren *ce* /t
incoherens   incoherence ⁺
incombustible
income /tax
incomensurat   incommensurate
incoming
incommensurate
incommod *e* ² /ious
incommunicado
incomparabl *e* /y
incompatib *le* /ility
incompatibul   incompatible ⁺
incompeten *ce* /t/tly
incompetens   incompetence ⁺
incomplete
incomprehensible
incomunicado   incommunicado
inconceivabl *e* /y
inconclusive /ly
incongru *ent* /ous
incongruit *y* /ies
incongruus   incongruous
inconseavable   inconceivable ⁺
inconsiderable
inconsiderate /ly
inconsistenc *y* /ies
inconsistensey   inconsistency ⁺
inconsistent /ly
inconsolable
inconsolabul   inconsolable

inconspicuous /ly
inconstan *cy* /t
incontestabl *e* /y
incontestabul   incontestable ⁺
incontinen *ce* /t
incontinens   incontinence ⁺
incontrovertibl *e* /y
inconvenien *ce* ² /t
inconveniens   inconvenience ²⁺
incorect   incorrect ⁺
incorigible   incorrigible ⁺
incorigibul   incorrigible ⁺
incorporat *e* ² /ion/or
incorrect /ly
incorrigib *le* /ility
incorruptib *le* /ility
increase ²
incredibl *e* /y
incredibul   incredible ⁺
incredul *ity* /ous
incredulus   incredulous
increment /al
increse   increase ²
incriminat *e* ² /ion
incrust   encrust ¹
incubat *e* ² /ion/or
inculcat *e* ² /ion
inculpat *e* ² /ion
incum   income ⁺
incumbenc *y* /ies
incumbensey   incumbency ⁺
incumbent
incur ³
incurab *le* /ility/ly
incurabul   incurable ⁺
incurshun   incursion ⁺
incurs *ion* /ive
indebted /ness
indecenc *y* /ies
indecensey   indecency ⁺
indecent /ly
indecipherable
indecishun   indecision
indecision
indecisive /ly

151

indecorous /ness
indecorum
indecorus — indecorous [+]
indeed
indefatigabl e /y
indefatigabul — indefatigable [+]
indefensibl e /y
indefensibul — indefensible [+]
indefinable
indefinabul — indefinable
indefinite /ly
indeks — index [1+]
indelibl e /y
indelibul — indelible [+]
indelicac y /ies
indelicasey — indelicacy [+]
indelicate /ly
indemnifi — indemnify [4+]
indemnif y [4] /ication
indemnit y /ies
indencher — indenture
indent [1] /ation/ure
independen ce /t
independens — independence [+]
indescribabl e /y
indescribabul — indescribable [+]
indesency — indecency [+]
indesensey — indecency [+]
indesent — indecent [+]
indesiferable — indecipherable
indestructib le /ility
indestructibul — indestructible [+]
indeted — indebted [+]
indeterminate /ly
ind ex [1] /exes/ices (pls.)
Indian
indicat e [2] /ion/ive/or
indict [1]*(accuse)/ment
indiference — indifference [+]
indiferens — indifference [+]
indiferent — indifferent
indifferen ce /t
indigen ce /t
indigenous
indigens — indigence [+]

indigenus — indigenous
indigeschun — indigestion [+]
indigestibl e /y
indigestibul — indigestible [+]
indigest ion /ive
indignant /ly
indignashun — indignation
indignation
indignit y /ies
indigo
indipendence — independence [+]
indipendens — independence [+]
indipendent — independent
indirect /ly
indiscre et /tion
indiscreshun — indiscretion
indiscriminate
indisishun — indecision
indisision — indecision
indisisiv — indecisive [+]
indispensabl e /y
indispensabul — indispensable [+]
indispos e [2] /ition
indisputabl e /y
indisputabul — indisputable [+]
indistinct
indistinguishable
indite [2]* (compose)
indite — indict [1]*[+]
indium
individual /ity/ly
individualis m /t
indivisibl e /y
indivisibul — indivisible [+]
indoctrinat e [2] /ion
indolen ce /t/tly
indolens — indolence [+]
indomitabl e /y
indomitabul — indomitable [+]
indoor /s
indubitabl e /y
indubitabul — indubitable [+]
induce [2] /ment
inducshun — induction [+]
inductance

inductans	inductance	inequity ★ (injustice)	
induct *ion* /ive/ively		inequity	iniquity ★
indulge ² /nce/nt		iner	inner +
indulgens	indulgence	ineradicabl *e* /y	
induse	induce ²+	ineradicabul	ineradicable +
industrey	industry +	inersha	inertia
industrial /ism/ist/ly		inert /ia/ly/ness	
industrialis *e* ² /ation		inescapabl *e* /y	
industrious /ly		inescapabul	inescapable +
industrius	industrious +	inesenshal	inessential
industr *y* /ies		inesential	inessential
inebriat *e* ² /ion		inessential	
inedib *le* /ility		inestimabl *e* /y	
inedibul	inedible +	inestimabul	inestimable +
inefectiv	ineffective +	inestinium	einsteinium
inefectual	ineffectual +	inevitability	
ineffective /ly/ness		inevitabl *e* /y	
ineffectual /ly		inevitabul	inevitable +
inefficienc *y* /ies		inexact /itude	
inefficient /ly		inexcusabl *e* /y	
ineficiency	inefficiency +	inexhaustibl *e* /y	
ineficient	inefficient +	inexorabl *e* /y	
inefishensey	inefficiency +	inexpedient /ly	
inefishent	inefficient +	inexpensive /ly	
inegsact	inexact +	inexperience /d	
inegsactitude	inexactitude	inexperiens	inexperience +
inegsawstible	inexhaustible +	inexplicabl *e* /y	
inekscusable	inexcusable +	inexpressibl *e* /y	
inekserable	inexorable +	inextinguishable	
inekspedient	inexpedient +	inextingwishabul	inextinguishable
inekspensive	inexpensive +	inextricabl *e* /y	
ineksperience	inexperience +	infalible	infallible +
ineksplicable	inexplicable +	infalibul	infallible +
inekspresible	inexpressible +	infallib *le* /ility/ly	
inekstricable	inextricable +	infamey	infamy
inekwitable	inequitable +	infamous /ly	
inekwity	inequity ★	infamus	infamous +
inelegan *ce* /cy/t		infamy	
inelegens	inelegance +	infancy	
ineligib *le* /ility		infansey	infancy
ineligibul	ineligible +	infant /icide/ile	
inept /itude/ly		infantrey	infantry +
inequalit *y* /ies		infantr *y* /ies	
inequitabl *e* /y		infatuat *e* ² /ion	
inequitabul	inequitable +	infecshun	infection

infecshus	infectious +	influx	
infect¹ /ion		inform¹ /ative/er	
infectious /ness		informal /ity/ly	
infer³ /ence		informant	
inferens	inference	informashun	information
inferier	inferior +	information	
inferior /ity		infracshun	infraction
inferm	infirm	infraction	
infermarey	infirmary +	infra-red	
infermitey	infirmity +	infrastructure	
infernal /ly		infrekwency	infrequency +
inferno /s		infrekwent	infrequent
infertil e /ity		infrequen cy /t/tly	
infest¹ /ant/ation		infringe² /ment	
infidel		infuriate²	
infidelit y /ies		infus e² /er/ion	
infiltrat e² /ion/or		ingenious /ly	
infinite /ly		ingenius	ingenious +
infinitesimal /ly		ingenuity	
infinitey	infinity +	ingenuous /ly/ness	
infinitive		ingenuus	ingenuous +
infinit y /ies		ingle-nook	
infirm		Inglish	English +
infirmar y /ies		inglorious /ly	
infirmit y /ies		inglorius	inglorious +
inflamable	inflammable +	ingot	
inflamabul	inflammable +	ingrained	
inflamashun	inflammation	ingrashiate	ingratiate²
inflamatrey	inflammatory	ingratiate²	
inflame²		ingratitude	
inflamma ble /tion		ingredient	
inflammatory		ingrowing	
inflashun	inflation +	ingulnook	ingle-nook
inflat e² /able		inhabit¹ /able/ant	
inflation /ary		inhal e² /ant/ation	
inflect¹ /ion		inherent /ly	
inflexib le /ility		inherit¹ /ance/or	
inflict¹ /ion		inheritans	inheritance
inflooenza	influenza	inhibishun	inhibition
influence²		inhibit¹ /ion/or/ory	
influens	influence²	inhospitabl e /y	
influenshal	influential +	inhospitabul	inhospitable +
influential /ly		inhuman /ity/ly	
influenza		inikwalitey	inequality +
influks	influx	inikwitey	iniquity ★

inikwitous	iniquitous
inikwitus	iniquitous
inimical	
inimitabl e /y	
inimitabul	inimitable +
inings	innings
iniquitey	iniquity *
iniquitous	
iniquitus	iniquitous
iniquity * (badness)	
iniquity	inequity *
inishal	initial 3+
inishativ	initiative
inishiashun	initiation
inishiate	initiate 2+
inishiation	initiation
initial 3 /ly	
initiat e 2 /ion/ive	
inject 1 /ion/or	
injer	injure 2+
injunction	
injunkshun	injunction
injur e 2 /ious	
injurey	injury +
injurius	injurious
injur y /ies	
injustice	
injustis	injustice

> If you cannot find your word
> under **ink** look under **inc**

ink 1 /-pot/-well	
inkalculable	incalculable +
inkeeper	innkeeper
inkling	
inkrement	increment +
inkwest	inquest
inkwire	enquire 2+
inkwisitiv	inquisitive +
inkwisitor	inquisitor
inlade	inlaid
inland	
in-law	
inla y /id	
inlet	

inmate	
inmost	
inn * (tavern) /keeper	
innate /ly	
inner /most	
innings	
innocen ce /t/tly	
innocuous /ly	
innovat e 2 /ion/ive	
innuendo /es	
innumerabl e /y	

inocence	innocence +
inocens	innocence +
inocent	innocent
inoculat e 2 /ion	
inocuous	innocuous +
inocuus	innocuous +
inofensiv	inoffensive +
inoffensive /ly/ness	
inoperative /ness	
inoportune	inopportune +
inopportune /ly	
inordible	inaudible +
inordinate /ly	
inorganic	
inorgural	inaugural
inorgurate	inaugurate 2+
inormitey	enormity +
inormous	enormous +
inormus	enormous +
inorspicious	inauspicious +
inorspishus	inauspicious +
inosent	innocent
inough	enough
inovashun	innovation
inovate	innovate 2+
inovation	innovation
inovativ	innovative
input	
inquest	
inquisitive /ly/ness	
inquisitor	
inroad	
inrode	inroad
insan e /ely/ity	

155

insanitar *y* /iness		insidius	insidious +
insanitey	insanity	insight ★ (keen	
insanitrey	insanitary +	understanding)	
insashable	insatiable +	insight	incite ²★+
insashabul	insatiable +	insignia	
insatiabl *e* /y		insignifican *ce* /t/tly	
inscribe ²		insincere /ly	
inscripshun	inscription	insincerity	
inscription		insinerate	incinerate ²+
inscrutab *le* /ility		insinerater	incinerator
insect /icide		insinsere	insincere +
insectiside	insecticide	insinseritey	insincerity
insecure /ly		insinuat *e* ² /ion/or	
insecurity		insipid /ly/ness	
inseminat *e* ² /ion		insipient	incipient
insendiarey	incendiary +	insiser	incisor
insense	incense ²	insishun	incision
insensib *le* /ility/ly		insision	incision
insensibul	insensible +	insisiv	incisive +
insensitive /ly		insist ¹ /ence/ent/ently	
insensitivity		insite	incite ²★
insentiv	incentive	insite	insight ★
inseparabl *e* /y		insivilitey	incivility +
inseprabul	inseparable +	insolen *ce* /t/tly	
insepshun	inception +	insolens	insolence +
inseption	inception +	insolub *le* /ility/ly	
insermountable	insurmountable +	insolubul	insoluble +
insert ¹ /ion		insolven *ce* /cy/t	
insertitude	incertitude	insolvens	insolvence +
insesant	incessant +	insomnia /c	
insest	incest +	insomuch	
insestuous	incestuous	inspecshun	inspection
insestuus	incestuous	inspect ¹ /ion	
inset ³		inspecter	inspector +
inshorance	insurance	inspector /ate	
inshorans	insurance	inspir *e* ² /ation	
inshore	ensure ²★	instability	
inshore	insure ²★+	instal	install ¹+
inside /r		install ¹ /ation	
insidence	incidence ★	instalment	
insidens	incidence ★	instance ²	
insidens	incidents ★	instans	instance ²
insident	incident +	instant /ly	
insidental	incidental	instantaneous /ly	
insidious /ly/ness		instantanius	instantaneous +

instead		intangibl *e* /y	
insted	instead	intangibul	intangible +
instep		integer	
instigat *e* ² /ion/or		integral /ly	
instigater	instigator	integrashun	integration
instill ¹		integrat *e* ² /ion/or	
instinct /ive/ively		integrity	
institushun	institution +	intelect	intellect
institut *e* ² /or		intelectual	intellectual +
institution /al		inteligence	intelligence +
institutionalis *e* ² /m		inteligens	intelligence +
instrement	instrument +	inteligensia	intelligentsia
instruct ¹ /ion/ive/or		inteligent	intelligent +
instrument /ation		inteligible	intelligible +
instrumental /ist		intellect	
insubordinashun	insubordination	intellectual / ly	
insubordinat *e*/ely/ion		intelligen *ce* /tsia	
insufferabl *e* /y		intelligent /ly	
insufficien *cy* /t/tly		intelligibl *e* /y	
insuficiency	insufficiency +	intelligibul	intelligible +
insuficient	insufficient	intemperance	
insufishensey	insufficiency +	intemperans	intemperance
insufishent	insufficient	intemperate /ly	
insufrable	insufferable +	intend ¹	
insular /ity		intense /ly	
insulat *e* ² /ion/or		intenshun	intention +
insulin		intensif *y* ⁴ /ication	
insult ¹		intensit *y* /ies	
insuperabl *e* /y		intensive /ly/ness	
insuprabul	insuperable +	intent	
insurance		intention /al/ally	
insurans	insurance	inter ³ /ment	
insure ²★(insurance)/r		interbred	
insure	ensure ²★	interbreeding	
insurecshun	insurrection	intercede ²	
insurection	insurrection	intercept ¹ /ion/or	
insurgen *ce* /t		interceshun	intercession +
insurgens	insurgence +	intercess *ion* /or	
insurmountabl *e* /y		interchange ² /able	
insurrection		interconnect ¹ /ion	
insurshun	insertion	intercorse	intercourse
insurt	insert ¹+	intercourse	
insurtion	insertion	interelate	interrelate ²
intact		interest ¹	
intake		interfere ² /nce	

interier	interior	intervenshun	intervention
interim		interview [1]	
interior		intervue	interview [1]
interject [1] /ion		interweav e /ing	
interlock [1]		interwoven	
interloper		intestin e /al	
interlude		intiger	integer
intermarie	intermarry [4]	intigral	integral +
intermarry [4]		intigrashun	integration
intermediar y /ies		intigrate	integrate [2]+
intermediate		intigration	integration
interment		intijer	integer
interminable		intimacy	
interminabul	interminable	intimasey	intimacy
intermingle [2]		intimate /ly	
intermingul	intermingle [2]	intimidashun	intimidation
intermishun	intermission	intimidat e [2] /ion	
intermission		intoksicant	intoxicant
intermittent		intoksicate	intoxicate [2]+
intern [1] /ment		intolerabl e /y	
internal		intoleran ce /t	
internashunal	international +	intolerans	intolerance +
international /ly		intolrabul	intolerable +
internecine		intonashun	intonation
internisine	internecine	intonation	
interogashun	interrogation	intoxicant	
interogate	interrogate [2]+	intoxicat e [2] /ion	
interogation	interrogation	intractable	
interplanetary		intractabul	intractable
Interpol		intramuscular	
interpolat e [2] /ion		intransigen ce /t	
interpret [1] /ation		intransigens	intransigence +
interrelate [2]		intransitive	
interrogat e [2] /ion/or		intreeg	intrigue [2]+
interrupt [1] /ion		intrepid /ly	
intersect [1] /ion		intricac y /ies	
interseed	intercede [2]	intricasey	intricacy +
intersepshun	interception	intricate /ly	
intersept	intercept [1]+	intrigue [2] /r	
intersepter	interceptor	intrinsic /ally	
interseshun	intercession +	introduc e [2]	
interupshun	interruption	introducshun	introduction +
interuption	interruption	introduct ion /ory	
interval		introduse	introduce [2]
interven e [2] /tion		introod	intrude [2]+

introoshun	intrusion +	invenshun	invention
introosion	intrusion +	invent¹ /ion/or	
introosiv	intrusive	inventer	inventor
introspect¹ /ion /ive		inventive /ness	
introver t¹ /sion		inventor y /ies	
intrude² /r		inventrey	inventory +
intrushun	intrusion +	invers e /ion	
intrus ion /ive		invershun	inversion
intuishun	intuition	invert¹ /er	
intuition		invertebrate	
intuitive /ly		invest¹ /ment	
inturn	intern ¹+	investicher	investiture
inturnal	internal	investigashun	investigation
inuendo	innuendo +	investigat e² /ion	
inuf	enough	investiture	
inumerable	innumerable +	inveterate	
inumerashun	enumeration	invidious /ly	
inumerate	enumerate ²+	invidius	invidious +
inumerater	enumerator	invigilat e² /ion/or	
inumeration	enumeration	invigilater	invigilator
inumrabul	innumerable +	invigorat e² /ion	
inunciashun	enunciation	invincibl e /y	
inunciate	enunciate ²+	invinsible	invincible +
inunciation	enunciation	inviolate	
inundat e² /ion		invisib le /ility/ly	
inunsiate	enunciate ²+	invisibul	invisible +
inure²		invitashun	invitation
inursha	inertia	invit e² /ation	
inurt	inert +	invoice²	
invade² /r		invois	invoice²
invalid /ity		invoke²	
invalidate²		involuntar y /ily	
invaluable		involuntrey	involuntary +
invaluble	invaluable	involve² /ment	
invalubul	invaluable	invulnerab le /ility	
invariabl e /y		invulnerabul	invulnerable +
invariabul	invariable +	invurs	inverse +
invashun	invasion	invurt	invert ¹+
invasion		invurtebrate	invertebrate
invay	inveigh¹	inward /ly/ness/s	
invaygul	inveigle²	inwud	inward +
invective		iodene	iodine
inveigh¹		iodine	
inveigle²		iodise²	
inveigul	inveigle²	ion /ic	

159

ionis *e*² /ation		ireverence	irreverence +
ionosfere	ionosphere	ireverens	irreverence +
ionosphere		ireverent	irreverent
iota		ireversible	irreversible +
ira	era +	irevocable	irrevocable +
iradiate	irradiate ²+	irevocabul	irrevocable +
iradicate	eradicate ²+	irideemable	irredeemable +
irascib *le* /ility		irideemabul	irredeemable +
irascibul	irascible +	iridium	
irase	erase ²+	irigashun	irrigation
irasher	erasure	irigate	irrigate ²+
irashonal	irrational +	irigation	irrigation
irasible	irascible +	iris	
irate		Irish	
irational	irrational +	irisistible	irresistible +
ire		irisistibul	irresistible +
ireclaimable	irreclaimable	iritable	irritable +
ireconcilable	irreconcilable +	iritant	irritant
ireconcilabul	irreconcilable +	iritashun	irritation
irecoverable	irrecoverable +	iritate	irritate ²+
irect	erect ¹+	iritation	irritation
irecuvrable	irrecoverable +	iriversible	irreversible +
irefutable	irrefutable +	irk ¹ /some	
iregular	irregular +	irode	erode ²
iregularitey	irregularity +	iron ¹ /monger	
ireguler	irregular +	ironeous	erroneous +
irelegious	irreligious	ironey	irony +
irelevance	irrelevance +	ironic /al/ally	
irelevans	irrelevance +	ironie	irony +
irelevansey	irrelevancy +	ironius	erroneous +
irelevant	irrelevant	iron *y* /ies	
ireligus	irreligious	iroshun	erosion
iremediable	irremediable +	irosion	erosion
iremediabul	irremediable +	irotic	erotic +
iremovable	irremovable +	irradiat *e*² /ion	
iremovabul	irremovable +	irrational /ly	
ireplacable	irreplaceable	irreclaimable	
ireplasable	irreplaceable	irreclaimabul	irreclaimable
ireprable	irreparable	irreconcilabl *e* /y	
ireprabul	irreparable	irreconcilabul	irreconcilable +
irepressible	irrepressible	irrecoverabl *e* /y	
iresolute	irresolute +	irrecoverabul	irrecoverable +
irespectiv	irrespective +	irredeemabl *e* /y	
iresponsible	irresponsible +	irredeemabul	irredeemable +
iresponsibul	irresponsible +	irrefutabl *e* /y	

irrefutabul	irrefutable +	ishuans	issuance
irregular /ly		ishue	issue 2+
irregularit y /ies		isicle	icicle
irrelevan ce /t		isight	eyesight
irrelevanc y /ies		isinglass	
irrelevansey	irrelevancy +	isite	eyesight
irreligious		islànd /er	
irreligus	irreligious	isle ★ (island)	
		isle	aisle ★
irremediabl e /y		islet ★ (small island)	
irremediabul	irremediable +	islet	eyelet ★
irremovabl e /y		isn't (is not)	
irremovabul	irremovable +	isnt	isn't
irreparable		isobar	
irreplacabul	irreplaceable	isolashun	isolation +
irreplaceable		isolate 2	
irreprabul	irreparable	isolation /ist	
irrepresibul	irrepressible	isometric /ally	
irrepressible		isosceles	
irresistibl e /y		isosilese	isosceles
irresolute /ly/ness		isotherm	
irrespective /ly		isotope	
irresponsibility		Israeli	
irresponsibl e /y		Isralie	Israeli
irresponsibul	irresponsible +	issuans	issuance
irretrievabl e /y		issu e 2 /ance	
irretrievabul	irretrievable +	isthmus	
irreveren ce /t/tly		Italian	
irreverens	irreverence +	italic /s	
irreversibl e /y		italicise 2	
irreversibul	irreversible +	italisize	italicise 2
irrevocabl e /y		Italyun	Italian
irrevocabul	irrevocable +	itch 1 /y	
irrigat e 2 /ion/or		item	
irrisistable	irresistible +	itemise 2	
irritab le /ility/ly		iternal	eternal +
irritabul	irritable +	iternally	eternally
irritant		iternitey	eternity +
irritashun	irritation	ither	either
irritat e 2 /ion		itinerant	
irrupt 1 /ion/ive		itinerar y /ies	
irrupshun	irruption	itinerey	itinerary +
irupt	irrupt 1+	it's ★ (it is)	
iruption	irruption	its ★ (possessive)	
ise	ice 2+	iun	iron 1+
ishuance	issuance		

iunmunger	ironmonger	jackdaw	
ivacuashun	evacuation	jackdoor	jackdaw
ivacuate	evacuate ² +	jacket ¹	
ivacuation	evacuation	jack-kni *fe* ² /ves (pl.)	
ivacuee	evacuee	Jacobean	
ivade	evade ² +	Jacobi *n* /te	
ivaluashun	evaluation	jade ²	
ivaluate	evaluate ² +	jaffa	
ivaluation	evaluation	jaffer	jaffa
ivangelise	evangelise ² +	jag ³	
ivangelist	evangelist	jaguar	
ivaperator	evaporator	jail ¹ /bird/er	
ivaporashun	evaporation	jam ³★ (preserve) /my	
ivaporate	evaporate ² +	jamb ★ (side post)	
ivaporation	evaporation	jamboree	
ivashun	evasion	jambori	jamboree
ivasion	evasion	jangle ²	
ivasiv	evasive +	jangul	jangle ²
I've (I have)		janiter	janitor
Ive	I've	janitor	
ivent	event +	January	
iventful	eventful	Janurey	January
iventual	eventual +	Japanese	
iventualitey	eventuality +	jar ³	
ivicshun	eviction	jargon	
ivict	evict ¹ +	jasmin	jasmine
iviction	eviction	jasmine	
ivie	ivy	jasper	
ivocashun	evocation +	jaundice ²	
ivocation	evocation +	jaundis	jaundice ²
ivocativ	evocative	jaunt ¹ /ily/iness/y	
ivoke	evoke ²	jauntie	jaunty
ivolve	evolve ²	javelin	
ivory		jaw /bone	
ivry	ivory	jawndice	jaundice ²
ivy		jawndis	jaundice ²
		jawnt	jaunt ¹ +
		jawntey	jaunty
		jay /-walker	

J

jab ³		jaz	jazz ¹ +
jabber ¹ /er		jazz ¹ /y	
jabot		jealous /ly/y	
jack ¹ /boot/pot		jeans	
jackal		jeep	
jackass /es		jeer ¹	

Jehovah		jingo /es/ism	
jelie	jelly +	jingul	jingle ²
jell y /ies		jirashun	gyration
jelous	jealous +	jirate	gyrate ²+
jelus	jealous +	jiration	gyration
jely	jelly +	jiro	giro ★
jemie	jemmy +	jiro	gyro ★+
jemm y /ies		jiroscope	gyroscope +
jemy	jemmy +	jist	gist
jenes	jeans	jiter	jitter ²+
jeopard ise ² /y		jitter ² /y	
jepadise	jeopardise ²+	jive ²	
jepardy	jeopardy	job ³ /less	
jeribilt	jerry-built	jockey ¹ /s	
jerie	jerry +	jockie	jockey ¹+
jerk ¹ /ily/iness/y		jocky	jockey ¹+
jerkin		jocose /ly	
jerry /-building/-built		jocular /ity/ly	
jersey /s		jocund /ity	
jersie	jersey +	jodhpurs	
jersy	jersey +	jodpers	jodhpurs
jery	jerry +	jodpurs	jodhpurs
jest ¹ /er		jog ³	
jet ³ /-propelled		joggle ²	
jetie	jetty +	jogul	joggle ²
jetison	jettison ¹	joi	joy +
jetsam		joiful	joyful
jettison ¹		join ¹ /er/ery	
jett y /ies		joint ¹ /er/ly	
jety	jetty +	joiride	joy-ride +
Jew /ish/ry		joist ¹	
jewel ³★ (gem)		joius	joyous +
jewel	duel ³★	jok e ² /er/ingly	
jewel	joule ★	joll y ⁴ /ier/iest/ily/ity	
jeweler	jeweller +	jolt ¹ /y	
jeweller /y		joly	jolly ⁴+
jewelrey	jewellery	jonkwil	jonquil
jib ³		jonquil	
jiffy		Joo	Jew +
jifie	jiffy	Jooish	Jewish
jify	jiffy	jool	joule ★
jig ³ /saw		joon	June
jilt ¹		joopiter	Jupiter
jim	gym +	joos	juice +
jingle ²		joosey	juicy

joot	jute	jugle	juggle ²⁺
jostle ²		jugular ★ (vein)	
josul	jostle ²	juic *e* /ier/iest/ily/y	
jot ³		Juish	Jewish
joule ★ (unit of energy)		jujoob	jujube
joule	duel ³★	jujube	
joule	jewel ³★	juke-box	
journal /ism/ist		jukstapose	juxtapose ²⁺
journey ¹ /s		jukstaposition	juxtaposition
jovial /ity/ly		Juli	July
jowl		July	
joy /ful/fully		jumble ²	
joyous /ly		jumbo	
joy-rid *e* /ing		jumbul	jumble ²
joyus	joyous ⁺	jump ¹ /er/iness/y	
ju	Jew ⁺	junkcher	juncture
jubilant /ly		junction	
jubilashun	jubilation	juncture	
jubilation		June	
jubilee		jungle	
jubili	jubilee	jungul	jungle
juce	juice ⁺	junier	junior
jucy	juicy	junior	
Judas		juniper	
judder ¹		junk	
judge ² /ment		junket ¹	
judicacher	judicature	junta	
judicature		Jupiter	
judicial /ly		jurer	juror
judiciar *y* /ies		juri	jury ⁺
judicious /ly		juridical /ly	
judishal	judicial ⁺	juriman	juryman ⁺
judisharey	judiciary ⁺	jurisdicshun	jurisdiction ⁺
judishus	judicious ⁺	jurisdiction /al	
judo		jurispruden *ce* /t	
juel	duel ³★	jurisprudens	jurisprudence ⁺
juel	jewel ³★	jur *ist* /or	
juel	joule ★	jurnal	journal ⁺
jueller	jeweller ⁺	jurnalism	journalism
juelrey	jewellery	jurnalist	journalist
jug ³		jurnie	journey ¹⁺
juge	judge ²⁺	jurny	journey ¹⁺
jugernawt	juggernaut	jur *y* /ies	
juggernaut		jury *man* /men (pl.)	
juggle ² /r ★ (conjurer)		juse	juice ⁺

jusie	juicy
just	
justice	
justifiabl *e* /y	
justifiabul	justifiable +
justificashun	justification
justif *y* ⁴ /ication	
justis	justice
jut ³	
jute	
juvenil *e* /ity	
juwel	jewel ³★
juweller	jeweller +
juwellrey	jewellery
juxtapos *e* ² /ition	
jym	gym +
jymkana	gymkhana
jymnasium	gymnasium +
jymnast	gymnast
jymnastics	gymnastics
jyroscope	gyroscope +

K

*If you cannot find your word
under* **k** *look under* **c**

kacao	cacao
kaen	cayenne
Kaiser	
kaison	caisson
kakey	khaki
kakie	khaki
kale	
kaleidoscop *e* /ic	
kalidascope	kaleidoscope +
kameliun	chameleon
kangaroo	
kaolin	
kaos	chaos +
kaotick	chaotic
karate	
karicter	character
karicterisashun	characterisation
karicterise	characterise ²⁺

karicteristic	characteristic +
karizma	charisma
kayak	
kedgeree	
keel ¹ /age	
keelige	keelage
keen ¹ /ly/ness	
keep /er/ing/sake	
keg	
kegeree	kedgeree
kejery	kedgeree
kelp	
kelsius	Celsius
kelt	Celt +
keltic	Celtic
kemical	chemical +
kemist	chemist +
kemistrey	chemistry
ken ³	
kenl	kennel
kennel	
kept	
kerb ¹★ (stone edging)	
kerb	curb ¹★
kerchief	
kernel ★ (seed)	
kernel	colonel ★
keropodie	chiropody +
keropody	chiropody +
keroseen	kerosene
kerosene	
kestrel	
ketch /es	
ketchup	
ketle	kettle +
kettle /drum	
ketul	kettle +
kew	cue ²★
kew	queue ★+
key ¹★† /hole/stone †(with lock)	
key	quay ★
khaki	
khan	
khrist	Christ

khristianity	Christianity	kiropodey	chiropody +
kiak	kayak	kiropodist	chiropodist
kibbutz		kiropody	chiropody +
kick ¹ /er		kiser	Kaiser
kick-off		kiss ¹ /er/es	
kid ³		kit ³	
kidd y /ies		kitchen	
kidie	kiddy +	kite	
kidnap ³ /per		kiten	kitten
kidney		kith	
kidy	kiddy +	kitie	kitty
kile	chyle	kitn	kitten
kill ¹ /er		kitten	
kiln		kitty	
kilo		kity	kitty
kilocycle		kiyak	kayak
kilogram		klorate	chlorate
kilohertz		kloride	chloride
kiloliter	kilolitre	klorinashun	chlorination
kilolitre		klorinate	chlorinate ²+
kilometer	kilometre	klorination	chlorination
kilometre		klorine	chlorine
kilotonne		klorofil	chlorophyll
kilotun	kilotonne	kloroform	chloroform ¹
kilowatt		klorophill	chlorophyll
kilowhat	kilowatt	knack /er	
kilt		knapsack	
kime	chyme	knave ★ (rascal) /ry	
kimono		knead ¹★ (press)	
kin /dred/ship		knee /-cap/d ★†/ing	
kinaesthesis		† (touch with knee)	
kind /ly/ness		kneel ¹	
kindergarten		knell ¹	
kindle ²		knelt	
kindrid	kindred	knew ★ (did know)	
kindul	kindle ²	knew	gnu ★
kinesthesis	kinaesthesis	knew	new ★+
kinetic		knickerbockers	
king /ly/-pin/-size		knickers	
kink /ier/iest/y		knick-knack	
kins *man* /woman/folk		kni *fe* ² /ves (pl.)	
kiosk		knight ★ (rank)	
kipper ¹		knit ³★ (with needles)	
kirk		knob ³★ (handle) /by	
		knob	nob ★

knock [1] /er/-kneed	
knoll [1]	
knot [3]★ (what you tie) /ty	
know ★† /ing/ingly/s ★†	
†(understand)	
knowledge /able	
knuckle [2] /duster	
koala ·	
Kodak	
kola	koala
koolom	coulomb
kopeck	copeck
koral	choral ★+
koral	coral ★
koral	corral [3]★
kord	chord ★
kord	cord ★+
Kremlin	
kresh	crèche
krisalis	chrysalis +
krisanthimum	chrysanthemum
Krishna	
kroisant	croissant
kromate	chromate
kromatic	chromatic +
kromatin	chromatin
kromatograf	chromatograph +
kromatogram	chromatogram
krome	chrome +
kromic	chromic
kromium	chromium
kromosome	chromosome
krone★(money)/r(pl.)	
krone	crone ★
kronicul	chronicle [2]+
kronie	crony +
kronik	chronic +
kronologey	chronology +
kuisine	cuisine
Ku-Klux-Klan	
kul de sac	cul-de-sac
kurb	curb [1]★
kurb	kerb [1]★
kurchif	kerchief
kurd	curd

kurdle	curdle [2]
kurdul	curdle [2]
kurk	kirk
kurl	curl [1]+
kurlew	curlew
kurlu	curlew
kurly	curly
kurnel	colonel ★
kurnel	kernel ★

> *If you cannot find your word*
> *under* **kw** *look under* **qu**

kwack	quack [1]
kwaff	quaff [1]
kwafur	coiffeur ★+
kwafur	coiffure ★
kwagmire	quagmire
kwail	quail [1]
kwaint	quaint +

L

label [3]	
laber	labour [1]+
labernum	laburnum
labirinth	labyrinth +
labium	
labor	labour [1]+
laborator *y* /ies	
laboratrey	laboratory +
laborious /ly	
laborius	laborious +
labour [1] /er	
Labrador	
labrum	
laburnum	
labyrinth /ine	
lac *e* [2] /y	
lacerat *e* [2] /ion	
lach	latch [1]+
lachrym *al* /ose	
lack [1] /-lustre	
lackadaisical	
lackadaysical	lackadaisical
lacker	lacquer [1]

167

lackey /s		lakrimal	lachrymal +
lacky	lackey +	lakross	lacrosse
laconic /ally		laks	lax +
lacquer [1]		laksativ	laxative
lacrimal	lachrymal +	lama ★ (Tibetan monk)	
lacros	lacrosse	lama	llama ★
lacrosse		lamb /'s-wool	
lactashun	lactation	lame [2] /ly/ness	
lactation		lament [1] /ation	
lactic		lamentabl *e* /y	
lad /die		lamentabul	lamentable +
ladder [1]		lamentashun	lamentation
lad *e* ★† /en/ing		laminate [2]	
†(load cargo)		lamp /light/shade	
lade	laid ★	lampoon [1] /er/ist	
lader	ladder [1]	lampray	lamprey
ladie	lady +	lamprey	
ladilike	ladylike +	lance [2] /r/t	
ladiship	ladyship	land [1] /lord	
ladle [2]		landau	
ladul	ladle [2]	landaw	landau
lad *y* /ies		landing /-place	
lady *like* /ship		landlad *y* /ies	
laer	lair ★	landlocked	
laer	layer [1]★	landlubber /ly	
laerd	laird	landmark	
laf	laugh [1]+	landoner	landowner
laffing stock	laughing-stock	landowner	
lafter	laughter	landscape [2]	
lag [3]		landsli *de* /p	
lagard	laggard	lane ★ (path)	
lager		lane	lain ★
laggard		langger	languor +
lagoon		language	
laid ★ (lay)		languid /ly/ness	
laid	lade ★+	languish [1]	
lain ★ (did lie on)		languor /ous	
lain	lane ★	langwid	languid +
lair ★ (den)		langwidge	language
lair	layer [1]★	langwige	language
laird		langwish	languish [1]
laitie	laity	lanjerie	lingerie
laity		lank /iness/y	
lake		lanladie	landlady +
laker	lacquer [1]	lanlord	landlord

lanolin		lateral	
lans	lance [2+]	lath ★ (wooden strip)	
lanset	lancet	lathe ★ (machine)	
lantern		lather [1]	
lanthanum		Latin	
lanyard		latis	lattice [+]
lap [3]		latitude	
lapel /led		latrine	
lapidary		latter ★ (last) /ly	
lapis lazuli		lattice /d	
lapse [2]		lattis	lattice [+]
larceny /ies/ous		laud [1]★ (praise)	
larch /es		laud	lord [1]★+
larconic	laconic [+]	lauda ble /bly/tory	
lard [1] /er		laugh [1] /ter	
large /ly/r/sse/st		laughing-stock	
lariat		launch [1] /er/es	
laringitis	laryngitis	launder [1] /erette/ress	
larinks	larynx [+]	laundrey	laundry [+]
larinx	larynx [+]	laundry /ies	
lark [1] /er		laureate	
larseny	larceny [+]	laurel [3]	
larva ★† /e (pl.)/l		lava ★ (of volcano)	
†(of insects)		lava	larva ★+
larva	lava ★	lavatory /ies	
larynx /gitis		lavatrey	lavatory [+]
lascivious /ly/ness		lavender	
lase	lace [2+]	lavish [1] /ly/ness	
laser		law ★ (rule) /-abiding	
laserashun	laceration	law	lore ★
laserate	lacerate [2+]	law court /suit/yer	
laseration	laceration	lawd	laud [1]★
lasitude	lassitude	lawd	lord ★+
lasivious	lascivious [+]	Lawd Maer	Lord Mayor
lasivius	lascivious [+]	lawdable	laudable [+]
lasoo	lasso [1+]	lawdabul	laudable [+]
lassitude ◄		lawdatorey	laudatory
lasso [1] /es		lawditrey	laudatory
last [1] /ly		lawful /ly	
latch [1] /key		lawless /ness	
late /ly/st		lawn	
latency /t		lawnch	launch [1+]
latensey	latency [+]	lawnder	launder [1+]
later ★ (afterwards)		lawnderet	launderette
later	latter ★+	lawndress	laundress

lawndrey	laundry +	lee *† /ward/way †(shelter)	
lax /ity/ly/ness			
laxative		lee	lea *
lay /by/ing/-out		leech * (worm) /es	
laybie	layby	leech	leach ¹*
laybye	layby	leed	lead *+
layer ¹* (thickness)		leef	leaf +
layer	lair *	leeflet	leaflet
layman		leeg	league
laz *e* ² /y		leege	liege
lazi *er* /est/ly/ness		leek * (vegetable)	
lea * (open ground)		leek	leak ¹*+
lea	lee *+	leen	lean ¹
leach ¹* (purge)		leep	leap +
leach	leech *	leep yeer	leap-year
lead * (direct) /er/ing		leer ¹ /y	
lead * (element) /en		leesh	leash ¹
lea *f* /flet/ves (pl.)		left /ist/ward	
leaf *y* /iness		leftenancy	lieutenancy +
league		leftenansey	lieutenancy +
leak ¹* (hole) /age/y		leftenant	lieutenant
leak	leek *	left-hand /ed	
lean ¹		leg ³ /gy	
leant * (inclined)		legac *y* /ies	
leant	Lent *	legal /ly	
leant	lent *	legalis *e* ² /ation	
leap /ing/t		legalit *y* /ies	
leap -*frog* /-year		legasey	legacy +
learn ¹ /er/t		legashun	legation
lease ²		legation	
leash ¹		legend /ary	
least /ways/wise		legendrey	legendary
leather /iness/n/y		leger	ledger
leav *e* /er/ing		legib *le* /ility/ly	
leaven ¹		legibul	legible +
lebra	libra	legion /ary/aries	
lecher /ous/y		legislacher	legislature
lecherus	lecherous	legislashun	legislation
lectern		legislat *e* ² /ion/or	
lecture ² /r/ship		legislature	
led * (did guide)		legitima *cy* /te/tely	
led	lead *+	legitimasey	legitimacy +
ledge		legitimis *e* ² /ation	
ledger		legonrey	legionary
ledo	lido	leisure /ly	

170

lejun	legion [+]	lest	least [+]
lejunrey	legionary	lesure	leisure [+]
leksicografer	lexicographer [+]	let /table/ting	
leksicographer	lexicographer [+]	leter	letter [1]
leksicon	lexicon	lethal /ly	
lemon /ade		lethargey	lethargy [+]
lemur		letharg y /ic	
lend /er/ing		lether	leather [+]
length /wise/y		letice	lettuce
lengthen [1]		letis	lettuce
lenienc e /y		letre	litre
leniens	lenience [+]	letter [1]	
lenient /ly		lettuce	
lens /es		letus	lettuce
Lent ★ (40 days)		leucocytes	
lent ★ (did lend)		leukaemia	
lent	leant ★	Levant	
lenth	length [+]	leve	leave [+]
lenthen	lengthen [1]	level [3] /ler/ly	
lenticel		level-headed	
lentil		levelheded	level-headed
Leo		leven	leaven [1]
leopard		lever [1] /age	
leotard		leves	leaves
lep er /rous		leviathan	
leperd	leopard	levie	levy [4+]
lepidopterous		levitashun	levitation
leprosy		levitat e [2] /ion	
lept	leapt	levity	
lerch	lurch [1+]	levy [4] /ies	
lerk	lurk [1]	lewd /ly/ness	
lern	learn [1+]	lexicografer	lexicographer [+]
les	less [+]	lexicograph er /y	
Lesbian		lexicon	
lese	lease [2]	lezbian	Lesbian
lesen	lessen [1★]	li	lie ★
lesher	leisure [+]	li	lye ★
leshon	lesion	lia	liar ★
lesion		liabilit y /ies	
leson	lessen [1★]	liable	
leson	lesson ★	liabul	liable
less /ee/er ★ (minor)		liaise [2]	
lessen [1★] (to belittle)		liaison [1]	
lesson ★ (learnt)		liar ★ (tells lies)	
lessor ★ (grants lease)		liar	lyre ★[+]

libel [3] /ler/lous		lignin	
libelus	libellous	lignite	
liberal /ity/ly		likable	
liberalis *e* [2] /ation		likabul	likable
liberashun	liberation	like [2] /ly/ness	
liberat *e* [2] /ion/or		likelihood	
libertey	liberty +	liken [1]	
libertine		liker	liqueur [1]★
libert *y* /ies		liker	liquor [1]★
libid *o* /inal/inous		likewise	
libra		likoris	liquorice
libralise	liberalise [2]+	likwefi	liquefy [4]+
librar *y* /ies/ian		likwid	liquid +
lice		likwidashun	liquidation
licee	lycée	likwidate	liquidate [2]+
licence ★ (n.)		likwidation	liquidation
license [2]★ (v.) /e/r		likwiditey	liquidity
licenshiate	licentiate	lilac	
licenshus	licentious +	lilak	lilac
licentiate		lile	lisle
licentious /ness		lilie	lily +
lichen /ed		Lilipushun	Lilliputian
lick [1]		Lilliputian	
licoriss	liquorice	lilt [1]	
lid /ded		lil *y* /ies	
lido		limb [1] /less	
lie ★ (untruth)		limber [1]	
lie	lye ★	limbo /s	
liege		lime /-kiln/light	
lieu ★ (place)		limelite	limelight
lieutenan *cy* /t		limerick	
li *fe* /ves (pl.)		limestone	
life *belt* /blood/less/long		limf	lymph +
life-size		limfatic	lymphatic
lift [1] /-off		limit [1] /ation	
ligacher	ligature	limoosene	limousine
ligament		limousine	
ligature		limp [1] /er/ness	
light /er/ing		limpet	
lighten [1]		limph	lymph +
light *est* /ly/ness		limphatic	lymphatic
lighthouse		limpid	
lightning		linage ★†	
light-weight		†(number of lines)	
light-year		linch	lynch [1]

line [2] /r		lire	lyre *+
lineage * (ancestry)		lirical	lyrical
lineament * (features)		lisay	lycée
lineament	liniment *	lise	lice
linear /ity/ly		lisen	listen [1]+
linet	linnet	lisence	licence *
linger [1]		lisence	license [2]*+
lingerie		lisener	listener
lingo /es		lisensee	licensee
lingual		lisenshiat	licentiate
linguist /ic/ics		lisenshus	licentious +
lingwal	lingual	lisentiate	licentiate
lingwist	linguist +	lisentious	licentious +
liniament	lineament *	lisle	
linier	linear +	lisp [1]	
liniige	lineage *	lissom	
liniment * (salve)		list [1]	
liniment	lineament *	listen [1] /er	
link [1] /age		listless /ly/ness	
links * (joins)		lisum	lissom
links	lynx *	lit	
linnet		litany /ies	
lino /cut/leum		lite	light +
linolium	linoleum	litehowse	lighthouse
linseed		litely	lightly
lint		liten	lighten [1]
lintel /led		liter	litre
lintul	lintel +	liter	litter [1]
linx	lynx *+	literacher	literature
lio	Leo	litera cy /te	
lion /ess (fem.)		literal /ly	
lion-hearted		literary /ily	
liotard	leotard	literasey	literacy +
lip [3] /stick		literat	literate
lip-read /er/ing		literature	
liquef y [4] /action		litergic	liturgic +
liquer	liquor [1]*	litergy	liturgy +
liqueur [1]*†		litewait	light-weight
†(sweet liquor)		lithe /ly/some	
liquid /ity		lithium	
liquidat e [2] /ion/or		lithograf	lithograph +
liquor [1]* (drink)		lithografey	lithography
liquor	liqueur [1]*	lithograph /ic/y	
liquorice		litig ant /ious	
liquoris	liquorice	litigashun	litigation

litigat *e*² /ion		loby	lobby⁴⁺
litijus	litigious	local ★ (of place)	
litle	little	locale ★ (locality)	
litmus paper		localis *e*² /ation	
litning	lightning	localit *y* /ies	
litracher	literature	locashun	location
litre		locat *e*² /ion/or	
litter¹		loch ★ (lake)	
little		lock¹★ (door) /er/jaw	
litul	little	locket	
liturgey	liturgy⁺	locksmith	
liturgic /al		lockwacious	loquacious⁺
liturg *y* /ies		lockwacity	loquacity
liv	live²⁺	lockwashus	loquacious⁺
livable		locomoshun	locomotion⁺
livabul	livable	locomot *ion* /ive	
live² /lihood/ly		locum	
liveli *er* /est/ness		locust	
liven¹		lode ★ (mineral) /stone	
liver /ish		lode	load¹★⁺
liver *y* /ies		lodge² /ment/r	
livid		lof	loaf¹⁺
living-room		loft¹ /ier/iest/ily/iness	
livlie	lively	log³ /ger	
livlier	livelier⁺	loganberie·	loganberry⁺
livrey	livery⁺	loganberr *y* /ies	
liying	lying	logarithm /ic	
lizard		log-book	
lizerd	lizard	loge	lodge²⁺
llama ★ (animal)		logerhed	loggerhead
lo	low⁺	loggerhead	
load¹★† /er		logic /al/ally/ian	
†(heavy weight)		logishun	logician
load	lode★⁺	logistics	
loa*f*¹ /ves (pl.)		loial	loyal⁺
loam /y		loialist	loyalist
loan¹★ (lending)		loialtey	loyalty⁺
loan	lone★⁺	loier	lawyer
loath ★ (reluctant)		loin	
loath *e*²★ (hate) /some		loiter¹ /er	
lob³		lokust	locust
lobby⁴ /ist		lol	loll¹
lobe		lolipop	lollipop
lobie	lobby⁴⁺	loll¹	
lobster		lollipop	

lom	loam [+]	lorgnette	
lone ★ (lonely) /r		loriat	laureate
lone	loan [1]★	lorie	lorry [+]
loneliness		lornch	launch [+]
lonesome		lornderet	launderette
lonesum	lonesome	lornyet	lorgnette
long [1] /er/est/wise		lorr y /ies	
longevity		lory	lorry [+]
longitud e /inal/inally		los	loss [+]
loo [1]★ (card game)		los e ★† /ing/er/t	
loo	lieu ★	†(fail to win)	
loobricant	lubricant	lose	loose [2]★[+]
loobricashun	lubrication	loshun	lotion
loobricate	lubricate [2+]	loss [+]	
loocrativ	lucrative	lotery	lottery [+]
loodicrous	ludicrous [+]	lothe	loathe [2]★[+]
loodicrus	ludicrous [+]	lothsum	loathsome
look [1]		lotion	
lookemia	leukaemia	lotter y /ies	
looker	lucre [+]	lotus	
looking-glass		loud /er/ly/ness	
lookwarm	lukewarm	loud-speaker	
loom [1]		lounge [2] /r	
loominus	luminous [+]	lous e /y	
loona	luna	lout /ish	
loop [1]		lov e [2] /able/ely/er	
loose [2]★† /ly/ness/r/st		loveli er /est/ness	
†(not tight)		loves	loaves
loose	lose ★[+]	low [1] /est/liness/ly	
loosen [1]		lowd	loud [+]
loosing	losing	lower [1]	
loot [1]★ (booty) /er		lownge	lounge [2+]
loot	lute ★	lowse	louse [+]
lop [3]		lowt	lout [+]
lope [2]		loyal /ism/ist/ly	
loquacious /ly/ness		loyalt y /ies	
loquacity		lozenge	
loquashus	loquacious [+]	lozinge	lozenge
lord [1]★ (noble) /ly/ship		lu	lieu.★
lord	laud [1]★	lu	loo [1]★
lord(s) justice(s)		lubber /ly	
Lord Mayor		luber	lubber [+]
lore ★ (teaching)		lubricant	
lore	law ★[+]	lubricat e [2] /ion	
lorel	laurel [3]	lucer	lucre [+]

lucid /ity/ly/ness		lusid	lucid +
luck /ier/iest/ily/y		lust¹ /ful	
lucr e /ative		luster	lustre +
lude	lewd +	lustie	lusty +
ludicrous /ly		lustr e /ous	
luff¹		lust y /ily/iness	
lug³ /ger		lute ★ (instrument)	
luggage		lute	loot¹★+
lugige	luggage	lutetium	
lugsuriant	luxuriant	Lutheran	
lugubrious		luv	love²+
lukemia	leukaemia	luver	lover
lukewarm		luvley	lovely
luksurey	luxury +	luvlier	lovelier +
luksuriant	luxuriant	luxurey	luxury +
luksuriate	luxuriate²	luxurian ce /t/tly	
luksurious	luxurious +	luxuriate²	
luksurius	luxurious +	luxurious /ly	
lul	lull¹	luxur y /ies	
lulabie	lullaby +	lycée	
lull¹		lye ★ (chemical)	
lullab y /ies		lye	lie ★
lumbago		lying	
lumbar ★ (back)		lymph /atic	
lumber¹★ (wood)		lynch¹	
lumberjack		lynx ★ (animal) /es	
luminary		lynx	links ★
lumino us /sity		lyre ★† /-bird	
luminus	luminous +	†(instrument)	
lump¹ /iness/y		lyre	liar ★
luna		lyric /al/ism/ist	
luna cy /tic			
lunasey	lunacy +		
lunch¹ /eon/es			
lung			
lunge²			
lurch¹ /er			

M

lure²		ma'am	
lurid /ly		mac ★ (macintosh)	
lurk¹		mac	mach ★
lurn	learn¹+	macabre	
lurner	learner	macadam /ise²	
lurnt	learnt	macaroni	
luscious		macaroon	
lushus	luscious	mace	
		macerat e² /ion	
		mach ★ (speed ratio)	

mach	match [1]+	magnificens	magnificence +
machate	machete	magnifisence	magnificence +
machete		magnifisent	magnificent
machiage	maquillage	magnif y [4] /ication	
Machiavellian		magnitude	
machination		magnolia	
machine [2] /ry		magnum	
machinist		magot	maggot +
mackerel		magpie	
mackintosh /es		Magyar	
macrocosm		mahara ja /nee (fem.)	
macroscopic		mahem	mayhem
mad /der/dest/ly/ness		mahjong	
madam /e (French)		mahogany	
madden [1]		maid * (girl) /en/enly	
made * (built)		maid	made *
made	maid *+	mail [1]* (letters)	
Madeira		mail	male *
mademoiselle		maim [1]	
mademwoisel	mademoiselle	main *† /land/ly	
maden	madden [1]	†(most important)	
madera	Madeira	main	mane *
madonna		maintain [1]	
madrigal		maintenance	
maelstrom		maintenans	maintenance
maer	mayor +	maisonette	
magazine		maize * (corn)	
magenta		maize	maze [2]*
maggot /y		majenta	magenta
Magi		majer	major [1]+
magic /al/ally/ian		majestey	majesty +
magishun	magician	majestic /ally	
magisterial /ly		majest y /ies	
magistrac y /ies		majong	mahjong
magistrat e /ure		major [1] /ette	
magnanim ity /ous		majorit y /ies	
magnanimus	magnanimous	mak	mac *
magnate *†		mak	mach *
†(prominent person)		makaber	macabre
magnesi a /um		makadam	macadam +
magnet *† /ic/ism		makaroon	macaroon
†(attracts iron)		mak e /ing/er/eshift	
magnetis e [2] /ation		Makiavelian	Machiavellian
magneto /s		makination	machination
magnificen ce /t/tly		maksila	maxilla +

maksim	maxim	malnutrishun	malnutrition
maksimise	maximise ²	malnutrition	
maksimum	maximum +	malodorous	
malachite		Malpighian (layer)	
maladey	malady +	malstrom	maelstrom
maladjust *ed* /ment		malt ¹ /ose	
maladministration		Maltese	
maladroit /ness		maltreat ¹ /ment	
malad *y* /ies		maltreet	maltreat ¹+
malaise		mam	ma'am
malakite	malachite	mamal	mammal +
malaprop *ism* /os		mamarey	mammary
malard	mallard	mame	maim ¹
malaria		mammal /ian	
malase	malaise	mammary	
malcontent		mammon	
male ★ (man)		mammoth	
male	mail ¹★	mamon	mammon
maledicshun	malediction	mamoth	mammoth
malediction		man ³ /fully/ly/-of-war	
malefactor		mana	manna ★
malet	mallet	manacle ²	
maleus	malleus	manacul	manacle ²
malevolen *ce* /t		manage ² /able/ment	
malevolens	malevolence +	manager /ial	
malform ¹ /ation		mandarin	
malformashun	malformation	mandat *e* ² /ary ★ (law)	
malfuncshun	malfunction ¹	mandatory ★(command)	
malfunction ¹		mandatrey	mandatory ★
maliable	malleable +	mandible	
malice		mandibul	mandible
malicious /ly/ness		mandolin	
malign ¹ /er/ity		mane ★ (hair)	
malignanc *y* /ies		mane	main ★+
malignansey	malignancy +	maner	manner ★+
malignant		maner	manor ★+
maline	malign ¹+	manganese	
malinger ¹ /er		mang *e* /y	
malis	malice	mangel-wurzel	
malishus	malicious +	manger	
mallard		mangle ²	
malleab *le* /ility		mango /es	
malleabul	malleable +	mangrove	
mallet		mangul	mangle ²
malleus		manhandle ²	

manhandul	manhandle [2]	maple	
manhole		mapul	maple
manhood		maquillage	
mania /c/cal		mar [3]	
manicur e [2] /ist		marathon	
manidge	manage [2+]	maraud [1] /er	
manie	many	marawd	maraud [1+]
manifest [1] /ation		marble [2]	
manifesto /s		marbul	marble [2]
manifold [1]		march [1] /er/es	
manige	manage [2+]	marchioness (fem.)	
manikin	mannequin	Marconi	
manila	manilla	mare	
manilla		mareen	marine +
manipulashun	manipulation	margarine	
manipulat e [2] /ion		margerit	marguerite
manipulat ive /or		margin /al/ally	
manjer	manger	marguerite	
manliness		mariage	marriage +
manna * (food)		marie	marry [4]
mannequin		marige	marriage +
manner *† /ed/ism/ly		marigold	
†(method)		marijuana	
manoeuvr e [2] /able		marina	
manoover	manoeuvre [2+]	marinade	
manoovrable	manoeuvrable	marinate [2]	
manoovrabul	manoeuvrable	marine /r	
manor * (estate) /ial		marionet	marionette
manshun	mansion	marionette	
mansion		marital	
manslaughter		maritime	
manslorter	manslaughter	maritul	marital
mantel *† /piece		mariwana	marijuana
†(shelf at fireplace)		marjoram	
mantilla		mark [1] /edly/er	
mantle [2*] (cloak)		market [1] /ability	
mantul	mantle [2*]	markey	marquee *
manual /ly		markey	marquis *+
manufaccher	manufacture [2+]	markoni	Marconi
manufactur e [2] /er		marksism	Marxism +
manure [2]		marksman	
manuscript		markwis	marquis *+
many		marline-spike	
maonaise	mayonnaise	marmalade	
map [3]		marmoreal	

marmorial	marmoreal	maserate	macerate [2+]
marmoset		mash [1]	
marmot		mashene	machine [2+]
maroon [1]		mashenerey	machinery
marow	marrow	mashenist	machinist
marquee ★ (tent)		mashine	machine [2+]
marquis ★ (noble)		mashinerey	machinery
marriage /able		mashinist	machinist
marrow		masiv	massive +
marry [4]		mask [1]★ (cover)	
Mars		mask	masque ★
Marseillaise		maskerade	masquerade [2]
Marselase	Marseillaise	masoch ism /ist/istic	
marsh /-mallow/y		masocism	masochism +
marshal [3]★†		masocist	masochist
†(arrange in order)		mason /ic/ry	
marshal	martial ★+	masonet	maisonette
marshoness	marchioness	masque ★ (ball)	
marshun	Martian	masque	mask [1]★
marsupial		masquerade [2]	
marten ★ (animal)		mass [1] /es	
marten	martin ★	massacer	massacre [2]
marter	martyr [1+]	massacre [2]	
marterdom	martyrdom	massage [2]	
marterise	martyrise [2]	masseu r /se (fem.)	
martial ★† /ly		massive /ly/ness	
†(relating to war)		massur	masseur +
martial	marshal [3]★	master [1] /ly	
Martian		masterbate	masturbate [2+]
martin ★ (bird)		masterful /ly/ness	
martin	marten ★	masterpeace	masterpiece
martinet		masterpiece	
martyr [1] /dom		masticat e [2] /ion	
martyrise [2]		mastiff /s	
marvel [3] /lous/lously		masturbat e [2] /ion	
Marxis m /t		mat [3]★ (rug)	
marv	marry [4]	mat	matt ★
marzipan		matador	
mas	mass [1+]	match [1] /es/less	
masacer	massacre [2]	mate [2]	
masacre	massacre [2]	mater	matter [1]
masage	massage [2]	material /ism/ist/ly	
mascot		materialis e [2] /ation	
masculin e /ity		maternal /ly	
mase	mace	maternit y /ies	

mathematic s /al/ian	
mathematishun	mathematician
maths	
matinay	matinée
matinée	
mating	matting
matins	
matress	mattress +
matriarch /al/y	
matriculat e ² /ion	
matriks	matrix +
matrikulate	matriculate ²+
matrimon y /ial	
matri x /ces/xes (pls.)	
matron /ly	
matt ★ (dull surface)	
matter ¹	
matting	
mattress /es	
mature ² /ly	
maturity	
maul ¹	
mausoleum	
mauve	
maverick	
mawgage	mortgage ²+
mawkish /ness	
mawl	maul ¹
mawsoleum	mausoleum
maxilla /e (pl.)	
maxim	
maximise ²	
maxim um /a (pl.)	
may /be	
May /day/-fly	
mayhem	
mayonnaise	
mayor /al/alty	
maypole	
maze ²★†	
†(confusing paths)	
maze	maize ★
mazurka	
mead	
meadow	

meager	meagre +
meagre /ly	
meak	meek +
meal /time/y	
mean ★ (nasty) /ing/t	
mean	mien ★
meander ¹	
mean er /est/ly/ness	
meaning /ful/fully/less	
means	
meantime	
meanwhile	
measl es /y	
measuls	measles +
measurable	
measure ² /less/ment	
meat ★ (flesh)	
meat	meet ★+
meat	mete ²★
mecanic	mechanic +
mecanise	mechanise ²+
mecanism	mechanism
mechanic /al/ally	
mechanis e ² /ation/m	
medal ★ (award) /list	
medal	meddle ²★+
medallion	
medalyon	medallion
medcine	medicine +
meddle ²★† /some/r ★	
†(interfere /r)	
meddler	medlar ★
medeval	medieval
medi an /al/ally	
medical /ly	
medicament	
medicat e ² /ion	
medicin e /al	
medieval	
mediocer	mediocre
mediocre	
mediocrit y /ies	
medisinal	medicinal
meditat e ² /ion/ive/or	
Mediterranean	

medi *um* /a/ums (pls.)		melifluus	mellifluous
medlar ★ (fruit)		mellifluous	
medle	meddle ²★+	mellow ¹	
medler	meddler ★	melodey	melody +
medler	medlar ★	melodic /ally	
medley		melodius	melodious
medly	medley	melodrama /tic	
medow	meadow	melod *y* /ies/ious	
medsin	medicine +	melon	
medul	meddle ²★+	melow	mellow ¹
medulla		melt ¹	
meed	mead	member /ship	
meek /ly/ness		membrain	membrane +
meel	meal +	membran *e* /ous	
meeltime	mealtime	memento /es	
meen	mean ★+	memo /s	
meener	meaner +	memoir	
meening	meaning +	memorabl *e* /y	
meeningful	meaningful	memorand *um*/a/ums(pls.)	
meens	means	memorey	memory +
meentime	meantime	memorial	
meenwile	meanwhile	memorise ²	
meerschaum		memor *y* /ies	
meershum	meerschaum	memrable	memorable +
meesels	measles +	men (pl. of man)	
meesley	measly	menace ²	
meet ★(encounter)/ing		menagerie	
meet	meat ★	menajerey	menagerie
meet	mete ²★	menas	menace ²
megacycle		mend ¹	
megafone	megaphone	mendacious /ly	
megalith /ic		mendacity	
megalomania /c		mendashus	mendacious +
megaphone		mendasitey	mendacity
meger	meagre +	mendelevium	
megohm		mendicity	
megom	megohm	menial /ly	
mekanic	mechanic +	meningitis	
mekanical	mechanical	meninjitis	meningitis
mekanise	mechanise ²+	menopause	
mekanism	mechanism	menopaws	menopause
melanchol *y* /ia/ic		menshun	mention ¹
melay	mêlée	menstrooal	menstrual
mêlée		menstrooate	menstruate ²+
melifluqus	mellifluous	menstrual	

menstruat *e* [2] /ion		mesofill	mesophyll
ment	meant	mesophyll	
mental /ity/ly		mess [1] /ier/iest/ily/y	
mentalitey	mentality	message	
menthol		messenger	
mention [1]		Messia *h* /nic	
mentor		mesur	monsieur
menu /s		mesurable	measurable
merang	meringue	mesurabul	measurable
mercantil *e* /ism		mesure	measure [2+]
mercenar *y* /ies		metabol *ic* /ism	
mercenrey	mercenary [+]	metacarpals	
merchandise		metafisical	metaphysical [+]
merchant		metafisics	metaphysics
mercur *y* /ial		metafor	metaphor
merc *y* /iful/ifully/iless		metaforical	metaphorical [+]
mere /ly/st		metal [3*] (material)	
meretricious		metal	mettle [*]
meretrishus	meretricious	metalic	metallic
merge [2] /r		metalise	metallise [2+]
meridian		metallic	
meridional		metallis *e* [2] /ation	
merie	merry [+]	metallurg *y* /ical/ist	
meriment	merriment	metalurgey	metallurgy [+]
meringue		metamorfose	metamorphose [2+]
merit [1]		metamorfosis	metamorphosis
meritorious		metamorphos *e* [2] /is/es (pl.)	
meritorius	meritorious	metaphor	
mermade	mermaid	metaphorical /ly	
mermaid		metaphysical /ly	
merr *y* /ier/ily/iment		metaphysics	
merry-go-round		metatarsals	
merry-making		mete [2*] (measure)	
mersenrey	mercenary [+]	mete	meat [*]
mersie	mercy [+]	mete	meet [*+]
mersiful	merciful	meteor /ic/ite	
mersy	mercy [+]	meteorolog *y* /ical	
mery	merry [+]	meter [1*] (machine)	
mesenger	messenger	meter	metre [*+]
mesh [1]		methane	
Mesia	Messiah [+]	methilate	methylate [2]
mesidge	message	method /ical/ically	
mesie	messy	methylate [2]	
mesige	message	meticulous /ly	
mesmeris *e* [2] /m		meticulus	meticulous [+]

metior	meteor +	midshipman	
metiorite	meteorite	midst	
metiorologey	meteorology +	midsummer	
metiorological	meteorological	midul	middle +
metr e * (measure) /ic		midwi fe /ves (pl.)/fery	
metre	meter [1]*	mien * (bearing)	
metricashun	metrication	mige	midge +
metricat e [2] /ion		might * (strength, may)	
metronome		might	mite *
metropoli s /tan		might ier /iest/ily/y	
mettle * (spirit)		migit	midget
mettle	metal [3]*	migraine	
metul	mettle *	migrane	migraine
mew [1] /s *†		migrant	
†(cat's cry, stable)		migrat e [2] /ion/or	
mezanin	mezzanine	mika	mica
mezzanine		miklmas	Michaelmas
mi	my +	miks	mix [1]+
miander	meander [1]	miksamatosis	myxomatosis
miaow		mikscher	mixture
mica		mikser	mixer
mice (pl. of mouse)		miksture	mixture
Michaelmas		mil	mill [1]+
microb e /ial		milch-cow	
microbiolog y /ist		mild /ly/ness	
microcosm		mildew /y	
microfilm		mildu	mildew +
microfone	microphone +	mile /age/stone	
micrometer		milenium	millennium +
micron		milet	millet
micro-organism		miligram	milligram +
microphon e /ic		milileter	millilitre
micropyle		milimeter	millimetre
microscop e /ic/ical/y		miliner	milliner +
microwave		milinerey	millinery
mid-brain		milinrey	millinery
midday		milion	million +
middle /-weight		milionair	millionaire
middling		milipede	millepede
midge /t		milisha	militia
Midlands		militan cy /t	
midling	middling	militansey	militancy +
midnight		militarey	military +
midnite	midnight	militar y /ily/ism/ist	
midriff		militate [2]	

militia	
milivolt	millivolt +
miliwot	milliwatt
milk ¹ /er/iness/y	
milkmade	milkmaid +
milk *maid* /sop	
mill ¹ /er	
millenni *um* /a (pl.)	
millepede	
millet	
milli *gram* /litre/metre	
milliner /y	
million /aire/th	
milli *volt* /watt	
milyun	million +
milyunair	millionaire
mime ²	
mimeograph ¹	
mimic /ry	
mimick *ed* /ing	
mimiograf	mimeograph ¹
mimosa	
minaret	
mince ² /meat/-pie/r	
mind ¹ /er/ful/less	
mine ² /sweeper	
miner *†	
†(works in a mine)	
miner	minor *
mineralog *y* /ical/ist	
minestrone	
minestrony	minestrone
mingle ²	
mingul	mingle ²
mini /skirt	
miniatur *e* /ist	
minicher	miniature +
minim /al/um/a (pl.)	
minimise ²	
minion	
miniscule	minuscule
minister ¹	
ministerial /ly	
ministra *tion* /nt	
ministrey	ministry +

ministr *y* /ies	
minit	minute ²+
mink	
minks	minx
minnow	
minor * (lesser)	
minor	miner *
minorit *y* /ies	
minow	minnow
minse	mince ²+
minsmeat	mincemeat
minspie	mince-pie
minster	
minstrel	
mint ¹	
minuet	
minus /sign	
minuscule	
minushia	minutia +
minute ² /ly	
minutia /e (pl.)	
minx	
minyouet	minuet
minyun	minion
miopia	myopia +
miow	miaow
mirac *le* /ulous	
miracul	miracle +
miraculus	miraculous
mirage	
mir *e* /y	
mirer	mirror ¹
miriad	myriad
mirror ¹	
mirth /ful/fully	
mis	miss ¹+
misadvencher	misadventure
misadventure	
misal	missal *
misal	missile *
misaliance	misalliance
misalians	misalliance
misalliance	
misanthrop *e* /ic/ist/y	
misapli	misapply ⁴+

misappl*y*[4] /ication		miserabul	miserable[+]
misapprehen*d*[1] /sion		miser*y* /ies	
misappropriat*e*[2] /ion		misfire[2]	
misaprehend	misapprehend[1+]	misfit	
misaprehenshun	misapprehension	misfortune	
misaprehension	misapprehension	misgave	
misapropriate	misappropriate[2+]	misgidance	misguidance
misbehav*e*[2] /iour		misgidans	misguidance
misbehavier	misbehaviour	misgide	misguide[2+]
misbihave	misbehave[2+]	misgiv*e* /en/ing	
miscalculat*e*[2] /ion		misgovern[1] /ment	
miscariage	miscarriage	misguid*e*[2] /ance	
miscarie	miscarry[4+]	misguven	misgovern[1+]
miscarige	miscarriage	mishandle[2]	
miscarr*y*[4] /iage		mishandul	mishandle[2]
miscast		mishap	
miscelanius	miscellaneous	mishun	mission
miscellaneous		mishunarey	missionary
miscellan*y* /ies		mishunrey	missionary
mischance		misile	missile ★
mischans	mischance	misinform[1] /ation	
mischie*f* /vous		misinterpret[1] /ation	
mischif	mischief[+]	misiv	missive
mischivus	mischievous	misjudge[2] /ment	
miscible		misjuge	misjudge[2+]
misconceive[2]		miskwotashun	misquotation
misconception		miskwotation	misquotation
misconcieve	misconceive[2]	miskwote	misquote[2+]
misconduct[1]		mislade	mislaid
misconsepshun	misconception	mislaid	
misconstru*e*[2] /ction		mislay /ing	
miscount[1]		misle	missal ★
miscownt	miscount[1]	misle	missile ★
miscreant		mislead /ing	
misdeed		misled	
misdemeanour		misleed	mislead[+]
misdemener	misdemeanour	misnomer	
mise	mice	misogyn*y* /ism/ist	
miselaneous	miscellaneous	misojinist	misogynist
miselaney	miscellany[+]	misojiny	misogyny[+]
miselanius	miscellaneous	mispell	misspell[+]
miself	myself	mispelt	misspelt
miselium	mycelium	mispend	misspend[+]
miser /liness/ly		mispent	misspent
miserabl*e* /y		misplace[2] /ment	

misplase	misplace [2+]	misultoe	mistletoe
misprint [1]		misunderstand /ing	
mispronounce [2]		misunderstood	
mispronownce	mispronounce [2]	misuse [2]	
misquot *e* [2] /ation		mite ★ (very small)	
misrable	miserable [+]	mite	might ★
misrabul	miserable [+]	miten	mitten
misread /ing		miter	mitre [2]
misred	misread [+]	mith	myth [+]
misrepresent [1] /ation		mithical	mythical
misrool	misrule [2]	mithologey	mythology [+]
misrule [2]		mitie	mighty
miss [1] /es		mitigat *e* [2] /ion	
missal ★(prayer book)		mitre [2]	
missal	missile ★	mitten	
missellaneous	miscellaneous	mix [1] /er/ture	
missellany	miscellany [+]	mixamatosis	myxomatosis
missel-thrush		mixcher	mixture
misshapen		mnemonic	
missible	miscible	mo	mow [1+]
missile ★ (weapon)		moan [1] /er	
mission /ary/aries		moat [1]	
missive		mob [3]	
misspell /ing		mobil *e* /ity	
misspelt		mobilis *e* [2] /ation	
misspend /ing		mobilitey	mobility
misspent		moca	mocha
misstate [2] /ment		moccasin	
mist /ily/iness/y		mocha	
mistak *e* /able/en/ing		mock [1] /ery	
misterey	mystery [+]	mod *e* /ish	
misterious	mysterious [+]	model [3]	
misterius	mysterious [+]	moderashun	moderation
mistic	mystic ★[+]	moderat *e* [2] /ion/or	
mistic	mystique ★	modern /ism/ity	
mistifi	mystify [4+]	modernis *e* [2] /ation	
mistime [2]		modest /y	
mistisism	mysticism	modicum /s	
mistletoe		modifi	modify [4+]
mistook		modificashun	modification
mistress /es		modif *y* [4] /ication	
mistrust [1] /ful		modul	model [3]
misul	missal ★	modulat *e* [2] /ion/or	
misul	missile ★	modul *us* /i (pl.)	
misul thrush	missel-thrush	mohair	

mohare	mohair	monkey /s	
moischer	moisture	monochord	
moisen	moisten [1]	monochrom e /atic/ic	
moist /ness/ure		monocle	
moisten [1]		monocotyledon	
moka	mocha	monocul	monocle
mokasin	moccasin	monogamus	monogamous
molar		monogam y /ist/ous	
molasses		monograf	monograph [1]
mold	mould [1+]	monogram	
molder	moulder [1]	monograph [1]	
moldey	mouldy	monokord	monochord
mole		monokrome	monochrome [+]
molecul e /ar		monokside	monoxide
molest [1] /ation		monolith /ic	
molicodle	mollycoddle [2]	monolog	monologue
molicodul	mollycoddle [2]	monologue	
mollify [4]		monomania /c	
mollusc		monophonic	
mollycoddle [2]		monoplane	
molt	moult [1]	monopoley	monopoly [+]
molten		monopolis e [2] /ation	
molusk	mollusc	monopolist /ic	
molybdenum		monopol y /ies	
moment /arily/ary		monorail	
momentous		monosilabic	monosyllabic
momentum		monosilable	monosyllable [+]
mònak	monarch [+]	monosyllab le /ic	
monakey	monarchy [+]	monothaism	monotheism [+]
monarch /al/ical		monotheis m /t/tic	
monarch y /ies		monotipe	Monotype
monaster y /ial/ies		monoton e /ic	
monastic /ism		monoton ous /y	
monastrey	monastery [+]	monotonus	monotonous [+]
Monday		Monotype	
mone	moan [1+]	monoxide	
monetar y /ism/ist		monsieur	
money /s (pl.)/ed		monsoon	
Mongol /ian		monst er /rous	
Mongol ism /oid		monstrosit y /ies	
mongoose /s		monstrus	monstrous
mongrel		month /ly	
moniter	monitor [1]	monument /al/ally	
monitor [1]		moo [1]	
monk /ish		mooch [1]	

mood /ily/iness/y	
moon [1] /beam/lit/y	
moonlight	
moor [1]*† /age	
†(waste ground)	
moor	more *+
moose * (animal)	
moose	mousse *
moot [1]	
moov	move [2]+
moovable	movable
moovabul	movable
mop [3]	
mope [2]	
moped	
moraine	
moral /e/ity/ly	
moralise [2]	
moralitey	morality
morass	
moratorium /s	
morbid /ity	
mordant	
more *† /over	
†(greater quantity)	
more	moor [1]*+
morfia	morphia +
morfine	morphine
morg	morgue
morgage	mortgage [2]+
morganatic /ally	
morgige	mortgage [2]+
morgue	
moribund	
morn * (morning)	
morn	mourn [1]*+
mornful	mournful +
moron /ic	
morose /ly	
morover	moreover
morow	morrow
morphi a /ne/nism	
morrow	
Morse	
morsel	

mortal /ity/ly	
mortar [1] /-board	
mortary	mortuary +
mortgag e [2] /ee/or	
mortifi	mortify [4]+
mortif y [4] /ication	
mortise [2]	
mortuar y /ies	
mos	moss +
mosaic	
moshun	motion [1]+
mosk	mosque
moskito	mosquito +
Moslem	
mosque	
mosquito /es	
moss /es/y	
most	
mote	
moteef	motif *+
motel	
moter	motor [1]+
moterboat	motorboat
motercycle	motorcycle
moterise	motorise [2]+
moterist	motorist
moterway	motorway
moth /-eaten	
mother [1] /ly	
mother-tongue	
motif * (ornament) /s	
motion [1] /less	
motivat e [2] /ion	
motive * (movement)	
motled	mottled
motley	
motlie	motley
motly	motley
moto	motto +
motor [1]/boat/cycle/way	
motoris e [2] /t	
mottled	
motto /es	
mould [1] /iness/y	
moulder [1]	

moult [1]	
mound [1]	
mount [1]	
mountain /eer/ous	
mountebank	
mountenus	mountainous
mourn [1]* (grieve) /er	
mournful /ly	
mous e * (rodent) /er/y	
mouse	moose *
mousse * (pudding)	
moustache	
mouth [1] /ful/piece	
movable	
movabul	movable
move [2] /ment	
move	mauve
mow [1] /er/n	
mownd	mound [1]
mownt	mount [1]
mowntain	mountain +
mowntbank	mountebank
mownten	mountain +
mowntenear	mountaineer
mowntenus	mountainous
mowse	mouse *+
mowth	mouth [1]+
mowthful	mouthful
mu	mew [1]+
much	
muchooal	mutual +
mucilag e /inous	
muck [1] /y	
mucous * (adj.)	
mucus * (n.)	
mud /dy/guard	
muddid	muddied +
muddi ed /er/est	
muddle [2] /r	
mudid	muddied +
mudie	muddy
mudul	muddle [2]+
muff [1]	
muffin	
muffle [2] /r	

mufin	muffin
mufti	
muful	muffle [2]+
mug [3] /gy	
mukus	mucous *
mukus	mucus *
mulatto /s	
mulberie	mulberry +
mulberr y /ies	
mulch [1]	
mulct [1]	
mul e /eteer/ish	
mulkt	mulct [1]
mullion	
multifarious	
multifarius	multifarious
multiform	
multilateral /ly	
multiple	
multipleks	multiplex
multiplex	
multipli	multiply [4]+
multiplicashun	multiplication
multiplicity	
multipl y [4] /ication	
multipul	multiple
multiracial	
multirashul	multiracial
multitud e /inous	
multitudinus	multitudinous
mulyun	mullion
mumble [2]	
mumbo-jumbo	
mumbul	mumble [2]
mumie	mummy +
mumifi	mummify [4]
mummify [4]	
mumm y /ies	
mumy	mummy +
munch [1]	
mundane	
Munday	Monday
munetarey	monetary +
munetrey	monetary +
mungrel	mongrel

municipal /ity/ities		mustang	
munie	money +	mustard	
munificen ce /t		muster 1	
munifisens	munificence +	mustie	musty +
munifisent	munificent	must y /iness	
munishun	munition 1	mutashun	mutation
munisipal	municipal +	mutation	
munisipalitey	municipality	mute 2 /ly	
munition 1		muter	mutter 1
munk	monk +	mutilat e 2 /ion/or	
munky	monkey +	mutinear	mutineer +
munth	month +	mutin eer /ous	
muny	money +	mutinus	mutinous
mur	myrrh	mutin y 4 /ies	
mural /ly		muton	mutton
murder 1 /er/ess/ous		mutter 1	
murk /ily/iness/y		mutton	
murmer	murmur 1	mutual /ly	
murmur 1		muzie	muzzy +
murth	mirth +	muzul	muzzle 2
murtle	myrtle	muzzle 2	
mus	mews ★	muzz y /ily/iness	
mus	muse 2★	my /self	
muscat /el		mycelium	
muscle 2★ (in body)		myopi a /c	
muscle	mussel ★	myriad	
muscular /ity		myrrh	
muse 2★ (think)		myrtle	
muse	mews ★	mysterious /ly/ness	
musel	muscle 2★	mysterius	mysterious +
musel	mussel ★	myster y /ies	
museum /s		mystic ★† /al/ism	
mush /y		†(spiritual)	
mushroom 1		mystif y 4 /ication	
music /al/ally/ian		mystique ★ (mystery)	
musilage	mucilage +	myth /ical/ology	
musishun	musician	myxomatosis	
musk			
musket /eer/ry			
muskwash	musquash	**N**	
musquash			
mussel ★ (shellfish)		nab 3	
mussel	muscle 2★	naber	neighbour +
must /n't		nabob	
mustach	moustache	nabour	neighbour +

nacher	nature
nacheral	natural +
nacheralise	naturalise 2+
nachural	natural +
nack	knack +
nacker	knacker
nader	nadir
nadir	
naftha	naphtha
nag 3 /ger	
nail 1	
naive /té/ty	
naked /ness	
nakid	naked +
nale	nail 1
namby-pamby	
name 2 /less/ly	
nanie	nanny +
nann y /ies	
nany	nanny +
nap 3	
napalm	
naparm	napalm
nape	
naphtha	
napie	nappy +
napkin	
napp y /ies	
napsack	knapsack
narate	narrate 2+
narativ	narrative
narcissis m /t/tic	
narcissus	
narcosis	
narcotic	
nar-do-well	ne'er-do-well
narl	gnarl 1
narow	narrow 1+
narrat e 2 /ion/or	
narrative	
narrow 1 /er/ly/ness	
narsissism	narcissism +
narsissist	narcissist
narsisus	narcissus
nasal /ly	

nascen ce /t	
nasel	nasal +
nash	gnash 1
nashanality	nationality +
nashnalism	nationalism +
nashun	nation +
nastie	nasty +
nast y /ier/iest/ily/iness	
nat	gnat
natal	
natie	natty
nation /al/ally	
nationalis e 2 /ation	
nationalis m /t/tic	
nationalit y /ies	
native	
Nativity	
natle	natal
natsi	Nazi
natty	
natul	natal
natural /ism/ist/ly	
naturalis e 2 /ation	
nature	
naty	natty
naught	
naughtie r /st	
naught y /ily/iness	
nause a /ous	
nauseate 2	
nautical	
naval ★ (navy)	
nave ★ (of church)	
nave	knave ★+
navel ★ (stomach)	
naverey	knavery
navie	navvy ★+
navie	navy ★+
navigab le /ility	
navigabul	navigable +
navigashun	navigation
navigat e 2 /ion/or	
navul	naval ★
navv y ★ (labourer) /ies	
nav y ★ (warships) /ies	

naw	gnaw [1]
nay ★ (no)	
nay	neigh [1]★
naybour	neighbour [+]
nayl	nail [1]
Nazi	
nead	knead [1]★
nead	need [1]★[+]
neadle	needle [2]
neadless	needless [+]
Neapolitan	
near /-by/ly/ness	
neat /er/est/ly/ness	
nebul a /ous	
nebulus	nebulous
necesarey	necessary [+]
necesitate	necessitate [2]
necesitey	necessity [+]
necessar y /ily	
necessitate [2]	
necessit y /ies/ous	
neck /lace/tie	
necksus	nexus
necrofilia	necrophilia
necrophilia	
necropolis	
nectar /y	
nee	knee [+]
need [1]★ (lack) /ful/y	
need	knead [1]★
need	kneed ★
needle [2]	
needless /ly	
needul	needle [2]
neel	kneel [1]
neer	near [+]
ne'er-do-well	
neet	neat [+]
nefarious /ly	
nefarius	nefarious [+]
nefew	nephew
negashun	negation
negation	
negative /ly	
neglect [1] /ful	

négligé	
negligen ce /t	
negligens	negligence [+]
negligibl e /y	
negligibul	negligible [+]
neglijay	négligé
negoshable	negotiable
negoshabul	negotiable
negoshiate	negotiate [2][+]
negotiable	
negotiat e [2] /ion/or	
negr o /oes/ess (fem.)	
negroid	
neice	niece
neigh [1]★ (horse's cry)	
neighber	neighbour [+]
neighberhood	neighbourhood
neighbour /ing/ly	
neighbourhood	
neither	
nek	neck [+]
neklace	necklace
necklis	necklace
nekrofilia	necrophilia
nekropolis	necropolis
nekst	next [+]
neksus	nexus
nell	knell [1]
nelt	knelt
Nemesis	
nemisis	Nemesis
nemonic	mnemonic
neodimium	neodymium
neodymium	
neolithic	
neon	
nephew	
nepotism	
Neptune	
neptunium	
nerv e [2] /y	
nervous /ly/ness	
nervus	nervous [+]
nesesarey	necessary [+]
nesesitate	necessitate [2]

nesesitey	necessity +	next /-of-kin	
neslin	nestling	nexus	
nest¹ /ling		ni	nigh
net³ /ball		nibble²	
netha	neither	nibul	nibble²
nether		nice /ly/ness/r/st	
nettle² /rash		nicet y /ies	
netul	nettle²⁺	nich	niche
network		niche	
neumatick	pneumatic	nick¹	
neural /gia		nickel	
neuritis		nickerbockers	knickerbockers
neurologist		nickers	knickers
neuron		nickle	nickel
neuro sis /tic		nicknack	knick-knack
neuter		nickname²	
neuton	newton	nicotine	
neutral /ity		niece	
neutralis e² /ation		niether	neither
neutron /s		nifarious	nefarious +
neva	never +	nifarius	nefarious +
never /more/theless		nife	knife²⁺
nevu	nephew	niftie	nifty +
new ★ (not old) /er/est		nift y /iness	
new	gnu ★	nigerd	niggard +
new	knew ★	niggard /ly	
newclear	nuclear	niggl e² /y	
newcleus	nucleus +	nigh	
new comer /fangled		night ★† /dress/gown †(the dark)	
new ly /ness			
newmatic	pneumatic	night	knight ★
newmonia	pneumonia	night fall /jar	
newral	neural +	nightingale	
newritis	neuritis	nightmar e /ish	
newrologist	neurologist	night -shift /-time	
newron	neuron	night-watch /man	
newrosis	neurosis +	nigle	niggle²⁺
newrotic	neurotic	niglect	neglect¹⁺
news /agent/-flash		nigul	niggle²⁺
news paper /print/y		niks	nix
newt		nilon	nylon
newter	neuter	nimble /ness	
newton		nimblie	nimbly
newtralise	neutralise²⁺	nimbly	
newtron	neutron	nimbul	nimble +

nimbus /es		nobie	knobby
nimf	nymph	nobility	
nimph	nymph	noble /man/men(pl.)/r/st	
nincompoop		noblie	nobly
nin *e* /th/thly		nobly	
nineteen /th		nobul	noble +
ninet *y* /ies/ieth		nock	knock [1]+
ningcumpoop	nincompoop	nocker	knocker
ninie	ninny +	nockneed	knock-kneed
ninn *y* /ies		nodes	
niobium		nodule	
nion	neon	noes * (negative)	
nip [3] /per/py		noes	knows *
nipie	nippy	noes	nose *+
nipple		noledge	knowledge +
nipul	nipple	nolidge	knowledge +
nipy	nippy	noll	knoll [1]
nise	nice +	nome	gnome +
nisitey	nicety +	nomon	gnomon
niss	niece	none * (not any)	
nit * (insect)		none	nun *+
nit	knit [3]*	nor	gnaw [1]
nite	knight *	norsia	nausea +
nite	night *+	norsiate	nauseate [2]
niter	nitre	nort	naught
nither	neither	nortey	naughty +
nitrate		nortickle	nautical
nitre		nortie	naughty +
nitric		Norwegian	
nitrifi	nitrify [4]	nose * (on face) /y	
nitrify [4]		nose	knows *
nitrite		nose	noes *
nitrogen /ous		nostril	
nitrogliserine	nitroglycerine	not * (no)	
nitroglycerine		not	knot [3]*+
nitrojen	nitrogen +	notie	knotty
nitrous /oxide		notty	knotty
nitrus	nitrous +	nova	
nitwit		nowing	knowing
nives	knives	nowledge	knowledge +
nix		nu	gnu *
no * (negative reply)		nu	knew *
no	know *+	nu	new *+
nob * (cribbage)		nuance	
nob	knob [3]*+	nuans	nuance

195

nuckle	knuckle [2]+	nuspaper	newspaper +
nuclear		nut /cracker/shell	
nucle *us* /i (pl.)		nuta	neuter
nud *e* /ist/ity		nuter	neuter
nudge [2]		nutie	nutty
nuge	nudge [2]	nutmeg	
nugget		nuton	newton
nulifi	nullify [4]+	nutralise	neutralise [2]+
nulitey	nullity	nutrishun	nutrition
null		nutrition	
nullif *y* [4] /ication		nutron	neutron
nullity		nutty	
numatic	pneumatic	nuty	nutty
numb [1] /ness		nuzul	nuzzle [2]
number [1] /-plate		nuzzle [2]	
numer *able* /acy/al		nylon	
numerabul	numerable +	nymf	nymph
numerasey	numeracy	nymph	
numerat *e* [2] /ion			
numerical			
numerous /ly/ness			
numerus	numerous +		

O

numismatic /s		O ★ (addressing)	
numonia	pneumonia	o	oh ★
numrable	numerable +	o	owe [2]★
numrabul	numerable +	oaf /ish	
numskull		oak /en	
nun ★ (religious) /nery		oakum	
nun	none ★	oar ★ (of a boat)	
nupshal	nuptial	oar	ore ★
nuptial		oas *is* /es (pl.)	
nural	neural +	oast	
nuralgia	neuralgia	oat /meal	
nurcher	nurture [2]	oath	
nuritis	neuritis	obay	obey [1]
nurologist	neurologist	obduracy	
nuron	neuron	obdurasey	obduracy
nurosis	neurosis +	obdurate /ly	
nurotic	neurotic	obedien *ce* /t	
nurse [2]		obediens	obedience +
nurser *y* /ies		obelisk	
nursrey	nursery +	obes *e* /ity	
nurture [2]		obey [1]	
nurv	nerve [2]+	obituar *y* /ies	
nus	news +	objecshun	objection +

196

object¹ /or		obstacul	obstacle	
objection /able		obstetric /ian/s		
objectiv e /ely/ity		obstetrishun	obstetrician	
obligashun	obligation⁺	obstinacy		
obligat ion /ory		obstinasey	obstinacy	
obligatrey	obligatory	obstinate /ly		
oblige²		obstreperous		
oblik	oblique⁺	obstreperus	obstreperous	
oblique /ly/ness		obstrucshun	obstruction	
obliterashun	obliteration	obstruct¹ /ion/ive		
obliterat e² /ion		obtain¹ /able		
obliv ion /ious		obtane	obtain¹⁺	
oblivius	oblivious	obtroode	obtrude²⁺	
oblivyun	oblivion⁺	obtrooshun	obtrusion⁺	
oblokwey	obloquy⁺	obtroosion	obtrusion⁺	
oblong		obtroosiv	obtrusive	
obloqu y /ies		obtrude² /r		
obnokshus	obnoxious⁺	obtrus ion /ive		
obnoxious /ly		obtuse /ly/ness		
obo	oboe⁺	obverse		
obo e /ist		obviate²		
obscene /ly		obvious /ly		
obscure² /ly		obvius	obvious⁺	
obscurit y /ies		ocasion	occasion¹⁺	
obseen	obscene⁺	ocasional	occasional	
obsekwies	obsequies	occashun	occasion¹⁺	
obsekwius	obsequious⁺	occasion¹ /al/ally		
obsequies		occident /al		
obsequious /ly		occlu de² /sion		
observable		occlushun	occlusion	
observabul	observable	occult¹ /ation		
observan ce /t		occupan cy /t		
observashun	observation	occupation /al		
observator y /ies		occupi	occupy⁴⁺	
observatrey	observatory⁺	occup y⁴ /ier		
observ e² /ation/er		occur³ /rence		
observence	observance⁺	occurens	occurrence	
observens	observance⁺	ocean		
obseshun	obsession	ocell us /i (pl.)		
obsess¹ /ion/ive		ocelot		
obsolescen ce /t		ochre		
obsolesens	obsolescence⁺	o'clock		
obsolesent	obsolescent	oclude	occlude²⁺	
obsolete		oclusion	occlusion	
obstacle		ocsident	occident⁺	

197

octagon /al
octane
octav e /o
octet
October
octogenarian
octopus /es
ocul ar /ist

ocult	occult [1+]
ocupancy	occupancy [+]
ocupant	occupant
ocupashun	occupation [+]
ocupation	occupation [+]
ocupi	occupy [4+]
ocur	occur [3+]
ocurence	occurrence
ocurens	occurrence
od	odd [+]

odd /er/est/ly/ment
oddit y /ies
ode

odecolone	eau-de-cologne
oder	odour [+]
oderiferus	odoriferous
oderous	odorous
oderus	odorous
odiferus	odoriferous

odious /ly

oditey	oddity [+]

odium

odius	odious [+]

odontology
odoriferous
odorous
odour /less

oesofagus	oesophagus

oesophagus
of * (belonging to)

of	oaf [+]
of	off [*+]
ofal	offal
ofence	offence
ofend	offend [1+]
ofens	offence
ofensiv	offensive [+]

ofer	offer [1]

off * (away from) /ing
offal
offence
offend [1] /er

offens	offence

offensive /ly/ness
offer [1]
offhand /ed/edness
office /r
official /ly
officiate [2]
officious /ly/ness

offis	office [+]
offishal	official [+]
offishus	officious [+]

offprint
offset /ting
offshoot
offside

ofhand	offhand [+]
oficial	official [+]
oficiate	officiate [2]
oficious	officious [+]
ofing	offing
ofis	office [+]
ofiser	officer
ofishal	official [+]
ofishiate	officiate [2]
ofishus	officious [+]
ofprint	offprint
ofset	offset [+]
ofshoot	offshoot
ofside	offside

oft /en

ofthalmia	ophthalmia [+]
ofthalmologist	ophthalmologist [+]
oger	ogre [+]

ogle [2] /r
ogre /ss (fem.)

ogul	ogle [2+]

oh * (exclaim)

oh	O *

ohm /ic/meter
oil [1] /y

ointment		omlet	omelette	
oister	oyster	omnibus /es		
oiyay	oyez	omnipoten *ce* /t		
ok	oak [+]	omnipotens	omnipotence [+]	
oks	ox [+]	omnipresent		
oksalic	oxalic	omniscien *ce* /t		
oksbridge	Oxbridge	omnisiens	omniscience [+]	
oksbrige	Oxbridge	omnisient	omniscient	
oksen	oxen	omnivorous /ly		
oksiasetilene	oxy-acetylene	omnivorus	omnivorous [+]	
oksidashun	oxidation	on	own [1]	
oksidation	oxidation	once		
okside	oxide [+]	oncoming		
oksident	occident [+]	oncore	encore [2]	
oksidise	oxidise [2+]	one ★ (single) /self		
oksigen	oxygen	oner	honour [1+]	
oksigenate	oxygenate [2+]	oner	owner [+]	
oksigenise	oxygenise [2]	onerable	honourable	
oksihemoglobin	oxyhaemoglobin	onerabul	honourable	
oksonian	Oxonian	onerous		
okstail	oxtail	onership	ownership	
okstale	oxtail	onerus	onerous	
okstung	ox-tongue	oniks	onyx	
okum	oakum	onion		
old /en/er		onist	honest [+]	
olfacshun	olfaction [+]	onistey	honesty	
olfact *ion* /ory		onley	only	
olfactrey	olfactory	onlook *er* /ing		
oligarch *y* /ies		only		
oligarkey	oligarchy [+]	onomatipea	onomatopoeia [+]	
olimpic	Olympic [+]	onomatopoei *a* /c		
oliv	olive	onorarey	honorary	
olive		onorarium	honorarium [+]	
Olympi *c* /an		onrable	honourable	
om	ohm [+]	onrabul	honourable	
ombudsman		onrush		
omega		onset		
omelet	omelette	onslaught		
omelette		onslawt	onslaught	
omen [1]		onslort	onslaught	
ominous /ly		onto		
ominus	ominous [+]	ontray	entrée	
omishun	omission	ontreprener	entrepreneur [+]	
omission		onus		
omit [3]		onward /s		

onyx		oppress ¹ /ion/ive	
oolit *e* /ic		oprable	operable ⁺
ooze ² /y		oprabul	operable ⁺
opacity		opreshun	oppression
opake	opaque ⁺	opresiv	oppressive
opal /ine		opress	oppress ¹⁺
opalescen *ce* /t		opshun	option ⁺
opalesens	opalescence ⁺	opshunal	optional
opaque /ly		opt ¹ /ative	
opasitey	opacity	opthalmia	ophthalmia ⁺
open ¹ /er		opthalmic	ophthalmic
open sesame		opthalmologist	ophthalmologist
opera /tic/tically		opthalmology	ophthalmology
operab *le* /ility		optic /al/ally	
operabul	operable ⁺	optician	
operashun	operation ⁺	optimise ²	
operat *e* ² /ive/or		optimism	
operater	operator	optimistic /ally	
operation /al		optimum	
operetta		option /al/ally	
ophthalmi *a* /c		optishun	optician
ophthalmolog *ist* /y		opulen *ce* /t	
opiate		opulens	opulence ⁺
opine ²		opus	
opinion /ated		or ★ (alternative)	
opinyun	opinion ⁺	or	awe ²★⁺
opium		or	oar ★
oponent	opponent	or	ore ★
oportune	opportune ⁺	ora	aura
oportunism	opportunism ⁺	orac *le* /ular	
oportunist	opportunist	oracul	oracle ⁺
oportunitey	opportunity ⁺	oral ★ /ly (verbal)	
opose	oppose ²⁺	oral	aural ★⁺
oposishun	opposition	orangatang	orang-outang
oposit	opposite ⁺	orange /ade	
oposition	opposition	orang-outang	
opossum		orashun	oration ⁺
oposum	opossum	orater	orator
opponent		orat *ion* /or	
opportune /ly/ness		oratorio /s	
opportun *ism* /ist		orator *y* /ies	
opportunit *y* /ies		oratrey	oratory ⁺
oppose ² /r		orb ¹	
opposishun	opposition	orbit ¹ /al	
opposit *e* /ion		orcestra	orchestra

orcestrate	orchestrate [2+]	original /ity/ly	
orchard		originat e [2] /ion/or	
orchestra		oringe	orange [+]
orchestrat e [2] /ion/or		oriole	
orchid		orkestrate	orchestrate [2+]
ordain [1]		orkid	orchid
ordane	ordain [1]	orlder	alder
ordeal		ornament [1] /al/ation	
ordenrey	ordinary [+]	ornate /ly	
order [1] /liness/ly		orning	awning
ordinal		ornitholog y /ist	
ordinance ★ (rule)		orphan [1] /age	
ordinance	ordnance ★	orspishus	auspicious
ordinar y /ily		orstralian	Australian
ordinat e [2] /ion		orstruck	awestruck
ordinrey	ordinary [+]	orsum	awesome
orditer	auditor	ort	aught ★
orditorey	auditory	ort	ought ★
orditrey	auditory	orthedoks	orthodox
ordnance ★ (survey, guns)		orthodox	
ordure		orthografey	orthography [+]
ore ★ (mineral)		orthograph y /ic/ical	
ore	awe [2★+]	orthopaedic	
ore	oar ★	orthopeadic	orthopaedic
orfan	orphan [1+]	orthoritarian	authoritarian [+]
orfanage	orphanage	ortolan	
orfanige	orphanage	oscilashun	oscillation [+]
orful	awful [+]	oscilation	oscillation [+]
organ /ist		oscillate [2★] (swing)	
organic		oscillat ion /or/ory	
organis e [2] /ation/er		oscillogra m /ph	
organism		oscilloscope	
orgasm		osculate [2★] (contact)	
orger	auger ★	oselot	ocelot
orger	augur [1★]	oshun	ocean
orgey	orgy [+]	osicul	ossicle
org y /iastic/ies		osier	
orical	auricle [+]	osifi	ossify [4+]
oriel		osius	osseous
orient /al/ally		osler	ostler
orientashun	orientation	osmium	
orientat e [2] /ion		osmosis	
orifice		ospray	osprey [+]
orifis	orifice	osprey /s	
origin		osseous	

osseus	osseous	outbid /ding	
ossicle		outbilding	outbuilding
ossifi	ossify [4+]	outboard	
ossif*y* [4] /ication		outbound	
ossilate	oscillate [2*]	outbownd	outbound
ossilation	oscillation [+]	outbrake	outbreak
ossilograf	oscillograph	outbreak	
ossilogram	oscillogram [+]	outbuilding	
ossiloscope	oscilloscope	outburst	
ost	oast	outcase	
ostensibl *e* /y		outclass [1]	
ostensibul	ostensible [+]	outcome	
ostentashun	ostentation [+]	outcri	outcry [+]
ostentashus	ostentatious	outcrop	
ostentat *ion* /ious		outcr*y* /ies	
osteo-arthritis		outdate [2]	
osteology		outdistance [2]	
osteopath /y		outdo /ing/ne	
ostintashun	ostentation [+]	outdoor /s	
ostioarthritis	osteo-arthritis	outer /most	
ostiologey	osteology	outface	
ostler		outfall	
ostracis *e* [2] /m		outfit /ter	
ostrasism	ostracism	outflank [1]	
ostrasize	ostracise [2+]	outflow	
ostrich /es		outgoing /s	
ote	oat [+]	outgrow /n/th	
oter	otter	outhouse	
oth	oath	outhowse	outhouse
other /wise		outlandish /ness	
otoman	ottoman	outlast [1]	
otter		outlaw [1] /ry	
ottoman		outlay	
ought [*] (should)		outlet	
ought	aught [*]	outliing	outlying
ouija		outline [2]	
ounce		outlive [2]	
ouns	ounce	outlook	
our [*] (belonging to us)		outlying	
our	hour [*+]	outmanoeuvre [2]	
ourly	hourly	outmanoover	outmanoeuvre [2]
ourselves		outmatch [1]	
oust [1]		outmoded	
out [1]		outnumber [1]	
outback		outpace [2]	

outpashent	out-patient	overawe [2]	
out-patient		overawl	overall [+]
outpoor	outpour [1]	overbalance [2]	
outpost		overbalans	overbalance [2]
outpour [1]		overbaring	overbearing
output		overbearing	
outrage [2] /ous/ously		overberden	overburden [1]
outragus	outrageous	overblown	
outran		overboard	
outreach [1]		overbord	overboard
outrid e /den/ing/er		overburden [1]	
outright		overcame	
outrite	outright	overcast	
outrun /ning		overcharge [2]	
outset		overcoat	
outshin e /ing		overcom e /ing	
outshone		overcrowd [1]	
outside /r		overdew	overdue
outsize		overdo /ing/ne	
outskirts		overdose [2]	
outspoken /ness		overdraft	
outstanding /ly		overdraw /n	
outstare [2]		overdrive	
outstay [1]		overdu	overdue
outstretch [1]		overdue	
outstrip [3]		overdun	overdone
outvote [2]		overeach	overreach [1]
outward /ly/s		overeat /en/ing	
outwit [3]		overeet	overeat [+]
outworn		overestimate [2]	
ov	of [*]	overflow [1]	
oval		overground	
ovarey	ovary [+]	overgrow /n/th	
ovarian		overgrownd	overground
ovar y /ies		overhand	
ovashun	ovation	overhang /ing	
ovation		overhaul [1]	
oven		overhawl	overhaul [1]
over		overhead /s	
overact [1]		overhear /ing	
overall /s		overheard	
overan	overran	overheat [1]	
overarm		overhed	overhead [+]
overate [*] (overeat)		overheet	overheat [1]
overate	overrate [2*]	overherd	overheard

overhere	overhear [+]	overstate [2] /ment	
overhung		overstep [3]	
overide	override [+]	overstock [1]	
overjoi	overjoy [+]	overstrung	
overjoy /ed		overt /ly	
overladen		overtak e /en/ing	
overland		overtaks	overtax [1]
overlap [3]		overtax [1]	
overla y /id		overtern	overturn [1]
overleaf		overthrow /n	
overleef	overleaf	overtime	
overload [1]		overtire [2]	
overlode	overload [1]	overtone	
overlook [1]		overtook	
overmuch		overture	
overnight		overturn [1]	
overnite	overnight	overwate	overweight
overore	overawe [2]	overweight	
overought	overwrought	overwelm	overwhelm [1+]
overpass		overwerk	overwork [1]
overpower [1]		overwhelm [1] /ingly	
overproduc e [2] /tion		overw ind /ound	
overproducshun	overproduction	overwork [1]	
overran		overwownd	overwound
overrate [2]★ (overvalue)		overwrought	
overrate	overate ★	oviduct	
overrawt	overwrought	ovine	
overreach [1]		oviparous	
overreech	overreach [1]	oviparus	oviparous
overrid e /den/ing		ovipositor	
overrool	overrule [2]	ovoid	
overrule [2]		ovoyd	ovoid
overrun /ning		ovulashun	ovulation
oversaw		ovulat e [2] /ion	
oversea ★ (abroad) /s ★		ovule	
oversee ★† /ing/n/r/s ★†		ov um /a (pl.)	
†(supervise)		owe [2]★ (in debt)	
overshadow [1]		ower	hour ★+
overshoot		ower	our ★
overshot		owerselves	ourselves
oversight		owl /ish	
oversite	oversight	own [1]	
oversle ep /pt		ownce	ounce
oversore	oversaw	owner /less/ship	
overspill [1]		owns	ounce

owst	oust [1]
owt	out [1]
owtbilding	outbuilding
owtbord	outboard
owtbound	outbound
owtbownd	outbound
owtbreak	outbreak
owtlaw	outlaw [1+]
ox /en (pl.)	
oxalic	
Oxbridge	
oxbrige	Oxbridge
oxidashun	oxidation
oxid *e* /ation	
oxidis *e* [2] /ation	
oxigenate	oxygenate [2+]
oxigenise	oxygenise [2]
oxihemoglobin	oxyhaemoglobin
Oxonian	
oxtail	
oxtale	oxtail
ox-tongue	
oxy-acetylene	
oxygen	
oxygenat *e* [2] /ion	
oxygenise [2]	
oxyhaemoglobin	
oyez	
oyster	
ozier	osier
ozone layer	

P

pace [2] /-maker	
pach	patch [1+]
pachwerk	patchwork
pachwork	patchwork
pachyderm /atous	
pacific /ally	
pacifis *m* /t	
pacif *y* [4] /ication/ier	
pack [1] /-horse/-ice	
package [2]	

packet	
packiderm	pachyderm [+]
packidge	package [2]
packing-case	
pact	
pad [3]	
paddle [2] /r/-wheel	
paddock	
paddy /-field	
pade	paid [+]
padie	paddy [+]
padlock [1]	
padock	paddock
padray	padre
padre	
padul	paddle [2+]
pady	paddy [+]
pagan /ism	
pag *e* [2] /ination	
pageant /ry	
pagentrey	pageantry
paginashun	pagination
pagoda	
paid /-up	
pail ★ (bucket)	
pail	pale [2★]
pain [1★] (suffering) /less	
pain	pane ★
painful /ly	
pain-killer	
painstaking	
paint [1] /er	
pair [1★] (two)	
pair	pare [2★]
pair	pear [★+]
pakiderm	pachyderm [+]
pakidurm	pachyderm [+]
pal /ly	
pala *ce* /tial	
paladium	palladium
palankwin	palanquin
palanquin	
palas	palace [+]
palashul	palatial
palatabl *e* /y	

palatabul	palatable +	pamphlet /eer	
palat *e* /al		pan³ /cake	
palatinate		panacea	
palaver		panache	
pale ²★ (whitish)		pan-African	
pale	pail ★	Panama	
paleografey	paleography	pan-American	
paleography		panasea	panacea
paleolithic		panash	panache
paleontolog *y* /ist		panchromatic	
paleozoic		pancrea *s* /tic	
pale *r* /ly/ness/st		pancromatic	panchromatic
palet	pallet ★	panda ★ (animal)	
palet	palette ★+	pandemonium	
palette ★† /-knife		pander ¹★ (indulge)	
†(artist's board)		pane ★ (of glass)	
palfrey		pane	pain ¹★+
paliass	palliasse	paneful	painful +
paliate	palliate ²+	panegyric	
palid	pallid +	panekiller	pain-killer
palindrome		panel³ /list	
palis	palace +	panestaking	painstaking
palisade		pang	
pall¹ /-bearer		panic /-stricken/-struck	
palladium		panick *ed* /ing/y	
pallet ★ (bed)		panickt	panicked +
pallet	palette ★+	panier	pannier
palliasse		panigiric	panegyric
palliat *e* ² /ive		panikey	panicky
pall *id* /or		panikstriken	panic-stricken
palm¹ /ist/istry		pannier	
palmie	palmy	panopl *y* /ied	
palmy		panorama /s	
palor	pallor	panoramic /ally	
palpabl *e* /y		pansie	pansy +
palpabul	palpable +	pansnay	pince-nez
palpitashun	palpitation	pans *y* /ies	
palpitat *e* ² /ion		pant¹	
palsie	palsy +	pantaloon	
pals *y* /ied		pantechnicon	
paltrie	paltry +	panteknicon	pantechnicon
paltr *y* /iness		pantheis *m* /t/tic	
pamflet	pamphlet +	pantheon	
pampas		panther	
pamper¹ /er		panthiism	pantheism +

206

panthion	pantheon	paraly *se* [2] /sis/tic	
pantile		parameter	
pantograf	pantograph [+]	paramilitary	
pantograph /y		paramilitrey	paramilitary
pantomime		paramiter	parameter
pantrey	pantry [+]	paramoor	paramour
pantr *y* /ies		paramount	
papa *cy* /l		paramour	
papasey	papacy [+]	paramownt	paramount
paper [1] /back/-chase		paranoi *a* /c/d	
paperwait	paperweight	parapet	
paperweight		paraphernalia	
papier-mâché		paraphrase [2]	
papirus	papyrus [+]	paraplegi *a* /c	
papist /ical		parapleja	paraplegia [+]
papoose		paraselene	
paprika		parashoot	parachute [2+]
papyamashay	papier-mâché	parashootist	parachutist
papyr *us* /i (pl.)		parasilene	paraselene
parable		parasit *e* /ic/ical	
parabol *a* /ic		parasol	
parabul	parable	paratifoid	paratyphoid
parachut *e* [2] /ist		paratroop /er	
parade [2]		paratyphoid	
paradigm		parboil [1]	
paradim	paradigm	parcel [3]	
paradise		parch [1] /ment	
paradoks	paradox [+]	pardon [1] /able/er	
paradox /ical/ically		pardonabul	pardonable
parafernalia	paraphernalia	pare [2]★ (trim)	
paraffin		pare	pair [1]★
parafrase	paraphrase [2]	pare	pear ★[+]
paragon		parent /age/al/ally	
paragraf	paragraph	parenthes *is* /es (pl.)	
paragraph		parenthesise [2]	
parakeet		parenthetic /ally	
paralaks	parallax	parentige	parentage
paralax	parallax	pariah	
paralel	parallel [1+]	parie	parry [4]
paralelogram	parallelogram	parish /es/ioner	
paralise	paralyse [2+]	parishoner	parishioner
paralisis	paralysis	Parisi *an* /enne (fem.)	
paralitic	paralytic	pariside	parricide [+]
parallax		parisidul	parricidal
parallel [1] /ogram/ism		parit *y* /ies	

park [1] /er
parket   parquet
parking-meter
parlament   parliament [+]
parlance
parlans   parlance
parlay [1]★ (bet)
parlay   parley [1]★
parlementarey   parliamentary
parlementarian   parliamentarian
parler   parlour [+]
parlermade   parlour-maid
parley [1]★ (discuss)
parley   parlay [1]★
parliament /arian/ary
parlour /-maid
parlous
parlus   parlous
parm   palm [1+]
Parmesan
parmist   palmist
parochial /ism/ly
parod y [4] /ies
parokial   parochial [+]
paroksism   paroxysm
parole [2]
parot   parrot [1+]
paroxysm
parquet
parricid e /al
parrot [1] /-fish
parry [4]
parse [2]
parsec
parsel   parcel [3]
parshal   partial [+]
parshialitey   partiality [+]
parsimon ious /y
parsimonius   parsimonious [+]
parsley
parslie   parsley
parsly   parsley
parsnip
parson /age/ic
parsonige   parsonage

part [1] /ly/-time
partak e /en/er/ing
partial /ly
partialit y /ies
participant
participat e [2] /ion/or
particip le /ial
participul   participle [+]
particle
particul   particle
particular /ity/ly
particularis e [2] /ation
partie   party [+]
partisan /ship
partishun   partition [1+]
partisipant   participant
partisipashun   participation
partisipate   participate [2+]
partisipation   participation
partisipul   participle [+]
partit ion [1] /ive
partly
partner [1] /ship
partook
partridge
partrige   partridge
part y /ies
parvenew   parvenu
parvenu
pary   parry [4]
pas   pass [+]
pasable   passable [+]
pasabul   passable [+]
pascher   pasture [+]
pase   pace [2+]
pasemaker   pace-maker
pasenger   passenger
paserbie   passer-by
paserby   passer-by
pasha
pashence   patience ★
pashens   patience ★
pashent   patient [+]
pashonat   passionate
pashun   passion [+]

pasidge	passage	pasturn	pastern
pasific	pacific +	past y /ies	
pasifier	pacifier	paswerd	password
pasifism	pacifism +	pasword	password
pasifist	pacifist	pat ³ /ly/ness	
pasify	pacify ⁴+	patay	pâté
pasige	passage	patch ¹ /es/work/y	
pasiv	passive +	pâté	
pasivitey	passivity	patella	
pasover	passover	paten	pattern ¹
paspartoo	passe-partout	patency	
pasport	passport	patensey	patency
pass /book/es/ing/key		patent ¹ /able/ee/ly	
passabl e /y		pater	patter ¹+
passage		patern	pattern ¹
passed ★ (did pass)		paternal /ism/ly	
passed	past ★	paternalist /ic	
passenger		paternity	
passe-partout		path /way	
passer /-by		pathetic /ally	
passige	passage	pathological /ly	
passion /ate/ately		patholog y /ist	
passive /ly		pathos	
passivity		patie	patty +
passover		patience ★†	
passport		†(forbearance)	
password		patient /s ★ (under	
past ★ (just over)		doctor's care)	
past	passed ★	patina	
pasta		patio /s	
paste ² /board		patiserey	pâtisserie
pastel		pâtisserie	
paster	pastor +	patois	
pasterise	pasteurise ²+	patriarch /al/y	
pastern		patriark	patriarch +
pasteuris e ² /ation		patrician	
pastie	pasty +	patricide	
pastil	pastille	patrimon y /ies	
pastille		patriot /ism	
pastime		patriotic /ally	
pastmaster		patrishun	patrician
pastor /al/ate		patriside	patricide
pastrey	pastry +	patrol ³	
pastr y /ies		patron /ess (fem.)	
pastur e /age		patron age /al	

patronige	patronage +	pay /able/ee/ing/ment	
patronise ² /r		payabul	payable
patten		paynt	paint ¹+
patter ¹ /er		pe	pea+
pattern ¹		pea /nut	
patt y /ies		peace ★ (calm)	
paturnal	paternal +	peace	piece ²★+
paturnitey	paternity	peaceabl e /y	
patwa	patois	peaceabul	peaceable +
paucity		peaceful /ly/ness	
paunch /y		peace-offering	
pauper /ism		peach /es	
pauperis e ² /ation		pea cock /fowl/hen	
pause ²★ (stop)		peak ¹★ (top)	
pause	paws★	peak	pique ★
pave ² /ment		peal ¹★ (of bells)	
pavier	paviour	peal	peel ¹★
pavilion		peap	peep ¹
pavilyun	pavilion	pear ★ (fruit) /-shaped	
paviour		pear	pare ²★
paw ¹★ (foot, feet) /s ★		pear	peer ¹★+
paw	pore ²★	pear	pier ★
pawcelain	porcelain	pearage	peerage +
pawch	porch +	pearce	pierce ²
pawferey	porphyry	pearl ★ (gem) /y	
pawk	pork +	pearl	purl ¹★+
pawkupine	porcupine	peasant /ry	
pawl	pall ¹+	peat	
pawlbarer	pall-bearer	pebbl e /y	
pawlfrey	palfrey	pebul	pebble +
pawltrey	paltry +	pecadillo	peccadillo
pawlzid	palsied	pecan	
pawlzy	palsy +	peccadillo	
pawn ¹ /broker/shop		peck ¹ /er/ish	
pawnch	paunch +	pecock	peacock +
pawnografey	pornography +	pectin	
pawnography	pornography +	pectoral	
pawper	pauper +	peculat e ² /ion/or	
pawperise	pauperise ²+	peculiar /ly	
pawpus	porpoise	peculiarit y /ies	
paws	pause ²★	pecuniary	
pawselane	porcelain	pedagog	pedagogue +
pawselin	porcelain	pedagogic /al	
pawshun	portion ¹	pedagog ue /y	
pawsitey	paucity	pedal ³★ (of bicycle)	

pedant /ic/ry		pelt [1]	
peddle [2]★ (sell)		pelusid	pellucid
pedestal		pelvi *s* /c	
pedestrian crossing		pemmican	
pediatric *s* /ian		pen [3] /-friend/-name	
pediatrishun	pediatrician	penal	
pedi *cure* /gree/ment		penalis *e* [2] /ation	
pedlar		penalt *y* /ies	
pedler	pedlar	penance ★ (repentance)	
pedometer		penance	pennants ★
pedul	pedal [3]★	penans	penance ★
pedul	peddle [2]★	penant	pennant +
peech	peach +	pence	
peel [1]★ (remove skin)		pencil [3]	
peel	peal [1]★	pendant ★ (ornament)	
peep [1]		pendent ★ (hanging)	
peer [1]★† /ess (fem.)		pending	
†(look, noble)		pendulous	
peer	pier ★	pendulum /s	
peer *age* /less/lessly		pendulus	pendulous
peet	peat	penetrab *le* /ility	
peev *ed* /ish/ishness		penetrabul	penetrable +
peg [3]		penetrashun	penetration
pehen	peahen	penetrat *e* [2] /ion/ive	
peice	piece [2]★+	penguin	
peiceofring	peace-offering	pengwin	penguin
pejorative		penicillin	
pekancy	piquancy +	penie	penny +
pekanese	pekinese	peniless	penniless +
pekansey	piquancy +	peninsula ★(n.) /r ★(adj.)	
pekant	piquant	penis	
peek	peak [1]★	penisilin	penicillin
peek	pique ★	peniten *ce* /t	
pekinese		penitens	penitence +
pekish	peckish	penitensharey	penitentiary +
pektin	pectin	penitentiar *y* /ies	
pektoral	pectoral	penkni *fe* /ves (pl.)	
pelican		pennant /s ★ (flags)	
pelit	pellet	pennife	penknife +
pellet		penniless /ness	
pell-mell		pennives	penknives
pellucid		pennon	
pelmel	pell-mell	penn *y* /ies	
pelmet		penon	pennon
pelota		pens	pence

penshun	pension [1+]	perchance	
penshunabul	pensionable	perchans	perchance
penshuner	pensioner	perchase	purchase [2+]
pensil	pencil [3]	percolat *e* [2] /ion/or	
pension [1] /able/er		percushun	percussion [+]
pensive /ly/ness		percuss *ion* /ive	
pentagon /al		perda	purdah
pentameter		perdishun	perdition
pentathlon		perdition	
Pentecost		peregrin *e* /ation	
penthouse		peremptor *y* /ily/iness	
penthows	penthouse	peremtrey	peremptory [+]
penticost	Pentecost	perenial	perennial [+]
penultimate /ly		perennial /ly	
penumbra		perfecshun	perfection [+]
penurey	penury [+]	perfect [1] /ible	
penurius	penurious	perfection /ist	
penur *y* /ious		perfidey	perfidy [+]
penut	peanut	perfidius	perfidious
peonie	peony [+]	perfid *y* /ious	
peon *y* /ies		perforashun	perforation
people [2]		perforat *e* [2] /ion/or	
peper	pepper [1+]	perforce	
pepercorn	peppercorn	perform [1] /ance/er	
peperey	peppery	performans	performance
pepper [1] /corn/mint/y		perfors	perforce
pepsin /ogen		perfume [2] /ry/ries	
pep-talk		perfunctor *y* /ily	
peptic		perfunctrey	perfunctory [+]
peptides		pergative	purgative [+]
pepul	people [2]	pergatrey	purgatory
per	purr [1]	perge	purge [2+]
per annum		perhaps	
per capita		pericarp	
peradvencher	peradventure	periferal	peripheral
peradventure		periferey	periphery [+]
perambulat *e* [2] /ion/or		periferic	peripheric
perblind	purblind	perifery	periphery [+]
perceiv *e* [2] /able		perigee	
percentage		peril /ous/ously	
percepshun	perception [+]	perilus	perilous
perceptibl *e* /y		perimeter	
perceptibul	perceptible [+]	period	
percept *ion* /ive		periodic /al/ally	
perch [1] /es		periosteum	

peripatetic		perpetrater	perpetrator
peripher *y* /al/ic		perpetual /ly	
periscope		perpetuat *e* ² /ion	
perish ¹ /able/ables		perpetuity	
peristalsis		perple .	purple
periton *eum* /itis		perpleks	perplex ¹⁺
periwinkle		perplex ¹ /ity/ities	
periwinkul	periwinkle	perport	purport ¹
perjur *e* ² /y ·		perpose	purpose ⁺
perk ¹ /iness/s/y		perse	purse ²⁺
perkushun	percussion ⁺	persecut *e* ² /ion/or	
perkusiv	percussive	persepshun	perception ⁺
perl	pearl ★⁺	perseptible	perceptible ⁺
perl	purl ¹★⁺	perseption	perception ⁺
perloin	purloin ¹	perseptiv	perceptive
perlu	purlieu	perseve	perceive ²⁺
perm ¹		persever *e* ² /ance	
permanenc *e* /y		pershun	Persian
permanens	permanence ⁺	Persian	
permanent /ly		persist ¹ /ent/ently	
permanganate		persistenc *e* /y	
permeab *le* /ility		persistens	persistence ⁺
permeabul	permeable ⁺	person /able/age	
permeat *e* ² /ion		persona /(non) grata	
permishun	permission ⁺	personal ★ (private) /ly	
permisibul	permissible	personal	personnel ★
permisiv	permissive ⁺	personalit *y* /ies	
permiss *ion* /ible		personat *e* ² /ion/or	
permissive /ness		personel	personal ★⁺
permit ³		personel	personnel ★
permutashun	permutation	personifi	personify ⁴⁺
permut *e* ² /ation		personif *y* ⁴ /ication/ier	
pernicious /ly/ness		personnel ★ (employees)	
pernickety		personnel	personal ★⁺
pernikitey	pernickety	perspective	
pernishus	pernicious ⁺	perspeks	perspex
perokside	peroxide	perspektiv	perspective
peroxide		perspex	
perpechooal	perpetual ⁺	perspicaci *ous* /ty	
perpechooate	perpetuate ²⁺	perspicashus	perspicacious ⁺
perpechual	perpetual ⁺	perspicu *ous* /ity	
perpechuate	perpetuate ²⁺	perspicuus	perspicuous ⁺
perpendicular /ity		perspirashun	perspiration
perpetrashun	perpetration	perspir *e* ² /ation	
perpetrat *e* ² /ion/or		persuad *e* ² /able/er	

persuashun	persuasion	pestle	
persuasion		pesul	pestle
persuasive /ly/ness		pet³ /-name	
perswadable	persuadable	petal³	
perswadabul	persuadable	peteat	petite
perswade	persuade ²⁺	peter¹ /sham	
perswasion	persuasion	peticoat	petticoat
perswasiv	persuasive ⁺	petie	petty⁺
pert /ly/ness		petiole	
pertain¹		petish	pettish
pertane	pertain¹	petishun	petition ¹⁺
pertinaci *ous* /ty		petite	
pertinashus	pertinacious⁺	petition¹ /er	
pertinen *ce* /t		petrel ★ (sea bird)	
pertinens	pertinence⁺	petrel	petrol ★⁺
perturb¹ /ation		petrifacshun	petrifaction
perva *de*² /sive		petrifaction	
perverse /ly/ness		petrifi	petrify⁴⁺
pervershun	perversion⁺	petrif *y*⁴ /ication	
pervers *ion* /ive		petrol ★ (gasoline) /eum	
pervert¹ /er		petrol	petrel ★
pervious		petrolog *y* /ist	
pervius	pervious	petrul	petrel ★
pervurs	perverse⁺	petrul	petrol ★⁺
pervurshun	perversion⁺	petticoat	
pervursiv	perversive	pettish	
pervurt	pervert ¹⁺	pett *y* /ier/iest/ily/iness	
pesable	peaceable⁺	petul	petal³
pesabul	peaceable⁺	petulan *ce* /t	
pesant	peasant⁺	petulans	petulance⁺
pesarey	pessary⁺	petunia	
pese	peace ★	peved	peeved⁺
pese	piece ²★⁺	pevish	peevish
peseful	peaceful⁺	pew	
peseofring	peace-offering	pewit	
peseta		pewter	
pesimism	pessimism⁺	phaeton	
pesimist	pessimist	phalanks	phalanx⁺
pesimistic	pessimistic	phalan *x* /ges/xes (pls.)	
pessar *y* /ies		phall *ic* /us	
pessimis *m* /t/tic		phantasm	
pest /icide		phantasmagori *a* /c	
pester¹		phantom	
pestilen *ce* /t/tial		Pharaoh	
pestilens	pestilence⁺	pharingeal	pharyngeal⁺

pharinx	pharynx	phisicist	physicist
Pharis *ee* /aic		phisics	physics
pharmaceutic /al		phisik	physique ★
pharmacist		phisiologey	physiology +
pharmacolog *y* /ist		phisionomey	physiognomy
pharmacopoeia		phisiotherapist	physiotherapist
pharmac *y* /ies		phisiotherapy	physiotherapy +
pharmasey	pharmacy +	phisique	physique ★
pharmasist	pharmacist	phlebitis	
pharmasutical	pharmaceutical	phlegm /atic	
pharo	Pharaoh	phlem	phlegm +
pharyng *eal* /itis		phloem	
pharynx		phloks	phlox ★
phase ²		phlox ★ (flower)	
phayton	phaeton	phobia	
pheasant		Phoebus	
phebus	Phoebus	phoenix	
pheniks	phoenix	phon ★ (unit of sound)	
phenix	phoenix	phone ²★ (telephone)	
phenobarbitone		phonetic /ally	
phenol		phonograf	phonograph +
phenomenal /ly		phonograph /ic	
phenomen *on* /a (pl.)		phonolog *y* /ical	
phesant	pheasant	phony	
phial ★ (bottle)		phosfate	phosphate
philander ¹ /er		phosforesence	phosphorescence
philanthrop *y* /ic/ist		phosforesent	phosphorescent
philarmonic	philharmonic	phosforous	phosphorous ★+
philatel *y* /ist		phosforus	phosphorus ★
philharmonic		phosphate	
philip	fillip	phosphoresce ² /nce/nt	
Philistine		phosphor *ous* ★ (adj.) /ic	
philolog *y* /ical/ist		phosphorus ★ (n.)	
philosofer	philosopher	photo /-electric/stat	
philosofey	philosophy +	photocopie	photocopy +
philosofical	philosophical +	photocop *y* /ies	
philosofise	philosophise ²	photo-finish	
philosoph *er* /y		photogenic	
philosophical /ly		photograf	photograph ¹+
philosophise ²		photograph ¹ /ic/y	
philter	philtre ★	photomet *er* /ric/ry	
philtre ★ (love potion)		photon	
phisic	physic ★	photosynthesis	
phisical	physical +	phototropism	
phisician	physician	phrase ²★ (words) /ology	

phrenetic		piece ²★ (part) /meal	
phrenolog y /ist		piece	peace ★
phthisis		piece-work	
phylum		pier ★ (jetty)	
physic ★ (remedy)		pier	peer ¹★+
physic	physique ★	pierce ²	
physical /ly		piers	pierce ²
physician		piety	
physicist		pig ³ /-iron/let	
physics		pigeon ★ (bird)	
physiognomy		pigeon	pidgin ★
physiolog y /ical/ist		pigeon-hole ²	
physiotherap ist /y		pigerey	piggery +
physique ★ (body)		pigger y /ies	
pi ★ (maths)		piggyback	
pi	pie ★+	pigheaded /ness	
pianist		pigheded	pigheaded +
piano /forte		pigiback	piggyback
piatsa	piazza	pigin	pidgin ★
piazza		pigin	pigeon ★
pibald	piebald	pigment ¹ /ation	
picador		pig skin /tail	
picalilli	piccalilli	pigsti	pigsty +
picancy	piquancy +	pigst y /ies	
picaniny	piccaninny	pigtale	pigtail
picant	piquant	pijamas	pyjamas
piccalilli		pikaxe	pickaxe
piccaninny		pike ² /staff	
piccolo /s		piks	pyx ¹
pich	pitch ¹+	piksy	pixie +
pichfork	pitchfork ¹	pil	pill +
pick ¹ /axe/pocket		pilage	pillage ²+
pickcher	picture ²+	pilchard	
picket ¹		pile ²	
pickle ²		piler	pillar +
picnic /ked/ker/king		pilerbox	pillar-box
Pict /ish		pilfer ¹ /age/er	
pictorial /ly		pilgrim /age	
picture ² /sque		pilgrimige	pilgrimage
picturesk	picturesque	pilige	pillage ²+
pidgin ★ (jargon)		pilion	pillion
pidgin	pigeon ★	pill /-box	
pie ★ (food) /crust		pillage ² /r	
pie	pi ★	pillar /-box	
piebald		pillion	

pillor*y*⁴ /ies		pirat*e*² /ical	
pillow		pire	pyre
pilon	pylon	piric	Pyrrhic
pilorey	pillory⁴⁺	pirite	pyrite
pilot¹ /age		pirooet	pirouette²
pilow	pillow	pirotecnic	pyrotechnic⁺
pilyun	pillion	pirouette²	
pimento		pirric	Pyrrhic
pimpernel		pistachio /s	
pimpl*e* /y		pistil ★ (flower)	
pimpul	pimple⁺	pistol ★ (gun)	
pin³ /-prick/-up		piston	
pinacle	pinnacle²	pit³ /fall/man	
pinacul	pinnacle²	pitance	pittance
pinafore		pitans	pittance
pince-nez		pit-a-pat /ter	
pincers		pitch¹ /blende/er/es	
pinch¹ /er/es		pitchfork¹	
pincushion		pitch-pine	
pincushun	pincushion	piteous /ly/ness	
pine² /-cone		pith /ily/iness/y	
pineapple		pithon	python
pineapul	pineapple	pitiabl*e* /y	
ping-pong		pitiabul	pitiable⁺
pinion¹		pitie	pity⁴⁺
pink¹		pitiful /ly	
pinnacle²		pitius	piteous⁺
pinpoint¹		pitsicato	pizzicato
pinsers	pincers	pittance	
pint		pittans	pittance
pinyun	pinion¹	pituitary	
pionear	pioneer¹	pituitrey	pituitary
pioneer¹		pit*y*⁴ /iless	
pious /ly		pius	pious⁺
pip³ /-squeak		pivot¹ /al	
pipe² /line/r		pix	pyx¹
pipe -*clay* /dream		pixie /s	
pipet	pipette	pixy	pixie⁺
pipette		pizzicato	
pippin		placab*le* /ility	
piquan*cy* /t		placabul	placable⁺
pique ★ (anger)		placard¹	
piracy		placat*e*² /ion	
piramid	pyramid⁺	place²★ (position)	
pirasey	piracy	place	plaice ★

217

placenta /l		plate	plait [1]
placid /ity/ly		plateau /x (pl.)	
placket		platelet	
plagarise	plagiarise [2+]	plater	platter
plage	plague [2]	platform	
plagiaris *e* [2] /m/t		platichood	platitude [+]
plague [2]		platinum	
plaice ★ (fish)		platipus	platypus [+]
plaid		platitud *e* /inous	
plain ★ (flat land)		platitudinus	platitudinous
plain	plane [2★]	plato	plateau [+]
plain *er* /ness/song		platonic /ally	
plaintiff ★ (legal)		platoon	
plaintive ★ (sad) /ly		platter	
plait [1]		platypus /es	
plait	plate [2+]	plaudit	
plajarise	plagiarise [2+]	plausib *le* /ility/ly	
plak	plaque	plausibul	plausible [+]
plaket	placket	plawdit	plaudit
plan [3] /ner		plawsible	plausible [+]
plane [2★] (smooth, aircraft)		play [1] /er/ing/mate	
		playfellow	
plane	plain ★	playful /ly/ness	
planet /arium/ary		playground	
planetrey	planetary	playgrownd	playground
plank		playrite	playwright
plankton		playwright	
plant [1] /ain/ation/er		ple	plea [+]
plantashun	plantation	plea /s ★ (appeal)	
plantif	plaintiff ★	plead [1] /er	
plantin	plantain	pleasant /ly/ry	
plantiv	plaintive ★+	please [2★] (request)	
plaque		pleasur *e* /able/ably	
plase	place [2★]	pleat [1]	
plase	plaice ★	plebean	plebeian
plasenta	placenta [+]	plebeian	
plasid	placid [+]	plebian	plebeian
plasma		plebiscite	
plasmolysis		plebisit	plebiscite
plaster [1] /cast/er		plectrum	
plastic /ally/ity		pledge [2]	
plasticine		pleed	plead [1+]
plastiseen	plasticine	pleet	pleat [1]
plastisine	plasticine	plege	pledge [2]
plate [2] /ful/-glass		plenary	

plenipotensharey	plenipotentiary	plumage	
plenipotentiary		plumb ¹★ (weight) /line	
plenitude		plumbago	
plentie	plenty +	plumber	
plentiful /ly/ness		plume ²	
plentius	plenteous	plumer	plumber
plent y /eous		plumet	plummet ¹
plesant	pleasant +	plumige	plumage
plese	pleas ★	plumline	plumbline
plese	please ²★	plummet ¹	
plesurable	pleasurable	plump ¹ /er/est/ness	
plesurabul	pleasurable	plunder ¹ /er	
plesure	pleasure +	plunge ² /r	
plethor a /ic		pluperfect	
pleural ★ (membrane)		plural ★ (a few) /ism/ity	
pleural	plural ★+	plural	pleural ★
pleurisy		plurisey	pleurisy
pli	ply ⁴+	plus	
pliab le /ility		plush /y	
pliabul	pliable +	Pluto	
plian cy /t		plutocrac y /ies	
pliansey	pliancy +	plutocrasey	plutocracy +
pliers		plutocrat /ic	
plight /ed		plutonium	
Plimsoll /line/mark		pluvial	
plimsolls		ply ⁴ /wood	
plinth		pnemonic	mnemonic
plite	plight +	pneumatic	
pliwood	plywood	pneumonia	
plod ³ /der		poach ¹ /er	
ploi	ploy	poch	poach ¹+
plooto	Pluto	pock /-marked	
plootocracy	plutocracy +	pocket ¹ /-book/-knife	
plootocrat	plutocrat +	pocket-money	
plootonium	plutonium	podgy	
ploovial	pluvial	podium	
plot ³ /ter		poem	
plough ¹ /man/share		poet /ess (fem.)	
plover		poetic /al/ally	
plow	plough ¹+	poetry	
ploy		pogo-stick	
pluck ¹ /ier/iest/ily/y		poignan cy /t/tly	
plug ³ /ger		poim	poem
plum ★ (fruit)		poinancy	poignancy +
plum	plumb ¹★+	poinansey	poignancy +

poinant	poignant	polip	polyp
point¹ /edly/er/less		polisey	policy+
point -*blank* /-duty		polish¹	
poise²		polisilable	polysyllable+
poisenous	poisonous	polite /ly/ness	
poisenus	poisonous	politecnic	polytechnic
poison¹ /er/ous		politey	polity
pok e² /er/y		politheism	polytheism+
poker-face /d		polithene	polythene
pokey	poky	politic /ian/s	
pokmarked	pock-marked	political /ly	
poks	pox	politishun	politician
pol	poll¹★+	polity	
polar /ity		polka /dot	
polar bear		poll¹★ (vote) /-tax	
polard	pollard+	poll	pole★+
Polaris		pollard /ed	
polaris e² /ation/er		pollen	
pole ★ (tall staff) /cat		pollinat e² /ion	
pole	poll¹★+	pollster	
pole-jump¹		pollut e² /ion	
polemic /al		polonaise	
polen	pollen	polonase	polonaise
poler	polar+	polo-neck	
polerbare	polar bear	polonium	
polerbear	polar bear	poltax	poll-tax
polese	police²+	poltegist	poltergeist
pole-star		polterer	poulterer
pole-vault¹		poltergeist	
poliandrey	polyandry+	poltice	poultice
poliandrus	polyandrous	poltis	poultice
polianthus	polyanthus	poltrey	poultry
police² /man/woman		polushun	pollution
polic y /ies		polute	pollute²+
poligamey	polygamy+	polution	pollution
poligamus	polygamous	polyandrey	polyandry+
poliglot	polyglot	polyandr y /ous	
poligon	polygon	polyanthus	
polihedron	polyhedron+	polygam y /ous	
polimer	polymer	polyglot	
polinashun	pollination	polygon	
polinate	pollinate²+	polyhedr on /al	
polination	pollination	polymer	
polinesian	Polynesian	polymeris e² /ation	
polio /myelitis		polyneshun	Polynesian

Polynesian		poor *er* /est/ly	
polyp		pop³ /corn/gun	
polysyllab *le* /ic		pop *e* /ery/ish	
polytechnic		popet	poppet
polytheis *m* /t/tic		pop-eyed	
polythene		popicock	poppycock
pomace ★ (pulp)		popie	poppy⁺
pomade²		popinjay	
pomegranate		poplar ★ (tree)	
pomegranit	pomegranate	poplar	popular ★⁺
pomel	pommel³	poplin	
Pomeranian		poppet	
pomfret /cake		popp *y* /ies	
pomfrit	pomfret⁺	poppycock	
pomiculcher	pomiculture	populace	
pomiculture		popular ★† /ity/ly	
pommel³		†(well known)	
pomology		popularis *e*² /ation	
pomp /osity/ous		popularitey	popularity
pompus	pompous	populas	populace
ponder¹ /able		populashun	population
ponderous /ly		populat *e*² /ion	
ponderus	ponderous⁺	populer	popular ★⁺
pondrabul	ponderable	populous	
poney	pony⁺	populus	populous
poniard		popy	poppy⁺
ponie	pony⁺	por	paw¹★⁺
ponitale	pony-tail	por	pore²★
pontiff		porcelain	
pontificate²		porch /es	
pontoon		porcupine	
pon *y* /ies /y-tail		pore²★ (of skin)	
ponyard	poniard	pore	poor ★
poo	pooh¹⁺	pore	pour¹★
poodle		porer	poorer⁺
poodul	poodle	porfrey	porphyry
poof	pouffe	poridge	porridge
pooh¹ /-pooh		porige	porridge
pool		poringer	porringer
pooley	pulley	pork /er/y	
poolit	pullet	porkupine	porcupine
poop¹		pornografey	pornography⁺
poor ★ (needy)		pornograph *y* /ic	
poor	pore²★	poro *us* /sity	
poor	pour¹★	porphyry	

porpoise		posse	
porpus	porpoise	possess¹ /ion/ive/or	
porridge		possi	posse
porringer		possib *le* /ility/ly	
porselin	porcelain	possibul	possible⁺
porshun	portion¹	possum	
porslin	porcelain	post¹ /-card	
port /age/-hole		post office	
portab *le* /ility		postage /-stamp	
portabul	portable⁺	postal	
portal		post-date²	
portcullis		poster	
portend¹		posterier	posterior
portent /ous		posterior	
portentus	portentous	posterity	
porter /house		postern	
portfolio		post-graduate	
portico		post-haste	
portion¹		posthumous /ly	
portkulis	portcullis	posthumus	posthumous⁺
portl *y* /iness		postige	postage⁺
portmanteau		postilion	
portrait /ure		postilyon	postilion
portray¹ /al		post-impressionist	
portrit	portrait⁺	post *man* /mark	
portul	portal	post *master* /mistress	
porus	porous⁺	post-meridiem	
poscher	posture²	post-mortem	
pose²		postofiss	post office
poseshun	possession	postpone² /ment	
posess	possess¹⁺	postulant	
posession	possession	postulate²	
posessiv	possessive,	postumus	posthumous⁺
posey	posy⁺	posture²	
posh		post-war	
poshun	potion	posum	possum
posibilitey	possibility	pos *y* /ies	
posible	possible⁺	potash	
posibul	possible⁺	potasium	potassium
posie	posy⁺	potassium	
posishun	position⁺	potato /es	
position /al		pot-bell *y* /ied	
positive /ly/ness		poteen	
positivism		poten *cy* /t	
positron		potene	poteen

potensey	potency [+]	praer	prayer [+]
potenshul	potential [+]	pragmati c /sm	
potentate		prairey	prairie
potential /ity/ly		prairie	
poter	potter [1]	praise [2] /worthy	
poterey	pottery [+]	prance [2]	
pot-hol e /er/ing		prank	
pot-hook		prans	prance [2]
potie	potty	prarey	prairie
potion		prase	praise [2+]
pot-pourri		prasee	précis [1]
potter [1]		praseworthey	praiseworthy
potter y /ies		prate [2]	
potty		prattle [2]	
pouch [1] /es		pratul	prattle [2]
pouffe		prawn [1]	
poulterer		pray [1]★ (say prayers)	
poultice		pray	prey [1]★
poultry		prayer /book/ful	
pounce [2]		preach [1] /er	
pound [1] /age		preamble [2]	
pour [1]★ (to flow)		preambul	preamble [2]
pour	poor ★	prearrange [2]	
pour	pore [2]★	precarious /ly/ness	
pout [1]		precarius	precarious [+]
poverty /-stricken		precaution /ary	
powch	pouch [1+]	precawshun	precaution [+]
powder [1] /y		precede [2]★ (go before)	
power [1] /less/-station		precede	proceed [1]★[+]
powerful /ly/ness		precedence ★ (priority)	
pownce	pounce [2]	precedent ★† /s ★†	
pownd	pound [1+]	†(previous law[s])	
powns	pounce [2]	precedent	president ★[+]
powt	pout [1]	precentor	
pow-wow [1]		precept /or	
pox		preceshun	procession
practicab le /ility		prech	preach [1+]
practicabul	practicable [+]	precinct	
practical /ity/ly		precious /ly	
practice ★ (n.)		precipice	
practician		precipis	precipice
practise [2]★ (v.)		precipitanc e /y	
practishun	practician	precipitans	precipitance [+]
practishuner	practitioner	precipitat e [2] /ion/or	
practitioner		precipitous /ly	

precipitus	precipitous +	preferens	preference
précis ¹		preferenshal	preferential +
precise /ly		preferential /ly	
preclu *de* ² /sion/sive		preferment	
preclushun	preclusion	prefiks	prefix ¹
precocious /ness		prefis	preface ²+
precocity		prefix ¹	
preconceive ²		pregnanc *y* /ies	
preconception		pregnansey	pregnancy +
preconsepshun	preconception	pregnant	
preconseve	preconceive ²	prehensile	
precoshus	precocious +	prehistor *ic* /y	
precositey	precocity	pre-ignition	
precursor /y		prejudge ²	
predater	predator +	prejudice ²	
predator /y		prejudicial /ly	
predecessor		prejudis	prejudice ²
predesesor	predecessor	prejudishal	prejudicial +
predestinashun	predestination	prejuge	prejudge ²
predestin *e* ² /ation		prelate	
predetermine ²		prelim	
predicament		preliminar *y* /ies	
predicate ²		preliminrey	preliminary +
predicshun	prediction	prelude ²	
predict ¹ /able/ion		premature /ly	
predictabul	predictable	premeditat *e* ² /ion	
predilecshun	predilection	premier *† /ship	
predilection		†(Prime Minister)	
predispos *e* ² /ition		première *†	
prediturmine	predetermine ²	†(first performance)	
predominance		premise ²★ (postulate)	
predominans	predominance	premises (house)	
predominant /ly		premiss ★ (logic)	
predominate ²		premium /s	
preegsist	pre-exist ¹+	premonishun	premonition +
pre-eminen *ce* /t		premonit *ion* /ory	
pre-empt ¹ /ion		prenatal	
preemshun	pre-emption	prene	preen ¹
preen ¹		preoccupi	preoccupy ⁴+
pre-exist ¹ /ence		preoccup *y* ⁴ /ation	
prefabricat *e* ² /ion		preocupashun	preoccupation
prefa *ce* ² /tory		preocupy	preoccupy ⁴+
prefect /orial/ure		prepade	prepaid
prefer ³ /able/ably		prepaid	
preference		preparashun	preparation

preparatrey	preparatory	presid *e*² /ial	
prepar *e*² /ation/atory		presidency	
prepay /ing/ment		presidensey	presidency
preponder *ance* /ant		presidenshal	presidential
preponderate ²		president *† /ial/s *†	
preposess	prepossess ¹⁺	†(elected head[s])	
preposishun	preposition ⁺	president	precedent *⁺
preposition /al		presidial	
prepossess ¹ /ion		presige	presage ²
preposterous /ly		presinct	precinct
preposterus	preposterous ⁺	presipice	precipice
prerekwisit	prerequisite	presipis	precipice
prerequisite		presipitance	precipitance ⁺
prerogative		presipitans	precipitance ⁺
pres	press ¹⁺	presipitate	precipitate ²⁺
presage ²		presipitation	precipitation
presbiterian	Presbyterian	presipitous	precipitous ⁺
Presbyterian		presipitus	precipitous ⁺
prescribe ²*†		presise	precise ⁺
†(give directions)		press ¹ /er	
prescribe	proscribe ²*	press-stud	
prescripshun	prescription ⁺	pressure ² /-cooker	
prescript *ion* /ive		pressuris *e*² /ation	
presede	precede ²*	prest	priest ⁺
presedence	precedence *	prestege	prestige ⁺
presedence	precedents *	presthood	priesthood
presedent	precedent *⁺	prestig *e* /ious	
presedent	president *⁺	prestigus	prestigious
preseed	precede ²*	presto	
presence		presum *e*² /ably	
presens	presence	presumpt *ion* /ive/uous	
present ¹ /ation/ly		presumshun	presumption ⁺
presentabl *e* /y		presumshus	presumptuous
presentashun	presentation	presumtuous	presumptuous
presentiment		presuppos *e*² /ition	
presentor	precentor	pretekst	pretext
presept	precept ⁺	pretence	
preservashun	preservation	pretend ¹ /er	
preservative		pretens	pretence
preserv *e*² /ation		pretenshun	pretension
preseshun	procession	pretenshus	pretentious ⁺
presession	procession	pretension	
presher	pressure ²⁺	pretentious /ly/ness	
presherise	pressurise ²⁺	preterite	
preshus	precious ⁺	pretext	

pretie	pretty +	principal ★ (chief) /ly	
prett y /ily/iness		principal	principle ★
prety	pretty +	principalit y /ies	
prevail ¹		principle ★†	
prevalen ce /t		†(moral code)	
prevalens	prevalence +	principle	principal ★+
prevaricat e ² /ion/or		prins	prince +
prevayl	prevail ¹	prinsess	princess
prevenshun	prevention	prinsipal	principal ★+
prevent ¹ /able/ion/ive		prinsipality	principality +
preview		print ¹ /er	
previous /ly		prior /ess (fem.)/y	
previus	previous +	priorit y /ies	
prevue	preview	prise ²★ (lever)	
pre-war		prise	price ²+
prey ¹★ (devour)		prise	prize ²★
prey	pray ¹★	prisie	prissy
prezbiterian	Presbyterian	prism /atic	
pri	pry ⁴	prison /er	
price ² /less		prissy	
prick ¹		pristene	pristine
prickl e ² /y		pristine	
pricul	prickle ²+	prithee	
pride ²		prity	pretty +
prier	prior +	privacy	
prierey	priory	privaricate	prevaricate ²+
priest /hood/ly		privasey	privacy
prig /gish		privashun	privation
prim /ly/mer/mest/ness		private /ly	
prima donna		privateer	
prima facie		privation	
prima cy /te		privet	
primar y /ies/ily		privie	privy
primasey	primacy +	privilege ²	
prime ² /r		privilige	privilege ²
Prime Minister		privit	private +
primeval		privy	
primitiv e /ism		prize ²★ (award)	
primogenit al /or/ure		prize	prise ²★
primordial		prizm	prism +
primrey	primary +	probab le /ility/ly	
primrose		probabul	probable +
primula		probashun	probation +
primus		probate	
prince /ly/ss (fem.)		probation /ary/er	

probe²	
problem	
problematic /al/ally	
proboscis	
procedure	
proceed¹★ (go on) /s	
proceed	precede²★
proceshun	procession
process¹ /ion/ional	
proclaim¹	
proclamashun	proclamation
proclamation	
proclaym	proclaim¹
procrastinat e² /ion	
procreat e² /ion	
proctor /ial	
procura ble /tion/tor	
procurabul	procurable⁺
procurater	procurator
procure² /ment	
prod³	
prodigal /ity	
prodigey	prodigy⁺
prodigious /ly/ness	
prodigus	prodigious⁺
prodig y /ies	
produc e² /er/ible	
product /ion/ive	
produse	produce²⁺
produser	producer
profan e² /ation	
profanit y /ies	
profecy	prophecy★
profecy	prophesy⁴★
profer	proffer¹
profeser	professor⁺
profesey	prophecy★
profeshonal	professional⁺
profeshun	profession⁺
profesi	prophesy⁴★
profesor	professor⁺
profess¹ /edly	
profession /alism	
professional /ly	
professor /ial	

profet	prophet⁺
profetical	prophetical
proffer¹	
proficien cy /t	
profilactic	prophylactic⁺
profile	
profishency	proficiency⁺
profishensey	proficiency⁺
profishent	proficient
profit¹ /less	
profitab le /ility/ly	
profitabul	profitable⁺
profiteer¹	
profliga cy /te	
profound /ly	
profownd	profound⁺
profundity	
profus e² /ion	
profushun	profusion
progenitor	
progeny	
prognos is /es (pl.)/tic	
prognosticat e² /ion	
program³★ (computer)	
programme ★†	
†(list of events)	
progreshun	progression
progress¹ /ion/ional	
progressive /ly	
prohibishun	prohibition
prohibit¹ /ion/ive/ory	
proibit	prohibit¹⁺
projecshun	projection
project¹ /ile/ion/or	
projeney	progeny
projeniter	progenitor
proksey	proxy⁺
proksimate	proximate⁺
proksimitey	proximity
prolapse²	
proletaria n /t	
proliferashun	proliferation
proliferat e² /ion	
prolific /ally	
prolog	prologue²

prologue ²		propitiat *e* ² /ion/or	
prolong ¹		propitious /ly	
prolongat *e* ² /ion		propolis	
promenade ² /r		proporshonal	proportional ⁺
promethium		proporshonate	proportionate
prominen *ce* /t		proporshun	proportion ¹⁺
prominens	prominence ⁺	proportion ¹ /ate	
promiscu *ous* /ity		proportional /ly	
promiscuus	promiscuous ⁺	proposal	
promis *e* ² /sory		propos *e* ² /ition	
promoshun	promotion ⁺	proposishun	proposition
promote ² /r		propound ¹	
promotion /al		propownd	propound ¹
prompt ¹ /er/ness		proprietary	
promulgat *e* ² /ion		proprieter	proprietor
prone /ly/ness		proprietey	propriety ⁺
prong ¹		proprietor	
pronoun		proprietrey	proprietary
pronounce ² /ment		propriet *y* /ies	
pronown	pronoun	propulshun	propulsion ⁺
pronowns	pronounce ²⁺	propuls *ion* /ive	
pronunciation		prorog	prorogue ²⁺
pronunsiashun	pronunciation	prorog *ue* ² /ation	
prood	prude ⁺	prosaic /ally	
proof ¹ /-reader		proscribe ²★ (outlaw)	
proon	prune ²	proscribe	prescribe ²★
proov	prove ²⁺	proscripshun	proscription ⁺
prop ³		proscript *ion* /ive	
propaganda		prose	
propagashun	propagation	prosecushun	prosecution
propagat *e* ² /ion		prosecut *e* ² /ion/or	
propane		prosedure	procedure
propel ³ /ler		proseed	proceed ¹★⁺
propell *ant* (n.) /ent (adj.)		proselight	proselyte ²
propensit *y* /ies		proselyte ²	
proper /ly		proselytise ² /r	
propert *y* /ies		prosess	process ¹⁺
prophecy ★ (n.)		prosicushun	prosecution
prophesy ⁴★ (v.)		prosilite	proselyte ²
prophet /ess (fem.)/ical		prosilitise	proselytise ²⁺
prophilactic	prophylactic ⁺	prosody	
prophyl *actic* /axis		prospect ¹ /ive/or	
propishiate	propitiate ²⁺	prospectus /es	
propishous	propitious ⁺	prosper ¹ /ity/ous	
propishus	propitious ⁺	prosperus	prosperous

prostate * (gland)		provision /al/ally	
prostitushun	prostitution	proviso /ry	
prostitut e ² /ion		provocat ion /ive	
prostrat e ²* (lay flat)		provok e ² /able	
protactinium		provost	
protagonist		prow	
protecshun	protection	prowd	proud +
protect ¹ /ion/ive/or		prowess	
protectorate		prowibishun	prohibition
proteen	protein	prowibition	prohibition
protégé /e (fem.)		prowl ¹ /er	
protein		proximate /ly	
protejay	protégé +	proximity	
protene	protein	prox y /ies	
protest ¹ /ation		prozaic	prosaic +
Protestant /ism		prud e /ery/ish	
protocol		pruden ce /t	
proton		prudens	prudence +
protoplasm		prudenshal	prudential +
prototipe	prototype +	prudential /ly	
prototyp e /al/ical		prune ²	
protract ¹ /ion/or		prurien ce /t	
protrood	protrude ²	pruriens	prurience +
protrooshun	protrusion +	prushan	Prussian
protrude ²		Prussian	
protrus ion /ive		pry ⁴	
protuberan ce /t		psalm /ist	
protuberans	protuberance +	psalter /y	
proud /ly/ness		pseudo /nym	
prov e ² /able		psycedelic	psychedelic
provenance		psyche	
provenans	provenance	psychedelic	
provender		psychiatr ist /y	
proverb /ial		psychic /al	
provide ² /r		psychoanal yse ² /ysis/yst	
providence		psychological /ly	
providens	providence	psycholog y /ist	
providenshul	providential	psychopath /ic	
provident/ial/ially		psycho sis /tic	
provijun	provision +	psychosomatic	
provijunal	provisional	psychotherap ist /y	
provinc e /ial		psycoanalise	psychoanalyse ²+
provins	province +	psycologey	psychology +
provinshal	provincial	psycological	psychological +
provishun	provision +	psycopath	psychopath +

psycosis	psychosis [+]	pulie	pulley
psycosomatic	psychosomatic	pulkritude	pulchritude
psycotherapist	psychotherapist [+]	pull [1]	
psykey	psyche	pullet	
psykick	psychic [+]	pulley	
ptarmigan		Pullman	
pterodactyl		pullover	
Ptolemaic system		pulman	Pullman
ptomaine		pulmonary	
ptyalin		pulmonrey	pulmonary
pu	pew	pulover	pullover
pub /lican		pulp [1] /y	
puberty		pulpit	
pubescen ce /t		pulsar	
pubesens	pubescence [+]	pulsashun	pulsation
pubesent	pubescent	pulsat e [2] /ion	
pubic		pulse [2] /less	
pubis		pulser	pulsar
public /ation/ly		pulveris e [2] /ation	
publicis e [2] /t		puma	
publicity		pumel	pummel [3]
publish [1] /er		pumice [2]★ (lava) /-stone	
publisitey	publicity	pumice	pomace ★
publisize	publicise [2+]	pumis	pomace ★
puce		pumis	pumice [2]★[+]
puck		pumkin	pumpkin
pucker [1]		pummel [3]	
pudding		pump [1] /er	
puddle [2]		pumpernickel	
puding	pudding	pumpkin	
pudul	puddle [2]	pumy	pumice [2]★[+]
pueril e /ity		pun [3] /ner/nist	
puff [1] /iness/y		punch [1] /eon/es	
puffin		punchun	puncheon
pufin	puffin	punctilious /ly/ness	
pug		punctilius	punctilious [+]
pugilis m /t/tic		punctual /ity/ly	
pugnaci ous /ty		punctuat e [2] /ion	
pugnashus	pugnacious [+]	puncture [2]	
pugnasitey	pugnacity	pundit	
puka	pucker [1]	pungen cy /t	
puke [2]		pungensey	pungency [+]
puker	pucker [1]	punie	puny [+]
pulchritude		punish [1] /able/ment	
pulcritude	pulchritude	punitive /ly	

punjency	pungency +
punjensey	pungency +
punjent	pungent
punt [1] /er	
pun y /ier/iest/ily	
pupa /e (pl.)	
pupat e [2] /ion	
pupie	puppy +
pupil	
pupit	puppet +
puppet /eer/ry	
pupp y /ies	

> *If you cannot find your word under* **pur** *look under* **per**

pur anum	per annum
puray	purée
purblind	
purceive	perceive [2+]
purcentige	percentage
purchas e [2] /able	
purchis	purchase [2+]
purda	purdah
purdah	
pure /ly/r/st	
purée	
purgat ive /ory	
purgatrey	purgatory
purg e [2] /ation	
purifi	purify [4+]
purif y [4] /ication	
purile	puerile +
purist	
puritan /ical	
purity	
purje	purge [2+]
purjer	perjure [2+]
purjerey	perjury
purl [1]★ (knitting) /y	
purl	pearl ★+
purlieu	
purloin [1]	
purlu	purlieu
puroolence	purulence +

purple	
purport [1]	
purpose /ful/fully/ly	
purpul	purple
purr [1]	
purse [2] /r	
pursuan ce /t	
pursue [2] /r	
pursuit	
pursute	pursuit
purulen ce /t	
purvay	purvey [1+]
purvey [1] /ance/or	
puse	puce
push [1] /-chair/y	
pusillanim ity /ous	
puss /y	
pussy-willow	
put [3]	
putative	
puter	pewter
putie	putty [4]
putrefi	putrefy [4+]
putref y [4] /action	
putrid	
putrifi	putrefy [4+]
putt [1] /er	
putty [4]	
puty	putty [4]
puzle	puzzle [2+]
puzzle [2] /ment	
pyatsa	piazza
pye	pie ★+
pygmy	
pyjamas	
pylon	
pyramid /al	
pyre	
pyrenoid	
pyric	Pyrrhic
pyrite	
pyrotechnic /als/s	
Pyrrhic victory	
python	
pyx [1]	

Q

quack [1]	
quad	
quadrang *le* /ular	
quadrangul	quadrangle +
quadrant	
quadratic	
quadrennial	
quadrenyal	quadrennial
quadril	quadrille
quadrilateral	
quadrille	
quadruped	
quadruple [2] /t/x	
quadruplicat *e* [2] /ion	
quadrupul	quadruple [2]+
quaff [1]	
quagmire	
quail [1]	
quaint /er/est/ly/ness	
quake [2]	
Quaker /ism	
qualifactory	
qualifi	qualify [4]+
qualif *y* [4] /ication	
qualitative	
qualit *y* /ies	
qualm	
quandar *y* /ies	
quandrey	quandary +
quantifi	quantify [4]+
quantif *y* [4] /ication	
quantitative	
quantit *y* /ies	
quant *um* /a (pl.)	
quarantine [2]	
quarel	quarrel [3]+
quarey	quarry +
quarrel [3] /some	
quarr *y* /ies	
quart	
quarter [1] /ly/master	
quartern	
quartet	

quarto /s	
quarts ★ (fluid measure)	
quartz ★ (mineral) /ite	
quasar	
quash [1]	
quaternary	
quatrain	
quaver [1]	
quay ★ (by sea)	
que	cue [2]★
que	queue [2]★
queas *y* /iness	
queen /ly	
queer [1] /er/est/ly/ness	
quell [1]	
quench [1] /able/less	
querey	query [4]+
quern	
querulous /ly/ness	
querulus	querulous +
quer *y* [4] /ies	
queschun	question [1]+
quest [1]	
question [1] /able/ably/naire	
quetzal	
queue [2]★ (line)	
quibble [2] /r	
quibul	quibble [2]+
quich	quitch
quick /er/est/ly/ness	
quicken [1]	
quick *sand* /silver	
quid	
quid pro quo	
quiescen *ce* /t	
quiesense	quiescence +
quiet [1] /er/est/ly	
quieten [1]	
quietude	
quiff	
quill [1]	
quilt [1]	
quin	
quince	
quincentenary	

quinine	
quins	quince
quinsy	
quintesence	quintessence +
quintessen ce /tial	
quintet	
quintupl e /et/icate	
quintupul	quintuple +
quip 3	
quire * (of paper)	
quire	choir *
quirk	
quisling	
quit 3 /ter	
quitch	
quite	
quits	
quiver 1	
quixot ic /ry	
quiz 3	
quizzical /ly	
quod	quad
quodrangul	quadrangle +
quodrant	quadrant
quodratic	quadratic
quodrenial	quadrennial
quodril	quadrille
quodrilateral	quadrilateral
quodrooped	quadruped
quodruplicate	quadruplicate 2+
quof	quaff 1
quogmire	quagmire
quoit	
quolitativ	qualitative
quolitey	quality +
quontify	quantify 4+
quontitativ	quantitative
quontitey	quantity +
quontum	quantum +
quorantine	quarantine 2
quorrel	quarrel 3+
quorrey	quarry +
quorum	
quoshent	quotient
quota	

quot e 2 /able/ation	
quotidian	
quotient	

R

rabbi /s	
rabbit 1* (animal)	
rabbit	rarebit *
rabble	
rabes	rabies
rabi	rabbi +
rabid /ly	
rabies	
rabit	rabbit 1*
rabit	rarebit *
rable	rabble
rabul	rabble
race /-course/-horse	
rachit	ratchet
racial /ism/ist/ly	
racis m /t	
rack 1* (shelf)	
rack	wrack *
racket 1 /eer	
racoon	
rac y /ily	
radar	
raddle 2	
rade	raid 1+
radial /ly	
radian ce /t	
radians	radiance +
radiashun	radiation
radiat e 2 /ion/or	
radiater	radiator
radical * (political) /ly	
radicle * (rootlet)	
radio 1 /wave	
radioactiv e /ity	
radio-astronomy	
radiografer	radiographer +
radiogram	
radiograph er /y	

radioisotope		ramifi	ramify [4+]
radiolog *y* /ist		ramificashun	ramification
radiotherapy		ramif *y* [4] /ication	
radish /es		ramp [1]	
radium		rampage [2] /ous	
radi *us* /i (pl.)		rampagus	rampageous
radon		rampan *cy* /t	
radul	raddle [2]	rampart	
radyal	radial [+]	rampige	rampage [2+]
raffia		ramshackle	
raffish		ramshacul	ramshackle
raffle [2]		ranch [1] /er/es	
rafia	raffia	rancid /ity	
rafish	raffish	rancor	rancour [★+]
raft [1] /er		ranco *ur* ★ (hate) /rous	
raful	raffle [2]	random	
rag [3] /ger/time/wort		randum	random
ragamuffin		rane	rain [1★+]
ragamufin	ragamuffin	ranee	
rage [2]		ranefall	rainfall
raglan		range [2] /finder/r	
raid [1] /er		rangle	wrangle [2+]
rail [1] /road/way		rangul	wrangle [2+]
raillery		rank [1] /er ★ (soldier)	
raiment		ranker	rancour [★+]
rain [1★] (water) fall/y		rankle [2]	
rain	reign [1★]	rankul	rankle [2]
rain	rein ★	ransack [1]	
raindeer	reindeer	ransid	rancid [+]
raise [2★] (lift)		ransom [1] /er	
raise	rays ★	ransum	ransom [1+]
raise	raze [2★]	rant [1] /er	
raisin		raon	rayon
raith	wraith	rap [3★] (knock) /per ★	
raja		rap	wrap [★+]
rak *e* [2] /ish		rapaci *ous* /ty	
rakoon	racoon	rapashus	rapacious [+]
rale	rail [1+]	rapasitey	rapacity
ralerey	raillery	rapcher	rapture [+]
ralie	rally [4+]	rap *e* [2] /er/ine/ist	
rall *y* [4] /ies		rapid /ity/ly	
ram [3] /mer/rod		rapier	
ramble [2] /r		rapper	wrapper ★
rambul	ramble [2+]	rapscallion	
rament	raiment	rapscalyon	rapscallion

rapsodey	rhapsody +	ratif *y* [4] /ication/ier	
rapsodise	rhapsodise [2]	ratio /s	
rapt ★ (absorbed)		ration [1]	
rapt	wrapped ★	rational ★ (adj.) /ity/ly	
raptur *e* /ous		rationale ★ (n.)	
rapturus	rapturous	rationalis *e* [2] /ation/m	
rare /ly/r/st		rattle [2] /snake	
rarebit ★ (food)		ratul	rattle [2]+
raref *y* [4] /ication		raucous /ly	
rarifi	rarefy [4]+	raucus	raucous +
rarit *y* /ies		ravage [2] /r	
rasberie	raspberry +	rave [2]	
rasbery	raspberry +	ravel [3]	
rascal /ity/ly		raven	
rase	raise [2]★	ravene	ravine
rase	raze [2]★	ravenous /ly/ness	
rasecorse	race-course	ravenus	ravenous +
rasehorse	race-horse	ravige	ravage [2]+
rash /er/est/ly/ness		ravine	
rashal	racial +	ravioli	
rashalism	racialism	ravish [1]	
rashalist	racialist	raw /er/est/ness	
rashio	ratio +	rawcus	raucous +
rashul	racial +	rayon	
rashun	ration [1]	rays ★ (light beams)	
rashunal	rational +	raze [2]★ (demolish)	
rashunalise	rationalise [2]+	raze	raise [2]★
rashunalitey	rationality	razer	razor +
rashyo	ratio +	razor /-bill/-blade	
rasie	racy +	reach [1]	
rasin	raisin	reacshun	reaction +
rasism	racism +	react [1] /ive/or	
rasist	racist	reaction /ary	
raskal	rascal +	read ★† /able/er/ing	
rasp [1]		†(book)	
raspberr *y* /ies		read	red ★+
rat [3] /-race/ter		read	reed [1]★
ratable	rateable	readdress [1]	
ratabul	rateable	readi *ly* /ness	
ratafia		readmishun	readmission
ratchet		readmission	
rate [2] /able/payer		readmit [3] /tance	
rath	wrath +	readress	readdress [1]
rather		ready /-made	
ratifi	ratify [4]+	reaf	reef [1]+

reagent	
reak	reek ¹★
reak	wreak ¹★
real ★ (actual) /ly	
real	reel ¹★
realey	really
realisashun	realisation
realis *e* ² /able/ation	
realis *m* /t	
realistic /ally	
realit *y* /ies	
realm	
realter	realtor
realtor	
ream	
reanimat *e* ² /ion	
reap ¹ /er	
reapear	reappear ¹⁺
reapearance	reappearance
reappear ¹ /ance	
rear ¹ /guard	
rear-admiral	
rearange	rearrange ²⁺
reargard	rearguard
rearm ¹ /ament	
rearrange ² /ment	
reasemble	reassemble ²
reasembul	reassemble ²
reasershun	reassertion
reasert	reassert ¹⁺
reasertion	reassertion
reasess	reassess ¹⁺
reashorance	reassurance
reashorans	reassurance
reashore	reassure ²⁺
reason ¹ /able/ably	
reassemble ²	
reassembul	reassemble ²
reassert ¹ /ion	
reassess ¹ /ment	
reassur *e* ² /ance	
reath	wreath ★
reath	wreathe ²★
rebate ²	
rebel ³ /lion	

rebellious /ly/ness	
rebelyun	rebellion
rebelyus	rebellious ⁺
reberth	rebirth
rebild	rebuild ⁺
rebilt	rebuilt
rebirth	
rebound ¹	
rebownd	rebound ¹
rebuff ¹	
rebuild /ing	
rebuilt	
rebuk *e* ² /ingly	
rebut ³ /tal	
rebutal	rebuttal
recalcitran *ce* /t	
recall ¹	
recalsitrance	recalcitrance ⁺
recant ¹ /ation	
recap ³	
recapcher	recapture ²
recapitulat *e* ² /ion	
recapture ²	
recast ¹	
recede ²	
receipt ¹★ (document)	
receit	receipt ¹★
receiv *e* ² /able/er	
recent ★ (of late) /ly	
recepshun	reception ⁺
recepshunist	receptionist
receptacle	
receptacul	receptacle
reception /ist/-room	
receptive /ly/ness	
receptivity	
receptor	
receshun	recession ⁺
recess ¹ /ive	
recession /al	
rech	retch ¹★
rech	wretch ★
recharge ² /able	
recicle	recycle ²
recidivis *m* /t	

236

recieve	receive [2+]
recipe	
recipi	recipe
recipient	
reciproc *al* /ally/ity	
reciprocat *e* [2] /ion	
recita *l* /tion/tive	
recitashun	recitation
recite [2]	
reck	wreck [1+]
reckage	wreckage
reckidge	wreckage
reckless /ly/ness	
reckon [1]	
reclaim [1]	
reclamashun	reclamation
reclamation	
reclaym	reclaim [1]
recline [2]	
recluse	
recognis *e* [2] /able/ably	
recognishun	recognition
recognition	
recoil [1]	
recolect	· recollect [1+]
recollect [1] /ion	
recomence	recommence [2+]
recomend	recommend [1+]
recomens	recommence [2+]
recommence [2] /ment	
recommend [1] /ation	
recommendabl *e* /y	
recompense [2]	
reconcil *e* [2] /able/iation	
reconcilement	
recondishun	recondition [1]
recondite	
recondition [1]	
reconker	reconquer [1]
reconnoitre [2]	
reconoiter	reconnoitre [2]
reconquer [1]	
reconsider [1] /ation	
reconsile	reconcile [2+]
reconstitut *e* [2] /ion	

reconstruct [1] /ion/ive	
recoop	recoup [1+]
record [1] /er/-player	
recorse	recourse
recount [1]★ (tell)	
re-count [1]★†	
†(count again)	
recoup [1] /ment	
recourse	
recover [1] /y	
recownt	recount [1]★
recownt	re-count [1]★
recreant /ly	
recreashun	recreation
recreat *e* [2]★ (entertain) /ion	
re-create [2]★ (form anew)	
recriminat *e* [2] /ion	
recriminat *ive* /ory	
recruit [1]	
rectang *le* /ular	
rectangul	rectangle [+]
recter	rector [+]
rectifi	rectify [4+]
rectifi *able* /er	
rectifiabul	rectifiable [+]
rectif *y* [4] /ication	
rectilinea *r* /l	
rectilinier	rectilinear [+]
rectitude	
recto	
rector /y/ies	
rect *um* /al	
recumben *cy* /t	
recuperat *e* [2] /ion/ive	
recur [3] /rence/rent	
recurens	recurrence
recycle [2]	
recycul	recycle [2]
red ★† /-handed	
†(colour)	
red	read ★[+]
redbreast	
redbrest	redbreast
redbrick	
redden [1]	

redd *er* /est/ish
redeem [1] /able/er
redempt *ion* /ive
redemshun   redemption +
reden   redden [1]
redeploi   redeploy [1+]
redeploy [1] /ment
reder   redder +
redevelop [1] /ment
redie   ready +
rediffusion
redifushun   rediffusion
redifusion   rediffusion
rediley   readily +
redimade   ready-made
rediploi   redeploy [1+]
rediploy   redeploy [1+]
redirecshun   redirection
redirect [1] /ion
redistribut *e* /ion
redivelop   redevelop [1+]
redolen *ce* /t
redouble [2]
redoubt /able
redound [1]
redress [1] /ment
redskin
reduble   redouble [2]
reduc *e* [2] /ible/tion
reducshun   reduction
redundanc *y* /ies
redundansey   redundancy +
redundant
reduplicat *e* [2] /ion
redwood
re-echo [1]
reed [1]★ (water-plant)
reed   read ★+
reef [1] /er/-knot
reegsamin   re-examine [2+]
reek [1]★ (smell)
reek   wreak [1]★
reeko   re-echo [1]
reeksport   re-export [1+]
reel [1]★ (wind in)

reel   real ★+
re-elect [1] /ion
reem   ream
re-enter [1]
re-entr *y* /ies
reep   reap [1+]
reer   rear [1+]
reer admiral   rear-admiral
reergard   rearguard
re-establish [1] /ment
reeve [2]
re-examin *e* [2] /ation
re-export [1] /ation
refashion [1]
refashun   refashion [1]
refector *y* /ies
refer [3] /able/ence
referee /d/ing
referend *um* /a/ums (pls.)
referens   reference
refewel   refuel [3]
refill [1] /able
refine [2] /ment
refiner *y* /ies
refit [3]
reflashun   reflation +
reflate [2]
reflation /ary
reflect [1] /ion/ive/or
refleks   reflex +
refleksiv   reflexive
reflex /ive
refloat [1]
reflote   refloat [1]
reform [1] /ation/er
reformashun   reformation
reformator *y* /ies
reformatrey   reformatory +
refracshun   refraction
refract [1] /able/ion/ive
refractor *y* /iness
refrain [1]
refresh [1] /er/ment
refrigerat *e* [2] /ion/or
refuel [3]

refuge * (shelter) /e *†
  †(fugitive)
refulgen *ce* /t
refulgens — refulgence +
refund [1]
refurbish [1]
refus *e* [2] /al
refutashun — refutation
refut *e* [2] /able/al/ation
regain [1]
regal *† /ia/ly
  †(of a king)
regale [2]* (to feast)
regane — regain [1]
regard [1] /less
regatta /s
regen *cy* /t
regenerat *e* [2] /ion/ive/or
regicid *e* /al
regime /n
regiment [1] /al/ation
region /al/alism/ally
regiside — regicide +
regist *er* [1] /ration
registrar
registrashun — registration
registr *y* /ies
regreshun — regression
regress [1] /ion/ive
regret [3] /ful/fully
regretabul — regrettable +
regrettabl *e* /y
regular /ity/ly
regularis *e* [2] /ation
regularitey — regularity
regulashun — regulation
regulat *e* [2] /ion/or
reguler — regular +
regurgitat *e* /ion
rehabilitat *e* [2] /ion
rehash [1]
rehears *e* [2] /al
rehersal — rehearsal
reherse — rehearse [2]+
Reich

reign [1]* (rule)
reimburse [2] /ment
rein * (of horse)
rein — reign [1]*
reincarnashun — reincarnation
reincarnat *e* [2] /ion
reindeer
reinforce [2] /able/ment
reinfors — reinforce [2]+
reinshore — re-insure [2]+
reinstate [2] /ment
re-insur *e* [2] /ance
reinvest [1] /ment
reiterashun — reiteration
reiterat *e* [2] /ion
rejecshun — rejection
reject [1] /ion
rejeme — regime +
rejoic *e* [2] /ingly
rejoin [1] /der
rejoise — rejoice [2]+
rejoovenate — rejuvenate [2]+
rejuvenat *e* [2] /ion
rekindle [2]
rekindul — rekindle [2]
rekwest — request [1]
rekwiem — requiem
rekwisishun — requisition
rekwisit — requisite +
rekwisition — requisition
rekwite — requite [2]+
relaks — relax [1]+
relaksashun — relaxation
relaksation — relaxation
relapse [2]
relashun — relation
relat *e* [2] /ion
relative /ly
relativity
relax [1] /ation
relay [1]
releaf — relief
release [2]
relegashun — relegation
relegat *e* [2] /ion

releif	relief	remitans	remittance
relent¹ /less/lessly		remnant	
relese	release²	remonstran *ce* /t	
relevan *ce* /t		remonstrans	remonstrance⁺
relevans	relevance⁺	remonstrat *e*² /ion/ive	
releve	relieve²⁺	remoov	remove²⁺
reli	rely⁴	remooval	removal
reliabilitey	reliability	remorse /ful/fully	
reliab *le* /ility/ly		remorseless /ly/ness	
reliabul	reliable⁺	remote /ly/r/st	
relian *ce* /t		remount¹	
relians	reliance⁺	removal	
relic		remov *e*² /able/ability	
relief		remownt	remount¹
reliev *e*² /able		remunerat *e*² /ion/ive	
religion		ren	wren
religious /ly/ness		Renaissance *†	
religun	religion	†(historic period)	
religus	religious⁺	renal	
relinkwish	relinquish¹⁺	renascen *ce* *† /t	
relinquish¹ /ment		†(rebirth)	
relish¹ /able		rench	wrench¹
relm	realm	rend¹	
reluctan *ce* /t/tly		render¹	
reluctans	reluctance⁺	rendezvous¹	
rely⁴		renegade²	
remain¹ /der/s		renew¹ /able/al	
remand¹		renit	rennet
remaridge	remarriage	renium	rhenium
remarie	remarry⁴⁺	rennet	
remarige	remarriage	renounce² /ment	
remark¹ /able/ably		renouns	renounce²⁺
remarr *y*⁴ /iage		renovashun	renovation
remed *y*⁴ /ies		renovat *e*² /ion/or	
rememb *er*¹ /rance		renown /ed	
remembrans	remembrance	renowns	renounce²⁺
remind¹ /er		rent¹ /al/er	
reminisce² /nce/nt		rentul	rental
reminisence	reminiscence	renue	renew¹⁺
reminisens	reminiscence	renunciat *e*² /ion	
reminisent	reminiscent	reorganis *e*² /ation	
reminiss	reminisce²⁺	re-orientat *e*² /ion	
remishun	remission	repade	repaid
remiss /ion/ly		repaid	
remit³ /tal/tance		repair¹ /er	

repara *ble* /tion		reprieve²	
reparashun	reparation	reprimand¹	
repartee /s		reprint¹	
repast		reprisal	
repatriashun	repatriation	reproach¹ /ful/fully	
repatriat *e*² /ion		reprobate²	
repay /able/ing/ment		reproduc *e*² /ible	
repeal¹		reproducshun	reproduction
repeat¹ /able/edly		reproduction	
repel³ /lent		reproof /s	
repent¹ /ance/ant		reprov *e*² /al/ingly	
repentans	repentance	reptil *e* /ian	
repercushun	repercussion	republic /an	
repercussion		repudiat *e*² /ion/or	
repertoire		repugnan *ce* /t	
repertory		repugnans	repugnance⁺
repetishun	repetition⁺	repuls *e*² /ion	
repetishus	repetitious	repulshun	repulsion
repetiti *on* /ous/ve		repulsive /ly/ness	
repetitiv	repetitive	reputashun	reputation
repetrey	repertory	reput *e*² /able/ation	
repine²		reputedly	
replace² /able/ment		request¹	
replase	replace²⁺	requiem	
replay¹		require² /ment	
replenish¹ /ment		requisishun	requisition
replet *e* /ion		requisit *e* /ion	
repli	reply⁴⁺	requit *e*² /al	
replica		rerite	rewrite⁺
repl *y*⁴ /ies		reritten	rewritten
report¹ /able/er		rerote	rewrote
repose² /ful		rescind¹	
repositor *y* /ies		rescue² /r	
repositrey	repository⁺	research¹ /er	
reprable	reparable⁺	reseat ★ (seat again)	
reprabul	reparable⁺	reseat	receipt¹★
reprehend		resede	recede²
reprehenshun	reprehension⁺	reseed	recede²
reprehensibul	reprehensible	reseipt	receipt¹★
reprehensi *on* /ble		resembl *e*² /ance	
represent¹ /ation		resembul	resemble²⁺
representashun	representation	resent¹★ (peeve) /ment	
representative		resent	recent ★⁺
represhun	repression	resentful /ly	
repress¹ /ible/ion/ive		resepshonist	receptionist

resepshun	reception [+]	resistans	resistance [+]
reseptacul	receptacle	resit /ting	
reseption	reception [+]	resitashun	recitation
reseptionist	receptionist	resitation	recitation
reseptiv	receptive [+]	resite	recite [2]
reseptor	receptor	resle	wrestle [2+]
reserch	research [1+]	resler	wrestler
reservashun	reservation	resole [2]	
reserv *e* [2] /ation/ist		resoloot	resolute [+]
reservoir		resolushun	resolution
reseshun	recession [+]	resolute /ly/ness	
resess	recess [1+]	resolution	
resession	recession [+]	resolve [2]	
resessiv	recessive	reson	reason [1+]
reset /ting		resonable	reasonable
reseve	receive [2+]	resonabul	reasonable
reshuffle [2]		resonan *ce* /t/tly	
reshuful	reshuffle [2]	resonans	resonance [+]
resicle	recycle [2]	resonat *e* [2] /or	
reside [2] /nce		resorce	resource [+]
residenc *y* /ies		resort [1]	
residens	residence	resound [1]	
residensey	residency [+]	resource /ful/fully	
residenshal	residential	respect [1] /ful/fully	
resident /ial		respectab *le* /ility/ly	
residivism	recidivism [+]	respectabul	respectable [+]
residivist	recidivist	respective /ly	
residu *e* /al/ary/um		respirashun	respiration
resign [1] /ation		respirater	respirator
resignashun	resignation	respir *e* [2] /ation/ator	
resilien *ce* /t/tly		respite	
resiliens	resilience [+]	resplenden *ce* /t	
resin /ous		respond [1] /ence/ent	
resind	rescind [1]	respons *e* /ive/iveness	
resinus	resinous	responsib *le* /ility/ly	
resipe	recipe	responsibul	responsible [+]
resipie	recipe	rest [1]★ (repose)	
resipient	recipient	rest	wrest [1]★
resiprocal	reciprocal [+]	restaurant	
resiprocate	reciprocate [2+]	resterant	restaurant
resiprositey	reciprocity	restful /ly/ness	
resist [1] /er/ive		restitushun	restitution
resistab *le* /ility/ly		restitution	
resistabul	resistable [+]	restive /ness	
resistan *ce* /t		restle	wrestle [2+]

restler	wrestler	retract¹ /able/ile/ion	
restless		retrase	retrace²
restorashun	restoration	retread ★ (walk again)	
restor e² /ation/ative		re-tread¹★ (tyre)	
restrain¹ /t		retreat¹	
restrict¹ /ion/ive		retred	retread ★
restruccher	restructure²	retred	re-tread¹★
restructure²		retreive	retrieve²⁺
resul	wrestle²⁺	retrench¹ /ment	
result¹ /ant		retribushun	retribution
resumay	résumé ★	retribut e² /ion	
resume²★ (restart)		retriev e² /able/al/er	
résumé ★ (summary)		retroactive	
resumption		retrograde	
resurecshun	resurrection	retrogress¹ /ion/ive	
resurection	resurrection	retrospect¹ /ion/ive	
resurgen ce /t		return¹ /able	
resurgens	resurgence ⁺	reunion	
resurrect¹ /ion		reunite²	
resus	rhesus	reunyun	reunion
resuscitat e² /ion		rev³	
resusitashun	resuscitation	revali	reveille
resusitate	resuscitate²⁺	revaluashun	revaluation
resusitation	resuscitation	revalu e² /ation	
retail¹ /er		reve	reeve²
retain¹ /er		reveal¹	
retale	retail¹⁺	reveille	
retaliat e² /ion/ory		revel³ /ler/ry	
retard¹ /ation/er		revelashun	revelation
retayn	retain¹⁺	revelation	
retch¹★ (vomit)		revelrey	revelry
retch	wretch ★	revenew	revenue
retenshun	retention ⁺	revenge² /ful/fully	
retent ion /ive		revenue	
reticen ce /t		reverberat e² /ion/or	
retina		revere² /nce	
retinew	retinue	reverend ★ (priest)	
retinue		reverens	reverence
retire² /ment		reverent ★† /ly	
retisens	reticence ⁺	†(respectful)	
retisent	reticent	reverey	reverie
retoric	rhetoric ⁺	reverie	
retorical	rhetorical	revers e² /al/ible/ion	
retort¹		revershun	reversion
retrace²		revert¹ /ible	

review [1]★ (survey) /er		rice ★ (food)	
review	revue ★	rich /er/es/est/ly/ness	
revijun	revision	ricital	recital [+]
revile [2]		ricite	recite [2]
revis e [2] /ion		rick [1] /ety	
revishun	revision	rickets	
reviv e [2] /al		rickshaw	
revocabl e /y		ricline	recline [2]
revokashun	revocation	ricluse	recluse
revo ke [2] /cation		ricochet [1]	
revolt [1]		ricooperate	recuperate [2+]
revolushun	revolution	ricroot	recruit [1]
revolushunise	revolutionise [2]	ricshore	rickshaw
revolushunrey	revolutionary [+]	ricumbent	recumbent
revolution		ricur	recur [3+]
revolutionar y /ies		ricuver	recover [1+]
revolutionise [2]		rid /dance	
revolve [2] /r		ridance	riddance
revue ★ (entertainment)		ridans	riddance
revue	review [1]★[+]	riddle [2]	
revulshun	revulsion	rid e /den/er/ing	
revulsion		rideem	redeem [1+]
reward [1]		rideemable	redeemable
rewrit e /ten/ing		rideemabul	redeemable
rewrote		rideemer	redeemer
rhapsodise [2]		ridemshun	redemption[+]
rhapsod y /ies		ridge [2]	
rhenium		ridicule [2]	
rhesus		ridiculous /ly/ness	
rhetoric /al		ridiculus	ridiculous [+]
rheumat ic /ism		ridownd	redound [1]
rhinoceros /es		ridowt	redoubt [+]
rhizome		ridress	redress [1+]
rhizomorph		riduce	reduce [2+]
rhodium		riducshun	reduction
rhododendron		ridul	riddle [2]
rhomb us /oid		ridundansey	redundancy [+]
rhubarb		ridundant	redundant
rhyme [2]★ (poetry)		riduse	reduce [2+]
rhythm		ridusible	reducible
rhythmic /al/ally		ridusibul	reducible
rib [3]		rie	rye ★
ribald /ry		rie	wry ★[+]
ribbon		rife	
ricalsitrant	recalcitrant	riff-raff	

rifinerey	refinery +	rikwest	request 1
rifle 2 /-range		rikwire	require 2+
riflecshun	reflection	rikwite	requite 2+
riflect	reflect 1+	rile 2	
riflecter	reflector	riluctance	reluctance +
riflectiv	reflective	riluctans	reluctance +
riform	reform 1+	riluctant	reluctant
rifract	refract 1+	rim 3	
rifrane	refrain 1	rimainder	remainder
rifresh	refresh 1+	rimand	remand 1
rifrigerate	refrigerate 2+	rimane	remain 1+
rifrigerater	refrigerator	rimark	remark 1+
rift /-valley		rimarkable	remarkable
rifulgens	refulgence +	rime 2★ (frost)	
rifulgent	refulgent	rime	rhyme 2★
rifusal	refusal	rimember	remember 1+
rifuse	refuse 2+	rimembrance	remembrance
rifutal	refutal	rimembrans	remembrance
rifute	refute 2+	rimind	remind 1+
rig 3 /ger		riminder	reminder
rigard	regard 1+	rimishun	remission
rigardless	regardless	rimiss	remiss +
rigata	regatta +	rimit	remit 3+
rige	ridge 2	rimitance	remittance
riger	rigor ★	rimitans	remittance
riger	rigour ★	rimonstrativ	remonstrative
riggle	wriggle 2	rimoov	remove 2+
right 1★ (correct)		rimorse	remorse +
right	rite ★	rimorsless	remorseless +
right	write ★+	rimote	remote +
righteous /ly/ness		rimunerate	remunerate 2+
rightful /ly		rimuneration	remuneration
rigid /ity/ly		rinasance	Renaissance ★
rigmarole		rinasance	renascence ★+
rigor ★ (stiffness)		rinasant	renascent
rigour ★ (severity)		rind	
rigreshun	regression	rinew	renew 1+
rigresiv	regressive	rinewable	renewable
rigress	regress 1+	rinewabul	renewable
rigret	regret 3+	rinewal	renewal
rigretable	regrettable +	ring 1★ (circle, bell)	
rigretabul	regrettable +	ring	wring 1★
rigretful	regretful	ring er ★† /leader/let	
rigul	wriggle 2	†(horse)	
rike	Reich	ringer	wringer ★

245

rink		ripublic	republic [+]
rinkle	wrinkle [2]	ripublican	republican
rinkul	wrinkle [2]	ripudiate	repudiate [2+]
rinoceros	rhinoceros [+]	ripugnance	repugnance [+]
rinoserus	rhinoceros [+]	ripugnans	repugnance [+]
rinounce	renounce [2+]	ripugnant	repugnant
rinownse	renounce [2+]	ripul	ripple [2]
rinse [2]		ripulse	repulse [2+]
rinuable	renewable	ripulshun	repulsion
rinuabul	renewable	ripulsiv	repulsive [+]
rinual	renewal	ripute	repute [2+]
rinue	renew [1+]	riquest	request [1]
rinunsiashun	renunciation	riquire	require [2+]
rinunsiate	renunciate [2+]	riquite	requite [2+]
rinunsiation	renunciation	ris *e* *(get up)/en/er/ing	
riot [1] /ous/ously		rise	rice *
riotus	riotous	risemblans	resemblance
rip [3] /per		risemble	resemble [2+]
ripair	repair [1+]	risembul	resemble [2+]
ripare	repair [1+]	risent	resent [1*+]
ripe /r/st/ly/ness		risentful	resentful [+]
ripeel	repeal [1]	riserch	research [1+]
ripeet	repeat [1+]	riserve	reserve [2+]
ripel	repel [3+]	riservist	reservist
ripen [1]		riside	reside [2+]
ripent	repent [1+]	risign	resign [1+]
ripentance	repentance	risilience	resilience [+]
ripentans	repentance	risilient	resilient
ripentant	repentant	risilyant	resilient
ripine	repine [2]	risilyens	resilience [+]
riple	ripple [2]	risist	resist [1+]
riplete	replete [+]	risistable	resistable [+]
ripli	reply [4+]	risistabul	resistable [+]
riport	report [1+]	resistance	resistance [+]
ripose	repose [2+]	risistans	resistance [+]
ripositrey	repository [+]	risistant	resistant
ripple [2]		risital	recital [+]
ripreshun	repression	risite	recite [2]
ripress	repress [1+]	risk [1] /ier/iest/y	
ripreve	reprieve [2]	riski *ly* /ness	
riprisal	reprisal	risolve	resolve [2]
riproch	reproach [1+]	risorce	resource [+]
riprochful	reproachful	risorceful	resourceful
riproof	reproof [+]	risort	resort [1]
riproov	reprove [2+]	risotto	

246

risound	resound [1]	riter	writer
risource	resource +	rithe	writhe [2]
risourceful	resourceful	rithm	rhythm
risownd	resound [1]	rithmic	rhythmic +
rispect	respect [1]+	riting	writing
rispectable	respectable +	ritire	retire [2]+
rispectful	respectful	ritort	retort [1]
rispectiv	respective +	ritracshun	retraction
rispire	respire [2]+	ritract	retract [1]+
rispite	respite	ritraction	retraction
risplendence	resplendence +	ritreet	retreat [1]
risplendens	resplendence +	retrevable	retrievable
risplendent	resplendent	retreval	retrieval
rispond	respond [1]+	ritreve	retrieve [2]+
rispondence	respondence	ritten	written
rispondens	respondence	ritual /ism/ist	
risponsible	responsible +	riturn	return [1]+
risponsibul	responsible +	rityoual	ritual +
risponsiv	responsive	rival [3] /ry	
rissole		riveal	reveal [1]
rist	wrist +	rivenge	revenge [2]+
ristband	wristband	rivengeful	revengeful
ristlet	wristlet	river	
ristore	restore [2]+	rivere	revere [2]+
ristrain	restrain [1]+	rivet [1]	
ristraint	restraint	rivijun	revision
ristrict	restrict [1]+	rivile	revile [2]
ristwatch	wrist-watch	rivise	revise [2]+
risult	result [1]+	rivishun	revision
risultant	resultant	rivision	revision
risume	resume [2]★	rivival	revival
risurgence	resurgence +	rivive	revive [2]+
risurgens	resurgence +	rivocable	revocable +
risurgent	resurgent	rivocabul	revocable +
rit	writ	rivoke	revoke [2]+
ritaliate	retaliate [2]+	rivolt	revolt [1]
ritard	retard [1]+	rivolv	revolve [2]+
ritchus	righteous +	rivolver	revolver
rite ★ (ceremony)		rivue	review [1]★+
rite	right [1]★	rivue	revue ★
rite	write ★+	rivulet	
riteful	rightful +	rivulshun	revulsion
ritenshun	retention +	rivulsion	revulsion
ritention	retention +	rivursal	reversal
ritentiv	retentive	rivurse	reverse [2]+

247

rivurt	revert [1]+	roli poli	roly-poly
riward	reward [1]	rolick	rollick [1]+
ro	roe *+	roll [1]* (move) /-call/er	
ro	row [1]*+	roller-skate [2]	
roach [1] /es		rollick [1] /er	
road * (highway)		rolling-pin	
road	rode *	roly-poly	
roadworth y /iness		Roman Catholic	
roam [1]		romance [2]	
roan		romans	romance [2]
roar [1] /er		romantic /ally/ism	
roast [1]		Romany	
rob [3] /ber		romboid	rhomboid
robber y /ies		rombus	rhombus +
robe [2]		rome	roam [1]
roberey	robbery +	romp [1] /er	
robin redbreast		rondayvoo	rendezvous [1]
robot		rondo /s	
robust /ly/ness		rone	roan
roch	roach [1]+	rong	wrong [1]+
rock [1] /er/y		rongful	wrongful +
rock -*cake* /garden		roo	rue [2]+
rocker y /ies		roobarb	rhubarb
rocket [1] /eer/ry		rooble	rouble
rocking -*chair* /-horse		roobul	rouble
rococo		rood * (church)	
rode *(did ride)		rood	rude *+
rode	road *	roodiment	rudiment +
rodedendron	rhododendron	roodimentrey	rudimentary
rodent		roof [1] /less	
rodeo /s		rooful	rueful
rodeworthey	roadworthy +	rooge	rouge [2]
rodio	rodeo +	rooin	ruin [1]+
rodium	rhodium	rooinashun	ruination
roe * (deer) /buck		rooination	ruination
roe	row [1]*+	rooinous	ruinous +
rog	rogue +	rooinus	ruinous +
rogish	roguish	rook [1] /ery/eries	
rogu e /ery/ish		rool	rule [2]+
roial	royal +	roolet	roulette
roialtey	royalty	room /ful/iness/y	
rol	role *	roomatic	rheumatic +
rol	roll [1]*+	roomatism	rheumatism
rolcall	roll-call	roomer	rumour [1]
role * (of an actor)		roomey	roomy

roon	rune	rough-and-tumble	
roopee	rupee	roughen [1]	
rooral	rural [+]	rough *er* /est/ly/ness	
roose	ruse	rough-shod	
roost [1] /er		rought	wrought [+]
root [1]★ /-crop/less		roulette	
root	route ★	round [1] /er/est/ly/ness	
roothless	ruthless [+]	roundabout	
rootine	routine	Roundhead	
rootstock		round -*table* /-up	
rop *e* [2] /iness/y		rous *e* [2] /ingly	
rope-ladder		rout [1]★ (defeat)	
ropey	ropy	route ★ (way)	
ror	roar [1+]	routeen	routine
rort	wrought [+]	routine	
rosarey	rosary [+]	rove [2] /r	
rosar *y* /ies		row [1]★ (boat) /er	
rose ★ /-bud/-tree		rowdie	rowdy [+]
rose	rows ★	rowd *y* /ies/ily/iness	
roset	rosette	rownd	round [1+]
rosette		rowndabout	roundabout
rosewood		rowndhed	Roundhead
rosie	rosy [+]	rowndup	round-up
rost	roast [1]	rows ★ (lines)	
roster		rowse	rouse [2+]
rostrum /s		rowt	rout [1]★
ros *y* /ily/iness		rowze	rouse [2+]
rot [3] /ter		royal /ly/ty	
rota /s		royaltey	royalty
rotarey	rotary [+]	rub [3] /ber	
rotar *y* /ies		rubarb	rhubarb
rotashun	rotation	rubbish /y	
rotat *e* [2] /able/ion		rubble	
rote ★ (repetition)		rubicund	
rote	wrote ★	rubie	ruby [+]
roten	rotten [+]	rubish	rubbish [+]
roter	rotor	rubric	
roth	wrath [+]	rubul	rubble
rotor		rub *y* /ies	
rotten /ly/ness		rucksack	
rotund /a/ity		rudder	
rouble		rudd *y* /iness	
rouge [2]		rude ★(offensive)/ly/r/st	
rough ★ (coarse) /age		rude	rood ★
rough-and-ready		ruder	rudder

rudie / ruddy +
rudiment /ary
rue² /ful/fully
ruf / rough *+
ruf / ruff *
ruf and redy / rough-and-ready
ruf and tumbul / rough-and-tumble
ruff * (collar, bird)
ruff / rough *+
ruffage / roughage
ruffen / roughen¹
ruffian /ism/ly
ruffle²
ruffley / roughly
rufidge / roughage
rufige / roughage
rufle / ruffle²
rufshod / rough-shod
ruful / rueful
rufyan / ruffian +
rugbe / Rugby
Rugby
rugged /ly/ness
rugid / rugged +
ruin¹ /ation
ruinashun / ruination
ruinous /ly
ruinus / ruinous +
ruksac / rucksack
rule² /r
rum /ba/my
rumatic / rheumatic +
rumatism / rheumatism
rumble²
rumbul / rumble²
rumer / rumour¹
rumidge / rummage²
rumige / rummage²
ruminat e² /ion/ive
rummage²
rumour¹
rump /steak
rumple²
rumpul / rumple²
rumpus /es

run /ner/ning/way
runaway
rune
runerup / runner-up
rung *†
   †(step, did ring)
rung / wrung *
runner-up
runt
rupcher / rupture²
rupea / rupee
rupee
rupture²
rural /ly
ruse
rush¹
rushun / Russian
rusit / russet
rusk
rusler / rustler
russet
Russian
rust¹ /less/y
rustic /ity
rusticat e² /ion
rusti er /est/ly/ness
rustle² /r
rust-proof
rusul / rustle²+
rut³
ruthenium
ruthless /ly/ness
rye * (grain)
rye / wry *+
ryly / wryly
rythm / rhythm
rythmic / rhythmic +

S

saans / seance
sabath / sabbath +
sabatical / sabbatical
sabbat h /ical

saber	sabre +	sail	sale ★+
sable		sailsman	salesman
sabotage 2		saint /hood/ly	
sabre /-toothed		sake	
sabul	sable	sakshorn	saxhorn
sacarin	saccharin	saksofone	saxophone +
saccharin		sakson	Saxon +
sacerdotal		saksophone	saxophone +
sachel	satchel	salar y 4 /ies	
sachet		sale ★† /ability/able	
sack 1 /ful		†(of goods)	
sackarin	saccharin	sale	sail 1★+
sacrament		salesman	
sacred /ly/ness		salie	sally 4+
sacrement	sacrament	salien ce /t	
sacrific e 2 /ial		saliens	salience +
sacrifise	sacrifice 2+	salin e /ity	
sacrifishal	sacrificial	saliva /ry/tion	
sacrileg e /ious		sallow /ness	
sacrilige	sacrilege +	sall y 4 /ies	
sacriligus	sacrilegious	salm	psalm +
sacrosanct		salmon	
sacsophone	saxophone +	salon	
sad /der/dest/ly/ness		saloon	
sadden 1		saloot	salute 2+
saddle 2 /r/ry		salow	sallow +
saden	sadden 1	salsify	
sadis m /t		salt 1 /iness/y	
sadul	saddle 2+	salt -cellar /-lick	
safari /s		salter	psalter +
safe /ly/r/st/ty		saltpeter	saltpetre
safegard	safeguard 1	saltpetre	
safeguard 1		salubri ous /ty	
saffron		salubrius	salubrious +
safire	sapphire	salutar y /iness	
saftie	safety	salutashun	salutation
sag 3		salut e 2 /ation	
saga /s		salvage 2	
sagaci ous /ty		salvashun	salvation
sagashus	sagacious +	salvation	
sagasitey	sagacity	salv e 2 /able	
sage /ly/ness		salver	
sago		salvidge	salvage 2
said		salvige	salvage 2
sail 1★ (of boat) /or		salvo /s	

samaritan		sap³	
samarium		saper	sapper
same /ness		sapien *ce* /t	
samon	salmon	sapiens	sapience⁺
samovar		sapling	
sample² /r		sapper	
sampul	sample²⁺	sapphire	
sanatorium /s		sarcasm	
sancshun	sanction¹	sarcastic /ally	
sanctifi	sanctify⁴⁺	sarcofagus	sarcophagus⁺
sanctif *y*⁴ /ication		sarcophag *us* /i (pl.)	
sanctimonious /ly		sardine	
sanctimonius	sanctimonious⁺	sardonic /ally	
sanction¹		sargant	sergeant⁺
sanctity		sari	
sanctuar *y* /ies		sarjent	sergeant⁺
sanctum /s		sarm	psalm⁺
sand¹ /y		sartorial	
sandal /-wood		sary	sari
sandle	sandal⁺	saserdotle	sacerdotal
sandpaper¹		sash /es	
sandwhich	sandwich¹⁺	sashable	satiable
sandwich¹ /es		sashabul	satiable
sane ★ (not mad) /ly/ness		sashay	sachet
sane	seine²★	sashiate	satiate²
sang-froid		Satan /ic	
sanguin *e* /ary		satchel	
sangwin	sanguine⁺	sate²	
sanitary		sateen	
sanitashun	sanitation	satelight	satellite
sanitation		satellite	
sanitey	sanity	saten	sateen
sanitrey	sanitary	saterday	Saturday
sanity		satiable	
sankshun	sanction¹	satiabul	satiable
sanktify	sanctify⁴⁺	satiate²	
sanktimonius	sanctimonious⁺	satin	
sanktitey	sanctity	satir *e* /ist	
sanktuarey	sanctuary⁺	satirical /ly	
sanktum	sanctum⁺	satirise²	
Sanskrit		satisfacshun	satisfaction
sant	saint⁺	satisfactor *y* /ily	
Santa Claus		satisfactrey	satisfactory⁺
Santa klaws	Santa Claus	satisfiabul	satisfiable
santeem	centime	satisf *y*⁴ /iable/action	

saturashun	saturation	say /ing	
saturat e² /ion		sayance	seance
Saturday		scab³ /by	
Saturn		scabbard	
sauce * (liquid) /boat/pan		scabees	scabies
sauce	source *	scabies	
saucer		scaffold	
saucerer	sorcerer⁺	scald¹	
saucerey	sorcery	scal e² /y	
sauci er /est/ly/ness		scaliwag	scallywag
saucy		scallop	
sauna		scallywag	
saunter¹		scalp¹ /er	
sausage		scalpel	
sausie	saucy	scamp¹	
savage² /ly/ry		scamper¹	
savana	savannah	scampi	
savannah		scan³ /ner	
save²		scandal /ous/ously	
saver	savour¹⁺	scandalise²	
savier	saviour	scandium	
savige	savage²⁺	scanshun	scansion
savigrey	savagery	scansion	
saviour		scant /ily/iness/y	
savorey	savoury	scapegoat	
savour¹ /iness/y		scapula /r	
savyer	saviour	scar³	
saw * (cut) /n		scarab	
saw	soar¹*	scarce /ly/ness/r	
saw	sore *⁺	scarcit y /ies	
sawcer	saucer	scare² /crow/y	
sawcy	saucy	scaremonger	
sawdid	sordid⁺	scarf /ves (pl.)	
sawdust		scarf-pin	
sawna	sauna	scarif y⁴ /ication	
sawnter	saunter¹	scarlatina	
saws	sauce *⁺	scarlet	
saws	source *	scarsitey	scarcity⁺
sawser	saucer	scathe² /less	
sawsey	saucy	scatter¹ /-brain	
sawsier	saucier⁺	scavenge² /r	
saxhorn		scavinge	scavenge²⁺
saxofone	saxophone⁺	sceme	scheme²⁺
Saxon /y		scenario /s	
saxophon e /ist		scene * (of a play) /ry	

253

scenic /ally		scot /ch/-free/tish	
scent [1]* (smell)		Scots *man* /woman	
scepter	sceptre	scoundrel /ism/ly	
sceptic /al/ally/ism		scour [1] /er	
sceptre		scourge [2]	
scerge	scourge [2]	scout [1]	
scermish	skirmish [1]+	scower	scour [1]+
schedule [2]		scowl [1]	
schematic /ally		scowndrel	scoundrel +
scheme [2] /r		scowt	scout [1]
scherzo /s		scrabble [2]	
schism /atic		scrabul	scrabble [2]
schist		scrag [3] /gy	
schizofrenia	schizophrenia +	scram [3]	
schizoid		scramble [2]	
schizophreni *a* /c		scrambul	scramble [2]
schnaps		scrap [3] /-book/-heap	
scholar /ly/ship		scrape [2] /r	
scholastic /ism		scrapie	scrappy +
school [1] /boy/girl		scrapp *y* /ily/iness	
schooner		scrapy	scrappy +
sciatic /a		scratch [1] /es	
scien *ce* /tist		scrawl [1]	
scientific /ally		scrawny	
scintillat *e* [2] /ion		scream [1] /er	
scion		scree	
scission		screech [1] /es/-owl	
scissors		screed	
scitsofrenia	schizophrenia +	screen [1]	
sclerosis		screw [1] /driver/y	
sclerotic		screwtinise	scrutinise [2]
scoff [1] /er		scribble [2] /r	
scolar	scholar +	scribe [2]	
scolarship	scholarship	scribul	scribble [2]+
scolastic	scholastic +	scrimige	scrimmage
scold [1] /er		scrimmage	
scone		scrimp [1] /y	
scool	school [1]+	scripcher	scripture +
scoop [1]		script /-writer	
scoot [1] /er		scriptur *e* /al	
scorch [1] /er/ingly		scroful *a* /ous	
score [2] /r		scroll	
scorn [1] /ful/fully		scroo	screw [1]+
scorpion		scrotum	
scorpyun	scorpion	scrounge [2] /r	

scrownge	scrounge [2+]	seam	seem [1]★
scrub [3] /ber/by		seaman /ship	
scruff /ier/iest/y		seamstress	
scrum half		seam y /ier/iest	
scrummage		sean	scene ★+
scrumptious /ly/ness		sean	seen ★
scrumshus	scrumptious [+]	seance	
scrunch [1] /es		seans	seance
scruple [2]		sear [1]★ (scorch)	
scrupul	scruple [2]	sear	seer ★
scrupulous /ly/ness		search [1] /es/er	
scrutinise [2]		sea shore /side/weed	
scrutin y /ies/eer		seasick /ness	
scud [3]		season [1] /able/ably	
scuffle [2]		seasonal /ly	
scuful	scuffle [2]	seasor	seesaw [1]
scul	scull [1]★+	seat [1]	
scul	skull ★+	seaworth y /iness	
sculerey	scullery [+]	sebaceous	
scull [1]★ (boat) /er		sebashus	sebaceous
sculler y /ies		secaters	secateurs
sculpcher	sculpture [2]	secateurs	
sculpt or /ress (fem.)		secede [2]	
sculpture [2]		seceshun	secession
scum [3] /my		secession	
scupper [1]		seclu de [2] /sion	
scurf /iness/y		second [1] /ly/-rate	
scurge	scourge [2]	secondar y /ily	
scurie	scurry [4]	secondrey	secondary [+]
scurilus	scurrilous [+]	secrecy	
scurrilous /ly		secresey	secrecy
scurry [4]		secret /ive/ly	
scurv y /ily		secretaria l /t	
scury	scurry [4]	secretar y /ies	
scuttle [2]		secret e [2] /ion	
scutul	scuttle [2]	sect /arian	
scythe [2]		section /al/ally	
sea ★ (water) /-gull		sector	
sea	see ★+	secular /ism	
seafar er /ing		secularis e [2] /ation	
seal /ed/er/ing ★ (fasten)		secur e [2] /able/ely	
sea -level /-lion		securitey	security [+]
sealing	ceiling ★	securit y /ies	
sealskin		sed	said
seam ★ (join in cloth)		sedashun	sedation [+]

sedate /ly/ness		seesfire	cease-fire
sedat *ion* /ive		seesher	seizure
sedentary		seeshore	seashore +
sedentrey	sedentary	seesick	seasick +
seder	cedar	seeside	seaside
sedge		seet	seat 1
sedila	cedilla	seeth	seethe 2
sediment /ation		seethe 2	
sedishun	sedition +	seeworthey	seaworthy +
sedishus	seditious	seeze	seize 2
sedit *ion* /ious		sefalic	cephalic +
seduce 2 /r		sefalitis	cephalitis
seducshun	seduction	sege	sedge
seduction		segment /ation	
seductive /ly		segregashun	segregation
sedulous /ly		segregat *e* 2 /ion/ive	
sedulus	sedulous +	seige	siege
seduse	seduce 2+	seine 2★ (fishing net)	
see ★† /ing/n ★†		seism *ic* /ometer	
†(with eyes)		seismograph /ic	
see	sea ★+	seismolog *y* /ist	
seed 1★ (of plants)		seize 2	
seed	cede 2★	seizure	
seed *iness* /ling/y		sekaters	secateurs
seefarer	seafarer +	sekstant	sextant
seege	siege	sekstet	sextet
seek /er/ing		sekston	sexton
seel	seal +	seksual	sexual +
seeling	ceiling ★	sekt	sect +
seeling	sealing ★	sekwel	sequel
seem 1★ (appear)		sekwence	sequence +
seem	seam ★	sekwens	sequence +
seeman	seaman +	sekwester	sequester 1
seemey	seamy +	sekwestrate	sequestrate 2+
seeml *y* /ier/iest/iness		sekwin	sequin
seemstress	seamstress	selandine	celandine
seen	scene ★+	selcius	Celsius
seenerey	scenery	seldom /ly	
seenic	scenic +	selebritey	celebrity +
seep 1 /age		select 1 /ion/or	
seepige	seepage	selective /ly	
seer ★ (prophet)		selenium	
seer	sear 1★	seler	cellar ★
seesaw 1		seler	seller ★
seese	cease 2+	selerey	celery

seleritey	celerity	semi-final	
self /ish/ishness		semikwaver	semiquaver
self-assured		semilunar	
self-centred		seminal	
self-confiden *ce* /t		seminar /y	
selfconfidens	self-confidence +	semi-precious	
self-conscious /ly/ness		semipreshus	semi-precious
selfconshus	self-conscious +	semiquaver	
self-contained		Semit *e* /ic	
self-control		semitone	
self-respect /ing		semitrey	cemetery +
self-righteous /ly/ness		semolena	semolina
self-service		semolina	
selibacy	celibacy +	sena	senna
selibasey	celibacy +	senario	scenario +
selibat	celibate	senat	senate +
selibrant	celebrant	senat *e* /or	
selibrate	celebrate 2+	senater	senator
sell ★ (goods) /er ★		send /er	
sell	cell ★	senil *e* /ity	
seller	cellar ★	senilitey	senility
Sellotape		senior /ity	
selofane	cellophane	senna	
selsius	Celsius	senotaf	cenotaph
selt	Celt +	sensashun	sensation
seltic	Celtic	sensashunal	sensational +
selular	cellular	sensation	
selule	cellule	sensational /ism/ly	
seluloid	celluloid	sense 2 /less	
selulose	cellulose	senser	censer ★
selvage		senser	censor 1★+
selvige	selvage	sensher	censure 2+
semafor	semaphore	senshience	sentience +
semantic /s		senshooal	sensual +
semaphore		sensib *le* /ility/ly	
semblance		sensibul	sensible +
semblans	semblance	sensitise 2	
semen		sensitiv *e* /ely/ity	
semester		sensitivitey	sensitivity
semibreve		sensorey	sensory
semicercul	semicircle +	sensorious	censorious
semicirc *le* /ular		sensorius	censorious
semicolon		sensory	
semi-conductor		sensual /ist/ity/ly	
semi-detached		sensus	census +

sent ★ (did send)		septer	sceptre
sent	cent ★	septic	
sent	scent ¹★	septicaemia	
sentenarey	centenary ⁺	septisemia	septicaemia
sentenarian	centenarian	sepulchr e /al	
sentence ²		sepulker	sepulchre ⁺
sentenial	centennial ⁺	sequel	
sentens	sentence ²	sequen ce /tial	
sentenshus	sententious ⁺	sequester ¹	
sententious /ly		sequestrat e ² /ion/or	
sentenyal	centennial ⁺	sequin	
senter	centre ²⁺	ser	sir
senter forwud	centre-forward	seraf	seraph ⁺
sentien ce /t		serafic	seraphic
sentigrade	centigrade	seramic	ceramic ⁺
sentigram	centigram	seraph /s/ic	
sentileter	centilitre	serch	search ¹⁺
sentiment		serebral	cerebral ⁺
sentimental /ist/ity/ly		serees	series
sentimentalise ²		serenade ²	
sentimeter	centimetre	serendipity	
sentinel		seren e /ely/ity	
sentipede	centipede	serenitey	serenity
sentor	centaur	seres	series
sentral	central ⁺	sereze	cerise
sentralise	centralise ²⁺	serf ★ (slave) /dom	
sentralitey	centrality	serf	surf ¹★⁺
sentrey	sentry ⁺	sergeant /-major	
sentrifugal	centrifugal ⁺	serial ★† /ly	
sentrifuge	centrifuge	†(part of a story)	
sentripetal	centripetal	serial	cereal ★
sentr y /ies		serialis e ² /ation	
sentuple	centuple	seribelum	cerebellum
senturey	century ⁺	seribrum	cerebrum
senturion	centurion	serid	serried
senyor	senior ⁺	series	
senyoritey	seniority	serimonial	ceremonial ⁺
separashun	separation	serimonius	ceremonious ⁺
separat e ² /ion/ist/or		serimuney	ceremony ⁺
sephalic	cephalic ⁺	serious /ly/ness	
sephalitis	cephalitis	serius	serious ⁺
sepia		serlier	surlier ⁺
sepoi	sepoy	serloin	sirloin
sepoy		serly	surly ★
September		sermise	surmise ²

sermon		sesmic	seismic [+]
sermonise [2]		seson	season [1+]
sermownt	surmount [1]	sesonable	seasonable
sername	surname	sesonabul	seasonable
serpass	surpass [1]	sesonal	seasonal [+]
serpent /ine		sespit	cesspit
serplis	surplice ★	sespool	cesspool
serplus	surplus ★	sessashun	cessation
serprise	surprise [2]	sessesion	secession
serrated		session ★ (period)	
serried		session	cession ★
sertaks	surtax [+]	set /ting/-square	
sertax	surtax [+]	setea	settee
sertifi	certify [4+]	seter	setter
sertifiable	certifiable [+]	setle	settle [2+]
sertificat	certificate [2+]	settee	
sertify	certify [4+]	setter	
sertintey	certainty [+]	settle [2] /ment/r	
sertitude	certitude	setul	settle [2+]
serum		setulment	settlement
servant		seudo	pseudo [+]
servay	survey [1+]	seudonim	pseudonym
servaylans	surveillance	sevear	severe [+]
serve [2] /r		seven /teen/teenth/th	
servical	cervical	sevent y /ies/ieth	
service [2] /ability/able		sever [1] /ance	
serviet	serviette	several /ly	
serviette		severans	severance
serviks	cervix [+]	sever e /ely/ity	
servil e /ity		severitey	severity
servitude		sew ★† /er ★† /ing/n ★†	
servival	survival	†(with a needle)	
servive	survive [2+]	sew er [1]★† /age/erage	
serviver	survivor	†(public drain)	
servix	cervix [+]	sewn	sown ★
sesashun	cessation	sex /ed/iness/less	
sese	cease [2+]	sextant	
seseed	secede [2]	sextet	
seseshun	secession	sexton	
seshun	cession ★	sexual /ity/ly	
seshun	session ★	sezarian	Caesarean
sesion	cession ★	Sezer	Caesar
sesion	session ★	sfere	sphere [2+]
sesium	caesium	sferical	spherical
sesless	ceaseless	sferoid	spheroid

sfincter	sphincter	shan't (shall not)	
sfinks	sphinx +	shant	shan't
sfinx	sphinx +	shant y /ies	
sha	shah	shape ² /liness/ly	
shabbi ly /ness		shaperon	chaperon ¹+
shabb y /ier/iest		sharad	charade
shaby	shabby +	share ² /holder/r	
shack		shark	
shackle ²		sharlot	charlotte
shad e ² /y		sharp /er/est/ly/ness	
shadervre	chef-d'oeuvre	sharpen ¹ /er	
shadow ¹ /y		sharpshooter	
shaft		shasee	chassis
shagay da fare	chargé-d'affaires	shater	shatter ¹
shagg y /iness		shatow	chateau +
shagie	shaggy +	shatter ¹	
shagrin	chagrin +	shave ² /n/r	
shah		shawl	
shak	shack	shea f ¹ /ves (pl.)	
shake *† /down/n/r		shear * (clip) /s	
†(agitate)		shear	sheer ¹*
shake	sheik *	sheath * (n.)	
shakey	shaky +	sheathe ²* (v.)	
shak y /ily/ing/iness		shed ³	
shal	shall	shedule	schedule ²
shalaton	charlatan	sheef	sheaf ¹+
shalay	chalet	sheek	chic *
shale		sheek	sheik *
shalet	chalet	sheen	
shall		sheep /-dog/skin	
shallot		sheepish /ly/ness	
shallow /er/est/ness		sheer ¹* (thin, steep)	
sham ³ /mer		sheer	shear *+
shamble ²		sheet ¹	
shambul	shamble ²	shef	chef
shame ² /-faced/less		sheik * (Arab chief)	
shameful /ly		sheik	chic *
shampane	champagne	sheild	shield ¹
shampoo ¹		shel	shell ¹+
shamrock		shelac	shellac +
shamwa	chamois	sheld	shield ¹
shandeleer	chandelier	shel f /ves (pl.)	
shandie	shandy +	shelfish	shellfish
shand y /ies		shell ¹ /fish	
shank		shellac /ked/king	

shelter¹ /er		shirt /ing/y	
shelve²		shivalrey	chivalry⁺
shemeez	chemise	shivalrous	chivalrous
sheperd	shepherd¹⁺	shivalrus	chivalrous
sheperds pie	shepherd's pie	shiver¹ /y	
shepherd¹ /ess (fem.)		shnaps	schnaps
shepherd's pie		shoal¹	
sherbet		shock¹ /-absorber/er	
sherie	sherry⁺	shoddi ly /ness	
sherif	sheriff⁺	shodd y /ier/iest	
sheriff /s		shodie	shoddy⁺
sheroot	cheroot	shody	shoddy⁺
sheropodey	chiropody⁺	shoe /lace/string	
sherr y /ies		shofer	chauffeur
shery	sherry⁺	sholder	shoulder¹
sheth	sheath ★	shole	shoal¹
sheth	sheathe²★	shoo	shoe⁺
shevaler	chevalier	shood	should⁺
sheves	sheaves	shook	
shevron	chevron	shoolace	shoelace
shi	shy⁴⁺	shoostring	shoestring
shic	chic ★	shoot ★ (gun) /er	
shic	sheik ★	shoot	chute ★
shicanerey	chicanery	shooting /-brake	
shield¹		shop³ /keeper/per	
shifon	chiffon	shoplift¹ /er	
shift¹ /ily/iness/less/y		shop-soiled	
shiling	shilling	shop-steward	
shilling		shore²★ (prop up)	
shilly-shall y⁴ /ier		shore	sure ★⁺
shily shaly	shilly-shally⁴⁺	shoretey	surety⁺
shimeric	chimeric⁺	shorley	surely
shimmer¹ /y		shorn	
shin³		short /age/ly	
shin e² /er/y		short bread /cake	
shingle²		short-circuit¹	
shingles		shorten¹	
shingul	shingle²	shorthand	
shinguls	shingles	short-sighted /ness	
ship³ /ment/per		short sited	short-sighted⁺
shipreck	shipwreck¹	shot	
ship shape /wright		should /n't	
shipwreck¹		shoulder¹	
shire		shout¹ /er	
shirk¹ /er		shove²	

shovel[3] /ler		siatic	sciatic[+]
shovinism	chauvinism[+]	sibernetics	cybernetics
shovinist	chauvinist	sibilant	
show /down/ily/ing/n/y		sibling	
shower[1] /-bath/y		sicamore	sycamore
showt	shout[1+]	sicedelic	psychedelic
shrank		siciatrey	psychiatry
shrapnel		sicick	psychic[+]
shred[3] /der		sick /ly/ness	
shreek	shriek[1]	sicken[1]	
shrew /ish/ishly		sickle	
shrewd /er/est/ly/ness		siclamate	cyclamate
shriek[1]		siclamen	cyclamen
shrift		siclic	cyclic[+]
shrike		siclist	cyclist[+]
shrill[1] /er/est/ness/y		siclometer	cyclometer
shrimp		siclone	cyclone[+]
shrine[2]		siclops	Cyclops
shrink /age/ing		siclostile	cyclostyle
shrivel[3]		siclotron	cyclotron
shroo	shrew[+]	sicoanalise	psychoanalyse[2+]
shrood	shrewd[+]	sicofant	sycophant[+]
shroud[1]		sicologey	psychology[+]
Shrovetide		sicological	psychological[+]
shrowd	shroud[1]	sicopath	psychopath[+]
shrub /bery		sicosomatic	psychosomatic
shrug[3]		sicosis	psychosis[+]
shrunk /en		sicotherapey	psychotherapy
shudder[1]		sicotherapist	psychotherapist[+]
shuffle[2] /r		sicotic	psychotic
shuful	shuffle[2+]	sicul	cycle[2]
shugar	sugar[+]	side[2] /board/line/ways	
shun[3]		sider	cider
shunt[1]		sidle[2]	
shurbet	sherbet	sie	sigh[1]
shurk	shirk[1+]	siege	
shurt	shirt[+]	sienna	
shut /ter/ting		siense	science[+]
shuttle[2] /cock		sientific	scientific[+]
shutul	shuttle[2+]	sientist	scientist
shuv	shove[2]	siesta	
shuvel	shovel[3+]	sieve[2]	
shy[4] /er/est/ly/ness		sieze	seize[2]
si	sigh[1]	sifer	cipher[1]
sianide	cyanide	sifilis	syphilis[+]

sifon	siphon [1]+	silidge	silage
sift [1]		silie	silly +
sigar	cigar +	silige	silage
sigaret	cigarette	silinder	cylinder
sigh [1]		silindrical	cylindrical +
sight [1]* (see) /less		silk /ily/iness/y	
sight	cite [2]*+	sill	
sight	site [2]*	sillable	syllable +
sightsee r /ing		sillabub	
sign [1]* /er/-writer		sill y /ier/iest/ily/iness	
sign	sine *	silo	
signacher	signature	silogise	syllogise [2]+
signal [3] /ler		silogism	syllogism
signalise [2]		silooet	silhouette [2]
signator y /ies		siluet	silhouette [2]
signature		silvan	
signet * (ring)		silver [1] /y	
signet	cygnet *	sily	silly +
signifi	signify [4]	simbiosis	symbiosis +
significan ce /t/tly		simbiotic	symbiotic
significans	significance +	simbol	cymbal *+
signify [4]		simbol	symbol *+
signpost [1]		simbolical	symbolical +
signul	signal [3]+	simbolise	symbolise [2]+
sikedelic	psychedelic	simbolism	symbolism
sikey	psyche	siment	cement [1]+
sikiatrist	psychiatrist +	simer	simmer [1]
sikiatry	psychiatry	simfoney	symphony +
sikick	psychic +	simian	
siks	six +	similar /ly	
sikstey	sixty +	similarit y /ies	
silable	syllable +	similer	similar +
silabus	syllabus +	similitude	
silage		simmer [1]	
silence [2] /r		simmetrey	symmetry +
silens	silence [2]+	simpathetic	sympathetic +
silent /ly		simpathise	sympathise [2]+
silestial	celestial +	simpathy	sympathy +
silf	sylph +	simper [1]	
silhouette [2]		simple /r/st/ton	
siliam	cilium	simplifi	simplify [4]+
silic a /osis		simplif y [4] /ication	
silicon * (hard mineral)		simplisitey	simplicity
silicone * (compound in polish)		simpl y /icity	
		simposium	symposium +

simptom	symptom +	sinopsis	synopsis +
simptomatic	symptomatic	sinoptic	synoptic
simpul	simple +	sinoshoor	cynosure
simpulton	simpleton	sinovial	synovial
simulashun	simulation	sinse	since
simulat e ² /ion/or		sinsere	sincere +
simultaneous /ly		sinseritey	sincerity
simultanius	simultaneous +	sintactic	syntactic
sin ¹ /ner		sintaks	syntax +
sinagog	synagogue	sintax	syntax +
sinamon	cinnamon	sinthesis	synthesis +
since		sinthesise	synthesise ²+
sincer e /ity		sinthetic	synthetic
sinch	cinch +	sinue	sinew +
sincopate	syncopate ²+	sinuous	
sindicalism	syndicalism +	sinus /es/itis	
sindicate	syndicate ²+	sinuus	sinuous
sindrome	syndrome	sion	scion
sine ★ (maths)		sip ³	
sine	sign ¹★+	sipher	cipher ¹
sinecamera	cine camera	siphon ¹ /age	
sinecure		sipress	cypress
sinepost	signpost ¹	sir	
sinew /y		sirca	circa
sinful /ly/ness		sircharge	surcharge ²
sing /er/ing		siren	
singe ²		siringe	syringe ²
single ² /-minded		sirloin	
singul	single ²+	siro stratus	cirro-stratus
singular /ity		sirocco	
singuler	singular +	sirocumulus	cirro-cumulus
sinic	cynic +	sirosis	cirrhosis
sinical	cynical +	sirup	syrup +
sinima	cinema +	sise	size +
sinimatograf	cinematograph +	sishun	scission
sinimatograph	cinematograph +	sismic	seismic +
sinisism	cynicism	sismograf	seismograph +
sinister		sismologey	seismology +
sink /er/ing		sissers	scissors
sinkromesh	syncromesh	sist	cyst +
sinkronise	synchronise ²+	sistem	system +
sinod	synod +	sistematic	systematic
sinonim	synonym +	sistematise	systematise ²+
sinonimus	synonymous	sister(s)/-in-law	
sinonym	synonym +	sistern	cistern

sistitis	cystitis	skeptic	sceptic +
sistole	systole	skepticul	sceptical
sit /-in/ter/ting		skeptisism	scepticism
sitadel	citadel	skermish	skirmish [1]+
sitashun	citation	skert	skirt [1]+
site [2]★ (place)		skerting bord	skirting-board
site	cite [2]★+	skertso	scherzo +
site	sight [1]★+	sketch [1] /ier/ily/iness/y	
siteseeing	sightseeing	skew [1] /-whiff	
siteseer	sightseer +	skewer [1]	
sitey	city +	ski [1]★ (sport) /er	
sithe	scythe [2]	ski	sky [4]★+
sitie	city +	skid [3]	
sitizen	citizen +	skiff	
sitologey	cytology	skil	skill +
sitric acid	citric acid	skilful /ly/ness	
sitron	citron +	skilite	skylight
sitrus	citrus	skill /ed	
situashun	situation	skim [3] /-milk	
situat e [3] /ion		skimp [1] /ily/iness/y	
siv	sieve [2]	skin [3] /ner/ny	
sivere	severe +	skin-deep	
sivic	civic +	skin-div er /ing	
sivil	civil +	skiney	skinny
sivilian	civilian	skinflint	
sivilisashun	civilisation	skintilate	scintillate [2]+
sivilise	civilise [2]+	skip [3]	
sivilitey	civility +	skipper	
sivit	civet	skirl [1]	
six /th/thly		skirmish [1] /es	
sixteen /th		skirt [1] /ing-board	
sixt y /ies/ieth		skiscraper	skyscraper
siythe	scythe [2]	skism	schism +
size /able/ably		skist	schist
sizemic	seismic +	skit /tish	
sizers	scissors	skitsofrenia	schizophrenia +
sizul	sizzle [2]	skittle [2]	
sizzle [2]		skitul	skittle [2]
skate [2] /r		skitzoid	schizoid
skedule	schedule [2]	sku	skew [1]+
skee	ski [1]★+	skulk [1]	
skein		skull ★ (head) /-cap	
skelet on /al		skull	scull [1]★+
skematic	schematic +	skunk	
skeme	scheme [2]+	skurl	skirl [1]

265

> *If you cannot find your word under* **skw** *look under* **squ**

skwable	squabble²
skwod	squad
skwodron	squadron
skwolid	squalid⁺
sky⁴*† /-blue/-high †(atmosphere)	
sky	ski¹*⁺
skyatic	sciatic⁺
skylark	
skylight	
skylite	skylight
skyscraper	
slack¹ /er/est/ly/ness	
slacken¹	
slain	
slake²	
slaken	slacken¹
slam³	
slander¹ /er/ous	
slane	slain
slang /y	
slant¹	
slap³ /dash/stick	
slash¹ /er	
slat e² /y	
slattern /ly	
slaughter¹ /-house	
Slav /onic	
slave² /ry	
slavish /ness	
slawter	slaughter¹⁺
slay *(kill) /ing	
slay	sleigh*
sleazy	
sled	
sledge /-hammer	
sleek /ness	
sleep /ing/y	
sleepi er /est/ly/ness	
sleepless /ness	
sleet¹ /y	

sleeve /d/less	
slege	sledge⁺
sleigh *(for snow)	
slender /ness	
sleuth	
slew	
sli	sly⁺
slice²	
slick¹	
slid e /ing	
slight¹ /er/est/ly/ness	
slim³ /mer/mest/ness	
slim e /ier/iest/y	
sling /er	
slip³ /way	
slipper /iness/y	
slipshod	
slise	slice²
slit /ting	
slite	slight¹⁺
slither¹	
sliver	
slo	sloe*
slo	slow¹*⁺
slobber¹ /er	
sloe *(plum)	
sloe	slow¹*⁺
slog³ /ger	
slogan	
sloop	
sloose	sluice²
slooth	sleuth
slop³ /py	
slope²	
sloppi er /est/ly/ness	
slosh¹	
slot³ /machine	
sloth /ful	
slouch¹	
slough¹* (dead skin)	
sloven /liness/ly	
slow¹*† /er/ly/-worm †(not quick)	
slow	slough¹*
slowch	slouch¹

slowerm	slow-worm
sludg *e* /y	
slue	slew
sluff	slough ¹★
slug /gard/gish	
sluge	sludge +
sluice ²	
slum ³ /mer/my	
slumber ¹ /ous	
slump ¹	
slung	
slunk	
slur ³	
slush /y	
slut /tish	
sly /er/est/ly/ness	
smack ¹	
small /er/est/pox	
smarmy	
smart ¹ /er/est/ly/ness	
smarten ¹	
smash ¹ /er	
smatter /ing	
smear ¹ /y	
smeer	smear ¹+
smell ¹ /ier/iest/ing/y	
smelling-salts	
smelt ¹ /er	
smirch ¹ /es	
smirk ¹	
smit *e* /ing	
smith /y/ies	
smithereens	
smithey	smithy
smitten	
smock ¹	
smog	
smoke ² /r/-stack	
smok *ier* /iest/y	
smolder	smoulder ¹
smooth ¹ /er/est/ly/ness	
smote	
smother ¹	
smoulder ¹	
smudg *e* ² /y	

smug /ger/gest/ly/ness	
smuge	smudge ²+
smuggle ² /r	
smugul	smuggle ²+
smurch	smirch ¹+
smurk	smirk ¹
smut /tiness/ty	
snack	
snag ³	
snail ¹	
snake ² /-bite	
snale	snail ¹
snap ³ /dragon/shot	
snapp *er* /ily/ish/y	
snare ²	
snarl ¹ /er	
snatch ¹ /es	
sneak ¹ /ingly/ily	
sneek	sneak ¹+
sneer ¹	
sneeze ²	
snicker ¹	
snide	
sniff ¹ /er/y	
sniffle ²	
sniful	sniffle ²
snigger ¹	
snip ³ /pet	
snipe ² /r	
snivel ³ /ler	
sno	snow ¹+
snobb *ery* /ish/ishness	
snoberie	snobbery +
snobish	snobbish
snooker ¹	
snoop ¹ /er	
snooze ²	
snore ² /r	
snorkel	
snorkle	snorkel
snort ¹ /er	
snot /ty	
snout	
snow ¹ /drift/drop/fall	
snowball ¹	

snow-plough		soften [1]	
snowt	snout	software	
snub [3]		softwear	software
snuff [1]		sogg *y* /iness	
snuffle [2]		sogie	soggy [+]
snuful	snuffle [2]	Soho	
snuggle [2]		soia	soya
snugul	snuggle [2]	soil [1]	
so ★ (in this way)		soiray	soirée
so	sew ★+	soirée	
so	sow [1]★	soiya	soya
soak [1]		sojern	sojourn [1+]
soap [1] /y		sojourn [1] /er	
soar [1]★ (to fly)		soke	soak [1]
soar	sore ★+	solace [2]	
sob [3]		solar /ium	
sober [1]		solar plexus	
sobriety		solar system	
sobrikay	sobriquet [+]	solas	solace [2]
sobriquet /s		solder [1]	
soccer		soldering iron	
sociab *le* /ility/ly		soldier [1] /ly/y	
sociabul	sociable [+]	sole ★ (shoe) /ly	
social /ite/ly		sole	soul ★+
socialis *e* [2] /ation		solecism	
socialis *m* /t/tic		soleful	soulful [+]
societ *y* /ies		solem	solemn [+]
sociolog *y* /ical/ist		solemn /ity/ly	
sock [1]		solemnis *e* [2] /ation	
socker	soccer	solemnitey	solemnity
socket		solenoid	
soda /-water		solesism	solecism
sodden		sol-fa	
soden	sodden	solger	soldier [1+]
sodium		solicit [1] /ation/ude	
sodom *y* /ite		solicit *or* /ous	
sofen	soften [1]	solid /er/est/ity/ly	
sofism	sophism [+]	solidarity	
sofist	sophist	solidifi	solidify [4+]
sofisticashun	sophistication	solidif *y* [4] /ication	
sofisticate	sophisticate [2+]	solilokwise	soliloquise [2]
sofistication	sophistication	solilokwy	soliloquy [+]
sofistrey	sophistry	soliloquise [2]	
sofmore	sophomore	soliloqu *y* /ies	
soft /er/est/ly/ness		solisit	solicit [1+]

solisiter	solicitor +	soop	soup
solisitous	solicitous	soot ★ (black powder) /y	
solisitus	solicitous	soot	suit ¹★+
solitar y /ily/iness		sooth /sayer	
solitrey	solitary +	soothe ²	
solitude		soovenir	souvenir
soljer	soldier ¹+	sop ³ /py	
solo /ist		sope	soap ¹+
solstice		sophis m /t/try	
solstis	solstice	sophisticat e ² /ion	
solub le /ility		sophomore	
solubul	soluble +	soporific	
solushun	solution	soprano /s	
solution		sorcer er /ess (fem.)/y	
solv e ² /able		sord	sword
solven cy /t		sordid /ly/ness	
solvensey	solvency +	sordust	sawdust
somber	sombre +	sore ★ (hurt) /ly/r/st	
sombraro	sombrero +	sore	saw ★+
sombre /ly/ness		sore	soar ¹★
sombrero /s		sorey	sorry +
some ★† /body/how		sorie	sorry +
†(a few)		sorna	sauna
some	sum ³★	sornter	saunter ¹
some one /what/where		sorow	sorrow ¹+
somersalt	somersault ¹	sorrel	
somersault ¹		sorrow ¹ /ful/fully	
somnolen ce /t		sorr y /ier/iest	
somnolens	somnolence +	sors	sauce ★+
son ★ (male child)		sors	source ★
sonar		sort ¹★ (kind) /er	
sonata		sort	sought ★
sonde		sortee	sortie
soner	sonar	sortie	
song /-bird/ster		sorul	sorrel
sonic		soshable	sociable +
son(s)-in-law		soshabul	sociable +
sonnet		soshal	social +
sonor ous /ity		soshalise	socialise ²+
sonorus	sonorous +	soshalism	socialism +
soo	sue ²	soshalist	socialist
soocher	suture	soshalistic	socialistic
sooflay	soufflé	soshiologey	sociology +
sooit	suet	soshiologist	sociologist
soon /er		sosidge	sausage

sosietey	society +	spanner	
sosige	sausage	Spanyard	Spaniard
sot /tish		spanyel	spaniel
sotto voce		spar³	
soufflé		spare²	
sought * (did seek)		spark¹ /ing-plug	
soul * (spirit) /less		sparkle² /r	
soul	sole *+	sparkul	sparkle²+
soulful /ly		sparo	sparrow +
sound¹ /er/est/less/ness		sparrow /-hawk	
soundproof¹		spars	sparse +
soup		sparse /ly/ness	
sour¹ /er/est/ish/ness		sparsity	
source * (origin)		Spartan	
source	sauce *+	spase	space²+
souse²		spashal	spatial
south /erly/ern		spashus	spacious
souvenir		spasm	
sou'-wester		spasmodic /ally	
sovereign /ty		spastic /ism	
soverin	sovereign +	spate	
soviet		spatial	
sovrentey	sovereignty	spatter¹	
sow¹* (cast seed, pig)		spatula /te	
sow	sew *+	spawn¹	
sown * (seed)		speak /er/ing	
sown	sewn *	spear¹ /head	
sownd	sound¹+	special /ist/ly	
sowndproof	soundproof¹	specialis e² /ation	
sowr	sour¹+	specialt y /ies	
sowse	souse²	species	
sowth	south +	specifi	specify⁴+
sow-wester	sou'-wester	specific /ally	
soya		specif y⁴ /ication	
spac e² /ious		specimen	
spade /-work		specious /ness	
spagetti	spaghetti	speck¹	
spaghetti		speckle²	
span³		spectacle	
spaner	spanner	spectacular /ly	
spangle		spectator	
spangul	spangle	specter	spectre +
Spaniard		spectr e /al	
spaniel		spectrograf	spectrograph
spank¹		spectrograph	

spectroscop *e* /ic
spectr *um* /a (pl.)
speculashun   speculation
speculat *e*² /ion/or
speculative /ly
speech /less
speed¹ /y
speedi *er* /est/ly/ness
speedometer

speek   speak⁺
speeker   speaker
speeking   speaking
speer   spear¹⁺
speerhed   spearhead
spekul   speckle²
spel   spell⁺
spelbownd   spellbound
spel *l* /ling/t
spellbound
spend /er/thrift
sperm /-whale
spermatoz *oon* /oa (pl.)

spern   spurn¹
spert   spurt¹
speshal   special⁺
speshalise   specialise²⁺
speshalist   specialist
speshaltey   specialty⁺
speshes   species
speshialtey   specialty⁺
speshus   specious⁺
spesifi   specify⁴⁺
spesific   specific⁺
spesificashun   specification
spesify   specify⁴⁺
spesimen   specimen
spew¹
spher *e*² /ical/ically
spheroid
sphincter
sphinx /es
spi   spy⁴⁺
spic *e*² /y
spici *er* /est/ly/ness
spick and span

spider /y
spik *e*² /y
spil *l* /ling/t
spin³ /ner/neret
spinach
spinaker   spinnaker
spindl *e* /y
spindul   spindle⁺
spin *e* /al/eless
spiney   spinney⁺
spinidge   spinach
spinige   spinach
spinnaker
spinney /s
spinster /hood
spiracle
spiral³ /ly
spire
spirichooal   spiritual⁺
spirichooalise   spiritualise²⁺
spirichooalist   spiritualist⁺
spirit¹ /less
spiritual /ly
spiritualis *e*² /ation
spiritualist /ic
spise   spice²⁺
spisey   spicy
spisier   spicier⁺
spit /ting/toon
spite /ful/fulness
spitfire
spittle
spitul   spittle
splash¹ /-down
splay¹
spleen
splender   splendour
splendid
splendour
splice²
splint¹
splinter¹
splise   splice²
split /ting
splutter¹

spoil [1] /sport/t		springtime	
spoke /n		spring y /iness/ing	
spokes *man* /woman		sprinkle [2] /r	
spoliashun	spoliation [+]	sprinkul	sprinkle [2+]
spoliat *ion* /or		sprint [1]	
spong *e* [2] /er/y		sprite /ly	
sponser	sponsor [1]	sprocket	
sponsor [1]		sproose	spruce [+]
spontaneity		sprout [1]	
spontaneous /ly/ness		sprowt	sprout [1]
spontanius	spontaneous [+]	spruce /ly	
spontenaitey	spontaneity	sprung	
spoof [1] /er		spry /er/est	
spool		spu	spew [1]
spoon [1] /-fed/ful		spume [2]	
spoonerism		spunge	sponge [2+]
spoor [1]★ (track)		spunk	
spoor	spore ★	spur [3]	
sporadic /ally		spurious /ly/ness	
sporan	sporran	spurius	spurious [+]
spore ★ (seed, germ)		spurm	sperm [+]
spore	spoor [1]★	spurn [1]	
sporn	spawn [1]	spurt [1]	
sporran		sputter [1]	
sport [1] /ive/ively		sputum	
sportsman		sp y [4] /ies	
spot [3] /-check/ty		squabble [2]	
spotlight [1]		squabul	squabble [2]
spotlite	spotlight [1]	squad	
spouse		squadron	
spout [1]		squalid /ly	
spowse	spouse	squall [1]	
spowt	spout [1]	squalor	
sprain [1]		squander [1]	
sprane	sprain [1]	square [2] /ly	
sprang		squash [1]	
sprawl [1]		squat [3] /ter	
spray [1] /er		squaw	
spread /ing		squawk [1] /er	
spread-eagle [2]		squeak [1] /er/y	
spred	spread [+]	squeal [1] /er	
spree		squeamish /ly/ness	
spri	spry [+]	squeeze [2]	
sprightl y /ier/iest		squelch [1]	
spring /-board/bok		squerm	squirm [1]

squert	squirt [1]	stale /ness	
squib		stalemate [2]	
squid		stalk [1] /er	
squiggle [2]		stall [1]	
squigul	squiggle [2]	stallion	
squint [1]		stalwart	
squir *e* [2] /archy		stalwert	stalwart
squirm [1]		stalyun	stallion
squirrel		stamen	
squirt [1]		stamer	stammer [1+]
squod	squad	stamina	
squodron	squadron	stammer [1] /er	
squoler	squalor	stamp [1] /er	
squolid	squalid [+]	stampede [2]	
squonder	squander [1]	stance	
squosh	squash [1]	stanch [1]★ (stop flow)	
squot	squat [3+]	stanch	staunch ★
stab [3]		stand /-by/point/still	
stabilis *e* [2] /ation/er		standard	
stability		standardis *e* [2] /ation	
stable [2]		standerd	standard
stabul	stable [2]	standerdise	standardise [2+]
staccato		stane	stain [1+]
stacher	stature	stank	
stachooery	statuary	stans	stance
stack [1]		stanza	
stadi *um* /a/ums (pls.)		stapes	
staf	staff [1+]	staple [2] /r	
staff [1] /s		stapul	staple [2+]
stag		star [3] /less/light/ry	
stage [2] /-coach		starboard	
stager	stagger [1]	starbord	starboard
stagger [1]		starch [1]	
stagnant		stare [2]★ (gaze)	
stagnashun	stagnation	stare	stair ★+
stagnat *e* [2] /ion		starecase	staircase
staid ★ (steady)		starie	starry
staid	stayed ★	stark	
stain [1] /less		starling	
stair ★ (step) /case		starry	
stair	stare [2]★	start [1] /er	
stake [2]★ (post)		startle [2]	
stake	steak ★	startul	startle [2]
stalactite ★ (down)		starvashun	starvation
stalagmite ★ (up)		starv *e* [2] /ation/eling	

stashun	station [1+]	stellar	
stashunrey	stationary ★	stelth	stealth [+]
stashunrey	stationery ★	stem [3]	
state [2] /less/ment		stench /es	
stately /ier/iest/iness		stencil [3] /ler	
static /ally/s		stenografey	stenography [+]
station [1] /ary ★ (at rest)		stenography /er/ic	
stationer /y ★ (paper)		stenotipe	stenotype [2]
statistic /ian/s		stenotype [2]	
statistical /ly		stensil	stencil [3+]
statistishun	statistician	step [3]★ (pace) /-ladder	
statuary		step	steppe ★
statue /sque/tte		step *brother* /sister	
statuesk	statuesque	step *daughter* /son	
statuet	statuette	step *father* /mother	
stature		steppe ★ (plain)	
status		ster	stir [3]
statute /ory		sterdey	sturdy [+]
staunch ★ (true)		stereo /phonic	
staunch	stanch [1]★	stereoscope /ic	
stave [2]		stereotype [2]	
stawk	stalk [1+]	sterile /ity	
stay /ed ★† /ing		sterilise [2] /ation	
†(remained)		sterilitey	sterility
stayed	staid ★	sterio	stereo [+]
steadfast /ly/ness		steriofonic	stereophonic
steadie	steady [4+]	sterioscope	stereoscope [+]
steady [4] /ier/iest/ily		steriotipe	stereotype [2]
steak ★ (beef)		sterjun	sturgeon
steak	stake [2]★	sterling	
steal ★ (to take) /ing		stern /er/est/ly/ness	
steal	steel [1]★+	sternum	
stealth /ily/iness/y		stethoscope	
steam [1] /er		stevedore	
stedfast	steadfast [+]	stew [1]	
stedy	steady [4+]	steward /ess (fem.)	
steed		sti	sty [4+]
steel [1]★ (metal) /y		stich	stitch [1+]
steel	steal ★+	stick /er/ing/s ★ (wood)	
steem	steam [1+]	sticking-plaster	
steep [1] /er/est/ly/ness		stickleback	
steeple /chase/jack		stickler	
steepul	steeple [+]	Sticks	Styx ★
steer [1] /able/age		sticky /ily/iness	
stelar	stellar	stif	stiff [+]

tifen	stiffen [1]+
stiff /er/est/ly	
stiffen [1] /er	
stifle [2]	
tiful	stifle [2]
stigma /s/ta (pls.)	
stigmatise [2]	
til	still [1]+
stilberth	still-birth +
stile ★ (steps)	
stile	style [2]★+
stiletto /s	
tilise	stylise [2]+
tilish	stylish
tilist	stylist
still [1] /ness	
still -birth /-born	
stilt [1]	
tilus	stylus +
timie	stymie +
timulashun	stimulation +
timulat e [2] /ion/ive/or	
timul us /i (pl.) /ant	
ting /er/ing	
sting y /ier/iest/ily/iness	
stink /er/ing	
stint [1]	
stipel	stipple [2]
stipend	
stipendiar y /ies	
stipple [2]	
tiptic	styptic
tipul	stipple [2]
tipulashun	stipulation
stipulat e [2] /ion/or	
stir [3]	
stirrup	
stirup	stirrup
stitch [1] /es	
stoat	
stock [1] /broker/taking	
stockade	
tockie	stocky +
stocking	
stockman	

stockpile [2]	
stock-still	
stock y /ier/iest/iness	
stodg e [2] /y	
stoge	stodge [2]+
stoic /al/ally	
stoicism	
stoisism	stoicism
stoke [2] /r	
stole /n	
stolid /ity	
stoma /ta (pl.)	
stomach [1] /-ache	
stone [2] /mason	
stonewall [1] /er	
ston y /ier/iest/ily	
stood	
stooge [2]	
stook [1]	
stool [1]	
stoop [1]	
stop [3] /cock/page/per	
stoper	stopper
storage	
store [2] /house	
storekeeper	
storey ★ (floor level) /s	
storey	story ★+
storidge	storage
storie	storey ★+
storie	story ★+
storige	storage
stork	
storm [1] /ier/iest/y	
stormi ly /ness	
stor y ★ (narrative) /ies	
story	storey ★+
stote	stoat
stout /er/est/ly/ness	
stove [2]	
stow [1] /age/away	
stowige	stowage
stowt	stout +
straddle [2]	
stradul	straddle [2]

straf	strafe [2]	streemline	streamline [2]
strafe [2]		street	
straggle [2] /r		strength	
stragul	straggle [2+]	strengthen [1]	
straight ★ (line)		strenth	strength
straight	strait ★	strenthen	strengthen [1]
straightaway		strenuous /ly/ness	
straighten [1]		strenuus	strenuous [+]
straightforward		streptococc *us* /i (pl.)/al	
strain [1] /er		stress [1]	
strait ★ (sea passage)		stretch [1] /er	
strait	straight ★	strew /ing	
straitaway	straightaway	strewn	
straiten	straighten [1]	striccher	stricture
straitforwerd	straightforward	stricken	
strait-jacket		stricneen	strychnine
strait-laced		strict /er/est/ly/ness	
strand [1]		stricture	
strane	strain [1+]	strid *e* /ing	
strange /ly/ness/r/st		striden *cy* /t	
strangle [2]		stridensey	stridency [+]
strangul	strangle [2]	strife	
strangulat *e* [2] /ion		strik *e* /er/ing	
strap [3] /hanger		strike-break *er* /ing	
stratagem		string /ing/y	
strate	straight ★	stringen *cy* /t	
strate	strait ★	stringensey	stringency [+]
strategey	strategy [+]	strip [3] /per	
strategic /ally		stripe /d	
strateg *y* /ies/ist		stripling	
stratifi	stratify [4+]	striv *e* /en/ing	
stratif *y* [4] /ication		stroboscop *e* /ic	
stratoscope		strode	
stratosfere	stratosphere [+]	stroke [2]	
stratospher *e* /ic		stroll [1] /er	
strat *um* /a (pl.)		strong /er/est/ly/ness	
straw		strontium	
strawberie	strawberry [+]	stroo	strew [+]
strawberr *y* /ies		strooen	strewn
stray [1]		strove	
streak [1] /y		struck	
stream [1]		struckcher	structure [+]
streamline [2]		structur *e* /al/ally	
streek	streak [1+]	struggle [2]	
streem	stream [1]	strugul	struggle [2]

strum³ /mer		sturgon ·	sturgeon	
strung		sturgun	sturgeon	
strut³		sturling	sterling	
strychnine		sturn	stern⁺	
stu ·	stew¹	sturnum	sternum	
stuard	steward⁺	stuter	stutter¹⁺	
stub³		stutter¹ /er		
stubbl e /y		stuward	steward⁺	
stubborn /ly/ness		st y⁴ /ies		
stubern	stubborn⁺	styl e²★† /ish/ist		
stubul	stubble⁺	†(manner)		
stucco¹		style	stile★	
stuck		stylis e² /ation		
stud³		stylus /es		
student		stymie /d		
studey	study⁴⁺	styptic		
studio /s		Styx★ (river)		
studious /ly/ness		suage	sewage	
studius	studious⁺	suav e /ely/ity		
stud y⁴ /ies		subaltern		
stuf	stuff¹⁺	subcomitee	subcommittee	
stuff¹ /y		subcommittee		
stuffi er /est/ly/ness		subconscious /ly		
stuko	stucco¹	subconshus	subconscious⁺	
stultifi	stultify⁴⁺	subcontinent		
stultif y⁴ /ication		subcontract¹ /or		
stumac	stomach¹⁺	subdivide²		
stumble²		subdivishun	subdivision⁺	
stumbul	stumble²	subdivisi on /ble		
stump¹		subdue²		
stun³		subedit¹ /or		
stung		suberb	suburb⁺	
stunk		suberban	suburban	
stunt¹		sub-human		
stupefi	stupefy⁴⁺	subjecshun	subjection	
stupef y⁴ /action		subject¹ /ion/ive/ivity		
stupendous /ly/ness		subjoogate	subjugate²⁺	
stupendus	stupendous⁺	subjugat e² /ion		
stuper	stupor	subjunctive		
stupid /er/est/ity/ly		sublet /ting		
stupify	stupefy⁴⁺	sublimat e² /ion		
stupor		sublim e /inal		
sturdie	sturdy⁺	submachine-gun		
sturd y /ier/iest/ily/iness		submarine		
sturgeon		submerg e² /ence/ible		

submershun	submersion +	subtenant	
submersi *on* /ble		subtend [1]	
submishun	submission +	subterfugé	
submisiv	submissive	subterranean	
submiss *ion* /ive		sub-title [2]	
submit [3]		subtitul	sub-title [2]
submurge	submerge [2+]	subtle /ness/r/st	
subnormal		subtlet *y* /ies	
subordinat *e* [2] /ion		subtly	
suborn [1] /ation/er		subtracshun	subtraction
subpena	subpoena [1]	subtract [1] /ion	
sub-plot		subtropical	
subpoena [1]		suburb /an/ia	
subscribe [2] /r		subvershun	subversion +
subscription		subvers *ion* /ive	
subsekwent	subsequent +	subversiv	subversive
subsequent /ly		subvert [1] /er	
subservien *ce* /t		subvurt	subvert [1+]
subserviens	subservience +	subway	
subsidarey	subsidiary +	succeed [1]	
subside [2] /nce		success /ful/fully	
subsidens	subsidence	success *ion* /ive/or	
subsidey	subsidy +	succinct	
subsidiar *y* /ies		succour [1]* (help)	
subsidis *e* [2] /ation		succulen *ce* /t	
subsid *y* /ies		succumb [1]	
subsist [1] /ence		such	
subsistens	subsistence	sucher	suture
subsoil		suck [1]	
subsonic		sucker * (victim, one who sucks)	
subsoyl	subsoil	sucker	succour [1]*
substance		suckle [2]	
substandard		sucksun	suction
substans	substance	suckulens	succulence +
substanshal	substantial +	suckulent	succulent
substanshiate	substantiate [2+]	suckumb	succumb [1]
substantial /ly/ity		sucrose	
substantiat *e* [2] /ion		sucseed	succeed [1]
substantive		sucseshun	succession +
substashun	substation	sucsess	success +
substation		sucsesser	successor
substitushun	substitution	sucsessful	successful
substitut *e* [2] /ion		sucsessiv	successive
substrat *um* /a (pl.)		sucsint	succinct
subtefuge	subterfuge		

suction		sulferus	sulphurous
sudden /ly/ness		sulfide	sulphide
sudo	pseudo +	sulfuric asid	sulphuric acid
sudonim	pseudonym	sulie	sully 4
suds		sulk 1 /ily/iness/y	
sue 2		sullen	
suède		sully 4	
suer	sewer 1★+	sulphate	
suet		sulphide	
sufer	suffer 1+	sulphur /ous	
suffer 1 /ance/er		sulphuric acid	
suffice 2		sultan /a (fem.) /ate	
sufficien cy /t		sultrey	sultry +
suffiks	suffix 1+	sultr y /ily/iness	
suffise	suffice 2	suly	sully 4
suffishency	sufficiency +	sum 3★ (total)	
suffishent	sufficient	sum	some ★+
suffix 1 /es		sumbody	somebody
suffocat e 2 /ion		sumhow	somehow
suffrage /tte		summari ly /ness	
suffus e 2 /ion		summarise 2	
sufocashun	suffocation	summar y /ies	
sufocate	suffocate 2+	summer /time/y	
sufocation	suffocation	summerise	summarise 2
sufrajet	suffragette	summit	
sufrance	sufferance	summon 1★ (call forth)	
sufrige	suffrage +	summons 1★ (before court)	
sufuse	suffuse 2+	sump	
sugar 1 /y		sumpshus	sumptuous +
sugeschun	suggestion	sumptuous /ly/ness	
sugest	suggest 1+	sumshus	sumptuous +
sugestion	suggestion	sumun	summon 1★
sugestiv	suggestive	sumuns	summons 1★
suggest 1 /ion/ive		sumwere	somewhere
suicid e /al		sumwun	someone +
suige	sewage	sun 3★† /beam/dial/ny	
suiside	suicide +	†(planet)	
suit 1★† /ability		sun	son ★
†(clothes)		sun inlaw	son(s)-in-law
suit	suet	sunbathe 2	
suitab le /ility/ly		sunbern	sunburn +
suite ★ (rooms)		sunburn /t	
suitor		sundae ★ (ice cream)	
sulfate	sulphate	Sunday ★ (day of week)	
sulfer	sulphur +	sundrey	sundry +

sundr *y* /ies	
sung	
sunk /en	
sunlight	
sunlite	sunlight
sunni *er* /est/ly/ness	
sun *rise* /stroke	
sun-tan³	
sup³ /per ★ (meal)	
super ★ (fantastic)	
super	supper ★
superabundan *ce* /t	
superannuat *e*² /ion	
superb /ly	
supercargo /es	
supercharge²	
supercilious /ly/ness	
superconductor	
superficial /ity/ly	
superfine	
superfishal	superficial⁺
superflooous	superfluous⁺
superflu *ous* /ity	
superhuman	
superier	superior⁺
superimpos *e*² /ition	
superintend¹ /ent	
superior /ity	
superlative	
super *man* /men (pl.)	
supermarket	
supernacheral	supernatural⁺
supernatural /ly	
supernova	
supernumerar *y* /ies	
superpos *e*² /ition	
supersede²	
supersilious	supercilious⁺
supersilius	supercilious⁺
supersonic	
superstishun	superstition⁺
superstishus	superstitious
superstitio *n* /us	
superstructure	
superven *e*² /tion	

supervis *e*² /ion/or/ory	
supervishun	supervision
supine	
suplant	supplant¹⁺
suple	supple⁺
suplement	supplement¹⁺
suplicate	supplicate²⁺
suport	support¹⁺
suposishun	supposition
suposition	supposition
supositrey	suppository⁺
supplant¹ /er	
supple /ness	
supplement¹ /ation	
supplementary	
suppli	supply⁴⁺
suppliant	
supplicat *e*² /ion/ory	
suppl *y*⁴ /ier/ies	
support¹ /er	
suppos *e*² /ition	
suppositor *y* /ies	
suppress¹ /ible/ion/or	
suppurat *e*² /ion	
supremasey	supremacy
suprem *e* /acy/ely	
supreshun	suppression
supress	suppress¹⁺
supression	suppression
suprintend	superintend¹⁺
supul	supple⁺
sur	sir
surayalism	surrealism⁺
surayalist	surrealist
surca	circa
surcharge²	
surcit	circuit¹★
surcitrey	circuitry
surcitus	circuitous
surcul	circle²
surcularise	circularise²⁺
surculashun	circulation
surculate	circulate²⁺
surculer	circular
surcumfleks	circumflex

surcumflex	circumflex	surogat	surrogate
surcumfrance	circumference	suround	surround [1]
surcumfrans	circumference	surownd	surround [1]
surcumnavigate	circumnavigate [2+]	surpass [1]	
surcumscribe	circumscribe [2]	surplice ★ (robe)	
surcumscripshun	circumscription	surplis	surplice ★
surcumscription	circumscription	surplus ★ (excess)	
surcumsise	circumcise [2+]	surprise [2]	
surcumsision	circumcision	surrealis *m* /t	
surcumspecshun	circumspection	surrender [1]	
surcumspect	circumspect +	surreptitious /ly/ness	
surcumstans	circumstance	surrogate	
surcumstanshul	circumstantial +	surround [1]	
surcumstantial	circumstantial +	surt	cert
surcumvent	circumvent [1+]	surtaks	surtax +
surcus	circus +	surtax /es	
sure ★† /ly ★†/r/st		surtin	certain +
†(certain[ly])		surtn	certain +
sure	shore [2]★	survant	servant
sureptishus	surreptitious +	survay	survey [1+]
sureptitious	surreptitious +	survaylans	surveillance
suret *y* /ies		surve	serve [2+]
surf [1]★ (sea) /er		surveillance	
surf	serf ★+	survey [1] /or	
surface [2]		survice	service [2+]
surfdom	serfdom	surviet	serviette
surfeet	surfeit [1]	survile	servile +
surfeit [1]		survilitey	servility
surfis	surface [2]	survis	service [2+]
surfit	surfeit [1]	surviv *e* [2] /al/or	
surge [2]		susceptib *le* /ility	
surgeon		suseptible	susceptible +
surger *y* /ies		suseptibul	susceptible +
surgun	surgeon	suspect [1]	
surley	surely ★	suspend [1] /er	
surli *er* /est/ly/ness		suspense	
surloin	sirloin	suspenshun	suspension +
surly ★ (uncivil)		suspens *ion* /ory	
surly	surely ★	suspicion	
surmise [2]		suspicious /ly/ness	
surmon	sermon	suspishun	suspicion
surmonise	sermonise [2]	suspishus	suspicious +
surmount [1]		sustain [1]	
surmownt	surmount [1]	sustayn	sustain [1]
surname		sustenance	

sustenans	sustenance	swerve [2]	
sut	soot *+	swet	sweat [1]+
sutable	suitable +	sweter	sweater
sutabul	suitable +	swich	switch [1]+
suter	suitor	swift /er/est/ly/ness	
suthen	southern	swig [3]	
sutherley	southerly	swill [1] /er	
sutle	subtle +	swim /mer/-suit	
sutletey	subtlety +	swimming /-pool	
sutul	subtle +	swindle [2] /r	
suture		swindul	swindle [2]+
swab [3]		swin e /ish	
swaddle [2]		swing * (move) /ing	
swade	suède	swinge * (beat) /ing	
swadul	swaddle [2]	swipe [2]	
swagger [1] /er		swirl [1]	
swain		swish [1]	
swallow [1] /er		Swiss /roll	
swam		switch [1] /back	
swamp [1] /y		swivel [3]	
swan [3] /sdown		swizul	swizzle [2]
swane	swain	swizzle [2]	
swank [1] /y		swob	swab [3]
sware	swear +	swollen	
swarm [1]		swollow	swallow [1]+
swarthy		swomp	swamp [1]+
swash [1]		swon	swan [3]+
swastika		swoon [1]	
swat [3] /ter		swoop [1]	
swath * (line of cut grass)		swop [3]	
swathe [2]* (bandage)		sword	
sway [1]		swor e /n	
swear /-word		swostika	swastika
sweat [1] /er/y		swot [3] /ter	
Swed e /ish		swum	
sweep /er/ing/stake		swung	
sweet * (sugary)		swurl	swirl [1]
sweet	suite *	swurv	swerve [2]
sweetchestnut		sybarit e /ic	
sweeten [1]		sycamore	
sweet *heart* /ly/meat		sycedelic	psychedelic
sweetpea		syciatrey	psychiatry
swell /ing		syciatrist	psychiatrist +
swelter [1]		sycick	psychic +
swept		sycoanalise	psychoanalyse [2]+

sycoanalisis	psychoanalysis
sycofant	sycophant +
sycologey	psychology +
sycological	psychological +
sycologist	psychologist
sycopath	psychopath +
sycophant /ic	
sycosis	psychosis +
sycosomatic	psychosomatic
sycotherapey	psychotherapy
sycotherapist	psychotherapist +
sycotic	psychotic
syfilis	syphilis +
sygnet	cygnet ★
sylf	sylph +
syllab *le* /ic	
syllabus /es	
syllogis *e*² /m	
sylph /like	
symbio *sis* /tic	
symbol ★ (sign) /ic	
symbol	cymbal ★+
symbolical /ly	
symbolis *e*² /m	
symmetr *y* /ical/ically	
sympathetic /ally	
sympathey	sympathy +
sympathise ² /r	
sympath *y* /ies	
symphon *y* /ies/ic	
symplify	simplify ⁴+
symposi *um* /a (pl.)	
symptom /atic	
synagog	synagogue
synagogue	
synchronis *e*² /ation/m	
syncopat *e*² /ion	
syncope	
syncromesh	
syndicalis *m* /t	
syndicat *e*² /ion	
syndrome	
synic	cynic +
synod /al/ical	
synonym /ous/ously	

synops *is* /es (pl.)	
synoptic	
synovial	
syntaks	syntax +
synta *x* /ctic	
synthes *is* /es (pl.)	
synthe *sise* ² /tic/tically	
sypher	cipher ¹
syphili *s* /tic	
syphon	siphon ¹+
syringe ²	
syrup /y	
system /atic/atically	
systematis *e* ² /ation	
systole	

T

tab ³	
tabard	
tabb *y* /ies	
tabernacle	
tabernacul	tabernacle
tabie	tabby +
table ²	
tableau /x (pl.)	
tablespoon /ful	
tabl *et* /oid	
tablit	tablet +
tablo	tableau +
tabloyd	tabloid
taboo ¹ /s	
tabor	
tabul	table ²
tabular	
tabulashun	tabulation
tabulat *e* ² /ion/or	
tabuler	tabular
tabulspoon	tablespoon +
taby	tabby +
tacit /ly	
taciturn /ity	
tack ¹	
tackey	tacky +

tackle² /r		tam *e*² /able	
tackul	tackle²⁺	tam-o'-shanter	
tack *y* /iness		tamper¹	
tact /less/lessly		tampon	
tactful /ly/ness		tan³ /ner/nery/neries	
tactic /al/ian/s		tandem	
tactile		taner	tanner
tactishun	tactician	tang	
tacul	tackle²⁺	tangent /ial	
tadpole		tangerine	
taffeta		tangib *le* /ility/ly	
tafita	taffeta	tangibul	tangible⁺
tag³		tangle²	
tail¹★† /less		tango¹ /s	
†(follow, of animals)		tangul	tangle²
tail	tale ★	tanic	tannic⁺
tailor¹ /-made		tanjent	tangent⁺
taint¹		tanjerene	tangerine
tak *e* /en/ing		tank /age/ard/er/ful	
takey	tacky⁺	tanni *c* /n	
taks	tax¹⁺	tant	taint¹
taksashun	taxation	tantalis *e*² /ingly	
taksi	taxi⁺	tantalum	
taksidermey	taxidermy⁺	tantamount	
talc /um		tantamownt	tantamount
tale ★ (story)		tantrum	
tale	tail¹★⁺	tap³ /-dancing/-root	
talent /ed		tape² /worm	
talie	tally⁴⁺	tape measure	
talie ho	tally-ho	tape recorder	
talisman /s		taper¹★ (candle, narrow)	
talk¹ /ative/er		taper	tapir ★
talk	talc⁺	tapestr *y* /ies	
talkum	talcum	tapioca	
tall /est/ness		tapir ★ (animal)	
tallow		tapistrey	tapestry⁺
tall *y*⁴ /ies		tar³	
tally-ho		taragon	tarragon
talon		tarantella ★ (dance)	
talor	tailor¹⁺	tarantula ★ (spider)	
talow	tallow	tardie	tardy⁺
tamarisk		tard *y* /ily/iness	
tamber	tambour⁺	tare ★ (weed)	
tamboreen	tambourine	tare	tear ★⁺
tambour /ine		target	

targit	target	tawny	
tarie	tarry [4]	tax [1] /able/ation	
tarif	tariff	taxashun	taxation
tariff		taxi /cab/meter/s	
tarmac		taxiderm y /ist	
tarmigan	ptarmigan	Te Deum	
tarn		tea ★ (drink) /cup/pot	
tarnish [1]		tea	tee ★+
tarpaulin		teach /able/er/ing	
tarporlin	tarpaulin	teajuncshun	T-junction
tarragon		teak	
tarr y [4]		teal	
tarsals		team [1] ★ (group) /ster	
tarsus		team	teem [1]★
tart /let		team-work	
tartan		tear ★ (crying) /ful	
tartar		tear ★ (rip) /ing	
tarter	tartar	tear	tier ★
tartrate		tease [2] /r	
tasit	tacit +	teaspoon /ful	
tasiturn	taciturn +	teat	
task /master		teath	teeth ★
tassel [3]		teathe	teethe [2]★
tassul	tassel [3]	teatime	
taste [2] /less/r		teatotler	teetotaller
tasteful /ly/ness		teatotul	teetotal +
tast ier /iest/y		tech	teach +
tatle	tattle [2]	techer	teacher
tatoo	tattoo [1]+	technical /ly	
tatter /ed		technicalit y /ies	
tattle [2]		techni cian /que	
tattoo [1] /er		technocrac y /ies	
tatul	tattle [2]	technocrat /ic	
taught ★ (did teach)		technolog y /ical/ically	
taught	tort ★	tecneek	technique
taunt [1] /er		tecnical	technical +
Taurus		tecnicalitey	technicality +
taut ★ (tight) /ly/ness		tecnician	technician +
taut	taught ★	tecnishun	technician +
taut	tort ★	tecnocracy	technocracy +
tauten [1]		tecnologey	technology +
tautolog y /ical		teddy-bear	
taven	tavern	tedibare	teddy-bear
tavern		tedi um /ous/ously	
tawdr y /ily/iness		tedius	tedious

tee * (golf) /d/ing		telex [1]	
tee	tea *+	telicomunications	telecommunications
teech	teach +	telie	telly
teek	teak	telifone	telephone [2]+
teel	teal	telifoto	telephoto +
teem [1]* (swarm)		teligraf	telegraph [1]+
teem	team [1]*+	teligram	telegram
teenage /r		telimeter	telemeter
teese	tease [2]+	teliprinter	teleprinter
teet	teat	teliscope	telescope [2]+
teeter [1]		teliscopic	telescopic
teeth * (pl. of tooth)		telitipe	teletype
teethe [2]* (develop teeth)		telivise	televise [2]
teetotal /ism/ler		telivishun	television
tegument		telivision	television
tekneek	technique	tell /er/ing/-tale	
teknical	technical +	tellurium	
teknicalitey	technicality +	telly	
teknician	technician +	telurium	tellurium
teknishun	technician +	temerity	
teknocracy	technocracy +	temper [1]	
teknocrasey	technocracy +	temperacher	temperature
teknologey	technology +	temperament /al	
teknological	technological	temperance	
tekscher	texture	temperans	temperance
tekst	text +	temperat e /ure	
tekstile	textile	temperit	temperate +
telecommunications		tempest /uous	
telefone	telephone [2]+	tempestuus	tempestuous
telefonist	telephonist	temple	
telegraf	telegraph [1]+	tempo /s	
telegram		temporal /ly	
telegraph [1] /ic/ist/y		temporar y /ily	
teleks	telex [1]	temporis e [2] /r	
telemeter		temprament	temperament +
telepath y /ic		temprecher	temperature
telephon e [2] /ic/ist		tempremental	temperamental
telephoto /graph		tempt [1] /ation/er	
teleprinter		temptashun	temptation
telescop e [2] /ic/y		tempul	temple
teletipe	teletype	temtashun	temptation
teletype		ten /fold/th/thly	
televise [2]		tenab le /ility	
televishun	television	tenabul	tenable +
television		tenacious /ly	

tenacity		terbine	turbine
tenanc *y* /ies		terbium	
tenansey	tenancy +	terbo	turbo +
tenant /ry		terbot	turbot
tenashus	tenacious +	terbulence	turbulence +
tenasitey	tenacity	terbulens	turbulence +
tend [1]		terbulent	turbulent
tendenc *y* /ies		tergid	turgid +
tendensey	tendency +	terible	terrible +
tendenshus	tendentious	teribul	terrible +
tendentious		terific	terrific +
tender [1] /er/est/ly/ness		terify	terrify [4]
tenderhooks	tenterhooks	teritorey	territory +
tendon		teritorial	territorial +
tendril		terjid	turgid +
tenement /-house		terkey	turkey +
tener	tenor ★	terkish	Turkish
tenet		terkwoise	turquoise
teniment	tenement +	term [1]	
tenis	tennis	termagant	
tennis		terminable	
tenon /-saw		terminabul	terminable
tenor ★ (voice)		terminal /ly	
tenor	tenure ★	terminat *e* [2] /ion	
tense /ly/ness/r/st		terminological /ly	
tenshun	tension	terminolog *y* /ies	
tensile		termin *us* /i (pl.)	
tension		termite	
tent		termoil	turmoil
tentacle		tern ★ (bird)	
tentacul	tentacle	tern	turn [1]★+
tentative /ly		ternip	turnip
tenterhooks		terodactil	pterodactyl
tenuous /ly/ness		teror	terror +
tenure ★ (possession)		terorism	terrorism
tenuus	tenuous +	terorist	terrorist
tenyer	tenure ★	terpentine	turpentine
tepid /ity/ly		terpitude	turpitude
teracota	terracotta	terra firma	
terafurma	terra firma	terrace [2]	
terain	terrain	terracotta	
terapin	terrapin	terrain	
terass	terrace [2]	terrapin	
terban	turban +	terrestrial	
terbid	turbid +	terribl *e* /y	

terribul	terrible +	thach	thatch [1]+
terrier		thalidomide	
terrifi	terrify [4]	thallium	
terrific /ally		than	
terrify [4]		thank [1] /less	
territorial /ly		thankful /ly	
territor y /ies		thanksgiving	
terror /ism/ist		that /'s (that is)	
terroris e [2] /ation		thatch [1] /er	
terse /ly/ness		thaw [1]	
tershan	tertian +	thay	they +
tertia n /ry		the	
tertle	turtle	theater	theatre
teselashun	tessellation	theatre	
teselate	tessellate [2]+	theatrical /ly	
teselation	tessellation	theft	
tespoon	teaspoon +	theif	thief +
tessellat e [2] /ion		their ★ (possession) /s ★	
test [1] /-tube		their	there ★
testament		theirs	there's ★
testat e /or/rix (fem.)		theis m /t/tical	
testes	testis +	theives	thieves
testicle		theivish	thievish
testicul	testicle	them /selves	
testie	testy +	them e /atic	
testifi	testify [4]+	thence /forth/forward	
testif y [4] /ier		thens	thence +
testimon y /ial		theocra cy /tic	
testimonyal	testimonial	theocrasey	theocracy +
test is /es (pl.)		theodolite	
test y /ily/iness		theolog y /ian/ical/ist	
tetanic	titanic	theolojun	theologian
tetanus		theorem	
tetatet	tête-à-tête	theoretic /al/ally	
tête-à-tête		theorey	theory +
tether [1]		theorise [2]	
tetragon /al		theor y /ies/ist	
tetrahedr on /al		theosofey	theosophy +
tetrarch /y		theosoph y /ical/ist	
tetrark	tetrarch +	therapeuti c /st	
Teutonic		therapey	therapy +
texcher	texture	theraputic	therapeutic +
text /ual/ually		therap y /ist	
textile		therd	third +
texture		there ★ (that place)	

here	their *+	thiroyd	thyroid
here	they're *	thirst [1] /ily/y	
herefore		thirteen /th	
herem	theorem	thirtie	thirty +
here's * (there is)		thirt y /ies/ieth	
heres	theirs *	thisis	phthisis
heretic	theoretic +	thisle	thistle +
heretical	theoretical	thisorus	thesaurus +
herey	theory +	thistl e /y	
herise	theorise [2]	thisul	thistle +
herist	theorist	thither	
herm /al/ally		tho	though
hermion /ic		thole	
hermite		thong	
hermocouple		thor	thaw [1]
hermocuple	thermocouple	thoraks	thorax +
hermodynamic /s		thora x /cic	
hermo-electric /ity		thorium	
hermomet er /ric/ry		thorn /y	
hermonuclear		thorough /ly	
hermos		thorough bred /fare	
hermostat /ic/ically		thort	thought
hersday	Thursday	thortful	thoughtful +
herst	thirst [1]+	thortless	thoughtless +
herstey	thirsty	those	
herteen	thirteen +	though	
herty	thirty +	thought	
hesaur us /i (pl.)		thoughtful /ly/ness	
hese		thoughtless /ly/ness	
hes is /es (pl.)		thousand /th	
hey /'re * (they are)		thowsand	thousand +
hi	thigh	thrall	
hick /er/est/ly/ness/set		thrash [1]	
hicken [1] /er		thread [1] /bare	
hie f /ves (pl.)/vish		threat	
high		threaten [1]	
himble /ful		thred	thread [1]+
himbul	thimble +	thredbare	threadbare
hime	thyme	three /fold/pence	
hin [3] /ly/ner/nest		three-dimensional	
hine		three-quarters	
hing		thresh [1] /er	
hink /er/ing		threshold	
hird /ly		thret	threat
hirm	therm +	threten	threaten [1]

threw ★ (did throw)		thurm	therm +
threw	through ★	thurmal	thermal
threwout	throughout	thurmion	thermion +
thrice		thurmite	thermite
thrift /less/y		thurmocuple	thermocouple
thrifti er /est/ly/ness		thurmodinamic	thermodynamic +
thrill ¹ /er		thurmoelectric	thermo-electric +
thrise	thrice	thurmometer	thermometer +
thriv e /en/ing		thurmonucliar	thermonuclear
throat /y		thurmos	thermos
throb ³		thurmostat	thermostat +
throe ★ (pain) /s ★		thurmyon	thermion +
throe	throw ★+	Thursday	
thrombosis		thurst	thirst ¹+
throne ★ (chair of state)		thurteen	thirteen +
throne	thrown ★	thurty	thirty +
throng ¹		thus	
throo	threw ★	thwack ¹	
throo	through ★	thwart ¹	
throt	throat +	thwort	thwart ¹
throttle ²		thyme	
throtul	throttle ²	thyroid	
through ★ (penetrated)		tialin	ptyalin
through	threw ★	tiara /s	
throughout		tibia	
throve		tic ★ (twitch)	
throw ★† /ing/n ★†/s ★†		tick ¹★ (sound) /er	
†(hurl[ed, s])		ticket	
throw	throe ★+	tickl e ² /er/ish	
thrum ³		tickul	tickle ²+
thrush /es		ticoon	tycoon
thrust /er/ing		tidal	
thud ³		tiddler	
thug /gery		tiddlywinks	
thulium		tide /less	
thum	thumb ¹	tidie	tidy ⁴+
thumb ¹		tidi ly /ness	
thump ¹		tidings	
thunder ¹ /bolt/ous		tidliwinks	tiddlywinks
thunderstorm		tidul	tidal
thunderstruck		tid y ⁴ /ier/iest/ily/iness	
thunderus	thunderous	tie /d	
thurer	thorough +	tier ★ (layer)	
thurerbred	thoroughbred +	tier	tire ²★+
thurerfare	thoroughfare	tier	tyre ★

iff[1]	
iffin	
ifin	tiffin
ifoid	typhoid
ifoon	typhoon+
ifus	typhus+
ig er /ress (fem.)	
ight /-laced/rope	
ighten[1]	
ight er /est/ly/ness	
ights	
ike	tyke
ile[2]	
ilige	tillage
ill[1] /able/age/er	
ilt[1]	
imber[1]	
ime[2] /keeper/less	
imepeace	timepiece
imepiece	
imid /er/est/ity	
imorous /ly/ness	
imorus	timorous+
impan o /i (pl.)/ist	
impanum	tympanum+
in[3] /foil/ny	
incture	
inder /y	
inge[2]	
ingle[2]	
ingul	tingle[2]
inie	tiny+
inkcher	tincture
inker[1]	
inkle[2]	
inkul	tinkle[2]
insel[3] /ly	
insul	tinsel[3]+
int[1]	
tin y /ier/iest/ily/iness	
·p[3] /ster	
ipe	type[2]+
iperiter	typewriter+
ipical	typical+
ipify	typify[4]

tipist	typist
tipit	tippet
tiple	tipple[2]+
tipografey	typography+
tippet	
tipple[2] /r	
tipsey	tipsy+
tips y /ily/iness	
tiptoe[2]	
tipul	tipple[2]+
tirade	
tiraney	tyranny+
tiranical	tyrannical+
tiranise	tyrannise[2]+
tirant	tyrant
tirannical	tyrannical
tiranus	tyrannous
tire[2]*† /less/lessly †(grow weary)	
tire	tyre*
tiresome /ly/ness	
tiresum	tiresome+
tiro	
tishoo	tissue+
tishue	tissue+
tissue /-paper	
Titan	
titanic	
titanium	
titbit	
tite	tight+
titen	tighten[1]
titer	tighter+
titerope	tightrope
tites	tights
tithe /-barn	
titillat e[2] /ion	
titivat e[2] /ion	
title /d	
titm ouse /ice (pl.)	
titmowse	titmouse+
titrat e[2] /ion	
titter[1]	
tittle-tattle	
titul	title+

titul tatul	tittle-tattle
titular	
tituler	titular
T-junction	
to ★ (towards) /day	
to	too ★
to	two ★+
to and fro	
toad /stool/y	
toast¹ /er	
tobacco /nist	
tobaco	tobacco +
toboggan¹ /er	
tocsic	toxic +
tocsicologey	toxicology +
tocsin ★ (bell)	
tocsin	toxin ★
toddle² /r	
toddy	
tode	toad +
todle	toddle ²+
todstool	toadstool
todul	toddle ²+
tody	toddy
toe ★ (on foot)	
toe	tow ¹★+
tofee	toffee
toffee	
together	
toggle	
togul	toggle
toi	toy ¹+
toil¹ /er	
toilet /ry	
token	
toksic	toxic +
toksicologey	toxicology +
tole	toll ¹+
tolemaic sistem	Ptolemaic system
tolerabl e /y	
tolerabul	tolerable +
toleran ce /t	
tolerans	tolerance +
tolerashun	toleration
tolerat e ² /ion	

toll¹ /-bar/-gate	
tolrable	tolerable +
tolrabul	tolerable +
tomahawk	
tomahork	tomahawk
tomane	ptomaine
tomato /es	
tomb /stone	
tomboi	tomboy
tomboy	
tome	
tomfoolery	
tomorrow	
tomtit	
ton ★ (weight) /nage	
ton	tun ★
tonal /ity	
tone /less	
tongs	
tongue² /-tied/-twister	
tonic	
tonight	
tonite	tonight
tonsher	tonsure +
tonsil /litis	
tons ure /orial	
too ★ (also)	
too	to ★+
too	two ★+
took	
tool¹	
toom	tomb +
toomstone	tombstone
toor	tour ¹+
toot¹	
tooth /ache/less	
toothake	toothache
tootle²	
tootul	tootle²
top³ /-heavy/sail	
topas	topaz
topath	towpath
topaz	
topic /al/ally	
tople	topple²

topografer	topographer	tortuus	tortuous +
topografey	topography +	torus	Taurus
topografic	topographic	Tor y /ies	
topograph y /er/ic/ical		toss 1 /-up	
topple 2		tost	toast 1+
topsy-turvy		total 3 /ity/ly	
topul	topple 2	totalis e 2 /ator	
torch /light		totalitey	totality
torcher	torture 2+	totem pole	
torchlite	torchlight	totter 1	
tordrey	tawdry +	totul	total 3+
toreador		touch 1 /ier/iness/y	
torenshal	torrential	touchstone	
torent	torrent +	touchwood	
torential	torrential	tough /er/est/ly/ness	
torero		toughen 1	
torey	Tory +	tour 1 /ism/ist	
torid	torrid	tournament	
torie	Tory +	tourniket	tourniquet
torism	tourism	tourniquet	
torist	tourist	tousle 2	
torment 1 /or		tout 1	
tornado /es		tow 1* (pull) /age	
tornament	tournament	tow	toe *
torney	tawny	toward /s	
tornt	taunt 1+	towel 3	
torpedo 1 /-boat/es		tower 1	
torper	torpor	town /hall	
torpid /ity		towpath	
torpor		towsl	tousle 2
torrenshal	torrential	towt	tout 1
torrent /ial		toxic /ity	
torrid		toxicolog y /ist	
torshun	torsion +	toxin * (poison)	
torsion /al		toxin	tocsin *
torso /s		toy 1 /s/shop	
tort * (law)		toylet	toilet +
tort	taught *	toyul	toil 1+
tort	taut *+	trace 2 /able/r/ry	
torten	tauten 1	trache a /otomy	
tortoise /-shell		tracing-paper	
tortologey	tautology +	track 1 /er	
tortuous /ly/ness		tracshun	traction
torture 2 /r		tract	
tortus	tortoise +	tract able /ion/or	

tracter	tractor	transendental	transcendental
trade² /r/sman		transept	
tradishun	tradition⁺	transfer³ /able/ence	
tradishunal	traditional	transferens	transference
tradition /al/ally		transfiger	transfigure²⁺
traduce²		transfigur e² /ation	
traduse	traduce²	transfiks	transfix¹
traffic /ked/king		transfix¹	
trafic	traffic⁺	transform¹ /ation/er	
traged y /ies		transformashun	transformation
tragic /al/ally		transfus e² /ion	
trail¹ /er		transfushun	transfusion
train¹ /ee/er		transgreshun	transgression
traipse²		transgress¹ /ion/or	
trait		tranship³ /ment	
traitor /ous		transien ce /t/tly	
trajector y /ies		transiens	transience⁺
trajectrey	trajectory⁺	transishun	transition⁺
trajedey	tragedy⁺	transister	transistor
trakia	trachea⁺	transistor	
trakiotomey	tracheotomy	transistoris e²	
trakshun	traction	transit /ive/ory	
tram /car/-line		transition /al	
trammel³		translashun	translation
tramp¹		translat e² /able/ion/or	
trample²		translater	translator
trampoline		translucen ce /t	
trampul	trample²	translusens	translucence⁺
tramul	trammel³	translusent	translucent
trance		transmigrat e² /ion	
trane	train¹⁺	transmishun	transmission
trankwil	tranquil⁺	transmission	
trankwilise	tranquillise²⁺	transmit³ /ter	
trankwilitey	tranquillity	transmut e /ation	
tranquil /lity/ly		transparen ce /cy/t	
tranquillis e² /er		transparens	transparence⁺
trans	trance	transparensey	transparency
transact¹ /ion		transpir e² /ation	
transatlantic		transplant¹ /ation	
transceiver		transport¹ /ation/er	
transcend¹ /ence/ental		transportashun	transportation
transcribe²		transpos e² /ition	
transcript /ion		transsever	transceiver
transend	transcend¹⁺	transverse /ly	
transendence	transcendence	transvershun	transversion

transversion		treetment	treatment
transvesti *sm* /te		trefoil	
trap³ /per		trefoyul	trefoil
trapez *e* /ium/oid		trek³ /ker	
trapse	traipse²	trellis-work	
trase	trace²⁺	tremble²	
trash /y		trembul	tremble²
trasing paper	tracing-paper	tremendous /ly	
trate	trait	tremendus	tremendous⁺
trater	traitor⁺	tremer	tremor
traterous	traitorous	tremor	
traterus	traitorous	tremulous	
trauma /tic		tremulus	tremulous
travail¹		trench¹ /es	
travale	travail¹	trenchan *cy* /t	
travel³ /ler/ogue		trenchansey	trenchancy⁺
travelog	travelogue	trend¹ /y	
traverse²		treo	trio⁺
travest *y* /ies		trepidashun	trepidation
trawl¹ /er		trepidation	
trawma	trauma⁺	treshur	treasure²⁺
tray /s		treshurey	treasury⁺
treacherey	treachery⁺	treson	treason⁺
treacher *y* /ous		trespass¹ /er/es	
treacl *e* /y		tressul	trestle
treacul	treacle⁺	trestle	
tread /ing/le		tri	try⁴⁺
treason /able/ous		trial	
treasonus	treasonous	triang *le* /ular	
treasure² /r		triangul	triangle⁺
treasur *y* /ies		triangulat *e*² /ion	
treat¹ /able/ment		trianguler	triangular
treatise		trib *e* /al/alism	
treatiss	treatise	tribul	tribal
treat *y* /ies		tribulashun	tribulation
trebl *e*² /y		tribulation	
trebul	treble⁺	tribun *e* /al	
trecherey	treachery⁺	tributar *y* /ies	
trecherus	treacherous	tribute	
tred	tread⁺	tributrey	tributary⁺
tree		trice	
treecul	treacle⁺	triceps	
treet	treat¹⁺	tricicul	tricycle
treetie	treaty⁺	trick¹ /ery/ster/y	
treetis	treatise	tricki *er* /est/ly/ness	

trickle [2]		trooant	truant
tricuspid		troobadoor	troubadour
tricycle		trooism	truism
trident		trooley	truly
trifle [2] /r		troop [1]★ (military)	
triful	trifle [2+]	troop	troupe ★
trigger [1]		troos	truce
trigonometr y /ic		trooth	truth
trill [1]		troothful	truthful [+]
trilogy		troph y /ies	
trim [3] /mer		tropic /al/ally	
trimaran		tropism	
trinity		troposfere	troposphere
trinket		troposphere	
trio /s		trorma	trauma [+]
triode		trormatic	traumatic
trip [3]★ (fall)		trot [3] /ter	
tripartite		troubadour	
tripe ★ (food)		trouble [2] /-maker	
triple [2] /t		troubleshooter	
triplicat e [2] /ion		troublesome	
tripod		trough	
tripos		trounce [2]	
triptick	triptych	trouns	trounce [2]
triptych		troup	troop [1]★
tripul	triple [2+]	troupe ★ (actors)	
trise	trice	trousers	
trisicul	tricycle	trousseau /x (pl.)	
trite /ly		trout	
triumf	triumph [1+]	trowel	
triumph [1] /al/ant		trownce	trounce [2]
trivia /l/ly		trowns	trounce [2]
trivialise [2]		trowsers	trousers
trivialit y /ies		trowt	trout
trod /den		truan cy /t	
trofey	trophy [+]	truansey	truancy [+]
troley	trolley [+]	truble	trouble [2+]
trolie	trolley [+]	trubul	trouble [2+]
troll [1]		truce	
trolley /s		truck	
trollop		truculen ce /t	
trolop	trollop	trudge [2]	
trombon e /ist		tru e /er/est/ism/ly/th	
troo	true [+]	truf	trough
trooancy	truancy [+]	truffle	

truful	truffle	tumultuus	tumultuous
truge	trudge [2]	tumulus	
trulie	truly	tun ★ (large cask)	
trump [1]		tun	ton ★+
trumpet [1] /er		tuna	
truncat e [2] /ion		tundra	
truncheon		tun e [2] /able/er	
trunchon	truncheon	tuneful /ly/ness	
trundle [2]		tuney	tunny +
trundul	trundle [2]	tung	tongue [2]+
trunk /-line		tungsten	
trusow	trousseau +	tungtied	tongue-tied
truss [1] /es		tunic	
trust [1] /ee/ful/fully		tunie	tunny +
trustwerthey	trustworthy +	tunige	tonnage
trustworth y /iness		tunnel [3] /ler	
truthful /ly/ness		tunn y /ies	
tr y [4] /ier/ies		tunul	tunnel [3]+
trycicle	tricycle	turban /ed	
tsar		turbid /ity	
tub [3] /biness/by		turbine	
tuba /s		turbo /-alternator	
tub e [2] /ular		turbo-generator	
tuber /cle/cular		turbo-jet	
tubercul osis /ous		turbo-prop	
tuch	touch [1]+	turbot	
tuchstone	touchstone	turbulen ce /t	
tuchwood	touchwood	turbulens	turbulence +
tuchy	touchy	tureen	
tuck [1] /er		turet	turret +
Tuesday		turf [1] /s/ves (pls.)	
tuf	tough +	turgid /ity	
tuffen	toughen [1]	turjid	turgid +
tuft [1]		turkey /s	
tug [3] /-of-war		Turkish	
tuishun	tuition	turkwoise	turquoise
tuition		turm	term [1]
tuk	tuck [1]+	turminable	terminable
tuksedo	tuxedo	turminabul	terminable
tulip		turminal	terminal +
tumble [2] /r		turminate	terminate [2]+
tumbul	tumble [2]+	turmination	termination
tumer	tumour	turminologey	terminology +
tumour		turminological	terminological +
tumult /uous		turminus	terminus +

turmite	termite	twilight	
turmoil		twilite	twilight
turn¹★ (rotate) /er		twill¹	
turn	tern★	twin³	
turn coat /key/pike		twine²	
turnikay	tourniquet	twinge²	
turniket	tourniquet	twinkle²	
turnip		twinkul	twinkle²
turn stile /table		twirl¹	
turpentine		twise	twice
turpitude		twist¹ /er	
turquoise		twit³	
turret /ed		twitch¹ /es	
turse	terse⁺	twitter¹	
turshan	tertian⁺	two★ (number) /-way	
tursharey	tertiary	two	to★⁺
turtian	tertian⁺	two	too★
turtle		twodle	twaddle²
turtul	turtle	two fold /pence	
tusday	Tuesday	twurl	twirl¹
tusk¹ /er		tyalin	ptyalin
tussle²		tycoon	
tusul	tussle²	tyfoid	typhoid
tutel age /ary		tyfoon	typhoon⁺
tutelige	tutelage⁺	tyfus	typhus⁺
tuter	tutor¹⁺	tyke	
tutonic	Teutonic	tympano	timpano⁺
tutor¹ /ial		tympan um /a (pl.)	
tuxedo		type² /script	
twaddle²		typeriter	typewriter⁺
twain		typewrit er /ing/ten	
twang¹		typho on /nic	
twayn	twain	typh us /oid	
tweak¹		typical /ly	
tweed		typifi	typify⁴
tweek	tweak¹	typify⁴	
tweezers		typist	
twel fth /ve		typografey	typography⁺
twelth	twelfth⁺	typograph y /er/ic	
twent y /ies/ieth		tyranical	tyrannical⁺
twice		tyrannical /ly	
twich	twitch¹⁺	tyrann ise² /ous	
twiddle²		tyran ny /t	
twidul	twiddle²	tyre★ (of a car)	
twig¹		tyre	tire²★⁺

U

u	ewe ★
U-boat	
ubikwitey	ubiquity +
ubikwitus	ubiquitous
ubiquit y /ous	
ucalyptus	eucalyptus +
Ucarist	Eucharist
uclid	Euclid
udder	
ufemism	euphemism
ufemistic	euphemistic +
ufoney	euphony +
uforia	euphoria +
uforic	euphoric
ug	ugh
ugenic	eugenic +
ugh	
uglie	ugly +
ugl y /ier/iest/iness	
ukaliptus	eucalyptus +
ukarist	Eucharist
ukelalee	ukulele
uksorius	uxorious
ukulele	
ulcer /ous	
ulcerat e ² /ion	
ulna	
ulogey	eulogy
ulogise	eulogise ²+
ulogism	eulogism
ulser	ulcer +
ulserate	ulcerate ²+
ulserous	ulcerous
ulserus	ulcerous
ulterier	ulterior
ulterior	
ultimate /ly	
ultimatum /s (pl.)	
ultramarine	
ultramicroscopic	
ultrasonic	
ultra-violet	
umbilical	

umbrage	
umbrella	
umbridge	umbrage
umpire ²★ (referee)	
umpire	empire ★
umpteen	
unable	
unabridged	
unabriged	unabridged
unabul	unable
unacceptable	
unaccompanied	
unaccompnid	unaccompanied
unaccountable	
unaccustomed	
unacowntable	unaccountable
unacquainted	
unacseptable	unacceptable
unacseptabul	unacceptable
unacumpanid	unaccompanied
unacustomd	unaccustomed
unaded	unaided
unadulterated	
unaffected	
unafrade	unafraid
unafraid	
unaided	
unalloyed	
unaloid	unalloyed
unanimity	
unanimous /ly	
unanimus	unanimous +
unanserable	unanswerable +
unanswer able /ed	
unapproachable	
unaprochable	unapproachable
unaprochabul	unapproachable
unarmed	
unashamed	
unasked	
unaskt	unasked
unassisted	
unassuming	
unatacht	unattached
unatainable	unattainable

unattached		uncann*y* /ily/iness	
unattainable		uncared-for	
unattended		unceremonious /ly	
unauthorised		unceremonius	unceremonious +
unavail *able* /ing		uncertain /ty/ties	
unavalabul	unavailable +	unchangable	unchangeable
unavaling	unavailing	unchangeable	
unavoidabl *e* /y		uncharitable	
unavoydable	unavoidable +	uncharitabul	uncharitable
unaware /s		uncharted	
unawthorised	unauthorised	unchristian	
unbalanced		uncivil /ised	
unbalanst	unbalanced	unclaimed	
unbarable	unbearable +	unclamed	unclaimed
unbarabul	unbearable +	uncle	
unbearabl *e* /y		unclean	
unbeat *able* /en		uncomfortabl *e* /y	
unbecoming		uncomfortabul	uncomfortable +
unbeknown		uncomftable	uncomfortable +
unbeleif	unbelief	uncomited	uncommitted
unbelevable	unbelievable +	uncommitted	
unbelevabul	unbelievable +	uncommon	
unbelief		uncommunicative	
unbeliev *able* /ing		uncompromising	
unbelievabul	unbelievable +	unconcern /ed	
unbend /ing		uncondishnal	unconditional +
unbenown	unbeknown	unconditional /ly	
unberden	unburden [1]	unconected	unconnected
unbeten	unbeaten	unconfirmed	
unbiased		unconfurmd	unconfirmed
unbiast	unbiased	uncongenial	
unbidden		unconnected	
unblemished		unconquerable	
unblemisht	unblemished	unconscionable	
unborn		unconscious /ly/ness	
unbounded		unconshonable	unconscionable
unbowed		unconshonabul	unconscionable
unbownded	unbounded	unconshus	unconscious +
unbridled		unconstitutional	
unbriduld	unbridled	uncontrolabul	uncontrollable
unbroken		uncontrollable	
unburden [1]		unconvenshunal	unconventional
unbutton [1]		unconventional	
uncalled-for		unco-operative	
uncanie	uncanny +	unco-ordinated	

uncooth	uncouth	underling	
uncorroborated		undermand	undermanned
uncouple ²		undermanned	
uncoupul	uncouple ²	undermine ²	
uncouth		underneath	
uncover ¹		undernourish ¹ /ment	
uncristian	unchristian	undernurish	undernourish ¹⁺
uncritical		underpass	
uncshun	unction ⁺	underprivileged	
unct *ion* /uous		underrate ²	
uncul	uncle	underrite	underwrite ⁺
uncultivated		underrote	underwrote
uncumftable	uncomfortable ⁺	undersell /ing	
uncuple	uncouple ²	undersigned	
uncuver	uncover ¹	undersined	undersigned
undated		undersised	undersized
undaunted		undersized	
undawnted	undaunted	understand /able	
undeceive ²		understatement	
undecided		understood	
undecieve	undeceive ²	understud *y* ⁴ /ies	
undefended		undertak *e* /er/ing	
undeniable		underto	undertow
undeniabul	undeniable	undertone	
under /arm/bid		undertook	
undercarige	undercarriage	undertow	
undercarriage		underwait	underweight
undercloth *es* /ing		underware	underwear
undercover		underwater	
undercurrent		underwear	
undercut /ting		underweight	
undercuver	undercover	underwerld	underworld
underdog		underworld	
underdone		underwrit *e* /ing/ten	
underdun	underdone	underwrote	
underfed		undeservd	undeserved
undergo /ing/ne		undeserved	
undergraduate		undeseve	undeceive ²
undergroth	undergrowth	undesirable	
underground		undesirabul	undesirable
undergrownd	underground	undeterd	undeterred
undergrowth		undetermind	undetermined
underhand		undetermined	
underl *ie* /ying		undeterred	
underline ²		undieing	undying

undifended	undefended	unfaned	unfeigned
undignifide	undignified	unfare	unfair +
undignified		unfasen	unfasten [1]
undisciplined		unfashionable	
undisided	undecided	unfashnable	unfashionable
undisiplind	undisciplined	unfasten [1]	
undo /ing/ne		unfathful	unfaithful +
undornted	undaunted	unfavourabl e /y	
undoubted /ly		unfavrable	unfavourable +
undowted	undoubted +	unfeigned	
undress [1]		unfit [3] /ness	
undu e /ly		unfold [1]	
undulat e [2] /ion/ory		unforeseen	
undying		unforgetabul	unforgettable
unearned		unforgettable	
unearth [1] /ly		unfortunate /ly	
uneas y /ily		unfounded	
uneatable		unfownded	unfounded
uneatabul	uneatable	unfriendl y /iness	
unecessary	unnecessary +	unfurl [1]	
uneconomic /al/ally		unfurnished	
uneducated		unfurnisht	unfurnished
uneek	unique +	ungainly	
unekspected	unexpected	unganley	ungainly
unekwal	unequal +	ungarded	unguarded
unemploiabul	unemployable +	ungodly	
unemploy able /ed/ment		ungovernable	
unenterprising		ungracious /ly	
unequal /led/ly		ungrammatical /ly	
unequivocal		ungrashus	ungracious +
unering	unerring	ungrateful	
unerned	unearned	ungreatful	ungrateful
unerring		unguarded	
unerth	unearth [1]+	unguent	
unesessary	unnecessary +	unguvernabul	ungovernable
unesey	uneasy +	unguvnable	ungovernable
unetable	uneatable	unguvnabul	ungovernable
uneven /ness		unhallowed	
uneventful		unhalowd	unhallowed
unexpected		unhapie	unhappy +
unfailing /ly		unhappi ly /ness	
unfaind	unfeigned	unhapp y /ier/iest	
unfair /ly/ness		unhealthy	
unfaithful /ly/ness		unheard-of	
unfaling	unfailing +	unhelthy	unhealthy

unherdov	unheard-of	unkshus	unctuous
unhinge ²		unkwalified	unqualified
unholesum	unwholesome	unkweschunable	unquestionable +
unholy		unlawful /ly	
unhurdov	unheard-of	unleash ¹	
unicellular		unleavened	
unicicle	unicycle	unlesh	unleash ¹
unicorn		unless	
unicycle		unlevend	unleavened
unidentified		unlicensed	
unifi	unify ⁴⁺	unlike /ly	
uniform /ity		unlimited	
unif y ⁴ /ication		unlisensd	unlicensed
unikwivocal	unequivocal	unload ¹	
unilateral /ly		unlock ¹	
unimpeachable		unlode	unload ¹
uninhabit able /ed		unluck y /ier/iest/ily	
uninteligibul	unintelligible +	unlukey	unlucky +
unintelligib le /ility		unmanageable	
union /ism/ist		unmanigable	unmanageable
unique /ly/ness		unmannerly	
uniquivocal	unequivocal	unmarid	unmarried
uniselular	unicellular	unmarried	
unisicul	unicycle	unmask ¹	
unison		unmenshunable	unmentionable
unit /ary		unmentionable	
unitarian /ism		unmistakabl e /y	
unite ²		unmistakabul	unmistakable +
unit y /ies		unmitigated	
uniun	onion	unmoovd	unmoved
universal /ity/ly		unmoved	
universe		unnacheral	unnatural +
universit y /ies		unnamd	unnamed
univursal	universal +	unnamed	
univurse	universe	unnatural /ly	
univursitey	university +	unnecessar y /ily	
unjust		unnerv ed /ing	
unjustifi able /ed		unnesessarey	unnecessary +
unjustifiabul	unjustifiable +	unnowing	unknowing +
unkempt		unnown	unknown
unkemt	unkempt	unnumberd	unnumbered
unkind /ness		unnumbered	
unknow ing /n		unnurvd	unnerved +
unkristian	unchristian	unobserv ant /ed	
unkshun	unction +	unobtrusive	

unoccupied		unread *y* /iness	
unocupied	unoccupied	unreal /istic	
unoffending		unreasnable	unreasonable [+]
unofficial /ly		unreasonabl *e* /y	
unoficial	unofficial [+]	unrecognis *able* /ed	
unofishul	unofficial [+]	unrecognisabul	unrecognisable [+]
unopend	unopened	unredabul	unreadable
unopened		unredey	unready [+]
unorthorised	unauthorised	unreel	unreal [+]
unpack [1]		unrekwited	unrequited
unpaid		unreleved	unrelieved
unparaleld	unparalleled	unreliab *le* /ility	
unparalleled		unreliabul	unreliable [+]
unparlamentrey	unparliamentary	unrelieved	
unparliamentary		unremitting	
unpayd	unpaid	unrequited	
unpick [1]		unreservedly	
unpleasant /ness		unresnable	unreasonable [+]
unplesant	unpleasant [+]	unresponsive	
unpopular /ity		unrest	
unpopuler	unpopular [+]	unrestraind	unrestrained
unpractical		unrestrained	
unprecedented		unrighteous	
unprejudiced		unrimitting	unremitting
unprejudist	unprejudiced	unripe	
unpremeditated		unritchus	unrighteous
unprepard	unprepared	unritten	unwritten
unprepared		unrivald	unrivalled
unprepossessing		unrivalled	
unpresedented	unprecedented	unroll [1]	
unpretenshus	unpretentious	unruffled	
unpretentious		unrufld	unruffled
unprincipled		unrufuld	unruffled
unprinsipld	unprincipled	unruly	
unprintable		unsafe	
unprintabul	unprintable	unsaid	
unprofeshnal	unprofessional [+]	unsatisfactor *y* /ily	
unprofessional /ly		unsatisfactrey	unsatisfactory [+]
unqualified		unsatisfied	
unquestionabl *e* /y		unsavorey	unsavoury [+]
unquestionabul	unquestionable [+]	unsavour *y* /iness	
unrap	unwrap [3]	unscathed	
unravel [3]		unscientific	
unreadable		unscrupulous /ly	
unreadabul	unreadable	unscrupulus	unscrupulous [+]

unseasnabul	unseasonable	unsucsesful	unsuccessful [+]
unseasonable		unsuitable	
unseat [1]		unsuitabul	unsuitable
unsed	unsaid	unsupported	
unseeing		unsurmountable	
unseeml y /iness		unsurmowntable	unsurmountable
unseen		unsurtan	uncertain [+]
unseet	unseat [1]	unsuspected	
unselfish /ly/ness		unsutable	unsuitable
unseremonius	unceremonious [+]	unsutabul	unsuitable
unsermowntable	unsurmountable	untactful /ly	
unsertan	uncertain [+]	untenable	
unsettle [2]		untenabul	untenable
unsetul	unsettle [2]	unthinkable	
unsientific	unscientific	unthinkabul	unthinkable
unsightl y /iness		unti	untie [+]
unsitely	unsightly [+]	untide	untied
unsivil	uncivil [+]	untid y /ier/iest/ily/iness	
unsivilised	uncivilised	unt ie /ied/ying	
unskathd	unscathed	untieing	untying
unskild	unskilled	until	
unskilful		untimely	
unskilled		untimley	untimely
unsociabl e /y		unto	
unsofisticated	unsophisticated	untold	
unsolicited		untouchable	
unsolisited	unsolicited	untouchabul	untouchable
unsootable	unsuitable	untoward	
unsootabul	unsuitable	untraceable	
unsophisticated		untrasable	untraceable
unsoshable	unsociable [+]	untrasabul	untraceable
unsoshabul	unsociable [+]	untroo	untrue
unsound		untrooth	untruth
unsownd	unsound	untroothful	untruthful [+]
unspeakabl e /y		untrue	
unspekabul	unspeakable [+]	untruth	
unspoiled		untruthful /ly/ness	
unspoyld	unspoiled	untuchable	untouchable
unstable		untuchabul	untouchable
unstabul	unstable	untuterd	untutored
unstead y /ily/iness		untutored	
unstedey	unsteady [+]	unuch	eunuch
unsubstanshiated	unsubstantiated	unuk	eunuch
unsubstantiated		unushual	unusual [+]
unsuccessful /ly		unusual /ly	

unvail	unveil[1]	upon	
unvareying	unvarying	upper /most	
unvarnished		uppish /ness	
unvarnisht	unvarnished	upright	
unvarying		upris e /ing	
unveil[1]		uprite	upright
unwanted		uproar /ious/iously	
unwarey	unwary[+]	uprore	uproar[+]
unwarrant able /ed		uprorius	uproarious
unwarrantabul	unwarrantable[+]	upset /ting	
unwar y /ily		upshot	
unweldey	unwieldy	upside-down	
unwell		upstairs	
unwerkable	unworkable	upstares	upstairs
unwerkabul	unworkable	upstart	
unwerthey	unworthy[+]	upstream	
unwholesome		upstreem	upstream
unwieldy		upward	
unwilling		upwerd	upward
unwind /ing		ur	err[1]
unwise /ly		uranium	
unwitting /ly		Uranus	
unworantable	unwarrantable[+]	Urazian	Eurasian
unworantabul	unwarrantable[+]	urban	
unworkable		urban e /ely/ity	
unworkabul	unworkable	urbanis e[2] /ation	
unworldl y /iness		urbun	urban
unworth y /iness		urchin	
unwound		urea	
unwownd	unwound	ureter	
unwrap[3]		urethra	
unwritten		urge[2] /ncy/nt	
unyun	onion	urinate[2]	
upbrade	upbraid[1]	urin e /al/ary	
upbraid[1]		urithmics	eurhythmics
upbringing		urjensey	urgency
update[2]		urjent	urgent
upheaval		url	earl[+]
upheld		urley	early[+]
upheval	upheaval	urlier	earlier[+]
uphill		urmin	ermine
uphold /ing		urn ★ (vase)	
upholster[1] /er/y		urn	earn[1★+]
uphoney	euphony[+]	urnest	earnest[+]
upkeep		urolog y /ist	

Uropian	European	vacseen	vaccine
erstwile	erstwhile	vacsinashun	vaccination
urth	earth ¹⁺	vacsination	vaccination
urthen	earthen ⁺	vacsine	vaccine
urthkwake	earthquake	vacu *ous* /ity	
urthquake	earthquake	vacuum	
us *e*² /able/age/er		vacuus	vacuous ⁺
useful /ly/ness		vagabond /age	
useless		vagar *y* /ies	
userp	usurp ¹⁺	vage	vague ⁺
usher ¹ /ette (fem.)		vagina	
usheret	usherette	vagran *cy* /t	
usless	useless	vagransey	vagrancy ⁺
usorius	usurious	vague /ly/r/st	
usual /ly		vail	vale ★
usurp ¹ /ation/er		vail	veil ¹★
usur *y* /ious		vain ★(proud)/er/est/ly	
utensil		vain	vane ★
uter	utter ¹⁺	vain	vein ¹★
uter *us* /ine		vainglor *ious* /y	
uthanasia	euthanasia	vainglorius	vainglorious ⁺
uther	other ⁺	vajina	vagina
utherwise	otherwise	valance	
utilis *e*² /able/ation		valans	valance
utilitarian /ism		valay	valet ³
utilit *y* /ies		vale ★ (valley)	
utmost		vale	veil ¹★
Utopia /n		valedicshun	valediction ⁺
utric *le* /ular/ulus		valedict *ion* /ory	
utter ¹ /ance/ly		valentine	
uvula /r		valer	valour ⁺
uxorious		valerus	valorous
uxorius	uxorious	valese	valise
		valet ³	
		valiant	
		valid /ity	
V		validashun	validation
		validat *e*² /ion	
vacanc *y* /ies		valise	
vacansey	vacancy ⁺	valley /s	
vacant /ly		valor	valour ⁺
vacashun	vacation	valo *ur* /rous	
vacat *e*² /ion		valt	vault ¹
vaccinat *e*² /ion/or		valuashun	valuation
vaccine		valu *e*² /able/ation/er	
vacillat *e*² /ion			

valueless	
valv *e* /ular	
valy	valley +
valyu	value ²+
valyuble	valuable
valyubul	valuable
valyuer	valuer
valyuless	valueless
vamp ¹	
vampire	
Van de Graaff generator	
vanadium	
vandal /ism	
vane ★ (weather)	
vane	vain ★+
vane	vein ¹★
vangard	vanguard
vanglorey	vainglory
vanglorious	vainglorious +
vanglorius	vainglorious +
vanguard	
vanilla	
vanish ¹	
vanity /-bag	
vankwish	vanquish ¹
vanquish ¹	
vantage	
vantidge	vantage
vantige	vantage
vaper	vapour +
vapid	
vaporis *e* ² /ation/er	
vaporus	vaporous
vapo *ur* /rous	
varia *ble* /bility/tion	
variabul	variable +
varian *ce* /t	
varians	variance +
variashun	variation
varicose	
varie	vary ⁴+
variegated	
variet *y* /ies	
varikose	varicose
varius	various

varnish ¹ /er	
var *y* ⁴ /iation/ious	
vascular	
vase	
Vaseline	
vasillate	vacillate ²+
vasleen	Vaseline
vast /er/est/ly/ness	
Vatican	
vault ¹	
vaunt ¹	
veal	
vech	vetch +
vector	
veel	veal
veemence	vehemence +
veemens	vehemence +
veement	vehement
veer ¹	
vegetable	
vegetarian /ism	
vegetashun	vegetation
vegetat *e* ² /ion/ive	
vegtable	vegetable
vegtabul	vegetable
vehemen *ce* /t	
vehic *le* /ular	
veiculer	vehicular
veil ¹★ (disguise)	
veil	vale★
vein ¹★ (blood)	
vein	vain ★+
vein	vane ★
veks	vex ¹+
veksashun	vexation
veksashus	vexatious
veksation	vexation
veksatious	vexatious
vekter	vector
veld	
vellum	
velocit *y* /ies	
veloors	velours
velositey	velocity +
velours	

velt	veld	verbiage	
velum	vellum	verbos *e* /ity	
velvet /een		verdant	
vena cava		verdict	
venal /ity/ly		verdur *e* /ous	
vencher	venture [2+]	verge [2]	
vend [1] /or		verger	
vendetta		verie	very
veneer [1]		verifi	verify [4+]
venerab *le* /ility		verif *y* [4] /iable/ication	
venerabul	venerable [+]	verily	
venerashun	veneration	verisimilitude	
venerat *e* [2] /ion		verit *y* /ies/able/ably	
venereal		vermicelli	
venerial	venereal	vermilion	
veneshun	Venetian	vermin /ous	
Venetian		vermouth	
venge *ance* /ful		vernacular	
vengence	vengeance [+]	vernal	
vengens	vengeance [+]	versatil *e* /ity	
venial		verse /s * (poetry)	
venison		verses	versus *
venom /ous		versif *y* [4] /ication	
venomus	venomous	version	
venous * (of veins)		versus * (against)	
venous	Venus *	vertebra /e (pl.)/l/te	
vent [1]		verteks	vertex [+]
ventilashun	ventilation	vert *ex* /ices (pl.)	
ventilat *e* [2] /ion/or		vertical /ly	
ventral /ly		vertig *o* /inous	
ventrical	ventricle	verve	
ventricle		very	
ventrilokwism	ventriloquism [+]	vesa	visa
ventriloquis *m* /t		vescher	vesture [2]
venture [2] /some		vespers	
venturous		vessel	
venturus	venturous	vest [1] /ment	
Venus * (planet)		vestal	
venus	venous *	vestibule	
venyet	vignette	vestig *e* /ial	
veraci *ous* /ty		vestrie	vestry [+]
veranda		vestr *y* /ies	
verashus	veracious [+]	vestul	vestal
verasitey	veracity	vesture [2]	
verb /al/ally/atim		vesul	vessel

vet [3]		victor y /ies	
vetch /es		victual [3] /ler	
vetenarey	veterinary +	video /-frequency	
vetenrey	veterinary +	vidio	video +
veteran		vie /d	
veterinar y /ies		vieing	vying
veto [1] /es		view [1] /er	
vex [1] /ation/atious		view-point	
vexashun	vexation	viger	vigour +
vexashus	vexatious	vigil /ance/ant/ante	
veza	visa	vigilans	vigilance
vezave	vis-à-vis	vignette	
vi	vie +	vigorus	vigorous
via		vigo ur /rous/rously	
viab le /ility		vijun	vision +
viabul	viable +	Viking	
viaduct		viksen	vixen
vial ★ (glass)		vilan	villain +
vial	vile ★+	vile ★† /ly/ness/r/st	
vial	viol ★+	†(loathsome)	
viands (pl.)		vile	vial ★
vibrant		vile	viol ★+
vibrashun	vibration	vilidge	village +
vibrat e [2] /ion/or		vilifi	vilify [4]+
vicar /age		vilif y [4] /ication/ier	
vicarious /ly		vilige	village +
vicarius	vicarious +	villa	
vice		village /r	
vice versa		villain /ous/y	
vice-chancellor		villaney	villainy
vice-president		villanus	villainous
vicer	vicar +	vill us /i (pl.)	
viceregal		vindicashun	vindication
viceroi	viceroy +	vindicat e [2] /ion/or	
viceroy /alty/alties		vindictive	
vicinity		vine /ry	
vicious /ly/ness		vinegar /y	
vicissitude		viniger	vinegar +
vicount	viscount +	vintage	
vicownt	viscount +	vintidge	vintage
victim		vintige	vintage
victimis e [2] /ation		vinul	vinyl
victor /ious/iously		vinyet	vignette
victorey	victory +	vinyl	
victorius	victorious	viol ★ (music) /a/in/inist	

viol	vial ★	visiditey	viscidity
viol	vile ★+	visinitey	vicinity
violashun	violation	vision /ary	
violat e² /ion/or		visionrey	visionary
violen ce /t		visissitude	vicissitude
violens	violence +	visit ¹ /ant/ation/or	
violet		visitashun	visitation
violoncello /s		visiter	visitor
violonchelo	violoncello +	viskositey	viscosity
viper /ish/ous		vista	
virgin /al/ity		visual /ly	
Virgo		visualis e² /ation	
viril e /ity		visul	visual +
virilitey	virility	visulise	visualise ²+
virolog y /ist		vital /ity/ly/s	
virtual /ly		vital	victual ³+
virtu e /osity/ous		vitalis e² /ation	
virtuoso		vitalitey	vitality
virulen ce /t		vitamin	
virulens	virulence +	vitaminis e² /ation	
virus		vitiat e² /ion	
visa		vitreous	
visage		vitrifi	vitrify ⁴+
vis-à-vis		vitrif y⁴ /ication	
viscera /l		vitriol /ic	
viscid /ity		vitrius	vitreous
viscos e /ity		vitul	vital +
viscositey	viscosity	vituperat e² /ion/ive/or	
viscount /ess (fem.)		viul	vial ★
viscous		viul	vile ★+
viscuus	viscous	viva voce	
vise	vice	vivac ious /ity	
vise chanseler	vice-chancellor	vivashus	vivacious +
vise president	vice-president	vivasitee	vivacity
visera	viscera +	vivavosi	viva voce
viseregal	viceregal	vivid /ly/ness	
viseroi	viceroy +	vivifi	vivify ⁴+
visevursa	vice versa	vivif y⁴ /ication	
vishiate	vitiate ²+	viviparous	
vishun	vision +	viviparus	viviparous
vishunrey	visionary	vivisecshun	vivisection
vishus	vicious +	vivisect ¹ /ion/or	
visib le /ility/ly		vixen	
visibul	visible +	vocabular y /ies	
visid	viscid +	vocal /ist/ly	

vocalis *e* [2] /ation	
vocashun	vocation [+]
vocation /al	
vocative	
vocifer *ate* [2] /ous	
vociferus	vociferous
vodka	
voge	vogue
vogue	
voice [2]	
void [1]	
voiige	voyage [2+]
voiiger	voyager
voile	
vois	voice [2]
volatil *e* /ity	
volatilis *e* [2] /ation	
volcanic	
volcano /es	
voley	volley [1+]
volishun	volition [+]
volition /al	
volkano	volcano [+]
volley [1] /s	
volt /age/meter	
volub *le* /ility/ly	
volubul	voluble [+]
volum *e* /etric/inous	
voluminus	voluminous
voluntar *y* /ily	
volunteer [1]	
voluntrey	voluntary [+]
voluptu *ous* /ary	
voluptuus	voluptuous [+]
vomit [1]	
voraci *ous* /ty	
vorashus	voracious [+]
vorasitey	voracity
vornt	vaunt [1]
vorteks	vortex [+]
vort *ex* /exes/ices (pls.)	
vorticella	
vosiferate	vociferate [2+]
vosiferus	vociferous
votar *y* /ies	

vote [2] /r	
votive	
vouch [1] /er	
vouchsafe [2]	
vow [1]	
vowch	vouch [1+]
vowchsafe	vouchsafe [2]
vowel	
vowul	vowel
voyage [2] /r	
voyd	void [1]
voys	voice [2]
vue	view [1+]
vulcanis *e* [2] /ation	
vulcher	vulture
vulgar /ity	
vulgaris *e* [2] /ation/m	
vulnerab *le* /ility	
vulnerabul	vulnerable [+]
vulnrable	vulnerable [+]
vulture	
vulva	
vurb	verb [+]
vurchoo	virtue [+]
vurchual	virtual [+]
vurchuous	virtuous
vurchuus	virtuous
vurgin	virgin [+]
vurginitey	virginity
vurgo	Virgo
vurtue	virtue [+]
vurtuoso	virtuoso
vurtuous	virtuous
vwal	voile
vye	vie [+]
vying	

W

wack	whack [1]
wad /ding	
waddle [2]	
wade [2] /r	
wadle	waddle [2]

wadul	waddle ²	walow	wallow ¹
wafe	waif	walrus /es	
wafer		walts	waltz ¹⁺
waffle ² /-iron		waltz ¹ /er	
wafle	waffle ²⁺	wan ★ (pale) /ness	
waft ¹		wan	won ★
waful	waffle ²⁺	wander ¹★ (roam) /er/lust	
wag ³ /gish/tail		wander	wonder ¹★⁺
wage ²		wane ²	
wager ¹		wangle ² /r	
waggle ²		wangul	wangle ²⁺
wagon /er/ette		wanskot	wainscot ¹⁺
wagul	waggle ²	want ¹	
waif		wanton /ness	
wail ¹★ (cry)		war ³ /-paint/-path	
wail	whale ★⁺	warant	warrant ¹⁺
wainscot ¹ /ing		warantee	warranty ⁺
waist ★ (body) /coat		warble ² /r	
waist	waste ²★⁺	warbul	warble ²⁺
wait ¹★† /er/ress (fem.)		ward ¹ /er/room	
†(stay for)		warden	
wait	weight ★⁺	wardrobe	
waitey	weighty	ware ★ (avoid) /s ★†	
waive ²★ (give up)		†(goods for sale)	
waive	wave ²★⁺	ware	wear ★⁺
waiver ¹★ (law)		ware	where ★
waiver	waver ¹★⁺	warehouse	
wake ² /ful/fulness		warehowse	warehouse
waken ¹		waren	warren
waks	wax ¹⁺	wares	wears ★
wakswork	waxwork	warey	wary ⁺
walabey	wallaby ⁺	warf	wharf ⁺
wale	wail ¹★	war *fare* /like	
wale	whale ★⁺	warior	warrior
walk ¹ /-over		warm ¹ /er/est/ly/ness/th	
walkie-talkie		warmonger ¹	
walking-stick		warn ¹	
wall ¹ /flower/paper		warp ¹	
wallab *y* /ies		warrant ¹ /able	
wallah		warrant *y* /ies	
wallet		warren	
wallop ¹		warrior	
wallow ¹		wart /y	
walnut		warves	wharves
walop	wallop ¹	war *y* /ily/iness	

was
wash[1] /able/er
washed-up
wasl   wassail[1]
wasn't (was not)
wasnt   wasn't
wasp /ish
wassail[1]
wast *e* [2]*† /age/er/rel
  †(squander)
waste   waist *+
wasteful /ly/ness
wat   watt *+
wat   what *+
watch[1] /ful/fulness
wate   wait[1]*+
wate   weight *+
water[1] /cress/fall
waterlogged
water *mark* /tight
waterproof[1]
watt * (power) /age
wave[2]*† /form/length
  †(water, gesture)
wave   waive[2]*
waver[1]* (falter) /er
waver   waiver[1]*
wawlts   waltz[1]+
wax[1] /en/work
way * (direction) /side
way   weigh[1]*+
way   whey *
waybridge   weighbridge
wayfare[2] /r
way *lay* /laid/laying
wayward
waywerd   wayward
we * (us)
we   wee *
weak *† /ling/ness
  †(feeble)
weak   week *+
weaken[1]
weak *er* /est/ly *† /ness
  †(sickly)

weakly   weekly *+
weal * (state)
weal   wheel[1]*+
weald * (district)
weald   wield[1]*
wealth /ier/iest/iness
wean[1]
weapon
wear *† /able/er/ing/s *†
  †(have on the body)
wear   ware *+
wear   where *
wearey   weary[4]+
wearisome
wears   wares *
wear *y* [4] /ier/iest/ily/iness
weasel
weat   wheat +
weather[1]*† /cock
  †(atmosphere)
weather   whether *
weathervane
weatmeal   wheatmeal
weave[2]* (make fabric) /r
weave   we've *
web[3] /-footed/-toed
wed[3] /ding/lock
wedge[2]
Wedensday   Wednesday
Wednesday
wee * (small)
weed[1] /s/y
weedul   wheedle[2]
week *† /day/end
  †(seven days)
week   weak *+
weeken   weaken[1]
weekling   weakling
weekl *y* * (every week) /ies
weel   weal *
weel   wheel[1]*+
weelbarrow   wheelbarrow
weeld   weald *
weeld   wield[1]*
weelrite   wheelwright

ween	wean [1]	were ★ (to be)	
weep /er/ing/y		were	where ★
weevil		were	whirr [1]★
weeze	wheeze [2]+	we're ★ (we are)	
wege	wedge [2]	wereabouts	whereabouts
weigh [1]★† /bridge		wereas	whereas +
†(how heavy)		wereby	whereby
weight ★† /less/lessness/y		werefor	wherefore
†(heaviness)		weren't (were not)	
weild	weald ★	werever	wherever
weild	wield [1]★	werewol f /ves (pl.)	
weir ★ (dam)		werey	weary [4]+
weird /er/est		werisum	wearisome
weja	ouija	werk	work [1]+
welch [1]★ (cheat)		werkbox	workbox +
welch	Welsh ★	werker	worker
welcome [2]		werkshop	workshop
weld [1] /er		werl	whirl [1]★+
welfare		werl	whorl [1]★
welk	whelk	werld	world +
welkin		werldwide	worldwide
we'll ★ (we will)		werligig	whirligig
well [1]★ (spring) /-advised		werm	worm [1]+
well-appointed		werse	worse +
well-balanced		wersen	worsen [1]
well-behaved		wership	worship [3]+
well-*being* /-bred		werst	worst
wellingtons		wersted	worsted
well-meaning		werth	worth +
well-*nigh* /-to-do		werthey	worthy +
welp	whelp [1]	werthwiul	worthwhile
Welsh ★ (from Wales)		werwoolf	werewolf +
welter [1]		wesel	weasel
welth	wealth +	Wesleyan	
wen	when +	weslian	Wesleyan
wence	whence	west /erly/ern/ward	
wench [1] /es		westernis e [2] /ation	
wend [1]		westwerd	westward
wenever	whenever	wet [3]★† /ness/ter/test	
went		†(soaked)	
wepon	weapon	wet	whet [3]★
wept		wether	weather [1]★+
wer	weir ★	wether	whether ★
werd	weird +	wethercock	weathercock
werd	word +	wethervane	weathervane

we've ★ (we have)	
weve	weave ²★+
wevil	weevil
whack ¹	
whal e ★† /er/ing	
†(mammal)	
whar f /ves (pl.)	
what ★† /ever/soever	
†(question)	
what	watt ★+
wheat /en/meal	
whedul	wheedle ²
wheedle ²	
wheel ¹★ /barrow	
wheelwright	
wheez e ² /ily/y	
whelk	
whelp ¹	
when /ever/soever	
whence	
whens	whence
where ★ (which place)	
where	ware ★+
where	wear ★+
where	were ★
whereabouts	
where as /by/ever	
wherefore	
where upon /withal	
wherl	whirl ¹★+
wherl	whorl ¹★
whet ³★ (sharpen)	
whether ★ (if)	
whether	weather ¹★+
whey ★ (milk)	
which ★ (which one)	
which	witch ★+
whiff ¹	
Whig ★ (political)	
whil e ★ (during) /st	
while	wile ²★+
whim /sical	
whimper ¹	
whimsie	whimsy +
whims y /ies	

whine ²★ (complain)	
whinn y ⁴ /ies	
whip ³ /cord	
whipper-snapper	
whippet	
whirl ¹★† /igig	
†(swing round)	
whirl	whorl ¹★
whirr ¹★ (whirl)	
whisk ¹	
whisker /ed	
whiskey ★†	
†(alcohol—Irish)	
whisky ★†	
†(alcohol—Scotch)	
whisper ¹ /er	
whist	
whistle ² /r	
whisul	whistle ²+
whit ★ (particle, jot)	
white /bait/r/st	
whiten ¹	
whitewash ¹	
whither ★ (where)	
whiting	
Whitsun	
whittle ²	
whitul	whittle ²
whiz ³	
who /ever	
whoa ★ (stop)	
whole ★ (complete)	
whole	hole ²★+
whole-hearted	
wholesale /r	
wholesome /ly	
wholly ★ (fully)	
wholly	holey ★
wholly	holy ★
whom	
whoop ¹★ (shout)	
whoop	hoop ¹★
whooping cough	
whop ³	
whore ² /monger	

whorl [1]*†	
†(ring of leaves)	
whorl	whirl [1]*+
who's * (who is or has)	
whose * (possessive)	
whur	whirr [1]*
whurl	whirl [1]*+
whurl	whorl [1]*
why	
wick /er/et	
wicked /er/est	
wide /ly/r/st	
wide awake /spread	
widen [1]	
widow [1] /er	
width	
wield [1]* (hold and use)	
wield	weald *
wife /ves (pl.)	
wiff	whiff [1]
wig [3]* (hair)	
wig	Whig *
wiggle [2] /y	
wigul	wiggle [2]+
wigwam	
wild /er/est/ly/ness	
wilderness	
wile [2]* (trick) /iness/y	
wile	while *+
wilful /ly/ness	
will [1] /power	
will-o'-the-wisp	
willow /y	
willy-nilly	
wilst	whilst
wilt [1]	
wim	whim +
wimin	women +
wimper	whimper [1]
wimsey	whimsy +
wimsical	whimsical
win /ner/ning	
wince [2]	
winch [1] /es	
wind /bag/ed/ward	

wind /er/ing	
window /-pane/-sill	
windy /ier/iest/iness	
wine * (drink) /-cellar	
wine	whine [2]*
wineglass /es	
wing [1]	
wink [1]	
winkle [2]	
winkul	winkle [2]
winnow [1]	
winsome /ness	
winter [1]	
wintrie	wintry
wintry	
wip	whip [3]+
wipcord	whipcord
wipe [2] /r	
wipper snapper	whipper-snapper
wippet	whippet
wire [2] /less	
wiriness /y	
wirl	whirl [1]*+
wirl	whorl [1]*
wirr	whirr [1]*
wisdom	
wise /acre/ly/r/st	
wish [1] /ful	
wishy-washy	
wisk	whisk [1]
wisker	whisker +
wiskey	whiskey *
wiskey	whisky *
wisp	
wisper	whisper [1]+
wist	whist
wistful /ly/ness	
wistle	whistle [2]+
wisul	whistle [2]+
wit * (flair, humour)	
wit	whit *
witch * (hag) /es	
witch	which *
witchery /ies	
wite	white +

witen	whiten [1]	wolop	wallop [1]
witer	whiter	wolow	wallow [1]
witewash	whitewash [1]	woman /kind/ly	
with /al		womb	
withdraw /al/ing/n		women (pl.) /folk	
withdrew		won * (did win)	
withdroo	withdrew	won	wan *+
wither [1]* (decay)		wonder [1]*† /ful/fully	
wither	whither *	†(remarkable thing)	
withers		wonder	wander [1]*+
withheld		wondrous	
withhold /ing		wondrus	wondrous
within		wont * (accustomed)	
without		wont	want [1]
withstand /ing		wont	won't *
witing	whiting	won't * (will not)	
witness [1] /es		wonton	wanton +
witsun	Whitsun	woo [1] /er	
witti cism /ness		wood * (lumber) /cut	
wittle	whittle [2]	wood	would *
witt y /ier/iest/ily		wooden /ly/ness	
witul	whittle [2]	woof	
wiz	whiz [3]	wool /len/liness	
wizard		woolf	wolf [1]+
wizened		wooll y /ies	
wo	whoa *	wooman	woman +
wo	woe *+	woomb	womb
wobbl e [2] /y		woond	wound [1]
woble	wobble [2]+	wop	whop [3]
wobul	wobble [2]+	wor	war [3]+
woch	watch [1]+	worant	warrant [1]+
wod	wad +	worantie	warranty +
wodle	waddle [2]	worble	warble [2]+
wodul	waddle [2]	worbul	warble [2]+
woe * (grief) /begone		word /ily/ing/y	
woe	whoa *	word	ward [1]+
woeful /ly		worden	warden
wofle	waffle [2]+	wordrobe	wardrobe
woft	waft [1]	wore	
woful	waffle [2]+	woren	warren
woful	woeful +	worf	wharf +
wolabey	wallaby +	worfare	warfare +
wolet	wallet	work [1] /able/aday/er	
wol f [1] /ves (pl.)		work box /shop	
wolla	wallah	worl	whirl [1]*+

worl	whorl ¹★
world /liness/ly/wide	
worm ¹ /wood	
worm	warm ¹⁺
wormunger	warmonger ¹
worn /-out	
worn	warn ¹
worp	warp ¹
worrey	worry ⁴⁺
worrier	warrior
worr y ⁴ /ies/ier	
wors e /t	
worsen ¹	
worship ³ /per	
worsted	
wort	wart ⁺
worth /less/while	
worth y /ier/iest/ily	
wos	was
wosh	wash ¹⁺
wosht up	washed-up
wosl	wassail ¹
wosnt	wasn't
wosp	wasp ⁺
wot	watt ★⁺
wot	what ★⁺
wotch	watch ¹⁺
wotchful	watchful
wotever	whatever
wotsoever	whatsoever
would ★ (conditional)	
would	wood ★⁺
wound ¹	
wove /n	
wrack ★ (seaweed)	
wraith	
wrangle ² /r	
wrangul	wrangle ²⁺
wrap ★ (pack) /per ★ /ping	
wrapped ★ (packed)	
wrath /ful	
wreak ¹★ (inflict)	
wreath ★ (flowers)	
wreathe ²★ (twist)	
wreck ¹ /age	

wren	
wrench ¹	
wrest ¹★ (pull away)	
wrestle ² /r	
wresul	wrestle ²⁺
wretch ★†	
†(unhappy person)	
wri	wry ★⁺
wriggle ²	
wrigul	wriggle ²
wring ¹★ (squeeze)	
wringer ★ (machine)	
wrinkle ²	
wrinkul	wrinkle ²
wrist /band/let/-watch	
writ	
writ e ★† /er/ing/ten	
†(put words on paper)	
writhe ²	
wrong ¹ /doer	
wrongful /ly	
wrort	wrought ⁺
wrote ★ (did write)	
wrought /-up	
wrung ★ (squeezed)	
wry ★ (distorted) /ly	
wun	one ★⁺
wunce	once
wunder	wonder ¹★⁺
wundrous	wondrous
wundrus	wondrous
wuns	once
wunself	oneself
wur	whirr ¹★
wurey	worry ⁴⁺
wurl	whirl ¹★⁺
wurl	whorl ¹★
wurligig	whirligig

X

xenofobia	xenophobia ⁺
xenophob ia /e/ic	
xeroks	Xerox ¹

Xerox[1]	
X-ray[1]	
xylofone	xylophone
xylophone	

Y

y	why
yacht[1] /sman	
yak	
yam	
yank[1]	
Yankee	
yap[3]	
yard /age	
yarn[1]	
yashmak	
yaw[1]★ (of ship)	
yaw	yore ★
yaw	your ★+
yawl[1]	
yawn[1]	
yay	yea
yea	
yeald	yield[1]
year /ling	
yearn[1]	
yeast	
yeer	year +
yeest	yeast
yeld	yield[1]
yell[1]	
yellow /ish	
yelow	yellow +
yelp[1]	
yeoman /ry	
yerling	yearling
yern	yearn[1]
yes	
yest	yeast
yesterday	
yet	
yeti	
yety	yeti

yew ★ (tree)	
yew	ewe ★
yew	you ★+
yewse	use[2]+
yewsery	usury +
yewshual	usual +
yewsual	usual +
yiddish	
yield[1]	
yodel[3] /ler	
yodle	yodel[3]+
yoga	
yogert	yogurt
yogurt	
yoke ★ (round neck)	
yoke	yolk ★
yokel	
yokle	yokel
yolk ★ (of egg)	
yolk	yoke ★
yoman	yeoman +
yonder	
yore ★ (years ago)	
yore	yaw[1]★
yore	your ★+
yorself	yourself +
yorselves	yourselves
yot	yacht[1]+
yotsman	yachtsman
you ★ (person)	
you	ewe ★
you	yew ★
youboat	U-boat
you'll ★ (you will)	
young /er/est/ster	
your ★† /s	
†(belonging to you)	
your	yaw[1]★
your	yore ★
your	you're ★
you're ★ (you are)	
yourself /ves (pl.)	
youth /ful	
ytterbium	
yttrium	

yule *† /tide	
†(Christmas)	
yule	you'll *
yung	young +
yungster	youngster
yurn	yearn [1]
yuse	use [2]+
yuseful	useful +
yuserey	usury +
yusual	usual +
yutensil	utensil
yuterine	uterine
yuterus	uterus +
yuth	youth +
yutilise	utilise [2]+
yutilitarian	utilitarian +
yutilitee	utility +
yutopia	Utopia +

Z

zan y /ies	
zar	tsar
zeal /ous	
zealot	
zebra	
zeel	zeal +
zefer	zephyr
zelot	zealot
zelus	zealous
zenith	

zenofobia	xenophobia +
zenophobia	xenophobia +
zepher	zephyr
zephyr	
zeplin	Zeppelin
Zeppelin	
zerconium	zirconium
zero /s	
zeroks	Xerox [1]
zerox	Xerox [1]
zest /ful	
Zeus	
zigospore	zygospore
zigote	zygote
zigzag [3]	
zilofone	xylophone
zilophone	xylophone
zinc	
zink	zinc
Zion /ism/ist	
zip [3] /per/-fastener	
zirconium	
zither	
zodiac	
zon e [2] /al	
zoo /logical/logy	
zoologey	zoology
zoom [1]	
Zulu	
zus	Zeus
zygospore	
zygote	

APPENDIX I
Some Spelling Rules

A. y always stays when adding -ing but changes to i before adding -ed, e.g.:

    carry, carrying, carried   terrify, terrifying, terrified

B. i before e except after c, e.g.:

    field, mischievous, relief   deceive, perceive, receipt

  Note that there are exceptions to the above rules.

C. q is always followed by u, e.g.:

    conquer, frequent, queen

D. all at the beginning of a word loses one l, e.g.:

    already, altogether, always

  The double l is retained in hyphenated words such as all-fours and all-round, but the words all right should always be written as two separate words and in that form only.

THE FORMATION OF PLURALS

The following is a summary of the main rules involved in the formation of plurals:

1. Most words, including those ending in silent -e, add -s, e.g.:
   airport, airports
   sausage, sausages

2. Words ending in -ay, -ey, -oy, or -uy add -s, e.g.:
   day, days   toy, toys
   abbey, abbeys   guy, guys

3. Words ending in -fe change f to v and add -s, e.g.:
   knife, knives

4. Some words ending in -f change f to v and add -es, e.g.:
   half, halves   loaf, loaves

5. Some words ending in -f add -s, e.g.:
   chief, chiefs
   handkerchief, handkerchiefs
   But note that some words ending in -f can either add -s or change f to v and add -es, e.g.:
   hoof, hoofs *or* hooves
   scarf, scarfs *or* scarves

6. Words ending in -ff usually add -s, e.g.:
   cliff, cliffs
   sheriff, sheriffs

7. Words ending in -o add -s or -es, e.g.:
   concerto, concertos
   dynamo, dynamos
   buffalo, buffaloes
   domino, dominoes

8. Words ending in -ch, -s, -sh, -x, or -z add -es, e.g.:
   church, churches   thrush, thrushes
   gas, gases   box, boxes
   dress, dresses   buzz, buzzes

9. Words ending in -y (but not -ay, -ey, -oy, or -uy: see Note 2) change the y to an i and add -es, e.g.:
   baby, babies
   family, families

10. Some words form their plurals mainly by changing their vowels (or some of their vowels), e.g.:
    foot, feet   mouse, mice
    goose, geese   tooth, teeth
    man, men   woman, women

11. One word adds -en:
    ox, oxen
    One word adds -ren:
    child, children

12. Words ending in -us change us to **i**, e.g.:

    bacillus, bacilli
    fungus, fungi
    radius, radii
    rhombus, rhombi
    terminus, termini

13. Words ending in -is change is to **-es**, e.g.:

    analysis, analyses
    basis, bases
    metamorphosis, metamorphoses

14. Words ending in -ex add **-es** or change -ex to **-ices**, e.g.:

    apex, apexes *or* apices
    index, indexes *or* indices
    vortex, vortexes *or* vortices

15. Words ending in -ix add **-es** or change -ix to **-ices**, e.g.:

    appendix, appendixes *or* appendices
    helix, helices
    matrix, matrixes *or* matrices

16. Some words ending in -a simply add **-s**, e.g.:

    aroma, aromas
    drama, dramas
    idea, ideas
    but note:
    alga, algae
    antenna, antennae
    formula, formulas *or* formulae
    stoma, stomas *or* stomata

17. Some words ending in -um simply add **-s**, e.g.:

    museum, museums
    pendulum, pendulums
    premium, premiums
    but note:
    aquarium, aquariums *or* aquaria
    bacterium, bacteria
    curriculum, curricula
    memorandum, memorandums
    			or memoranda
    spectrum, spectra
    stadium, stadiums *or* stadia

18. Words ending in -on usually add **-s** e.g.:

    electron, electrons
    neutron, neutrons
    but note:
    phenomenon, phenomena

19. Words ending in -eau add **-x**, e.g.:

    bureau, bureaux
    chateau, chateaux
    plateau, plateaux
    Note that some dictionaries allow a plural in **-s** for some of these words

20. Some words have the same spelling for both the singular and the plural forms e.g.:

bison	grouse	sheep
deer	salmon	trout

21. Compound words.

    Logically, the most important word should be changed into the plural, as for example:
    brother-in-law, brothers-in-law
    man-of-war, men-of-war
    but note:
    court-martial, court-martials
    lord justice, lords justices

22. Some words are used only in the singular form, e.g.:

arithmetic	goodness	magic
courage	logic	music

23. Some words are used only in the plural form, e.g.:

    mathematics
    Among words frequently used in their plural form are:

acoustics	physics	tactics
athletics	politics	

24. Pairs.

    The following nouns do not have a singular form:

entrails	pliers	trousers
pincers	scissors	tweezers

324

APPENDIX II
Abbreviations in General Use

A. Advanced (level of G.C.E.)
A.A. Automobile Association
A.B.M. anti-ballistic missile
acc., a/c account
A.D. in the year of our Lord
A.D.C. aide-de-camp
A.F.C. Air Force Cross
A.F.M. Air Force Medal
a.m. before noon
Ave. avenue
A.W.O.L. absent without leave

B.A. Bachelor of Arts
Bart. Baronet
B.B.C. British Broadcasting Corporation
B.C. before Christ
B.D. Bachelor of Divinity
B.Ed. Bachelor of Education
B.E.M. British Empire Medal
Benelux Belgium–Netherlands–Luxembourg Union
B.M. Bachelor of Medicine
B.M.A. British Medical Association
B.Mus. Bachelor of Music
B.R. British Rail
B.R.C.S. British Red Cross Society
B.Sc. Bachelor of Science
B.S.T. British standard time, British summer time

C. Centigrade
c., ca. about
C.A.B. Citizens' Advice Bureau
C.A.C.M. Central American Common Market
CARICOM. Caribbean Community
C.B.E. Commander of the British Empire
C.B.I. Confederation of British Industry
C.C. County Council
C.E.N.T.O. Central Treaty Organisation
C.G.M. Conspicuous Gallantry Medal
C.G.S. Chief of General Staff
C.H. Companion of Honour
Ch.B. Bachelor of Surgery

C.I.D. Criminal Investigation Department
C.-in-C. Commander-in-Chief
C.M.E.A. (COMECON) Council for Mutual Economic Assistance
C.N.D. Campaign for Nuclear Disarmament
C.O. Commanding Officer
c/o care of
C.O.D. cash on delivery
Con. Conservative
C.S.E. Certificate of Secondary Education

D.B.E. Dame Commander of the British Empire
D.C.L. Doctor of Civil Law
D.C.M. Distinguished Conduct Medal
D.D. Doctor of Divinity
D.D.T. dichlor-diphenyl-trichlorethane (insecticide)
D.F.C. Distinguished Flying Cross
D.F.M. Distinguished Flying Medal
D.M. Doctor of Medicine
D.Mus. Doctor of Music
DNA deoxyribonucleic acid
D.O.E. Department of the Environment
D.Phil. Doctor of Philosophy
Dr. Doctor
D.Sc. Doctor of Science
D.S.C. Distinguished Service Cross
D.S.M. Distinguished Service Medal
D.S.O. Distinguished Service Order

E.E.C. European Economic Community
E.F.T.A. European Free Trade Association
e.g. for example
E.S.N. educationally subnormal
E.S.P. extrasensory perception
Esq. Esquire

F. Fahrenheit
F.A. Football Association

325

F.A.O. Food and Agriculture Organisation

F.B.A. Fellow of the British Academy

f.o.c. free of charge

F.R.S. Fellow of the Royal Society

G.A.T.T. General Agreement on Tariffs and Trade

G.B. Great Britain

G.B.E. Dame or Knight Grand Cross of the British Empire

G.C. George Cross

G.C.E. General Certificate of Education

G.D.P. gross domestic product

G.D.R. German Democratic Republic

G.H.Q. General Headquarters

G.L.C. Greater London Council

G.M. George Medal

G.M.T. Greenwich mean time

G.N.P. gross national product

G.P. general practitioner

G.P.O. General Post Office

H.E. His Excellency; His Eminence

H.M. Her Majesty

H.M.I. Her Majesty's Inspector

H.M.S. Her Majesty's Ship

H.M.S.O. Her Majesty's Stationery Office

H.N.C. Higher National Certificate

H.N.D. Higher National Diploma

Hon. honorary; Honourable

h.p. hire purchase; horsepower

H.Q. Headquarters

H.R.H. Her (His) Royal Highness

I.B.R.D. International Bank for Reconstruction and Development (World Bank)

I.C.C. International Chamber of Commerce

I.C.F.T.U. International Confederation of Free Trade Unions

I.C.I. Imperial Chemical Industries

i.e. that is

I.L.O. International Labour Organisation

I.M.F. International Monetary Fund

I.O.U. I owe you

I.Q. intelligence quotient

I.R.A. Irish Republican Army

I.T.V. Independent Television

J.P. Justice of the Peace

Jr. Junior

K.B.E. Knight Commander of the British Empire

K.C.B. Knight Commander of the Bath

Kt. Knight

Lab. Labour

L.A.F.T.A. Latin American Free Trade Association

lat. latitude

lbw leg before wicket

L.E.A. Local Education Authority

Lib. Liberal

LL.B., LL.D. Bachelor, Doctor of Laws

long. longitude

L.P. long-playing (of gramophone records, etc.)

L.S.D. lysergic acid diethylamide (hallucinogenic drug)

L.T.A. Lawn Tennis Association

Ltd. Limited

L.V. luncheon voucher

M.A. Master of Arts

M.B. Bachelor of Medicine

M.B.E. Member of the British Empire

M.C. Military Cross; Master of Ceremonies

M.C.C. Marylebone Cricket Club

M.D. Doctor of Medicine

M.F.H. Master of Foxhounds

M.O.H. Medical Officer of Health

M.P. Member of Parliament

m.p.g. miles per gallon

m.p.h. miles per hour

MS., MSS. manuscript(s)

M.Sc. Master of Science

N.A.S.A. National Aeronautics and Space Administration

N.A.T.O. North Atlantic Treaty Organisation

N.B. note well

N.C.O. non-commissioned officer

N.H.S. National Health Service

N.I. National Insurance

No. number

nr. near

N.S.P.C.C. National Society for the Prevention of Cruelty to Children

O. Ordinary (level of G.C.E.)
O.A.P. old aged pensioner
O.A.S. Organisation of American States
O.A.U. Organisation of African Unity
O.B.E. Officer of the British Empire
O.D.E.C.A. Organisation of Central American States
O.E.C.D. Organisation for Economic Co-operation and Development
O.H.M.S. On Her Majesty's Service
O.M. Order of Merit
O.N.C. Ordinary National Certificate
O.N.D. Ordinary National Diploma
op. cit. in the work named
O.P.E.C. Organisation of the Petroleum Exporting Countries

P.A.Y.E. pay as you earn
P.E. physical education
Ph.D. Doctor of Philosophy
P.M. Prime Minister
P.O. post office; postal order
P.O.W. prisoner of war
P.S. postscript
P.T.O. please turn over

Q.C. Queen's Counsel

R. Regina; Rex
R.A. Royal Academy; Royal Artillery
R.A.C. Royal Automobile Club
R.A.D.A. Royal Academy of Dramatic Art
R.A.F. Royal Air Force
R.A.M. Royal Academy of Music
R.C. Roman Catholic
R.C.A. Royal College of Arts
R.C.M. Royal College of Music
Rev., Revd. Reverend
R.G.S. Royal Geographical Society
R.H.S. Royal Horticultural Society
R.I.P. may he (she, they) rest in peace
R.M. Royal Marines; Royal Mail
R.N. Royal Navy
r.p.m. revolutions per minute
R.S.P.C.A. Royal Society for the Prevention of Cruelty to Animals
R.S.V.P. please reply
Rt. Hon. Right Honourable

s.a.e. self-addressed envelope
S.A.L.T. Strategic Arms Limitation Talks

S.A.Y.E. save as you earn
S.C.M. State Certified Midwife
S.E.A.T.O. South-East Asia Treaty Organisation
S.O.S. distress signal
S.R.N. State Registered Nurse
St. Saint; street
S.T.D. subscriber trunk dialling

T.A.S.S. Soviet Telegraph Agency
T.B. tuberculosis
T.N.T. trinitrotoluene (high explosive)
T.U.C. Trades Union Congress

U.A.R. United Arab Republic
U.D.C. Urban District Council
U.D.I. Unilateral Declaration of Independence
U.F.O. unidentified flying object
U.N. United Nations
U.N.D.P. United Nations Development Programme
U.N.E.S.C.O. United Nations Educational, Scientific and Cultural Organisation
U.N.I.C.E.F. United Nations International Children's Emergency Fund
U.S. United States
U.S.A. United States of America
U.S.S.R. Union of Soviet Socialist Republics

V.A.T. value added tax
V.C. Victoria Cross
V.D. venereal disease
V.H.F. very high frequency
V.I.P. very important person

W.C.C. World Council of Churches
W.H.O. World Health Organisation
W.I. West Indies; Women's Institute
W.R.A.C. Women's Royal Army Corps
W.R.A.F. Women's Royal Air Force
W.R.N.S. Women's Royal Naval Service
W.R.V.S. Women's Royal Volunteer Service

Y.H.A. Youth Hostels Association
Y.M.C.A. Young Men's Christian Association
Y.W.C.A. Young Women's Christian Association

APPENDIX III
Common Forenames

MEN
Adrian
Alan, Allan
Andrew
Anthony, Antony
Barry
Brian, Bryan
Bruce
Charles
Christopher
Claude
Clive
Cyril
Derek
Desmond
Douglas
Edmund
Edward, Ted
Eugene
Ewen, Ewin
Francis
Frederick, Fred
Gareth
Gary
Geoffrey
George
Gerald, Gerry
Giles
Gordon
Graham
Guy
Harold, Harry
Howard, Howerd
Hugh
Humphrey
Ian
Jack
James, Jim
Jeremy, Jerry
John
Jonathan
Julian
Keith
Kenneth
Leonard

Lewis
Malcolm
Mathew, Matt
Michael, Mike
Neil
Nicholas, Nick
Nigel
Oliver
Patrick, Paddy
Peter
Philip
Richard, Dick
Robert, Bob
Roger
Ronald
Roy
Sean
Sidney
Simon
Stephen, Steven
Terence, Terry
Thomas
Timothy
Tony
Trevor
Wayne
William

WOMEN
Alice
Alison
Angela, Angie
Ann, Anne
Anthea
Barbara
Belinda
Bridget
Carol, Carole
Caroline
Carolyn
Catherine, Cathy
Charlotte
Christine
Clare
Daphne

Dawn
Deborah, Debby
Denise
Diana
Doreen
Eileen
Elaine
Elizabeth, Betty
Ellen
Emily
Emma
Evelyn
Felicity
Fiona
Frances
Gillian, Jill
Hazel
Heather
Helen
Hilary
Irene
Isabel, Isobel
Jacqueline
Jane
Janet
Janice
Jean
Jennifer, Jenny
Jill
Joan
Joanna
Joy
Joyce
Judith, Judy
Julia
Julie
Karen
Laura
Lesley
Lilian
Linda, Lynda
Lisa, Liza
Lorna
Louise
Lynn

Margaret, Maggie
Marian
Marie
Marilyn
Marion
Marjorie
Mary
Miranda
Miriam
Monica
Natalie
Olivia
Pamela
Patricia
Paula
Pauline
Penelope, Penny
Phillipa
Phillis, Phyllis
Rachel
Rebecca
Rosemary
Ruth
Sally
Sandra, Sandy
Sarah
Sharon
Sheila
Shirley
Sonia
Stephanie
Susan, Sue
Suzanne
Sylvia
Theresa, Tessa
Tina
Tracy
Vera
Veronica
Victoria, Vicky
Virginia
Vivian
Wendy
Yvonne
Zoe

APPENDIX IV

The British Isles

APPENDIX V

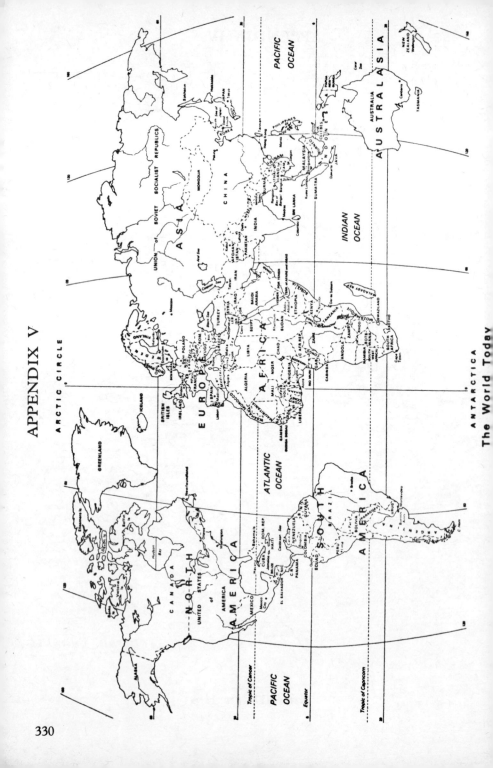

ANTARCTICA

The World Today

APPENDIX VI

Metric Measures | Imperial Measures

Length

		Metric		Imperial
1 millimetre (mm)		= 0.039 in	1 inch (in)	= 2.540 cm
1 centimetre (cm)	= 10 mm	= 0.394 in	1 foot (ft)	= 30.48 cm
1 metre (m)	= 100 cm	= 1.094 yd	1 yard (yd)	= 0.914 m
1 kilometre (km)	= 1000 m	= 0.621 mile	1 mile	= 1.609 km
			1 nautical mile	= 1.852 km

Surface or Area

		Metric		Imperial
1 sq cm (cm^2)		= 0.155 in^2	1 sq in (in^2)	= 6.452 cm^2
1 sq m (m^2)	= 100 mm^2	= 1.196 yd^2	1 sq ft (ft^2)	= 9.290 dm^2
1 sq km (km^2)	= 10000 cm^2	= 0.386 mile^2	1 sq yd (yd^2)	= 0.836 m^2
1 hectare (ha)	= 100 ha	= 11960 yd^2	1 rood	= 1012 m^2
	= 10000 m^2		1 acre	= 0.405 ha
			1 sq mile	= 259.0 ha

Note: 1 sq in = 144 in^2; 1 sq ft = 9 ft^2; 1 sq yd = 1210 yd^2; 1 rood = 4840 yd^2; 1 acre = 640 acres.

Volume and Capacity

		Metric		Imperial
1 cu cm (cm^3)		= 0.061 in^3	1 cu in (in^3)	= 16.39 cm^3
1 cu dm (dm^3)	= 1000 cm^3	= 61.02 in^3	1 cu ft (ft^3)	= 0.028 m^3
1 cu m (m^3)	= 1000 dm^3	= 1.308 yd^3	1 cu yd (yd^3)	= 0.765 m^3
1 litre (l)	= 1 dm^3	= 1.760 pints	1 pint	= 0.568 l
1 hectolitre (hl)	= 100 l	= 2.750 bushels	1 gallon (gal)	= 4.546 l
			1 bushel	= 36.37 l
			1 fluid ounce	= 28.41 cm^3
			1 pint	= 568.2 cm^3

Note: 1 cu in = 1728 in^3; 1 cu ft = 27 ft^3; 1 pint = 4 gills; 1 gallon = 8 pints; 1 bushel = 8 gal; 1 fluid ounce = 8 fl drachms; 1 pint = 20 fl oz.

Weight

		Metric		Imperial
1 milligram (mg)		= 0.015 grain	1 ounce (oz)	= 28.35 g
1 gram (gm)	= 1000 mg	= 0.035 oz	1 pound (lb)	= 0.454 kg
1 kilogram (kg)	= 1000 g	= 2.205 lb	1 stone	= 6.350 kg
1 tonne (t)	= 1000 kg	= 0.984 ton	1 cwt	= 50.80 kg
			1 ton	= 1.016 tonnes

Note: 1 ounce = 437.4 grains; 1 pound = 16 oz; 1 stone = 14 lb; 1 cwt = 8 st; 1 ton = 20 cwt.

Temperature Conversion

$$C = \tfrac{5}{9}(F - 32) \qquad F = (\tfrac{9}{5}C) + 32$$

98.4° Fahrenheit	= 36.9° Centigrade
32° Fahrenheit	= 0° Centigrade
50° Fahrenheit	= 10° Centigrade
68° Fahrenheit	= 20° Centigrade
212° Fahrenheit	= 100° Centigrade

Time

1 min	= 60 sec
1 hr	= 60 min = 3600 sec
1 day	= 24 hr
1 year	= 365 days (366 in leap year)

APPENDIX VII
Common Chemical Compounds

Common name	Chemical name	Formula
Alcohol, grain	Ethanol	CH_3CH_2OH
Alcohol, wood	Methanol	CH_3OH
Baking soda	Sodium hydrogen carbonate	$NaHCO_3$
Borax	Disodium tetraborate	$Na_2B_4O_7$
Brimstone	Sulphur	S
Calomel	Mercury(I) chloride	Hg_2Cl_2
Carbolic acid	Phenol	C_6H_5OH
Carbon tetrachloride	Tetrachloromethane	CCl_4
Carborundum	Silicon carbide	SiC
Chalk	Calcium carbonate	$CaCO_3$
Chloroform	Trichloromethane	$CHCl_3$
Cooking salt	Sodium chloride	NaCl
Corn syrup	Glucose, dextrose	$C_6H_{12}O_6$
Diamond	Carbon	C
Dry ice	Carbon dioxide (solid)	CO_2
Ethyl	Lead tetraethyl	$Pb(C_2H_5)_4$
Fire damp	Methane	CH_4
Glycerine	Glycerol	$C_3H_5(OH)_3$
Graphite	Carbon	C
Iron pyrites	Iron disulphide	FeS_2
Laughing gas	Dinitrogen oxide	N_2O
Lime water	Calcium hydroxide solution	$Ca(OH)_2$
Lye (or caustic soda)	Sodium hydroxide	NaOH
Magnesia	Magnesium oxide	MgO
Marble	Calcium carbonate	$CaCO_3$
Marsh gas	Methane	CH_4
Milk of magnesia	Magnesium hydroxide (with water)	$Mg(OH)_2$
Moth balls	Naphthalene	$C_{10}H_8$
Muriatic acid	Hydrochloric acid	HCl
Oil of vitriol	Sulphuric acid	H_2SO_4
Peroxide	Hydrogen peroxide	H_2O_2
Potash	Potassium carbonate	K_2CO_3
Quartz	Silicon dioxide	SiO_2
Quicklime	Calcium oxide	CaO
Quicksilver	Mercury	Hg
Sal ammoniac	Ammonium chloride	NH_4Cl
Saltpetre	Potassium nitrate	KNO_3
Sand	Silicon dioxide (impure)	SiO_2
Soap	Sodium stearate	$C_{17}H_{35}COONa$
Sugar (cane or beet)	Sucrose	$C_{12}H_{22}O_{11}$
Vinegar	Ethanoic acid (with water)	CH_3COOH
Water glass	Sodium silicate	Na_2SiO_3
Zinc white	Zinc oxide	ZnO

APPENDIX VIII

Physical Constants, Conversion Factors and Units

There are nine basic units in the SI system (Système international d'unités)

Quantity	Name of unit	Symbol
length	metre	m
mass	kilogram	kg
time	second	s
electric current	ampere *	A
thermodynamic temperature	kelvin *	K
amount of substance	mole	mol
luminous intensity	candela	cd
plane angle	radian	rad
solid angle	steradian	sr

In addition there are a number of derived units, including the following

Quantity	Name of unit	Symbol
force	newton *	N
energy	joule *	J
power	watt *	W
electric charge	coulomb *	C
potential difference	volt *	V
electric resistance	ohm *	Ω
frequency	hertz *	Hz
customary temperature	degree Celsius	°C

The asterisk (*) indicates that the names of the relevant units begin with a small letter when they are written out in full, but are symbolised by a capital letter.

Special prefixes and symbols are used to indicate multiples and sub-multiples of the basic units in powers of ten

Multiple	Prefix	Symbol
10^{12}	tera	T
10^{9}	giga	G
10^{6}	mega	M
10^{3}	kilo	k
10^{-1}	deci	d
10^{-2}	centi	c
10^{-3}	milli	m
10^{-6}	micro	μ
10^{-9}	nano	n
10^{-12}	pico	p
10^{-15}	femto	f
10^{-18}	atto	a

APPENDIX IX

PERIODIC TABLE OF THE ELEMENTS

H 1 Hydrogen																	He 2 Helium
Li 3 Lithium	Be 4 Beryllium											B 5 Boron	C 6 Carbon	N 7 Nitrogen	O 8 Oxygen	F 9 Fluorine	Ne 10 Neon
Na 11 Sodium	Mg 12 Magnesium											Al 13 Aluminium	Si 14 Silicon	P 15 Phosphorus	S 16 Sulphur	Cl 17 Chlorine	Ar 18 Argon
K 19 Potassium	Ca 20 Calcium	Sc 21 Scandium	Ti 22 Titanium	V 23 Vanadium	Cr 24 Chromium	Mn 25 Manganese	Fe 26 Iron	Co 27 Cobalt	Ni 28 Nickel	Cu 29 Copper	Zn 30 Zinc	Ga 31 Gallium	Ge 32 Germanium	As 33 Arsenic	Se 34 Selenium	Br 35 Bromine	Kr 36 Krypton
Rb 37 Rubidium	Sr 38 Strontium	Y 39 Yttrium	Zr 40 Zirconium	Nb 41 Niobium	Mo 42 Molybde–num	Tc 43 Technetium	Ru 44 Ruthenium	Rh 45 Rhodium	Pd 46 Palladium	Ag 47 Silver	Cd 48 Cadmium	In 49 Indium	Sn 50 Tin	Sb 51 Antimony	Te 52 Tellurium	I 53 Iodine	Xe 54 Xenon
Cs 55 Caesium	Ba 56 Barium	La 57 Lanthanum	Hf 72 Hafnium	Ta 73 Tantalum	W 74 Tungsten	Re 75 Rhenium	Os 76 Osmium	Ir 77 Iridium	Pt 78 Platinum	Au 79 Gold	Hg 80 Mercury	Tl 81 Thallium	Pb 82 Lead	Bi 83 Bismuth	Po 84 Polonium	At 85 Astatine	Rn 86 Radon
Fr 87 Francium	Ra 88 Radium	Ac 89 Actinium	104	105													

Ce 58 Cerium	Pr 59 Praseody–mium	Nd 60 Neodymium	Pm 61 Promethium	Sm 62 Samarium	Eu 63 Europium	Gd 64 Gadolinium	Tb 65 Terbium	Dy 66 Dysprosium	Ho 67 Holmium	Er 68 Erbium	Tm 69 Thulium	Yb 70 Ytterbium	Lu 71 Lutetium
Th 90 Thorium	Pa 91 Protactin–ium	U 92 Uranium	Np 93 Neptunium	Pu 94 Plutonium	Am 95 Americium	Cm 96 Curium	Bk 97 Berkelium	Cf 98 Californium	Es 99 Einsteinium	Fm 100 Fermium	Md 101 Mendelev–ium	No 102 Nobelium	Lr 103 Lawrencium

Acknowledgements

In preparing this dictionary the following books have been particularly useful to me as resource material:

Cassell's New Spelling Dictionary
L. B. & D. Firnberg, Cassell, 1976

Collins Authors and Printers Dictionary
F. Howard Collins, Oxford University Press, 11th rev. ed., 1973

The Concise Oxford Dictionary
Ed. C. T. Onions, Oxford University Press, 3rd rev. ed., 1976

Maxwell's Illustrated Colour Dictionary
Eds. J. P. Brasier-Creach, M.A. and
B. A. Workman, M.A. ILSC, London, 1969

The Oxford School Dictionary
Joan Pusey, Oxford University Press, 3rd rev. ed., 1974

The Perfect Speller
Harriet Wittels and Joan Griesman, Grosset & Dunlap, New York, 1973

I have benefited greatly from the help and advice of many people and schools. I would specially like to acknowledge the help of: Miss Judy Black, Miss Georgina Cox, Mr. Gordon Files, Mrs. Edna Goldman, Mr. Oliver Gregory, Mrs. Gretchen Ingram, Mr. C. R. Jacobs, Mrs. Jean Price, Mrs. Olive Robinson, Miss Avital Talmor and the teachers of Shepherds' Hill Middle School, Oxford. However, any mistakes contained in the dictionary are entirely my responsibility.

The final acknowledgement goes to my family who helped me out in so many ways and particularly to my father, without whose invaluable advice, constant encouragement and support this project would never have got off the ground.